CALLS TO ARMS

CALLS TO ARMS

*Presidential Speeches, Messages,
and Declarations of War*

EDITED BY
RUSSELL D. BUHITE

A Scholarly Resources Inc. Imprint
Wilmington, Delaware

Scholarly Resources Inc.
104 Greenhill Avenue
Wilmington, DE 19805-1897
www.scholarly.com

LIBRARY OF CONGRESS CATALOGING-IN-PUBLICATION DATA

Calls to arms : presidential speeches, messages, and declarations of war / edited by Russell D. Buhite.
    p. cm.
  Includes bibliographical references.
  ISBN 0-8420-2592-8 (alk. paper) — ISBN 0-8420-2593-6 (pbk. : alk. paper)
1. Presidents—United States—Messages. 2. War, Declaration of—United States—History—Sources. I. Buhite, Russell D.
J81.4 C35 2003
355.02'0973—dc21   2002015775

For my grandson Nicholas

May he never receive a call to arms

ACKNOWLEDGMENTS

A number of talented individuals have contributed to the publication of this book. My friend and colleague in the History Department at the University of Tennessee, Professor Bruce Wheeler, first introduced me to the idea of studying war messages. My graduate research assistant at Tennessee, Gary Vaughan, searched out and copied nearly all of the presidential speeches. Vaughan's successor, John Hendrickson, helped annotate some of the documents. Linda Musumeci, senior editor at Scholarly Resources, took the rough edges off the manuscript and guided it toward the finish line. Her efforts on this project, as on my previous work, have been cheerfully skillful and painstakingly professional. I owe her a huge debt. Richard Hopper, vice president and general manager at Scholarly Resources, encouraged this study and helped mold it into shape. Finally, I must express gratitude to my former student, Mary Brennan, from whose creative mind came the title "Calls to Arms," and to my wife, Mary Buhite, as always, for her love, friendship, and perseverance. To all of the above I offer a resounding "thank you" and the obligatory absolution for any errors or missteps that may have infected the final product.

CONTENTS

INTRODUCTION

The speeches or "calls to arms" reprinted in this volume evoke at least three critical questions: how has presidential speech changed over the years; which presidents stand out as superior rhetoricians and why; and to what degree and by what processes have presidents challenged the war powers delimited in the U.S. Constitution? The word "speech" here is used to convey both written and oral presentations; however, where oratorical skill is addressed in this introduction, "speeches" refers precisely to oral presentations. Sometimes presidential war messages have been written and then sent to Congress to be read; sometimes they have been delivered orally.

Late-eighteenth- and early-nineteenth-century presidents gave few speeches of any kind. Examination of the objectives of the Founding Fathers reveals the reason why founding intent tended to restrict oratory. The Founders, as befitted their Enlightenment heritage and their fear of tyranny, sought to create only a limited government, a small public sector. To them a system that protected freedom, guaranteed security, and promoted opportunity through private initiative was superior to any other, and government should extend no further than necessary to facilitate those goals. In such an environment the general public would not, as a matter of course, turn to government for answers to problems; it would not, in fact, pay much attention to government. Under these circumstances, presidents would have little need for oratory. Constitutionalism, from this perspective, tended to constrain executive appeal to the people through much of the first one hundred years of the nation's history.

The mere suggestion of arousing public passion always generated deep disquiet among the Founders. This concern manifested itself in important institutional ways. The president was to be elected by the people, but only indirectly; an electoral college would ultimately name the chief executive. The upper house of the Congress would be elected, again only indirectly, and state legislatures would choose U.S. senators (until the enactment of the Seventeenth Amendment). Supreme Court justices would be nominated by the president but would be approved by the Senate.

Demagoguery was a particular concern. A demagogue, in either the presidency or Congress, could divide the nation and, more worrisome still, could undermine the separation of powers by turning the people against one of the other branches of government. Because Congress's sheer numbers would always dispose it to harbor a multitude of potential demagogues, it would be easy for any members who were so inclined to overcome and diminish the presidency. Hence it was thought that presidential oratory could backfire and undercut the office of the president.

In accord with the Founders' expectations presidential speech in the early days of the Republic was written and nearly always directed to the Congress. Article 2, Section 3 of the Constitution states that the president "shall from time to time give to the Congress information of the state of the Union, and recommend to their consideration such measures as he shall judge necessary and expedient." It was assumed that any laws or policy initiatives, including those on foreign-policy matters originating with the president, would be communicated in writing to Congress without recourse to public posturing or mass appeal of any sort.

Inaugural addresses were the exception to these written communications. President George Washington spoke only briefly in the public ceremony in which he took the first oath of office. He delivered an oral address immediately thereafter to the assembled members of Congress. Washington disdained direct appeal to the public; he preferred to speak to the people only indirectly through Congress. His second inaugural address—only two paragraphs long—could hardly qualify as a speech. John Adams, as Washington's successor, utilized the method of the first inaugural. Those who followed Adams changed the procedure—and the form of address—over time. All delivered some oral speeches, some of which were merely hortatory, and, although most were delivered to the people, not all stressed high-blown principle. As the nineteenth century progressed, however, presidents increasingly began to invoke policy issues.

Other presidential speech during the nineteenth century consisted of (1) presidential proclamations, which included (among others) Washington's pronouncement of the first Thanksgiving and Abraham Lincoln's Emancipation Proclamation; and (2) the annual message to Congress, now called the State of the Union address, and veto messages returned to the house of a bill's origin. The Emancipation Proclamation notwithstanding, a great many proclamations were written for public release and dealt with matters that were not compelling. Veto messages were simply to be read by Congress, rather than presented orally. Thomas Jefferson, who possessed a weak voice and experienced pronounced discomfort before an audience, began the practice of submitting all State of the Union messages in writing, a custom followed thereafter until Woodrow Wilson's presidency. Ironically, although Jefferson refused to speak directly to the people or Congress, his reputation as the embodiment of democratic principle endured. (Historians are quick to note this inconsistency as only one of many manifested by this aristocratic, slave-owning drafter of the Declaration of Independence.)

In his book *The Rhetorical Presidency*, Jeffrey K. Tulis provides a useful enumeration of eighteenth- and nineteenth-century presidential speeches. The numbers are noteworthy and surprising. In his four-year administration, John Adams gave an estimated six speeches. In eight years, Jefferson delivered only three addresses, as did James Madison—Jefferson's closest friend, confidant, and successor—in his two terms. James Monroe gave forty-two in one term, whereas John Quincy Adams—introverted, sardonic, and abrasive—gave only five. James K. Polk delivered fifteen. Lincoln gave seventy-eight in his four-plus years in office, including two of the most memorable in all of U.S. history. Most presidents after Lincoln, enjoying greater accessibility of audiences, substantially increased the numbers. Railroad travel facilitated the assembly of masses of people and increased the frequency and efficiency with which presidents could travel to them. President William McKinley, for instance, gave an estimated 130 speeches on various and sundry topics. For a variety of reasons, by the turn of the twentieth century, presidents had clearly moved away from the earlier perceived constitutional constraints.

Throwing caution to the wind, Theodore Roosevelt began the trend of the twentieth century. He went directly to the people, frequently and flamboyantly. Wilson and most others followed suit. And as the century wore on, rather than merely release manuscript drafts, they increasingly delivered oral speeches, first over the new medium of radio and then on television.

Wilson justified his speechifying as necessary to counter the excessive power of Congress. That had been one of Theodore Roosevelt's reasons as well. Franklin D. Roosevelt, arguably the greatest orator in the history of the presidency, later became the master of the radio address. Subsequent presidents, including the photogenic John F. Kennedy, Ronald Reagan, and Bill (William Jefferson) Clinton, utilized television to gain access to millions of people, in the hope that they could mobilize the public to elicit support for particular policies or to gain political advantage.

What presidents said and how well they said it—either delivered orally or released in written manuscripts—is pertinent to a study of this nature. But assessing presidential speech is not an easy task. Evaluating oratory, the art of effective public speaking, is a lot like evaluating leadership. Leaders may have ambition, dynamism, intellect, communication skills, and charisma (though possession of these qualities alone does not make a leader); unless they have followers, however, they are not of much account. Although followers may be "made," they usually arise from a particular set of historical circumstances and are energized by a leader with whom they share a set of goals or values. By the same token, to be considered a successful orator, an individual must succeed in influencing audiences toward particular deeds or thoughts. A message delivered well and with rhetorical flourish must meet at least a moderately receptive crowd or the orator's efforts will fall flat. And a speaker whose historical circumstances prompt repeated inability to move listeners will often be judged a failure as an orator.

If an orator is defined as a person who has mastered and polished the techniques of delivering a speech, then very few U.S. presidents were orators. Lincoln, Theodore Roosevelt, Wilson, Franklin Roosevelt, Richard M. Nixon, Reagan, and Clinton probably come the closest. But scholars in the discipline now called "communication" agree not only that these chief executives exhibited flaws in their deliveries but also that any definition of "orator" must go beyond mere technique.

Scholars have evaluated oratory according to the ancient canons of that art. The Greeks and Romans not only practiced public speaking but also analyzed it and theorized about it as early as 90 B.C. to 80 B.C.; these analyses have become part of the modern lexicon. *Actio* is the Latin term for delivery, by which is meant verbal cadence, body gesture, eye contact, tone of voice, posture on the platform, personal appearance, and the like. Every student of communication knows the importance of delivery, which affects how a speech is received and determines to some degree how the speaker is assessed as a communicator. Critics have historically invoked the canon *memoria* (memory) in evaluating oration as well. Until recent times good delivery meant memorization. A speech delivered from memory was considered superior to one read from a manuscript because it allowed the orator to speak directly to his or her audience in a properly forceful or focused manner.

Perhaps the most important canon is *elocutio*, which means word choice, rhetorical or syntactical skill, and the use of prose or prose-poetry for effect. Scholars always address the question of the message a speaker conveyed in terms of whether he or she spoke simply and directly in plain, everyday, common language or utilized alliteration, rhetorical questions, epistrophe, the hortatory subjunctive, or other examples of flourish long associated with elegant speech (forms that decreased in favor during the twentieth century). How language is adorned, most critics would agree, can determine how well it is remembered—even if it is embellished in what may seem questionable taste.

Inventio, how a given speech originated, and *despositio*, how a speech was organized, are the other canons. *Depositio* in classical speech—which is historically well regarded—involved an appropriate introduction to capture the reader's attention, a body that developed the main points, and a conclusion in which the speaker might argue forcefully for a given course of action or particular way of thinking. *Inventio*, in large measure, concerns the topics the speaker addresses and such choices in writing a speech as what kind of appeal—logical or otherwise—to make to the listeners. In a sense this standard is the strategy of composition. No scholar can critique a speaker's work without attention to what he or she was attempting to accomplish in writing a given address.

It is worth noting that few of the calls to arms of U.S. presidents are masterpieces by any standard. All were written and read to Congress, to the American people, or to both. None was memorized for forceful and effective delivery. With few exceptions the messages contained little rhetorical sophistication and minimal stylistic flourish. Many of them constituted raw, emotional appeals to self-defense, nationalism, patriotism, economic self-interest, the protection of lives and property, the promotion of democracy, or the thwarting of some foreign ideology. Often—at least to some degree—they were intended to mislead.

A full accounting of presidential rhetoric is a massive undertaking, which space does not permit in this volume. A cursory examination of a few presidents is all that is practicable here. Either because they wrote their own speeches, formally studied rhetoric, were accomplished at delivery, or some combination of the three, attention is focused on Lincoln, Theodore Roosevelt, Wilson, and Franklin Roosevelt. Only brief comment is given to others who presided over wars or interventions.

Most historians and communication scholars consider Abraham Lincoln the greatest orator among U.S. presidents of the nineteenth century and rank his first and second inaugural addresses and his Gettysburg Address among the greatest speeches in human history. Lincoln relied heavily on biblical allusion and expression as well as on such literary devices as grammatical parallelism, repetition, and antithesis, in many of his presidential addresses. He also made frequent use of alliteration, assonance, and anaphora—the last a linguistic device in which parallelism and repetition are united as a prelude in successive expressions of thought. Later opinion of Lincoln's orations, however, does not agree with that of his contemporaries. His speeches were often less than well received by audiences of his own time. Some, such as his Gettysburg Address and his first inaugural, would have benefited from the excerption and replay that has been practiced on speeches in the twentieth-century television age. By giving listeners an opportunity to reflect on the subtlety and complexity of an oration, such revisiting allows for greater appreciation.

Theodore Roosevelt marked the beginning of the rhetorical presidency. He studied rhetoric in college, he read widely, he wrote extensively (including on topics such as the War of 1812 and the "winning" of the American West), and he served as president of the American Historical Association; but most important of all, as a young man he began to practice giving speeches in such places as the New York legislature. As president of the United States he considered it his mission to educate the public on a broad array of issues. His addresses are known for their balanced sentences, literary allusions, and vigor and enthusiasm of delivery. Though Roosevelt had an intense interest in foreign affairs and saw himself as a highly effective foreign-policy president who understood balance of power and the role of the United States in preserving it, most of his presidential speeches concerned domestic issues. In accord with his status as the first of the progressive reform presidents, his orations took on many of the ills of U.S. society.

Among the presidents who led the nation into war and military interventions, Wilson was probably the one who most prized rhetorical performance. Because his father was a Presbyterian minister, his earliest memories involved listening to sermons. His father also served as a professor of rhetoric at one point in his career. Young Wilson studied rhetoric at Davidson College and Princeton University and so admired the great speeches of the English political tradition that he kept copies of them for easy reference. He joined debating clubs at both Princeton and the University of Virginia, where he attended law school. On days when no services took place, he practiced public speaking in his father's churches. As a professor of history and political science at Princeton and later as president of that institution, he became a popular lecturer. As president of the United States, Wilson drafted most of his own speeches. He used public oration to secure popular support for his policies before taking them to Congress. Skillful at the formal cadences—even the bombast—of nineteenth-century orators, Wilson also cultivated the art of the conversational tone—the manner of repartee common in the British Parliament. If Theodore Roosevelt was the first of the rhetorical presidents, Wilson clearly continued that trend and even did him one better.

But no president of the twentieth century, and probably none in all of U.S. history, equaled Franklin Roosevelt as a public speaker. Having come along in the radio era, Roosevelt made the most of the new medium. In his famous Fireside Chats, beginning with the start of his term in 1933 and continuing until 1945, Roosevelt conducted informal seminars with the American people on critical issues of the day. He perfected the conversational style for the radio, but he performed brilliantly as an orator in other settings as well. He had a deep, powerful voice, which he used in near perfect verbal pacing as he waved his head from side to side and raised and lowered his eyebrows, often flashing a toothy smile. Humor and sarcasm were his forte. He often alternated them in the same address and used them effectively against his enemies, who—at least during World War II—were also portrayed as enemies of the American people. Though he did not draft his own speeches, he usually revised and put his own imprint on them. His addresses made liberal use of literary and biblical allusions in addition to antithesis, anaphora, and epistrophe. But the critical factor in his success was his ability to convince his audiences that he shared their feelings, values, aspirations, and goals—that he was the right person to lead them through domestic crisis and war.

Although other presidents who took the country into war, military crisis, or some manner of intervention had studied rhetoric, none of them met the oratorical standard set by Lincoln, Theodore Roosevelt, Wilson, and Franklin Roosevelt. John Adams reflected a biliousness that did not wear well. Jefferson had a weak voice and a profound fear of public speaking. The brilliant Madison did not like public speaking either, and he did not make an imposing appearance. Andrew Jackson—though rough-hewn, given to vulgarity, emotion, and volatility, and poorly educated in a formal sense—was not a bad stump speaker, if feelings could carry an issue. Polk, Ulysses S. Grant, and McKinley were not orators of note, though McKinley gave many speeches during his political career. No one considered McKinley a match for the likes of William Jennings Bryan, his opponent in the 1896 election. The presidents of the 1920s could express themselves clearly and directly, but not one of the three stands out as a speaker. Warren G. Harding was ponderous. Calvin Coolidge was taciturn and edgy. Herbert Hoover was often stiff, formal, and humorless.

Alhough some had training in rhetoric, most presidents in the post World War II era gained their speaking skills by trial and error. Harry S. Truman and Dwight D. Eisenhower spoke in simple, clear language with little flourish. Truman often revealed a flinty or abrasive manner, and Eisenhower, especially after suffering a heart attack and a stroke, stumbled over his words. When Kennedy stuck to the scripts prepared for him by such talented speechwriters as Theodore Sorenson, he could be quite eloquent; otherwise his speech grew pedestrian, often only marginally coherent. Still, his personal style was elegant and his handsome demeanor won him friends and followers. Though Lyndon B. Johnson tried to rely on sincerity, folksiness, or Texas cornpone to carry an issue, sometimes—as in his well-written addresses on civil rights—he managed a surprising eloquence. His inability to communicate American goals in Vietnam adequately (quite likely an impossible task in any case) contributed to the failure of U.S. policy in that part of the world and to the end of his presidency.

Among the presidents in the post-Vietnam War years, Richard Nixon had training in rhetoric, but his pathological propensity for mendacity, his self-serving conniving, and his personal insecurity kept him from achieving his potential as a speaker. One of the most intellectually talented men ever to occupy the presidency, Nixon could never fully evoke the trust or the empathy inspired by the superior oratorical leader. Though some of his speeches were memorable and showed technical excellence, he achieved his foreign-policy successes in spite of his speaking performances. Because Reagan spent his entire adult life in acting and in radio and television, he could certainly deliver a line. George Herbert Walker Bush was given to short sentences, brief paragraphs, and colloquial expressions; he did not win support for his policies with eloquence. Clinton could speak knowledgeably about more issues than most presidents before him, but his public addresses tended to include lists, and his style was more conversational than formal. Like Bush before him, Clinton's rhetoric did not account for his popularity or for his ability to lead the nation into military involvements. George W. Bush's fractured syntax, not to say his seeming indifference to audience or occasion, made him an ineffective speaker.

If the framers of the U.S. Constitution could evaluate American behavior in the latter half of the twentieth century, they would find cause for annoyance and concern. Few developments would be likely to bother them more, however, than the erosion of congressional warmaking power. Since World War II, the United States, in its quest for enhanced security or the furtherance of its professed ideals, has participated in three major wars and countless military skirmishes and has sent troops to far-flung trouble spots around the world. In none of these instances has the president asked Congress for a declaration of war; in all of them, in fact, the president has assumed extraordinary executive prerogative. The framers opposed a system that vested in an executive the exclusive authority to determine when or how a war should begin. To relinquish this power, they believed, would risk the establishment of monarchy by another name, thus undermining the very freedom they sought to secure. Thus, they proposed the division of authority. The president could make treaties, but with the advice and consent of the Senate. The president could appoint ambassadors if the

Senate approved the nominations. The president would become commander in chief of the army and navy and of the state militias if they were called up but would not be permitted to issue letters of marque and reprisal. Most important, the delegates to the Constitutional Convention granted Congress, not the president, the legal right to control international commerce, to raise and support armies and navies, to call up the militia, and to declare war.

What concerned the framers most was that the chief executive not have control of both the purse and the sword. That development would allow the president to make war and then create parliamentary or extraparliamentary ways to pay for it. In short, it would permit the president to engage in practices long associated with European monarchs, thus violating deeply held principles of free government. As Madison so trenchantly observed, "Those who are to conduct a war cannot in the nature of things, be proper or safe judges, whether a war ought to be commenced, continued, or concluded" (Fisher 1995: 9).

Twentieth-century presidents, particularly after World War II, consistently maintained that reliance on slow-moving congressional warmaking power exposes the nation to dire security threats. The advent of nuclear weapons and their possession by U.S. adversaries could require a nearly instantaneous executive decision to use military force. Cold War competition with the Soviet Union and the consequent commitment of U.S. power thousands of miles from the nation's borders made it all the more necessary to act quickly if the United States came under attack, they argued. But the constitutional fathers took emergency threat into consideration. Although they reserved to Congress the right to declare war, they gave the president the power to repel sudden attacks or threats to U.S. troops on foreign soil. They expressly rejected the notion, however, that the chief executive could send troops into harm's way and keep them there for extended periods. They accepted neither the idea that the president as commander in chief could initiate offensive military action or decide on general war nor the notion that troops or naval forces—once sent abroad to address a threat—could remain deployed at the president's discretion.

Generally speaking, late eighteenth- and nineteenth-century presidents respected the framers' intentions. In the 1790s, when France and Great Britain engaged in the war that led to French compromises of U.S. neutrality, President John Adams faced the decision of war or peace. In waging the undeclared war with France between 1798 and 1800, he did not act without congressional authority. At the president's request, Congress enacted bills improving coastal defense, enlarging the fledgling U.S. Navy, building new armaments, and authorizing the seizure of French ships. Although the Treaty of Amity and Commerce with France was not formally abrogated until the signing of the Franco-American Convention of 1800, Congress effectively suspended the agreement in 1798. In other words, although Congress did not declare war, it complied with Adams in supporting the U.S. position. In decisions made at the turn of the nineteenth century, the Supreme Court judged the arrangement adequate; by enacting legislation, Congress could undertake a de facto as well as a de jure authorization of war. Either approach was sufficient, but one or the other was necessary.

In the early years of the Constitution no one was sure what would be the best procedure in the event that another nation declared war on the United States. Alexander Hamilton, always wont to expand presidential authority, argued that if war were declared on the United States, the president would only need to proceed with military action. Because a state of war would already exist, the chief executive would not have to seek a declaration of war, and Congress would not have to submit one. Jefferson disagreed. A longtime advocate of force against the Barbary pirates from the North African states of Tunis, Tripoli, Morocco, and Algiers who preyed on American cargoes and crews, President Jefferson sent a naval squadron into the Mediterranean for defense. But when Tripoli declared war on the United States in 1801, Jefferson—believing that the Constitution required it—asked Congress for approval before undertaking offensive action. As it had in the undeclared war with France, Congress passed several pieces of legislation allowing the president to order the seizure or destruction of Tripolitan vessels and authorized military moves against the pirates in a number of other ways. Jefferson saw a clear distinction between emergency defensive action, which he—as president—could undertake of his own volition, and offensive action, which required the approval of Congress.

Madison, who, like Jefferson, his close friend and mentor from Monticello, was a foe of excessive executive prerogative, continued Jefferson's military efforts against the Barbary states. In 1815 he asked Congress for a declaration of war against Algiers. Reluctant to give a formal declaration, Congress once again passed legislation sanctioning force. The authorization granted Madison the right to send a naval squadron against Algerian shipping and to seize its ships and sailors. Through these actions and the maneuvers of British naval power, which turned against the Barbary corsairs following the defeat of Napoleon, the United States obtained a measure of security for its Mediterranean and Atlantic shipping.

During the Anglo-French war, the United States's neutrality was seriously violated by both European nations. When British impressment of American seamen, confiscation of U.S. cargoes, incitement of Indian attacks on frontier settlements, and general violations of American honor became too severe to overlook, Madison asked Congress for a declaration of war. Congress responded in a split vote that represented deep-seated sectional differences. An inconclusive military struggle ensued, followed by a peace that initially restored the status quo ante bellum. This was the first war in American history declared under the Constitution. The conflict may not have been definitive or even wise, but it was constitutional.

President Jackson would later refrain from extending recognition to the independent Republic of Texas out of fear that the action would provoke a war with Mexico that Congress might oppose. Still, he did not express the same reluctance as Jefferson and Madison in addressing the defense-offense conundrum. In February 1831 a group of Sumatran natives killed ten merchant seamen and wounded three others in a vicious attack on the crew of an American ship engaged in the area's pepper trade, when the vessel was docked at Kuala Batu, just off the northwest coast of Sumatra. When the ship and its remaining crew arrived back in the United States in June 1831, President Jackson—wasting little time in his decision to pursue restitution, indemnity, and punishment of the perpetrators of the attack—sent the U.S. frigate *Potomac* to the Sumatran village. The commander in charge of the mission, Commodore John Downes, took the assignment seriously: on February 6, 1832, he landed 250 marines, burned the village of Kuala Batu, and killed approximately 100 natives. Jackson later insisted—rightly, in all likelihood—that Downes had exceeded his instructions, but he maintained that authorization for the action derived from concern for the defense of American interests and the lawful protection of U.S. seamen.

In the same message to Congress in which he addressed the Sumatran problem, President Jackson called attention to a minor conflict with Argentina. In August 1831 an Argentine governor and proprietor in the Falkland Islands, then under claim by Argentina, had seized three American fishing schooners. Jackson told Congress he was sending a squadron to the South Atlantic to protect U.S. fishing rights, again in defensive action. The president later defended the peremptory military moves of the commander of the USS *Lexington*, though he had not consented to them in advance: the commander had seized all the guns on East Falkland, arrested all the inhabitants, and declared the island free and independent. The resulting crisis with Argentina abated the next year when Great Britain reasserted its control of the Falklands. Jackson had confounded defensive and offensive behavior in this instance, just as he had done with the natives of Kuala

Batu. In each case the military action was criticized in the United States, but the president had not bypassed Congress and claimed warmaking power as post–World War II chief executives would do.

Although President Polk followed constitutional procedure, asking Congress for a declaration of war against Mexico in May 1846, his policies raised the question of how to proceed in the event that a U.S. president actually provoked a war. The military conflict between Mexico and the United States has spawned an enormous corpus of scholarship. Suffice it to say that after years of tense relations, following the independence of Texas, and U.S. annexation of the state in March 1845, the situation quickly came to a head. Breakdown and war resulted when President Polk attempted to negotiate a favorable U.S. settlement of three issues: the purchase of California and New Mexico (which he desperately wanted to accomplish); monetary claims of U.S. citizens against Mexico, concerning which that government was in arrears; and the boundary of the new state of Texas. The United States claimed the Rio Grande; Mexico claimed the Nueces River. When Mexico refused to deal with Polk's envoy, John Slidell of Louisiana, Polk sent General Zachary Taylor and a contingent of troops from Corpus Christi to the Rio Grande. This action constituted a U.S. occupation of disputed territory and led to Mexico's April 25, 1846, attack, which killed or wounded sixteen of Taylor's men. Having already considered a request to Congress for a war declaration based on the Mexicans' refusal to satisfy the claims issue and on their rejection of the Slidell mission, Polk seized the opportunity. The Mexicans, fortuitously, had fired the first shot.

Wildly misrepresenting the facts, Polk's war message stressed that American blood had been shed on American soil. American blood had been shed, at best, on disputed soil. In any event, Congress responded with a 174–14 vote for war in the House and a 40–2 vote in the Senate. After initial anger toward the Mexicans subsided, many, especially in the Whig opposition, seriously questioned the war. Congressman Abraham Lincoln joined the critics: "Allow the President to invade a neighboring nation, whenever he shall deem it necessary to repel an invasion, and you allow him to do so, whenever he may choose to say he deems it necessary . . . and you allow him to make war at pleasure" (Fisher 1995: 34).

When South Carolinians precipitated the Civil War by firing on Fort Sumter in Charleston Harbor on April 12, 1861, President Lincoln took several steps that he might well have criticized at an earlier time. He placed a blockade on the Confederate states, called up the state militias, and—most momentous of all from a constitutional perspective—suspended habeas corpus. To his great credit, however, Lincoln did not claim broader executive power than that sanctioned in the Constitution. When Congress —which was in recess during the attack on Fort Sumter—reconvened, Lincoln explained his actions as an emergency measure taken to defend the nation from insurrection and ultimate destruction, and he asked Congress to approve his decisions. His message was a model of eloquence, of respect for congressional prerogative. Congress granted his request: "making valid all the acts, proclamations, and orders of the President as if . . . done under . . . the Congress of the United States" (Fisher 1995: 39). In this instance, Congress clearly had approved war in the same sense as if it had declared it.

Although President Grant acted without congressional authorization in ordering a punitive expedition against Korea in June 1871 (see the footnote to Grant's December 4, 1871, State of the Union message), he demonstrated proper respect for Congress in explaining his actions. A minor issue, it neither called forth exceptional presidential rhetoric nor triggered a constitutional confrontation.

The third declared war in U.S. history occurred in 1898 against Spain. Spain's inability to subdue a rebellion in Cuba that had begun in 1895, Spanish atrocities on that island, damage to U.S. trade and investments caused by the disruptions in the area, and sensationalized publicity from American newspapers that aroused the ire of the public and of Congress prompted the administration of President McKinley to pressure Spain to solve the Cuban problem diplomatically. On April 11, 1898, when it had become clear that Spain could not do so in a humane manner, or with sufficient dispatch, the president asked Congress for a declaration of war. By an overwhelming vote in the House and a fairly close margin in the Senate, Congress granted McKinley's request, passing a resolution authorizing war. The act, which was finally endorsed by the president on April 25, declared war to have existed as of April 21. Given the long-standing prowar sentiments of many congressmen, McKinley's recommendation reflected not so much a move toward aggressive executive action as an attempt by a leader to keep up with his followers. In the process, McKinley conformed to constitutional requirements for congressional authorization of force.

One of the products of the war with Spain was the acquisition of the Philippine Islands and the beginning of a U.S. empire. But, as President McKinley quickly realized, becoming an imperial power had its complications. Filipinos, who had resented Spanish domination and took no more kindly to U.S. rule, soon began an insurrection that lasted several years, became exceedingly bloody, and required a major expenditure of U.S.

military power to quell. McKinley regularly reported to Congress on the steps taken to put down the rebellion. Congress, though buffeted by public debate over the whole imperialist issue at the turn of the century, did not terminate funding for the requisite military activity, thus giving at least tacit support.

As a nation with growing overseas aspirations, the United States became involved in other matters that had gone unforeseen when President McKinley asked Congress to declare war against Spain. In one case the United States extended military power into China during that country's so-called Boxer Rebellion. In the opinion of McKinley his decision to send five thousand marines during the summer of 1900 as part of an international force to lift the siege of the legations in Peking fit the description of an emergency measure designed to save American lives. He duly informed Congress of his moves without seeking to disguise them in any way. McKinley's use of force against Spain, the Filipino rebels, and the Boxers in China was thus far more in accord with the framers' intentions than that of many of his twentieth-century successors.

Between 1900 and World War II, Theodore Roosevelt, William H. Taft, and Woodrow Wilson intervened in Latin America on several occasions. Primarily in Caribbean countries and in Central America, these interventions were informed by three overarching objectives: to secure U.S. trade and investments, to ensure peace and stability on the routes to the interoceanic canal in Panama (opened in 1914), and to promote democracy in each of the countries. The three presidents in question placed differing weights on these goals, but all were motivating factors as the chief executive deployed the U.S. military to the Dominican Republic, Haiti, Cuba, Panama, Nicaragua, and Mexico.

Roosevelt's preemption of Congress's sole authority to sanction military force was nothing if not breathtaking. He wrote a treaty with Colombia to obtain the access necessary to build a canal across the Isthmus of Panama. When the Colombian Senate refused to ratify the treaty as written, Roosevelt supported a Panamanian revolt against Colombian rule, and he sent U.S. naval vessels to Panamanian waters to prevent Colombia from suppressing the rebellion. Then he wrote a similar treaty with an independent Panama. In his December 1903 message to Congress, Roosevelt justified his use of force as in the interests of the United States, the world, and Colombia itself. He later bragged that he took the Canal Zone while Congress debated.

In December 1904, Roosevelt introduced a sweeping enlargement of the Monroe Doctrine, thereafter known as the Roosevelt Corollary.

Flagrant cases of Latin American wrongdoing or impotence, Roosevelt asserted, could entice European nations to become involved in the issues of Western Hemisphere nations, which could in turn become inimical to U.S. interests. This sort of scenario would force the United States to initiate "the exercise of an international police power." The United States, in other words, would intervene to prevent intervention by others. The president accordingly announced the new policy that he expected Congress to support.

A primary precipitating factor for the Roosevelt Corollary was a debt crisis in the Dominican Republic that brought the nation to bankruptcy and led to fear of intervention by four European creditors. The Corollary was thus implemented first in this small Caribbean country. Roosevelt concluded an agreement with the Dominican president by which the United States would take over the Dominican customhouses and use receipts to retire the debt. When Congress balked at this executive agreement, Roosevelt wrote a treaty and undertook military intervention. The treaty did not receive Senate approval, but Roosevelt was able to conclude a modus vivendi of 1905 that put the essence of the accord into effect until an acceptable treaty was negotiated in 1907. Through the vehicle of the customhouses, the United States controlled the Dominican Republic until 1911.

Roosevelt also sent troops to Cuba, informing Congress only after he had done so. In August 1906 a Cuban insurrection occurred that the existing government proved powerless to put down. The U.S. president dispatched a naval force to Cuban waters to help stabilize the situation. Then he sent in the marines, who propped up a provisional government established under the U.S. secretary of war until the selection of a new government.

President Taft, whose foreign policy was known as "dollar diplomacy," intervened militarily in Nicaragua and Cuba as well. The theory of dollar diplomacy was that official administration encouragement of investments and trade would promote increased economic activity while affording the United States a greater political presence in strategically important areas of the world. In practice, dollar diplomacy worked effectively only in regions where the United States could either send or threaten to send troops. If Taft's policy succeeded in Nicaragua, it was because a contingent of U.S. marines took over the country in 1912. In 1909 the Taft administration had helped precipitate the overthrow of President José Santos Zelaya of Nicaragua after he threatened to cancel U.S. business concessions and to contract with Japan for canal rights across his country. In 1912, Santos

Zelaya's pro-American successor, Adolfo Díaz, a man who sought to promote stability and good government, requested U.S. assistance when his
administration was threatened by an insurrection. Taft sent in two thousand
marines, who put down the revolt and deported the rebel leader. The
marines, or a segment of them, stayed on as a legation guard for the next
thirteen years to "stabilize" the country. Taft informed Congress of his
Nicaraguan policy after the fact, in his November 1912 State of the Union
address. In that same address he announced that in May 1912 he had sent
marines from the U.S. naval station at Guantánamo Bay into the heart of
Cuba to protect American lives and property by helping the Havana government put down an uprising.

As a constitutional scholar and committed anti-imperialist, Wilson came
to the presidency assuming his administration would neither trouble itself
in any primary way with foreign affairs nor engage in the interventionism
of his two immediate predecessors. Because of his powerful predisposition
toward the promotion of democracy and "good government," however, he
proved more interventionist than either one. To his credit, however, he paid
attention to the issue of congressional approval. In 1914, when the
Mexican government of General Victoriano Huerta became a problem that
in Wilson's opinion required the use of U.S. troops, he requested congressional authorization. He used it to occupy the port city of Vera Cruz as the
first step in an effort to bring down Huerta's government, which Wilson
considered an illegitimate aggregation presided over by a brutal murderer.
The occupation of Vera Cruz and subsequent U.S.-Mexican actions almost
led to full-scale war with Mexico, which Wilson did not want. But, using
tacit congressional approval, he proceeded to take military action against
Mexico—even after the country's removal of the Huerta regime—to deal
with border incursions led by the bandit Francisco (Pancho) Villa.

Although he understood his questionable legal authority to do so,
Wilson intervened in both the Dominican Republic and Haiti, primarily
in vain attempts to promote representative governments and sufficient stability in both countries so that imperial Germany would not find itself
tempted to move in. These interventions resulted in U.S. military occupation of the Dominican Republic from 1916 to 1924 and of Haiti from
1915 until 1934.

War with Germany was a far different matter from the establishment of
protectorates in the Caribbean and Central America. On April 2, 1917,
Wilson sent a message to Congress requesting a declaration of war against
Germany, which Congress overwhelmingly approved four days later. The
vote was 373–50 in the House and 82–6 in the Senate. War came after

nearly three years of U.S. maneuvering between the Allied and Central powers, during which time Wilson's policies became increasingly pro-Allied, specifically pro-British. The president, for a variety of reasons well documented in a large body of scholarship, essentially acquiesced in British violations of U.S. neutrality while holding Germany to strict accountability because of its use of the submarine. A primary factor influencing Wilson was that Great Britain's violations compromised American property, and Germany's—because of the nature of the submarine—took American lives.

As an extension of the war against Germany, Wilson joined Great Britain, France, and Japan in an intervention in Russia during the summer of 1918. The purpose of Wilson's decisions was multifold: to prevent large stocks of arms and munitions, given to Russia before the Bolshevik Revolution, from falling into the hands of Germany; to check the motives of the other intervening powers; and to aid in overthrowing the Bolshevik government, which the president deemed illegitimate, barbaric, and contrary to the interests of humanity itself. This action took place in northern European Russia. When the intervention extended to Siberia and went on into 1919, the Senate asked Wilson to explain the dispatching of U.S. soldiers to that part of the world. The president satisfactorily honored the request in July 1919. All U.S. troops left Russian territory in the spring of 1920.

Beginning with Warren G. Harding, Republican presidents in the 1920s became highly critical of the array of Wilsonian interventions and, particularly in Latin America, attempted a policy of gradual withdrawal of U.S. forces. Harding removed marines from the Dominican Republic. In 1925, President Calvin Coolidge pulled the remaining contingent of marines out of Nicaragua. But continuing political turmoil in Nicaragua led Coolidge to send a small naval force there in 1926, followed by U.S. marines in early 1927. Coolidge defended these actions as necessary to maintain control of a revolutionary situation provoked by other (particularly Mexican) outside intervention. He further claimed U.S. proprietary rights to a canal route through Nicaragua. His renewed military intrusion, however, did not meet with overwhelming approval in Congress or the press, and Congress threatened to cut off funds for the U.S. occupation. It did not do so, but the continuing debate on the matter kept it in public view. Despite the unpopularity of the intervention, the marines stayed until January 1933, just two months before the beginning of Franklin Roosevelt's presidency. In Nicaragua and in China, where Coolidge sent U.S. marines and warships in 1927, he held that protection of American lives and property under revolutionary circumstances took precedence over constitutional liberalism.

World War II was the United States's fifth declared war and its most popular. In September 1939, when war began in Europe with Nazi Germany's invasion of Poland, President Roosevelt began a policy of neutrality, though it deliberately favored the democracies. Between 1939 and December 1941 he progressively led the United States toward alignment, as he tried to convince the public and Congress of the wisdom of opposition to the Axis powers. The Destroyers-for-Bases deal with Great Britain, Cash-and-Carry trade policies, and the Lend-Lease Act were all designed to give maximum support—short of war—to opponents of Germany and Italy. Ultimately, U.S. refusal to accept Japan's domination of China—which it had invaded in 1931—as well as its efforts to control Southeast Asia and a major portion of the Pacific led to a breakdown of Japanese-U.S. relations in the fall of 1941. Moreover, with the move into Southeast Asia, Axis aggression in Europe and Asia became linked. When Roosevelt and his advisers put in place a tough regimen of economic sanctions against Japan and then refused to compromise them away, Japan prepared and carried out its aggressive December 7, 1941, attack on the U.S. naval base at Pearl Harbor. Roosevelt's war message the following day not only accorded with constitutional imperatives but also met with resounding approval. The Senate voted 82–0 for war, the House 388–1. Only Congresswoman Jeannette Rankin of Montana stood in opposition.

Following World War II the United Nations became a complicating entity in the U.S. war power issue. The question that arose on multiple occasions was whether U.S. responsibility to the United Nations took precedence over the warmaking power of Congress in those instances in which the international body voted to take military action. Several U.S. presidents advanced the specious argument that UN authority was enough for them to commit American forces abroad. Beginning with President Truman's intervention in the Korean conflict, the United States engaged in a number of undeclared wars over the succeeding forty-five years. In many of the cases, interestingly, the United Nations functioned as an arm of U.S. foreign policy.

War in Korea came after nearly five years of conflict on that peninsula between the United States, the Soviet Union, and indigenous Korean forces, sometimes under the control of the two superpowers. War broke out on June 25, 1950, following Joseph Stalin's decision, earlier that same year, to give North Korean leader Kim Il Sung the green light to unify the country under Communist domination. In 1945 the United States had accepted the Japanese surrender south of the 38th parallel and occupied that part of the peninsula along with South Korean nationalists. At the end of the 1940s—having determined to concentrate U.S. efforts at containing Soviet/Communist power in Europe—the United States had taken the Korean matter to the United Nations, had arranged a UN solution, and had withdrawn its forces. By early 1950, with only token troops left in South Korea, U.S. actions and Secretary of State Dean Acheson's statement to the National Press Club had made it clear to all observers that Korea lay outside the U.S. defense perimeter. The UN solution of 1948 had called for elections in all of Korea under UN auspices, a scheme concocted by the United States to internationalize the problem and allow it to withdraw without losing face. U.S. policymakers knew full well that North Korea and the Soviet Union would not permit UN elections in the North, and hence such elections could take place only in the South. The plan would not unify the peninsula, but it would provide cover for the Americans to leave. Once the United States departed, Kim applied increased pressure on his patron in the Soviet Union to secure approval and assistance to defeat the government left behind in the South.

Having already decided that Korea lay outside its defense perimeter, the United States could have allowed Communist domination of the entire country when the North Korean invasion occurred. That approach would have been in accord with official policy. Ultimately, however, the United States had concerns that transcended the territorial and the strategic— including such intangible considerations as promoting its credibility as a guarantor and ensuring the sanctity and viability of the United Nations as an international agency to combat aggression. Upon learning of the invasion, President Truman determined to send air and naval forces to Korean waters, and a few days later he committed troops. Almost simultaneously, he took the matter to the United Nations Security Council, where he secured a vote demanding that North Korea pull back across the 38th parallel. When he committed American air, land, and sea power, it was under the authority, he announced, of the United Nations. Without asking Congress for a declaration of war and with only the sanction of the United Nations, Truman took his country into a major war that lasted three years, cost over $15 billion, led to armed conflict with the Chinese Communists, and resulted in thirty-three thousand American deaths. Other countries committed small contingents of troops, but the United States and South Korea carried on the lion's share of the fighting, dying, and paying.

Despite President Truman's pronouncement to the contrary, the Korean conflict was, in fact, an American war in which the United Nations made few significant decisions. Moreover, when Truman informed congressional leaders of U.S. actions on June 27, he signaled his determination to go ahead with or without the approval of Congress. Subsequent meetings with members of Congress were characterized by the president's policy of sharing information without seeking direct congressional authorization. Such sanction was unnecessary, declared Truman, because the United States was engaged not in a war but in a UN "police action." Among Truman's reasons for proceeding as if the country were not at war was the fear that the conflict might lead to World War III. It is important to note, however, that nothing in the United States's decision to join the United Nations, nothing in Congress's deliberations, or otherwise, could accurately be construed as altering the constitutional requirements for the initiation of a major military effort. Truman, in other words, had acted contrary to the Constitution, even though he almost certainly did so in the nation's interests.

As the Republican candidate for the presidency in 1952, General Eisenhower made a major issue of the Korean War and Truman's mistakes in prosecuting it. Accordingly, when in office, he chose to request advance congressional authorization in cases where intervention would be necessary. In one such instance, the Taiwan Strait crisis of 1954–55, he asked Congress for extraordinary a priori approval to use U.S. military power against the People's Republic of China in defense of Taiwan and the Pescadores Islands. This conflict arose when the Chinese Communists began shelling the tiny offshore islands of Quemoy and Matsu, on which Chiang Kai-shek had left troops when he had fled the mainland to Taiwan in 1949. Angered that the United States, by becoming a protector of Taiwan, had prevented them from completing their revolution, the Communists had initiated these military moves. Their purpose was either to take a first step toward seizing Taiwan; to test their February 1950 alliance with the Soviet Union; or to put strains on the relationship between Chiang and the United States, which relationship was moving toward a mutual defense treaty in 1954. Only one day after Eisenhower submitted his message, the House of Representatives passed the Formosa Resolution (Formosa was the old Portuguese name for Taiwan) with a vote of 410–3. Shortly thereafter the Senate gave its approval with a vote of 85–3. The Formosa Resolution was extraordinary because of deliberations following its passage. The Eisenhower administration gave serious consideration to the use of nuclear weapons against China, which could have triggered the Sino-Soviet alliance and could have led to war with the Soviet Union. As it turned out, the crisis ended peacefully when the Chinese, who learned that the Soviets were not prepared to support them, stopped the shelling.

Two years later, Eisenhower asked for congressional support in the event that U.S. military intervention became necessary in the Middle East. He was worried that the increasingly close relationship between the government of Egypt's Gamal Abdel Nasser and the Soviet Union would encourage both regimes to seize upon instability in the region to advance Soviet influence. Congress debated this request at length before passing a joint resolution that allowed the president to send troops to any country asking for U.S. protection against any nation controlled by international communism. This resolution, which also permitted economic and military aid to Middle Eastern countries, became known as the Eisenhower Doctrine. It was under this doctrine that Eisenhower sent fourteen thousand marines to Lebanon in July 1958.

The intervention in Lebanon represented some degree of misapprehension on the part of Eisenhower and his advisers. Early in 1958, Egypt, Syria, and Yemen had established the United Arab Republic, a nominal unification of the three countries, with Nasser as its leader. Determined not to be isolated, Jordan and Iraq subsequently founded the Arab Union. When a coup seemed imminent in Jordan, the United States, assuming that the uprising had been instigated by Nasser, feared that both Iraq and Jordan would move closer to Egypt and the Soviet Union. The Lebanese president's plea for help in preventing his government from being the next to topple fell on sympathetic ears in Washington. U.S. military intervention was carried out until October when, under the aegis of Middle Eastern leaders and the United Nations, the situation stabilized. Political instability in the region clearly resulted more from competing Arab nationalisms than from attempts by the Soviets to purvey their influence. In the Cold War context, Eisenhower had overreacted, but he had not done so without some measure of congressional authority.

During the Cuban Missile Crisis, President Kennedy assumed sweeping executive authority, and the words and deeds of members of Congress indicated that it was quite all right with them. They were happy to see someone else assume responsibility for a crisis that could mean life or death for much of humanity. In October 1962, Kennedy had received definitive proof of the Soviets' emplacement of medium- and intermediate-range missiles in Cuba. His response included naming a group of advisers known as the Executive Committee of the National Security Council to consider all the options, and the decision was made to place a blockade on Cuba and insist that Soviet leaders agree to withdraw the weapons. On the evening of October 22, Kennedy went on national television to announce the blockade. As the world watched in sheer terror, the president and his advisers—notably, Attorney General Robert F. Kennedy, his brother; Secretary of State Dean Rusk; and Secretary of Defense Robert McNamara—negotiated with Soviet premier Nikita Khrushchev for the missiles' removal. On October 28 the Soviet leader—under intense pressure and aware that if he did not comply, the United States would invade Cuba, carry out attacks on the missile sites, and (in the event of Soviet retaliation) launch the full weight of its nuclear force against the Soviet Union—agreed to dismantle and remove the missiles. What Khrushchev knew and Kennedy did not was that Soviet forces in Cuba numbered over forty thousand and their commander had tactical nuclear weapons at his disposal for use against a U.S. invading force. American restraint in the use of its own nuclear arsenal would therefore have been almost impossible in the event of armed combat.

The only congressional mandate operative during the crisis, and one that Kennedy claimed he did not need, came before the confrontation: on October 3 the House and Senate agreed that the United States should, by whatever means it deemed necessary, prevent Cuba from extending its aggressive or subversive atrocities in the Western Hemisphere. Congress did not delegate authority to the president; it merely stated its sentiments. But some of its members supported Kennedy's views that he could take action as circumstances required. During the crisis itself, Kennedy did not seek a declaration of war. He relied on the emergency powers of defense considered inherent in his role as commander in chief.

As President Johnson escalated U.S. involvement in Vietnam, the closest he came to a war message was his request to Congress for a resolution expressing congressional support for all necessary actions to protect U.S. troops and assist countries party to the Southeast Asia Treaty Organization (SEATO). He wanted a resolution similar to Eisenhower's during the Taiwan Strait crisis, the 1957 resolution on the Middle East, or Kennedy's in the matter of Cuba. The occasion for Johnson's message was a series of incidents in North Vietnam's Gulf of Tonkin on August 2 and 4, 1964. North Vietnamese torpedo boats reportedly attacked U.S. destroyers deployed in the gulf, and U.S. aircraft retaliated. Whether the assaults actually occurred as the president described is unclear, but there is no doubt that he was searching for a pretext to ask Congress for a supporting resolution. He and his advisers had prepared a draft the previous spring. Congress acted on Johnson's request with enthusiasm and virtually no dissent. On August 7 the House passed the fateful resolution, 416–0, as did the Senate, 88–2. What followed this resolution—one that gave the president carte blanche in his actions to protect U.S. armed forces and support

SEATO countries—was America's longest war, its most costly conflict, and its first major defeat. Tremendous national disruption and turmoil that put in question not only the United States's international purposes but also many of its domestic institutions ensued. Some of the reevaluation focused on the president's war powers.

After the initial buildup in Vietnam, Johnson undertook an intervention in the Western Hemisphere that was reminiscent of those of the Progressive era. On April 24, 1965, followers of the Dominican Republic's Juan Bosch, including some leftists and Communists, launched a coup against the regime of Donald Reid Cabral. Bosch, himself an anti-Communist liberal poet and philosopher, had held power a few years before but had demonstrated less than superior ability to govern the country. Johnson favored Reid Cabral, and he feared that Communist support of Bosch could lead to another Cuba. Under the guise of protecting American nationals, Johnson sent in a small contingent of marines. Soon realizing that a favorable, pro-U.S. outcome to the political uncertainty would require more effort, he dispatched a force of over twenty-two thousand to the small Caribbean country. Consulting congressional leaders along the way, he received fairly strong support for his actions. At least in the initial phase of the operation, he enjoyed public backing as well. This was the last intervention during the Vietnam era to receive such endorsement.

On January 20, 1969, when Richard Nixon became president and assumed direction of the Vietnam War, he was fully aware that it was draining U.S. resources and limiting the nation's ability to address other foreign-policy concerns. He and his National Security Council adviser, Henry Kissinger, understood the need to end the war. How to do so was the problem. Nixon believed it necessary to achieve a peace with U.S. credibility intact, a peace "with honor." Unfortunately, terminating the conflict in this way—when his leverage with the North Vietnamese was limited to the issue of the pace of U.S. withdrawal—proved impossible. He inherited a conflict in which over thirty-one thousand Americans had been killed; he concluded it after nearly twenty-seven thousand more had lost their lives. In the process of disengaging from the war with honor, he put into use such extreme military measures as intensified bombing of the North, and he also launched an invasion of Cambodia. Having authorized the foray into Cambodia—which triggered a wave of protest the likes of which the United States had never seen before—as an extension of the Vietnam War, he did not seek congressional approval.

In large measure because of the Vietnam tragedy but also owing to increased presidential encroachments on congressional warmaking power in the entire post-World War II era, Congress in 1973 passed the War Powers Resolution. It came into existence following a number of statutory and court challenges of President Nixon's authority to continue waging war in Southeast Asia, particularly in Cambodia. In short the War Powers Resolution required that the president and Congress arrive at a collective judgment before commitment of U.S. forces to battle; it also gave the president up to ninety days to use military force without the approval of Congress, after which time such action would have to be ended. The resolution specified as well that the president must report these military exploits to Congress.

The War Powers Resolution was first applied in May 1975 when President Gerald R. Ford reported his exercise of force to free the *Mayaguez*, a U.S. merchant vessel en route from Hong Kong to Thailand. The president and his advisers apparently made use of this incident, which took place only a month after the denouement in Vietnam, to prove that the United States was not a pitiful, helpless giant. They also sought to avoid a repetition of the 1968 *Pueblo* incident, when North Korea had seized an American intelligence ship and held its crew in brutal confinement for approximately eleven months. In the case of the *Mayaguez*, Cambodian patrol boats stopped the vessel on May 12 and escorted it to Koh Tong Island, apparently as a prelude to taking the crew hostage. Rather than pursue diplomatic initiatives, and thereby giving the Cambodians time to transfer the crew to the mainland, President Ford ordered a marine assault on Koh Tong to retake the ship and rescue the men. As noted in his War Powers Report to Congress, which came one day after the completion of the mission, the operation was a success. What Ford did not disclose, however, was that forty-one marines were killed in rescuing the thirty-nine crewmen.

On April 25, 1980, President Jimmy (James Earl) Carter announced to the American people the failure of a military mission to rescue American hostages then being held in Tehran. The following day he made his War Powers Report to Congress on the action. Because it was a covert operation, Carter had not told members of Congress about its execution in advance. Informing them might have had a salutary effect, however, since they might have urged caution and spared the county considerable embarrassment. The mission, in brief, involved eight helicopters and six cargo planes undertaking a rendezvous in the Iranian Salt Desert, after which the copters would fly the men on to Tehran and attempt a daring rescue of the hostages. As it turned out, U.S. military planners had failed to secure helicopters with fuel filters to keep sand out of the engines. When two copters developed engine trouble and a third was found to have a hydraulic mal-function, the operation was scrapped. Then as one of the remaining heli-copters was preparing to leave, it crashed into one of the transport planes, killing three crewmen on the copter and five on the plane. If that were not enough, the U.S. mission subsequently encountered an Iranian bus, a fuel truck, and a pickup in the desert. Despite the best efforts of U.S. personnel to detain the Iranians, at least one driver escaped into the night.

President Reagan may have confused indigenous unrest in Central America caused by generations of grinding poverty and inequality with Cuban and Soviet incitement to revolution. But he was convinced, as had been other presidents before him, that turmoil in the United States's back-yard could not go unattended. The countries of main concern to him were El Salvador and Nicaragua. He particularly worried that the Soviet Union, acting through the Cubans and the leftist Sandinista regime in Nicaragua, might gain influence and even military bases in the region. Consequently, on April 27, 1983, Reagan delivered a special communication to Congress, not a war message but clearly an interventionist one, asking for congres-sional support for the administration's policies in four areas: promoting democracy in Central America, fostering economic development, granting military aid to forces opposing radical solutions in the area (in the case of El Salvador, defeating leftist guerrillas; in Nicaragua, undercutting the Sandinista regime), and encouraging negotiated settlement of regional problems. From that time forward, Reagan moved aggressively—usually within the law but occasionally outside it (through the sale of arms to Iran and the diversion of profits to rebels fighting the Sandinistas)—to stop the perceived advance of communism in the region.

Reagan conducted military operations in a number of areas of the world but did not always abide by the spirit of the War Powers Resolution. He sent some sixteen hundred marines to Lebanon, over two hundred of whom were killed in a terrorist attack on October 23, 1983. He also refused to accept a resolution by Congress giving him a full eighteen months to keep the marines in place; this was a small force to which the War Powers Act should not apply, he stated, implying that he could deploy the marines for as long as he wished, consonant with U.S. interests. Given the terrorist action and the public outcry in the United States about the continued dan-ger to the marines, however, he withdrew the force in the spring of 1984. Partly to divert attention from the tragedy in Lebanon, Reagan, in the same message to the American people in which he noted the terrorist attack, announced a U.S. invasion of Grenada conducted on October 25, 1983, to restore order to the island, purportedly to protect American medical students and prevent a Cuban occupation. Although he did not request prior congressional authorization for this action, he agreed to withdraw U.S. troops within a sixty-day period.

Because terrorism was a major U.S. concern during the 1980s, Reagan —capitalizing on Carter's inability to terminate the hostage crisis in Iran— promised a tough policy of nonnegotiation and strong retribution whenever Americans were put at risk. Although his rhetoric far exceeded his actions, some of which resulted in more Americans being killed by terrorists than had been killed in all the previous presidential administrations put together, Reagan occasionally did act in what appeared to be an appropriately forceful manner. On March 24, 1986, in response to surface-to-air missile attacks on U.S. ships and planes in the Gulf of Sidra, the United States sank three Libyan patrol boats. This move, Reagan informed Congress, was made purely in self-defense. On April 14, less than a month later, Reagan authorized a series of air strikes on the "headquarters, terrorist facilities, and military assets" of President Mu'ammar Gadhafi of Libya. Carried out in retaliation for a Libyan-sponsored terrorist bombing of a discotheque in West Berlin that had killed a U.S. serviceman and wounded 230 others, these attacks resulted in—among other things—the death of Gadhafi's adopted daughter. In an effort to deter further terrorism, Reagan claimed that his evidence of Libyan terrorism was irrefutable and his response justifiable self-defense. Acting in accord with the War Powers Resolution, in his view, he did not consult with Congress in advance but reported the air strikes two days later.

Also included in Reagan's behavior under the War Powers Resolution were revelations of an October 1987 military action against Iran in the Persian Gulf. On this occasion the United States had moved in reprisal for an October 15 Iranian missile attack on a U.S. tanker. Reagan had ordered a naval bombardment of Rashadat Platform, an Iranian military installation in the gulf. This time he not only reported the U.S. attack but also consulted with some members of Congress about it beforehand.

President Bush undertook three military campaigns, two of which comprised major military efforts involving the commitment of many thousands of U.S. troops. In all three he acted in agreement with the War Powers Resolution; in one he received congressional support tantamount to a declaration of war. In the first, Operation Just Cause, he sent eleven thousand troops to Panama to join the thirteen thousand already there, in order to defeat and capture General Manuel Noriega. An execrable dictator who had misgoverned Panama for several years, Noriega profited heavily from drug running and other forms of vice, threatened Americans living in the Canal Zone, and seemed a menace to future democracy, peace, and security in the region. In particular, he seemed an obstacle to the successful culmination of the Canal Treaty, through which Panama would assume control of this important waterway by the year 2000. Few Panamanians or Americans mourned when U.S. forces captured Noriega on January 3, 1990, and brought him to the United States, where he was tried and convicted on multiple criminal charges. Bush promptly began withdrawing troops; by the end of February all but those previously stationed in the country were gone. Though Bush's action may not have been fully consistent with either U.S. or international law, it appeared to conform with the interests of both the United States and the Panamanian people. It also received ex post facto endorsement from Congress.

When Iraqi leader Saddam Hussein sent nearly one hundred thousand troops into Kuwait in the summer of 1990, President Bush responded promptly and aggressively. In the knowledge that, by this act alone, Saddam Hussein had gained control of over 29 percent of the world's proven oil reserves, Bush immediately dispatched U.S. forces to prevent further aggression into Saudi Arabia, another huge oil producer. He called this action Operation Desert Shield. Then he set about building a U.S. alliance led by most of the rest of the world's developed nations to apply sanctions on Iraq and pressure its withdrawal from Kuwait. He secured a UN resolution demanding Iraqi withdrawal, and then he began preparing the United States, and the coalition of nations, for Iraq's forceful eviction from its neighbor's territory. To his credit he kept Congress informed of his actions. Although he insisted that with the UN resolution he did not need congressional authorization for war against Iraq, nevertheless he requested the approval. On January 12, by a close vote, Bush received it in the form of legislation that he signed into law on January 14, 1991. On February 24, following a month of intense bombing, the U.S.-led coalition, which included over three hundred thousand troops, began a land war against Iraq—a campaign that lasted one hundred hours and resulted in the deaths of over one hundred thousand Iraqi soldiers. One hundred and thirty-six Americans were killed in the conflict.

During any one year in the early 1990s, millions of people around the world suffered from starvation or malnutrition. For reasons that remain unclear, in 1992 the international and U.S. news media chose to focus on conditions in Somalia, a country on the Horn of Africa that previously had been an object of Soviet-U.S. Cold War competition. By the fall of 1992 an estimated three hundred thousand people had starved to death in Somalia, and one million more were on the verge of dying of hunger.

Moreover, civil government had totally collapsed, as armed gangs roamed the countryside; anarchy made it impossible for the United Nations to deliver food shipments to the needy. Huge quantities of UN-supplied provisions, to a large degree from the United States, piled up at the port of Mogadishu. In December 1992, under intense pressure to take humanitarian steps and ameliorate the suffering, Bush—by then a defeated, lame-duck president—decided to send in U.S. military forces to impose order and aid food distribution. These troops, numbering twenty-eight thousand, were part of a UN group acting pursuant to a December 3 resolution by that body. Bush's letter to Congress, in which he noted that his reporting was consistent with the War Powers Resolution, emphasized that this was a limited mission to restore order and deliver food. U.S. forces, he said, would remain "only as long as necessary to establish a secure environment for humanitarian relief operations."

Critics warned that no nation, no matter how limited its initial objective, could intervene in Somalia without becoming entangled in that country's political life. They were right. In June 1993 twenty-three Pakistani members of the UN peacekeeping mission were killed, probably by forces under the control of Somali warlord Mohammed Farah Aideed. On June 11, UN military units under U.S. leadership attacked some of Aideed's military positions, in the name of restoring order so the humanitarian mission could proceed. By August 1993 at least eight U.S. soldiers had lost their lives and several more had been wounded, also at the hands of Aideed's thugs. The American public and Congress finally became fed up with the operation in the fall of 1993, when it seemed that the Clinton administration had moved toward nation building in Somalia. The last straw came when Somali gangs desecrated the bodies of murdered U.S. servicemen and displayed a captured pilot. In October, Clinton ordered army troops into the country (the initial U.S. force of twenty-eight thousand had been reduced to five thousand) and stationed an aircraft carrier offshore, along with thirty-six hundred combat-ready marines. In response to pressure building in the United States, Clinton then announced to Congress that all American forces, except for a few hundred support troops, would be withdrawn by March 31, 1994.

President Clinton subsequently involved the United States in another African humanitarian intervention, when tribal, factional fighting led to slaughter in Rwanda in 1994. When thousands upon thousands of refugees flowing from Rwanda to Tanzania became subject to violence and bitter privation, Clinton ordered delivery of relief aid in large quantities in order to alleviate suffering. To avoid the type of violence to

Americans that had occurred in Somalia, he exercised caution. His limited actions neither invoked the war powers legislation nor elicited the direct concern of Congress.

Although Clinton did not have a military background and had avoided the draft during the Vietnam War—a conflict that he and many of his generation strenuously opposed—he took his role as commander in chief seriously, utilizing military force on several occasions. On June 26, 1993, he ordered a Tomahawk cruise-missile attack on Iraqi intelligence headquarters in Baghdad. Twenty-three such missiles were fired from U.S. naval vessels in the Red Sea and the Arabian Gulf. Precise amounts of damage were impossible to measure; however, Clinton claimed a high level of destruction to the complex. He had taken this action, he informed Congress, as part of his constitutional authority for national self-defense after the discovery of an elaborate Iraqi intelligence plan to assassinate Bush during the forrmer president's visit to Kuwait in April 1993. It was, Clinton boldly stated, an act of U.S. retribution that he hoped would make Iraq wary of pursuing further nefarious plots.

Concern about both the nonhumanitarian actions of the military dictatorship in Haiti and the thousands of refugees coming to U.S. shores led President Clinton to an intervention in the Caribbean not dramatically different from those of his early twentieth-century predecessors. Haiti had held an election in 1990 that had brought President Jean-Bertrand Aristide to power. A 1991 military coup had removed Aristide, beginning the rule of the Haitian military commander, Lieutenant General Raoul Cedras. Clinton deplored the Cedras dictatorship but was not prepared to do much about it until news of atrocities against women, children, and the regime's opponents became a daily feature in U.S. papers. The matter became further complicated as Haitians increasingly risked their lives— many of them dying—by taking to the sea in marginally seaworthy vessels, in the hope of making it to the United States. On July 3, 1993, the Organization of American States, meeting at Governors Island, New York, reached agreement on a plan to remove the dictatorship from power. Haiti's military leaders seemed prepared to cave in to U.S., Latin American, and UN sanctions at this point. In October 1993, however, when Clinton sent some six hundred U.S. troops as part of a UN mission to return Aristide to power, an unruly, armed mob of Haitians prevented the force from landing. This action caused the president to place even greater rhetorical and economic pressure—including the threat of imminent U.S. military intervention—on the Cedras regime. As a result, Congress became involved in a spirited debate about executive authority, which led to Clinton's bold announcement that as commander in chief he should have no limitation on his freedom of action to pursue U.S. interests.

When it became clear that no amount of diplomatic pressure would induce Cedras's resignation, the Clinton administration urged more direct action through the United Nations. In July 1994 the United Nations Security Council passed a resolution authorizing the use of any means, including force, to remove the dictatorship from power, and the United States agreed to lead an international military expedition to carry out the resolution. In a September 15 message to the American people, Clinton then announced the decision to invade Haiti. Having put the military option in place, Clinton sent former president Carter; General Colin Powell, former chairman of the Joint Chiefs of Staff; and Senator Sam Nunn of Georgia, chairman of the Senate Armed Services Committee, to undertake a last diplomatic effort to secure the Cedras regime's peaceful departure. This mission proved successful. The agreement enabled the opposition-free landing of a 15,000-member international force, the restoration of a degree of stability to Haiti, and—through the continued UN-U.S. occupation of that country—the return of Aristide to power.

Whereas the Caribbean was an area of vital U.S. interest, turmoil in the Balkans region of Southeast Europe did not evoke the same degree of concern. Yet a peculiar set of circumstances drew President Clinton's attention to that part of the world as well. The breakup of Yugoslavia in the aftermath of the Cold War led to intense ethnic fighting among Serbs, Croats, and Muslims—ancient rivals held together under Josip Broz Tito's Balkan empire since World War II. Bosnia, the most troublesome area and the one in which the Serbs were probably the most responsible for military aggression, caused the nations of the North Atlantic Treaty Organization (NATO) the greatest worry. In its forty-plus-year leadership of the West European alliance, the United States had moved well away from its historic nonentangled position in the affairs of Europe, and it could not help but address the questions that European governments found compelling. Conflict in Southeast Europe had sparked one world war; it could not be permitted to destabilize the whole of Europe. And Europe, moreover, could not allow Hitler-like atrocities to go unattended again.

In April 1993, NATO began the enforcement of a no-fly zone in Bosnia. The United States deployed combat aircraft to that effort. Through the remaining months of 1993 the United States participated in innumerable air drops of medical supplies, food, and other assistance over Bosnia, and it prevented intrusion into Bosnian air space. President Clinton reported U.S. involvement to Congress in April. Six months later, in October, he informed Congress of his policies in accordance with the War Powers Resolution, but he implied that membership in NATO allowed him to continue this involvement indefinitely, in effect superseding his constitutional authority. Congress debated cutting off funds but never did so.

Enforcing a no-fly zone did little to stop the bloodshed in Bosnia or to solve the ongoing problem of the Balkans. President Clinton increased U.S. involvement in the fall of 1995. Before the American people, he defended his plans for the expansion of NATO, extolled the alliance's virtues, and then stressed the role that NATO and the United States would play in Bosnia. In negotiations held in Dayton, Ohio, in November 1995, the United States helped broker a peace for Bosnia. The discussions resulted in an arrangement for shared power—a kind of Bosnian federation in which Muslims, Croats, and Serbs would hold sway in their own sectors of the country. Then Clinton reported to Congress and to the American people how the United States would participate in preserving the agreement: NATO, he said, would commit about sixty thousand troops to Bosnia; the United States would provide about twenty thousand of that number; and these forces would remain for approximately one year. This arrangement did not bring a permanent peace, but it ended the worst of the suffering and allowed the warring factions to begin the rebuilding process.

If the trouble in Bosnia seemed complicated, the crisis of 1999 in Kosovo proved even more complex and difficult. Serbian leader Slobodan Milosevic sought to suppress the Kosovo Liberation Army, cleanse Kosovo of its huge Albanian majority, and assert Serbian domination. In the process he authorized pillage, rape, and mayhem on a grand scale, thereby evoking outrage in the rest of Europe and among NATO countries in particular. The crisis created roughly eight hundred thousand refugees, who fled from the violence into Albania and Macedonia. After warning Milosevic, President Clinton, beginning on March 24, took the lead among U.S. allies and authorized an air bombardment of Serbian targets in the Federal Republic of Yugoslavia (Serbia and Montenegro). This air war went on until mid-June when Milosevic capitulated. He subsequently lost the presidency in the election of 2000, and the new government arrested him in the spring of 2001. In an address to the American people on March 24, 2000, President Clinton announced his decision to intervene. On March 26, in a follow-up message to Congress, he promised to abide by the War Powers Resolution.

President George W. Bush faced an unprecedented American crisis when, on September 11, 2001, small groups of terrorists took over three U.S. commercial jetliners, then flew them on suicide missions into the

World Trade Center buildings in New York City and into the Pentagon in Washington, DC, killing and injuring thousands of people. In another attempt at hitting a government building, apparently thwarted by passengers, they crashed a fourth plane into a field in southwestern Pennsylvania. Outraged, Congress shortly thereafter authorized a military response. President Bush issued a public statement as well as a statement to Congress, announcing a general war on terrorism and, specifically, a war to rid Afghanistan of its government, run by Muslim extremists known as the Taliban. The Taliban allowed a terror network, called al-Qaida, to operate on Afghan territory. Defeat of the Taliban proved quick and decisive. Defeat of terrorism would come slowly, if ever.

Readers will undoubtedly note a number of recurring themes in this presentation of calls to arms. In many cases presidents did not deliver a single war message requesting congressional and public approval for their use of force. Instead, they gave several addresses in varying venues, outlining the issues involved and detailing reasons for military action. Where there was more than one specific presidential message, I have reprinted all of the statements around and about the perceived need for force. Needless to say, such cumulative calls to arms occurred more frequently in instances of intervention than in formal, declared war. I should also note that I have reprinted presidential explanations of, defenses of, and requests for support of all of the major and most of the minor military interventions in U.S. history. Because this book concerns presidents' statements about what they planned to do, or what they had already done, I have excluded those uses of force that were brief and transitory. By the same token, I have included every war message following which Congress issued a formal, constitutional declaration of war. For clarity, I have provided textual or annotated identifications of people and events and have made emendations where necessary.

1

JOHN ADAMS

DOCUMENT 1
PRESIDENT JOHN ADAMS'S MESSAGE TO SPECIAL SESSION
OF CONGRESS. MAY 16, 1797.

Gentlemen of the Senate and Gentlemen of the House of Representatives:

The personal inconveniences to the members of the Senate and of the House of Representatives in leaving their families and private affairs at this season of the year are so obvious that I the more regret the extraordinary occasion which has rendered the convention of Congress indispensable.

It would have afforded me the highest satisfaction to have been able to congratulate you on a restoration of peace to the nations of Europe whose animosities have endangered our tranquillity; but we have still abundant cause of gratitude to the Supreme Dispenser of National Blessings for general health and promising seasons, for domestic and social happiness, for the rapid progress and ample acquisitions of industry through extensive territories, for civil, political, and religious liberty. While other states are desolated with foreign war or convulsed with intestine divisions, the United States present the pleasing prospect of a nation governed by mild and equal laws, generally satisfied with the possession of their rights, neither envying the advantages nor fearing the power of other nations, solicitous only for the maintenance of order and justice and the preservation of liberty, increasing daily in their attachment to a system of government in proportion to their experience of its utility, yielding a ready and general obedience to laws flowing from Reason and resting on the only solid foundation —the affections of the people.

It is with extreme regret that I shall be obliged to turn your thoughts to other circumstances, which admonish us that some of these felicities not be lasting. But if the tide of our prosperity is full and a reflux commencing, a vigilant circumspection becomes us, that we may meet our reverses with fortitude and extricate ourselves from their consequences with all the skill we possess and all the efforts in our power.

In giving to Congress information of the state of the Union and recommending to their consideration such measures as appear to me to be necessary or expedient, according to my constitutional duty, the causes and the objects of the present extraordinary session will be explained.

After the President of the United States received information that the French Government had expressed serious discontents at some proceedings of the Government of these States said to affect the interests of France, he thought it expedient to send to that country a new minister, fully instructed to enter on such amicable discussions and to give such candid explanations as might happily remove the discontents and suspicions of the French Government and vindicate the conduct of the United States. For this purpose he selected from among his fellow-citizens a character whose integrity, talents, experience, and services had placed him in the rank of the most esteemed and respected in the nation. The direct object of his mission was expressed in his letter of credence to the French Republic, being "to maintain that good understanding which from the commencement of the alliance had subsisted between the two nations, and to efface unfavorable impressions, banish suspicions, and restore that cordiality which was at once the evidence and pledge of a friendly union." And his instructions were to the same effect, "faithfully to represent the disposition of the Government and people of the United States (their disposition being one), to remove jealousies and obviate complaints by showing that they were groundless, to restore that mutual confidence which had been so unfortunately and injuriously impaired, and to explain the relative interests of both countries and the real sentiments of his own."

A minister thus specially commissioned it was expected would have proved the instrument of restoring mutual confidence between the two Republics. The first step of the French Government corresponded with that expectation. A few days before his arrival at Paris the French minister of foreign relations informed the American minister then resident at Paris of the formalities to be observed by himself in taking leave, and by his successor preparatory to his reception. These formalities they observed, and on the 9th of December presented officially to the minister of foreign relations, the one a copy of his letters of recall, the other a copy of his letters of credence.

These were laid before the Executive Directory. Two days afterwards the minister of foreign relations informed the recalled American minister that the Executive Directory had determined not to receive another minister plenipotentiary from the United States until after the redress of grievances demanded of the American Government, and which the French Republic had a right to expect from it. The American minister immediately endeavored to ascertain whether by refusing to receive him it was intended that he should retire from the territories of the French Republic, and verbal answers were given that such was the intention of the Directory. For his own justification he desired a written answer, but obtained none until toward the last of January, when, receiving notice in writing to quit the territories of the Republic, he proceeded to Amsterdam, where he proposed to wait for instruction from this Government. During his residence at Paris cards of hospitality were refused him, and he was threatened with being subjected to the jurisdiction of the minister of police; but with becoming firmness he insisted on the protection of the law of nations due to him as the known minister of a foreign power. You will derive further information from his dispatches, which will be laid before you.

As it is often necessary that nations should treat for the mutual advantage of their affairs, and especially to accommodate and terminate differences, and as they can treat only by ministers, the right of embassy is well known and established by the law and usage of nations. The refusal on the part of France to receive our minister is, then, the denial of a right; but the refusal to receive him until we have acceded to their demands without discussion and without investigation is to treat us neither as allies nor as friends, nor as a sovereign state.

With this conduct of the French Government it will be proper to take into view the public audience given to the late minister of the United States on his taking leave of the Executive Directory. The speech of the President discloses sentiments more alarming than the refusal of a minister, because more dangerous to our independence and union, and at the same time studiously marked with indignities toward the Government of the United States. It evinces a disposition to separate the people of the United States from the Government, to persuade them that they have different affections, principles, and interests from those of their fellow-citizens whom they themselves have chosen to manage their common concerns, and thus to produce divisions fatal to our peace. Such attempts ought to be repelled with a decision which shall convince France and the world that we are not a degraded people, humiliated under a colonial spirit of fear and sense of inferiority, fitted to be the miserable instruments of foreign influence, and regardless of national honor, character, and interest.

I should have been happy to have thrown a veil over these transactions if it had been possible to conceal them; but they have passed on the great theater of the world, in the face of all Europe and America, and with such circumstances of publicity and solemnity that they can not be disguised and will not soon be forgotten. They have inflicted a wound in the American breast. It is my sincere desire, however, that it may be healed.

It is my sincere desire, and in this I presume I concur with you and with our constituents, to preserve peace and friendship with all nations; and believing that neither the honor nor the interest of the United States absolutely forbid the repetition of advances for securing these desirable objects with France, I shall institute a fresh attempt at negotiation, and shall not fail to promote and accelerate an accommodation on terms compatible with the rights, duties, interests, and honor of the nation. If we have committed errors, and these can be demonstrated, we shall be willing to correct them; if we have done injuries, we shall be willing on conviction to redress them; and equal measures of justice we have a right to expect from France and every other nation.

The diplomatic intercourse between the United States and France being at present suspended, the Government has no means of obtaining official information from that country. Nevertheless, there is reason to believe that the Executive Directory passed a decree on the 2d of March last contravening in part the treaty of amity and commerce of 1778, injurious to our lawful commerce and endangering the lives of our citizens. A copy of this decree will be laid before you.

While we are endeavoring to adjust all our differences with France by amicable negotiation, the progress of the war in Europe, the depredations on our commerce, the personal injuries to our citizens, and the general complexion of affairs render it my indispensable duty to recommend to your consideration effectual measures of defense.

The commerce of the United States has become an interesting object of attention, whether we consider it in relation to the wealth and finances or the strength and resources of the nation. With a seacoast of near 2,000 miles in extent, opening a wide field for fisheries, navigation, and commerce, a great portion of our citizens naturally apply their industry and enterprise to these objects. Any serious and permanent injury to commerce would not fail to produce the most embarrassing disorders. To prevent it from being undermined and destroyed it is essential that it receive an adequate protection.

The naval establishment must occur to every man who considers the injuries committed on our commerce, the insults offered to our citizens, and the description of vessels by which these abuses have been practiced. As the sufferings of our mercantile and seafaring citizens can not be ascribed to the omission of duties demandable, considering the neutral situation of our country, they are to be attributed to the hope of impunity arising from a supposed inability on our part to afford protection. To resist the consequences of such impressions on the minds of foreign nations and to guard against the degradation and servility which they must finally stamp on the American character is an important duty of Government.

A naval power, next to the militia, is the natural defense of the United States. The experience of the last war would be sufficient to show that a moderate naval force, such as would be easily within the present abilities of the Union, would have been sufficient to have baffled many formidable transportations of troops from one State to another, which were then practiced. Our seacoasts, from their great extent, are more easily annoyed and more easily defended by a naval force than any other. With all the materials our country abounds; in skill our naval architects and navigators are equal to any, and commanders and seamen will not be wanting.

But although the establishment of a permanent system of naval defense appears to be requisite, I am sensible it can not be formed so speedily and extensively as the present crisis demands. Hitherto I have thought proper to prevent the sailing of armed vessels except on voyages to the East Indies, where general usage and the danger from pirates appeared to render the permission proper. Yet the restriction has originated solely from a wish to prevent collisions with the powers at war, contravening the act of Congress of June, 1794, and not from any doubt entertained by me of the policy and propriety of permitting our vessels to employ means of defense while engaged in a lawful foreign commerce. It remains for Congress to prescribe such regulations as will enable our seafaring citizens to defend themselves against violations of the law of nations, and at the same time restrain them from committing acts of hostility against the powers at war. In addition to this voluntary provision for defense by individual citizens, it appears to me necessary to equip the frigates, and provide other vessels of inferior force, to take under convoy such merchant vessels as shall remain unarmed.

The greater part of the cruisers whose depredations have been most injurious have been built and some of them partially equipped in the United States. Although an effectual remedy may be attended with difficulty, yet I have thought it my duty to present the subject generally to your consideration. If a mode can be devised by the wisdom of Congress to prevent the resources of the United States from being converted into the means of annoying our trade, a great evil will be prevented. With the same view, I think it proper to mention that some of our citizens resident abroad have fitted out privateers, and others have voluntarily taken the command, or entered on board of them, and committed spoliations on the commerce of the United States. Such unnatural aud iniquitous practices can be restrained only by severe punishments.

But besides a protection of our commerce on the seas, I think it highly necessary to protect it at home, where it is collected in our most important ports. The distance of the United States from Europe and the well-known promptitude, ardor, and courage of the people in defense of their country happily diminish the probability of invasion. Nevertheless, to guard against sudden aud predatory incursions the situation of some of our principal seaports demands your consideration. And as our country is vulnerable in other interests besides those of its commerce, you will seriously deliberate whether the means of general defense ought not to be increased by an addition to the regular artillery and cavalry, and by arrangements for forming a provisional army.

With the same view, and as a measure which, even in a time of universal peace, ought not to be neglected, I recommend to your consideration a revision of the laws for organizing, arming, and disciplining the militia, to render that natural and safe defense of the country efficacious.

Although it is very true that we ought not to involve ourselves in the political system of Europe, but to keep ourselves always distinct and separate from it if we can, yet to effect this separation, early, punctual, and continual information of the current chain of events and of the political projects in contemplation is no less necessary than if we were directly concerned in them. It is necessary, in order to [achieve] the discovery of the efforts made to draw us into the vortex, in season to make preparations against them. However we may consider ourselves, the maritime and commercial powers of the world will consider the United States of America as forming a weight in that balance of power in Europe which never can be forgotten or neglected. It would not only be against our interest, but it would be doing wrong to one-half of Europe, at least, if we should voluntarily throw ourselves into either scale. It is a natural policy for a nation that studies to be neutral to consult with other nations engaged in the same studies and pursuits. At the same time that measures might be pursued with this view, our treaties with Prussia and Sweden, one of which is expired and the other near expiring, might be renewed.

Gentlemen of the House of Representatives:

It is particularly your province to consider the state of the public finances, and to adopt such measures respecting them as exigencies shall be found to require. The preservation of public credit, the regular extinguishment of the public debt, and a provision of funds to defray any extraordinary expenses will of course call for your serious attention. Although the imposition of new burdens can not be in itself agreeable, yet there is no ground to doubt that the American people will expect from you such measures as their actual engagements, their present security, and future interests demand.

Gentlemen of the Senate and Gentlemen of the House of Representatives:

The present situation of our country imposes an obligation on all the departments of Government to adopt an explicit and decided conduct. In my situation an exposition of the principles by which my Administration will be governed ought not to be omitted.

It is impossible to conceal from ourselves or the world what has been before observed, that endeavors have been employed to foster and establish a division between the Government and people of the United States. To investigate the causes which have encouraged this attempt is not necessary; but to repel, by decided and united councils, insinuations so derogatory to the honor and aggressions so dangerous to the Constitution, union, and even independence of the nation is an indispensable duty.

It must not be permitted to be doubted whether the people of the United States will support the Government established by their voluntary consent and appointed by their free choice, or whether, by surrendering themselves to the direction of foreign and domestic factions, in opposition to their own Government, they will forfeit the honorable station they have hitherto maintained.

For myself, having never been indifferent to what concerned the interests of my country, devoted the best part of my life to obtain and support its independence, and constantly witnessed the patriotism, fidelity, and perseverance of my fellow-citizens on the most trying occasions, it is not for me to hesitate or abandon a cause in which my heart has been so long engaged.

Convinced that the conduct of the Government has been just and impartial to foreign nations, that those internal regulations which have been established by law for the preservation of peace are in their nature proper, and that they have been fairly executed, nothing will ever be done by me to impair the national engagements, to innovate upon principles which have been so deliberately and uprightly established, or to surrender in any manner the rights of the Government. To enable me to maintain this declaration I rely, under God, with entire confidence on the firm and enlightened support of the National Legislature and upon the virtue and patriotism of my fellow-citizens.

SOURCE: James D. Richardson, ed., *Messages and Papers of the Presidents*, 20 vols. (New York: Bureau of National Literature, 1912), 1:223–29.

DOCUMENT 2

PRESIDENT ADAMS REPLIES TO CONGRESS. JUNE 3, 1797.

Mr. Speaker and Gentlemen of the House of Representatives:

I receive with great satisfaction your candid approbation of the convention of Congress, and thank you for your assurances that the interesting subjects recommended to your consideration shall receive the attention which their importance demands, and that your cooperation may be expected in those measures which may appear necessary for our security or peace.*. . .

I pray you, gentlemen, to believe and to communicate such assurance to our constituents that no event which I can foresee to be attainable by any exertions in the discharge of my duties can afford me so much cordial satisfaction as to conduct a negotiation with the French Republic, to a removal of prejudices, a correction of errors, a dissipation of umbrages, an accommodation of all differences, and a restoration of harmony and affection to the mutual satisfaction of both nations. And whenever the legitimate organs of intercourse shall be restored and the real sentiments of the two Governments can be candidly communicated to each other, although strongly impressed with the necessity of collecting ourselves into a manly posture of defense, I nevertheless entertain an encouraging confidence that a mutual spirit of conciliation, a disposition to compensate injuries and accommodate each other in all our relations and connections, will produce

*On June 2, 1797, both the Senate and House responded to President Adams's Special Session Message of May 1797 with such enthusiastic commentary as "with singular satisfaction the vigilance, firmness, and promptitude exhibited by you in this critical state of our public affairs, and from thence derive an evidence and pledge of the rectitude and integrity of your Administration."

an agreement to a treaty consistent with the engagements, rights, duties, and honor of both nations.

SOURCE: Richardson, *Messages and Papers of the Presidents*, 1: 234–35.

DOCUMENT 3
PRESIDENT ADAMS'S FIRST ANNUAL MESSAGE TO CONGRESS. NOVEMBER 22, 1797.

... Our envoys extraordinary to the French Republic embarked ... to join their colleague in Holland [Elbridge Gerry and John Marshall joined Charles C. Pinckney]. I have received intelligence of the arrival of both of them in Holland, from which they all proceeded on their journeys to Paris. ... Whatever may be the result of this mission, I trust that nothing will have been omitted on my part to conduct the negotiation to a successful conclusion, on such equitable terms as may be compatible with the safety, honor, and interest of the United States. Nothing, in the meantime, will contribute so much to the preservation of peace and the attainment of justice as a manifestation of that energy and unanimity of which on many former occasions the people of the United States have given such memorable proofs, and the exertion of those resources for national defense which a beneficent Providence has kindly placed within their power.

It may be confidently asserted that nothing has occurred since the adjournment of Congress which renders inexpedient those precautionary measures recommended by me to the consideration of the two Houses at the opening of your late extraordinary session. If that system was then prudent, it is more so now, as increasing depredations strengthen the reasons for its adoption.

Indeed, whatever may be the issue of the negotiation with France, and whether the war in Europe is or is not to continue, I hold it most certain that permanent tranquillity and order will not soon be obtained. The state of society has so long been disturbed, the sense of moral and religious obligations so much weakened, public faith and national honor have been so impaired, respect to treaties has been so diminished, and the law of nations has lost so much of its force, while pride, ambition, avarice, and violence have been so long unrestrained, there remains no reasonable ground on which to raise an expectation that a commerce without protection or defense will not be plundered.

The commerce of the United States is essential, if not to their existence, at least to their comfort, their growth, prosperity, and happiness. The genius, character, and habits of the people are highly commercial. Their cities have been formed and exist upon commerce. Our agriculture, fisheries, arts, and manufactures are connected with and depend upon it. In short, commerce has made this country what it is, and it can not be destroyed or neglected without involving the people in poverty and distress. Great numbers are directly and solely supported by navigation. The faith of society is pledged for the preservation of the rights of commerce and seafaring no less than of the other citizens. Under this view of our affairs, I should hold myself guilty of a neglect of duty if I forbore to recommend that we should make every exertion to protect our commerce and to place our country in a suitable posture of defense as the only sure means of preserving both. . . .

The numerous captures of American vessels by the cruisers of the French Republic and of some by those of Spain have occasioned considerable expenses in making and supporting the claims of our citizens before their tribunals. The sums required for this purpose have in divers instances been disbursed by the consuls of the United States. By means of the same captures great numbers of our seamen have been thrown ashore in foreign countries, destitute of all means of subsistence, and the sick in particular have been exposed to grievous sufferings. The consuls have in these cases also advanced moneys for their relief. For these advances they reasonably expect reimbursements from the United States.

The consular act relative to seamen requires revision and amendment. The provisions for their support in foreign countries and for their return are found to be inadequate and ineffectual. Another provision seems necessary to be added to the consular act. Some foreign vessels have been discovered sailing under the flag of the United States and with forged papers. It seldom happens that the consuls can detect this deception, because they have no authority to demand an inspection of the registers and sea letters.

SOURCE: Richardson, *Messages and Papers of the Presidents*, 1:240–43.

DOCUMENT 4
PRESIDENT ADAMS REPORTS THAT A FRENCH PRIVATEER RAIDS AN ENGLISH MERCHANT SHIP IN AMERICAN WATERS. FEBRUARY 5, 1798.

I have received a letter from His Excellency Charles Pinckney, esq., governor of the State of South Carolina, dated the 22d of October, 1797, inclosing a letter of depositions of witnesses to several captures and outrages committed within and near the limits of the United States by a French privateer belonging to Cape Francois, or Monte Christo, called the *Vertitude* or *Fortitude*, and commanded by a person of the name of Jordan or Jourdain [NFI], and particularly upon an English merchant ship named the *Oracabissa*, which he first plundered and then burned, with the rest of her cargo, of great value, within the territory of the United States, in the harbor of Charleston, on the 7th day of October last, copies of which letter and depositions, and also of several other depositions relative to the same subject, received from the collector of Charleston, are herewith communicated.

Whenever the channels of diplomatic communication between the United States and France shall be opened, I shall demand satisfaction for the insult and reparation for the injury.

I have transmitted these papers to Congress not so much for the purpose of communicating an account of so daring a violation of the territory of the United States as to show the propriety and necessity of enabling the executive authority of Government to take measures for protecting citizens of the United States and such foreigners as have a right to enjoy their peace and the protection of their laws within their limits in that as well as some other harbors which are equally exposed.

SOURCE: Richardson, *Messages and Papers of the Presidents*, 1:252.

DOCUMENT 5

PRESIDENT ADAMS ASKS CONGRESS FOR INCREASED SPENDING FOR MILITARY READINESS IN PREPARATION FOR WAR. MARCH 19, 1798.

The dispatches from the envoys extraordinary of the United States to the French Republic, which were mentioned in my message to both houses of Congress of [March] 5th, have been examined and maturely considered.

While I feel a satisfaction in informing you that their exertions for the adjustment of the differences between the two nations have been sincere and unremitted, it is incumbent on me to declare that I perceive no ground of expectation that the objects of their mission can be accomplished on terms compatible with the safety, the honor, or the essential interests of the nation.

This result can not with justice be attributed to any want of moderation on the part of this Government, or to any indisposition to forego secondary interests for the preservation of peace. Knowing it to be my duty, and believing it to be your wish, as well as that of the great body of the people, to avoid by all reasonable concessions any participation in the contentions of Europe, the powers vested in our envoys were commensurate with a liberal and pacific policy and that high confidence which might justly be reposed in the abilities, patriotism, and integrity of the characters to whom the negotiation was committed. After a careful review of the whole subject, with the aid of all the information I have received, I can discern nothing which could have insured or contributed to success that has been omitted on my part, and nothing further which can be attempted consistently with maxims for which our country has contended at every hazard, and which constitute the basis of our national sovereignty.

Under these circumstances I can not forbear to reiterate the recommendations which have been formerly made, and to exhort you to adopt with promptitude, decision, and unanimity such measures as the ample resources of the country afford for the protection of our seafaring and commercial citizens, for the defense of any exposed portions of our territory, for replenishing our arsenals, establishing foundries and military manufactures, and to provide such efficient revenue as will be necessary to defray extraordinary expenses and supply the deficiencies which may be occasioned by depredations on our commerce.

The present state of things is so essentially different from that in which instructions were given to the collectors to restrain vessels of the United States from sailing in an armed condition that the principle on which those orders were issued has ceased to exist. I therefore deem it proper to inform Congress that I no longer conceive myself justifiable in continuing them, unless in particular cases where there may be reasonable ground of suspicion that such vessels are intended to be employed contrary to law.

In all your proceedings it will be important to manifest a zeal, vigor, and concert in defense of the national rights proportioned to the danger with which they are threatened.

SOURCE: Richardson, *Messages and Papers of the Presidents*, 1:254-55.

DOCUMENT 6
PRESIDENT ADAMS'S PROCLAMATION REVOKING THE FRENCH REPUBLIC'S CONSULAR RIGHTS AND PRIVILEGES IN THE UNITED STATES. JULY 13, 1798.

The citizen Joseph Philippe Létombe having heretofore produced to the President of the United States his commission as consul-general of the

French Republic within the United States of America, and another commission as consul of the French Republic at Philadelphia; and, in like manner, the citizen [Jean Antoine] Rosier having produced his commission as vice-consul of the French Republic at New York; and the citizen [Louis] Arcambal having produced his commission as vice-consul of the French Republic at Newport; and citizen Théodore Charles Mozard having produced his commission as consul of the French Republic within the States of New Hampshire, Massachusetts, and Rhode Island; and the President of the United States having thereupon granted an exequatur to each of the French citizens above named, recognizing them in their respective consular offices above mentioned, and declaring them respectively free to exercise and enjoy such functions, powers, and privileges as are allowed to a consul-general, consuls, and vice-consuls of the French Republic by their treaties, conventions, and laws in that case made and provided; and the Congress of the United States by their act passed the 7th day of July, 1798, having declared "that the United States are of right freed and exonerated from the stipulations of the treaties and of the consular convention heretofore concluded between the United States and France, and that the same shall not henceforth be regarded as legally obligatory on the Government or citizens of the United States," and by a former act, passed the 13th day of May, 1798, the Congress of the United States having "suspended the commercial intercourse between the United States and France and the dependencies thereof," which commercial intercourse was the direct and chief object of the consular establishment; and

Whereas actual hostilities have long been practiced on the commerce of the United States by the cruisers of the French Republic under the orders of its Government, which orders that Government refuses to revoke or relax; and hence it has become improper any longer to allow the consul-general, consuls, and vice-consuls of the French Republic above named, or any of its consular persons or agents heretofore admitted in these United States, any longer to exercise their consular functions:

These are therefore to declare that I do no longer recognize the said citizen Létombe as consul-general or consul, nor the said citizens Rosier and Arcambal as vice-consuls, nor the said citizen Mozard as consul of the French Republic in any part of these United States, nor permit them or any other consular persons or agents of the French Republic heretofore admitted in the United States to exercise their functions as such; and I do hereby wholly revoke the exequaturs heretofore given to them respectively, and do declare them absolutely null and void from this day forward.

SOURCE: Richardson, *Messages and Papers of the Presidents*, 1:260–61.

DOCUMENT 7
PRESIDENT ADAMS'S SECOND ANNUAL MESSAGE
TO CONGRESS. DECEMBER 8, 1798.

. . . To the usual subjects of gratitude I can not omit to add one of the first importance to our well-being and safety; I mean that spirit which has arisen in our country against the menaces and aggression of a foreign nation. A manly sense of national honor, dignity, and independence has appeared which, if encouraged and invigorated by every branch of the Government, will enable us to view undismayed the enterprises of any foreign power and become the sure foundation of national prosperity and glory.

The course of the transactions in relation to the United States and France, which have come to my knowledge during your recess, will be made the subject of a future communication. That communication will confirm the ultimate failure of the measures which have been taken by the Government of the United States toward an amicable adjustment of differences with that power. You will at the same time perceive that the French Government appears solicitous to impress the opinion that it is averse to a rupture with this country, and that it has in a qualified manner declared itself willing to receive a minister from the United States for the purpose of restoring a good understanding. It is unfortunate for professions of this kind that they should be expressed in terms which may countenance the inadmissible pretension of a right to prescribe the qualifications which a minister from the United States should possess, and that while France is asserting the existence of a disposition on her part to conciliate with sincerity the differences which have arisen, the sincerity of a like disposition on the part of the United States, of which so many demonstrative proofs have been given, should even be indirectly questioned. It is also worthy of observation that the decree of the Directory alleged to intend to restrain the depredations of French cruisers on our commerce has not given, and can not give, any relief. It enjoins them to conform to all laws of France relative to cruising and prizes, while these laws are themselves the sources of the depredations of which we have so long, so justly, and so fruitlessly complained.

The law of France enacted in January last, which subjects to capture and condemnation neutral vessels and their cargoes if any portion of the latter are of British fabric or produce, although the entire property belong to neutrals, instead of being rescinded has lately received a confirmation by the failure of a proposition for its repeal. While this law, which is an un-equivocal act of war on the commerce of the nations it attacks, continues in force those nations can see in the French Government only a power regardless of their essential rights, of their independence and sovereignty; and if they possess the means they can reconcile nothing with their interest and honor but a firm resistance.

Hitherto, therefore, nothing is discoverable in the conduct of France which ought to change or relax our measures of defense. On the contrary, to extend and invigorate them is our true policy. We have no reason to regret that these measures have thus far adopted and pursued, and in proportion as we enlarge our view of the portentous and incalculable situation of Europe we shall discover new and cogent motives for the full development of our energies and resources.

But in demonstrating by our conduct that we do not fear war in the necessary protection of our rights and honor we shall give no room to infer that we abandon the desire of peace. An efficient preparation for war can alone insure peace. It is peace that we have uniformly and persever-ingly cultivated, and harmony between us and France may be restored at her option. But to send another minister without more determinate assur-ances that he would be received would be an act of humiliation to which the United States ought not to submit. It must therefore be left with France (if she is indeed desirous of accommodation) to [take] the requisite steps. The United States will steadily observe the maxims by which they have hitherto been governed. They will respect the sacred rights of embassy; and with a sincere disposition on the part of France to desist from hostility, to make reparation for the injuries heretofore inflicted on our commerce, and to do justice in [the] future, there will be no obstacle to the restoration of a friendly intercourse. In making to you this declaration I give a pledge to France and the world that the Executive authority of this country still adheres to the humane and pacific policy which has invariably governed its proceedings, in conformity with the wishes of the other branches of the Government and of the people of the United States. But considering the late manifestations of her policy toward foreign nations, I deem it a duty deliberately and solemnly to declare my opinion that whether we negotiate with her or not, vigorous preparations for war will be alike indispensable. These alone will give to us an equal treaty and insure its observance.

Among the measures of preparation which appear expedient, I take the liberty to recall your attention to the naval establishment. The beneficial effects of the small naval armament provided under the acts of the last session are known and acknowledged. Perhaps no country ever experienced more sudden and remarkable advantages from any measure of policy than we have derived from the arming for our maritime protection and defense. We ought without loss of time to lay the foundation for an increase of our Navy to a size sufficient to guard our coast and protect our trade. Such a naval force as it is doubtless in the power of the United States to create and maintain would also afford to them the best means of general defense by facilitating the safe transportation of troops and stores to every part of our extensive coast. To accomplish this important object, a prudent foresight requires that systematical measures be adopted for procuring at all times the requisite timber and other supplies. In what manner this shall be done I leave to your consideration.

SOURCE: Richardson, *Messages and Papers of the Presidents*, 1:261–64.

2

THOMAS JEFFERSON

DOCUMENT 8

PRESIDENT THOMAS JEFFERSON'S FIRST ANNUAL MESSAGE TO CONGRESS. DECEMBER 8, 1801.

Fellow-Citizens of the Senate and House of Representatives:

It is a circumstance of sincere gratification to me that on meeting the great council of our nation I am able to announce to them on grounds of reasonable certainty that the wars and troubles which have for so many years afflicted our sister nations have at length come to an end, and that the communications of peace and commerce are once more opening among them. Whilst we devoutly return thanks to the beneficent being who has been pleased to breathe into them the spirit of conciliation and forgiveness, we are bound with peculiar gratitude to be thankful to Him that our own peace has been preserved through so perilous a season, and ourselves permitted quietly to cultivate the earth and to practice and improve those arts which tend to increase our comforts. The assurances, indeed, of friendly disposition received from all the powers with whom we have principal relations had inspired a confidence that our peace with them would not have been disturbed. But a cessation of irregularities which had affected the commerce of neutral nations and of the irritations and injuries produced by them can not but add to this confidence, and strengthens at the same time the hope that wrongs committed on unoffending friends under a pressure of circumstances will now be reviewed with candor, and will be considered as founding just claims of retribution for the past and new assurance for the future. . . .

To this state of general peace with which we have been blessed, one only exception exists. Tripoli, the least considerable of the Barbary States, had come forward with demands unfounded either in right or in compact, and had permitted itself to denounce war on our failure to comply before a given day. The style of the demand admitted but one answer. I sent a small squadron of frigates into the Mediterranean, with assurances to that power of our sincere desire to remain in peace, but with orders to protect our commerce against the threatened attack. The measure was seasonable and salutary. The Bey had already declared war. His cruisers were out. Two had arrived at Gibraltar. Our commerce in the Mediterranean was blockaded and that of the Atlantic in peril. The arrival of our squadron dispelled the danger. One of the Tripolitan cruisers having fallen in with and engaged the small schooner *Enterprise*, which had gone as a tender to our larger vessels, was captured, after a heavy slaughter of her men, without the loss of a single one on our part. The bravery exhibited by our citizens on that element will, I trust, be a testimony to the world that it is not the want of that virtue which makes us seek their peace, but a conscientious desire to direct the energies of our nation to the multiplication of the human race, and not to its destruction. Unauthorized by the Constitution, without the sanction of Congress, to go beyond the line of defense, the vessel, being disabled from committing further hostilities, was liberated with its crew. The Legislature will doubtless consider whether, by authorizing measures of offense also, they will place our force on an equal footing with that of its adversaries. I communicate all material information on this subject, that in the exercise of this important function confided by the Constitution to the Legislature exclusively their judgment may form itself on a knowledge and consideration of every circumstance of weight.

I wish I could say that our situation with all the other Barbary States was entirely satisfactory. Discovering that some delays had taken place in the performance of certain articles stipulated by us, I thought it my duty, by immediate measures for fulfilling them, to vindicate to ourselves the right of considering the effect of departure from stipulation on their side. From the papers which will be laid before you you will be enabled to judge whether our treaties are regarded by them as fixing at all the measure of their demands or as guarding from the exercise of force our vessels within their power, and to consider how far it will be safe and expedient to leave our affairs with them in their present posture.

SOURCE: James D. Richardson, ed., *Messages and Papers of the Presidents*, 20 vols. (New York: Bureau of National Literature, 1912), 1:314–15.

DOCUMENT 9
PRESIDENT JEFFERSON'S SECOND ANNUAL MESSAGE
TO CONGRESS. DECEMBER 15, 1802.

... There was reason not long since to apprehend that the warfare in which we were engaged with Tripoli might be taken up by some other of the Barbary Powers. A reenforcement, therefore, was immediately ordered to the vessels already there. Subsequent information, however, has removed these apprehensions for the present. To secure our commerce in that sea with the smallest force competent, we have supposed it best to watch strictly the harbor of Tripoli. Still, however, the shallowness of their coast and the want of smaller vessels on our part has permitted some cruisers to escape unobserved, and to one of these an American vessel unfortunately fell prey. The captain, one American seaman, and two others of color remain prisoners with them unless exchanged under an agreement formerly made with the Bashaw [from the Turkish "pasha," a subordinate ruler within the Ottoman Empire], to whom, on the faith of that, some of his captive subjects had been restored.

... A small force in the Mediterranean will still be necessary to restrain the Tripoline cruisers, and the uncertain tenure of peace with some other of the Barbary Powers may eventually require that force to be augmented. The necessity of procuring some smaller vessels for that service will raise the estimate, but the difference in their maintenance will soon make it a measure of economy.

SOURCE: Richardson, *Messages and Papers of the Presidents*, 1:331–33.

DOCUMENT 10
PRESIDENT JEFFERSON'S REPORT TO CONGRESS ON THE
FRIGATE *PHILADELPHIA* IN THE MEDITERRANEAN SEA.
NOVEMBER 4, 1803.

By the copy now communicated of a letter from Captain [William] Bainbridge, of the *Philadelphia* frigate, to our consul at Gibraltar, you will learn that an act of hostility has been committed on a merchant vessel of the United States by an armed ship of the Emperor of Morocco. This conduct on the part of that power is without cause and without explanation.

It is fortunate that Captain Bainbridge fell in with and took the capturing vessel and her prize, and I have the satisfaction to inform you that about the date of this transaction such a force would be arriving in the neighborhood of Gibraltar, both from the east and from the west, as leaves less to be feared for our commerce from the suddenness of the aggression.

On the 4th of September the *Constitution* frigate, Captain [Edward] Preble, with Mr. [Tobias] Lear on board, was within two days' sail of Gibraltar, where the *Philadelphia* would then be arrived with her prize, and such explanations would probably be instituted as the state of things required, and as might perhaps arrest the progress of hostilities.

In the meanwhile it is for Congress to consider the provisional authorities which may be necessary to restrain the depredations of this power should they be continued.

SOURCE: Richardson, *Messages and Papers of the Presidents*, 1:352.

DOCUMENT 11
PRESIDENT JEFFERSON'S REPORT ON THE MOROCCAN SEIZURE OF AN AMERICAN MERCHANT SHIP.
DECEMBER 5, 1803.

To the Senate and House of Representatives of the United States:

I have the satisfaction to inform you that the act of hostility mentioned in my message of the 4th of November to have been committed by a cruiser of the Emperor of Morocco on a vessel of the United States has been disavowed by the Emperor. All differences in consequence thereof have been amicably adjusted, and the treaty of 1786 between this country and that has been recognized and confirmed by the Emperor, each party restoring to the other what had been detained or taken. I inclose the Emperor's orders given on this occasion.

The conduct of our officers generally who have had a part in these transactions has merited [our] entire approbation.

The temperate and correct course pursued by our consul, Mr. [James] Simpson, the promptitude and energy of Commodore Preble, the efficacious cooperation of Captains [John] Rodgers and [Hugh] Campbell, of the returning squadron, the proper decision of Captain Bainbridge that a vessel which had committed an open hostility was of right to be detained for inquiry and consideration, and the general zeal of the other officers and men are honorable facts which I make known with pleasure. And to these I add what was indeed transacted in another quarter—the gallant enterprise of Captain Rodgers in destroying on the coast of Tripoli a corvette of that power of 22 guns.

I recommend to the consideration of Congress a just indemnification for the interest acquired by the captors of the *Mishouda* and *Mirboha*, yielded by them for the public accommodation.

SOURCE: Richardson, *Messages and Papers of the Presidents*, 1:353–54.

DOCUMENT 12

PRESIDENT JEFFERSON ANNOUNCES THE CAPTURE OF THE FRIGATE *PHILADELPHIA* AND HER CREW. MARCH 20, 1804.

I communicate to Congress a letter received from Captain Bainbridge, commander of the *Philadelphia* frigate, informing us of the wreck of that vessel on the coast of Tripoli, and that himself, his officers and men, had fallen into the hands of the Tripolitans. This accident renders it expedient to increase our force and enlarge our expenses in the Mediterranean beyond what the last appropriation for the naval service contemplated. I recommend, therefore, to the consideration of Congress such an addition to that appropriation as they may think the exigency requires.

SOURCE: Richardson, *Messages and Papers of the Presidents*, 1:356.

DOCUMENT 13

PRESIDENT JEFFERSON'S FOURTH ANNUAL MESSAGE TO CONGRESS. NOVEMBER 8, 1804.

...The activity and success of the small force employed in the Mediterranean in the early part of the present year, the reenforcements sent into that sea, and the energy of the officers having command in the several vessels will, I trust, by the sufferings of war, reduce the barbarians of Tripoli to the desire of peace on proper terms. Great injury, however, ensues to ourselves, as well as to others interested, from the distance to which prizes must be brought for adjudication and from the impracticability of bringing hither such as are not seaworthy.

The Bey of Tunis [the title 'bey' denoted the ruler of a state within the Ottoman Empire] having made requisitions unauthorized by our treaty, their rejection has produced from him some expressions of discontent. But to those who expect us to calculate whether a compliance with unjust demands will not cost us less than a war we must leave as a question of calculation for them also whether to retire from unjust demands will not cost them less than a war. We can do to each other very sensible injuries by war, but the mutual advantages of peace make that the best interest of both.

Peace and intercourse with the other powers on the same coast continue on the footing on which they are established by treaty.

SOURCE: Richardson, *Messages and Papers of the Presidents*, 1:357.

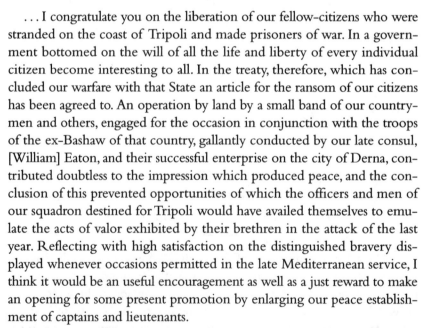

DOCUMENT 14
PRESIDENT JEFFERSON'S FIFTH ANNUAL MESSAGE
TO CONGRESS. DECEMBER 3, 1805.

... I congratulate you on the liberation of our fellow-citizens who were stranded on the coast of Tripoli and made prisoners of war. In a government bottomed on the will of all the life and liberty of every individual citizen become interesting to all. In the treaty, therefore, which has concluded our warfare with that State an article for the ransom of our citizens has been agreed to. An operation by land by a small band of our countrymen and others, engaged for the occasion in conjunction with the troops of the ex-Bashaw of that country, gallantly conducted by our late consul, [William] Eaton, and their successful enterprise on the city of Derna, contributed doubtless to the impression which produced peace, and the conclusion of this prevented opportunities of which the officers and men of our squadron destined for Tripoli would have availed themselves to emulate the acts of valor exhibited by their brethren in the attack of the last year. Reflecting with high satisfaction on the distinguished bravery displayed whenever occasions permitted in the late Mediterranean service, I think it would be an useful encouragement as well as a just reward to make an opening for some present promotion by enlarging our peace establishment of captains and lieutenants.

With Tunis some misunderstandings have arisen not yet sufficiently explained, but friendly discussions with their ambassador recently arrived and a mutual disposition to do whatever is just and reasonable can not fail of dissipating these, so that we may consider our peace on that coast, generally, to be on as sound a footing as it has been at any preceding time. Still, it will not be expedient to withdraw immediately the whole of our force from that sea.

SOURCE: Richardson, *Messages and Papers of the Presidents*, 1:373–74.

DOCUMENT 15
PRESIDENT JEFFERSON DECLARES RENEWED TENSION WITH THE BEY OF TUNIS OVER TRIBUTE PAYMENTS. APRIL 14, 1806.

During the blockade of Tripoli by the squadron of the United States a small cruiser, under the flag of Tunis, with two prizes, all of trifling value, attempted to enter Tripoli; was turned back, warned, and, attempting again to enter, was taken and detained as prize by the squadron. Her restitution was claimed by the Bey of Tunis with a threat of war in terms so serious that on withdrawing from the blockade of Tripoli the commanding officer of the squadron thought it his duty to repair to Tunis with his squadron and to require a categorical declaration whether peace or war was intended. The Bey preferred explaining himself by an ambassador to the United States, who on his arrival renewed the request that the vessel and her prizes should be restored. It was deemed proper to give this proof of friendship to the Bey, and the ambassador was informed the vessels would be restored. Afterwards he made a requisition of naval stores to be sent to the Bey, in order to secure a peace for the term of three years, with a threat of war if refused. It has been refused, and the ambassador is about to depart without receding from his threat or demand.

Under these circumstances, and considering that the several provisions of the act of March 25, 1804, will cease in consequence of the ratification of the treaty of peace with Tripoli, now advised and consented to by the Senate, I have thought it my duty to communicate these facts, in order that Congress may consider the expediency of continuing the same provisions for a limited time or making others equivalent.

SOURCE: Richardson, *Messages and Papers of the Presidents*, 1:388–89.

3

JAMES MADISON

DOCUMENT 16
PRESIDENT JAMES MADISON REQUESTS DECLARATION OF WAR AGAINST GREAT BRITAIN. JUNE 1, 1812.

To the Senate and House of Representatives of the United States:

I communicate to Congress certain documents, being a continuation of those heretofore laid before them on the subject of our affairs with Great Britain.

Without going back beyond the renewal in 1803 of the war in which Great Britain is engaged, and omitting unrepaired wrongs of inferior magnitude, the conduct of her Government presents a series of acts hostile to the United States as an independent and neutral nation.

British cruisers have been in the continued practice of violating the American flag on the great highway of nations, and of seizing and carrying off persons sailing under it, not in the exercise of a belligerent right founded on the law of nations against an enemy, but of a municipal prerogative over British subjects. British jurisdiction is thus extended to neutral vessels in a situation where no laws can operate but the law of nations and the laws of the country to which the vessels belong, and a self-redress is assumed which, if British subjects were wrongfully detained and alone concerned, is that substitution of force for a resort to the responsible sovereign which falls within the definition of war. Could the seizure of British subjects in such cases be regarded as within the exercise of a belligerent right, the acknowledged laws of war, which forbid an article of captured property to be adjudged without a regular investigation before a competent tribunal, would imperiously demand the fairest trial where the sacred rights of persons were at issue. In place of such a trial these rights are subjected to the will of every petty commander.

The practice, hence, is so far from affecting British subjects alone that, under the pretext of searching for these, thousands of American citizens, under the safeguard of public law and of their national flag, have been torn from their country and from everything dear to them; have been dragged on board ships of war of a foreign nation and exposed, under the severities of their discipline, to be exiled to the most distant and deadly climes, to risk their lives in the battles of their oppressors, and to be the melancholy instruments of taking away those of their own brethren.

Against this crying enormity, which Great Britain would be so prompt to avenge if committed against herself, the United States have in vain exhausted remonstrances and expostulations, and that no proof might be wanting of their conciliatory dispositions, and no pretext left for a continuance of the practice, the British Government was formally assured of the readiness of the United States to enter into arrangements such as could not be rejected if the recovery of British subjects were the real and the sole object. The communication passed without effect.

British cruisers have been in the practice also of violating the rights and the peace of our coasts. They hover over and harass our entering and departing commerce. To the most insulting pretensions they have added the most lawless proceedings in our very harbors, and have wantonly spilt American blood within the sanctuary of our territorial jurisdiction. The principles and rules enforced by that nation, when a neutral nation, against armed vessels of belligerents hovering near her coasts and disturbing her commerce are well known. When called on, nevertheless, by the United States to punish the greater offenses committed by her own vessels, her Government has bestowed on their commanders additional marks of honor and confidence.

Under pretended blockades, without the presence of an adequate force and sometimes without the practicability of applying one, our commerce has been plundered in every sea, the great staples of our country have been cut off from their legitimate markets, and a destructive blow aimed at our agricultural and maritime interests. In aggravation of these predatory measures they have been considered as in force from the dates of their notification, a retrospective effect being thus added, as has been done in other important cases, to the unlawfulness of the course pursued. And to render the outrage the more signal these mock blockades have been reiterated and enforced in the face of official communications from the British Government declaring as the true definition of a legal blockade "that particular ports must be actually invested and previous warning given to vessels bound to them not to enter."

Not content with these occasional expedients for laying waste our neutral trade, the cabinet of Britain resorted at length to the sweeping system of blockades, under the name of orders in council, which has been molded and managed as might best suit its political views, its commercial jealousies, or the avidity of British cruisers.

To our remonstrances against the complicated and transcendent injustice of this innovation the first reply was that the orders were reluctantly adopted by Great Britain as a necessary retaliation on decrees of her enemy proclaiming a general blockade of the British Isles at a time when the naval force of that enemy dared not issue from his own ports. She was reminded without effect that her own prior blockades, unsupported by an adequate naval force actually applied and continued, were a bar to this plea; that executed edicts against millions of our property could not be retaliation on edicts confessedly impossible to be executed; that retaliation, to be just, should fall on the party setting the guilty example, not on an innocent party which was not even chargeable with an acquiescence in it.

When deprived of this flimsy veil for a prohibition of our trade with her enemy by the repeal of his prohibition of our trade with Great Britain, her cabinet, instead of a corresponding repeal or a practical discontinuance of its orders, formally avowed a determination to persist in them against the United States until the markets of her enemy should be laid open to British products, thus asserting an obligation on a neutral power to require one belligerent to encourage by its internal regulations the trade of another belligerent, contradicting her own practice toward all nations, in peace as well as in war, and betraying the insincerity of those professions which inculcated a belief that, having resorted to her orders with regret, she was anxious to find an occasion for putting an end to them.

Abandoning still more all respect for the neutral rights of the United States and for its own consistency, the British Government now demands as prerequisites to a repeal of its orders as they relate to the United States that a formality should be observed in the repeal of the French decrees nowise necessary to their termination nor exemplified by British usage, and that the French repeal, besides including that portion of the decrees which operates within a territorial jurisdiction, as well as that which operates on the high seas, against the commerce of the United States should not be a single and special repeal in relation to the United States, but should be extended to whatever other neutral nations unconnected with them may be affected by those decrees. And as an additional insult, they are called on for a formal disavowal of conditions and pretensions advanced by the French Government for which the United States are so far from having made themselves responsible that, in official explanations which have been published to the world, and in a correspondence of the American minister at London with the British minister for foreign affairs such a responsibility was explicitly and emphatically disclaimed.

It has become, indeed, sufficiently certain that the commerce of the United States is to be sacrificed, not as interfering with the belligerent rights of Great Britain; not as supplying the wants of her enemies, which she herself supplies; but as interfering with the monopoly which she covets for her own commerce and navigation. She carries on a war against the lawful commerce of a friend that she may the better carry on a commerce with an enemy—a commerce polluted by the forgeries and perjuries which are for the most part the only passports by which it can succeed.

Anxious to make every experiment short of the last resort of injured nations, the United States have withheld from Great Britain, under successive modifications, the benefits of a free intercourse with their market, the loss of which could not but outweigh the profits accruing from her restrictions of our commerce with other nations. And to entitle these experiments to the more favorable consideration they were so framed as to enable her to place her adversary under the exclusive operation of them. To these appeals her Government has been equally inflexible, as if willing to make sacrifices of every sort rather than yield to the claims of justice or renounce the errors of a false pride. Nay, so far were the attempts carried to overcome the attachment of the British cabinet to its unjust edicts that it received every encouragement within the competency of the executive branch of our Government to expect that a repeal of them would be followed by a war between the United States and France, unless the French edicts should also be repealed. Even this communication, although silencing forever the plea of a disposition in the United States to acquiesce in those edicts originally the sole plea for them, received no attention.

If no other proof existed of a predetermination of the British Government against a repeal of its orders, it might be found in the correspondence of the minister plenipotentiary of the United States at London and the British secretary for foreign affairs in 1810, on the question whether the blockade of May, 1806, was considered as in force or as not in force. It had been ascertained that the French Government, which urged this blockade as the ground of its Berlin decree, was willing in the event of its removal to repeal that decree, which, being followed by alternate repeals of the other offensive edicts, might abolish the whole system on both sides. This inviting opportunity for accomplishing an object so important to the United States, and professed so often to be the desire of both the belligerents, was made known to the British Government. As that Government admits that an actual application of an adequate force is necessary to the existence of a legal blockade, and it was notorious that if such a force had ever been applied its long discontinuance had annulled the blockade in question, there could be no sufficient objection on the part of Great Britain to a formal revocation of it, and no imaginable objection to a declaration of the fact that the blockade did not exist. The declaration would have been consistent with her avowed principles of blockade, and would have enabled the United States to demand from France the pledged repeal of her decrees, either with success, in which case the way would have been opened for a general repeal of the belligerent edicts, or without success, in which case the United States would have been justified in turning their measures exclusively against France. The British Government would, however, neither rescind the blockade nor declare its nonexistence, nor permit its nonexistence to be inferred and affirmed by the American plenipotentiary. On the contrary, by representing the blockade to be comprehended in the orders in council, the United States were compelled so to regard it in their subsequent proceedings.

There was a period when a favorable change in the policy of the British cabinet was justly considered as established. The minister plenipotentiary [Augustus John Foster] of His Britannic Majesty here proposed an adjustment of the differences more immediately endangering the harmony of the two countries. The proposition was accepted with the promptitude and cordiality corresponding with the invariable professions of this Government. A foundation appeared to be laid for a sincere and lasting reconciliation. The prospect, however, quickly vanished. The whole proceeding was disavowed by the British Government without any explanations which could at that time repress the belief that the disavowal proceeded from a spirit of hostility to the commercial rights and prosperity of the United States; and it has since come into proof that at the very moment when the public minister was holding the language of friendship and inspiring confidence in the sincerity of the negotiation with which he was charged a secret agent of his Government was employed in intrigues having for their object a subversion of our Government and a dismemberment of our happy Union.

In reviewing the conduct of Great Britain toward the United States our attention is necessarily drawn to the warfare just renewed by the savages on one of our extensive frontiers—a warfare which is known to spare neither age nor sex and to be distinguished by features peculiarly shocking to humanity. It is difficult to account for the activity and combinations which have for some time been developing themselves among tribes in constant intercourse with British traders and garrisons without connecting their hostility with that influence and without recollecting the authenticated examples of such interpositions heretofore furnished by the officers and agents of that Government.

Such is the spectacle of injuries and indignities which have been heaped on our country, and such the crisis which its unexampled forbearance and conciliatory efforts have not been able to avert. It might at least have been expected that an enlightened nation, if less urged by moral obligations or invited by friendly dispositions on the part of the United States, would have found in its true interest alone a sufficient motive to respect their rights and their tranquillity on the high seas; that an enlarged policy would have favored that free and general circulation of commerce in which the British nation is at all times interested, and which in times of war is the best alleviation of its calamities to herself as well as to other belligerents; and more especially that the British cabinet would not, for the sake of a precarious and surreptitious intercourse with hostile markets, have persevered in a course of measures which necessarily put at hazard the invaluable market of a great and growing country, disposed to cultivate the mutual advantages of an active commerce.

Other counsels have prevailed. Our moderation and conciliation have had no other effect than to encourage perseverance and to enlarge pretensions. We behold our seafaring citizens still the daily victims of lawless violence, committed on the great common highway of nations, even within sight of the country which owes them protection. We behold our vessels, freighted with the products of our soil and industry, or returning with the honest proceeds of them, wrested from their lawful destinations, confiscated by prize courts no longer the organs of public law but the instruments of arbitrary edicts, and their unfortunate crews dispersed and lost, or forced or inveigled in British ports into British fleets, whilst arguments are employed in support of these aggressions which have no foundation but in a principle equally supporting a claim to regulate our external commerce in all cases whatsoever.

We behold, in fine, on the side of Great Britain a state of war against the United States, and on the side of the United States a state of peace toward Great Britain.

Whether the United States shall continue passive under these progressive usurpations and these accumulating wrongs, or, opposing force to force in defense of their national rights, shall commit a just cause into the hands of the Almighty Disposer of Events, avoiding all connections which might entangle it in the contest or views of other powers, and preserving a constant readiness to concur in an honorable reestablishment of peace and friendship, is a solemn question which the Constitution wisely confides to the Legislative department of the Government. In recommending it to their early deliberations I am happy in the assurance that the decision will be worthy of the enlightened and patriotic councils of a virtuous, a free, and a powerful nation.

Having presented this view of the relations of the United States with Great Britain and of the solemn alternative growing out of them, I proceed to remark that the communications last made to Congress on the subject of our relations with France will have shown that since the revocation of her decrees, as they violated the neutral rights of the United States, her Government has authorized illegal captures by its privateers and public ships, and that other outrages have been practiced on our vessels and our citizens. It will have been seen also that no indemnity had been provided or satisfactorily pledged for the extensive spoliations committed under the violent and retrospective orders of the French Government against the property of our citizens seized within the jurisdiction of France. I abstain at this time from recommending to the consideration of Congress definitive measures with respect to that nation, in the expectation that the result of unclosed discussions between our minister plenipotentiary at Paris and the French Government will speedily enable Congress to decide with greater advantage on the course due to the rights, the interests, and the honor of our country.

SOURCE: James D. Richardson, ed., *Messages and Papers of the Presidents*, 20 vols. (New York: Bureau of National Literature, 1912), 1:484–90.

DOCUMENT 17

PRESIDENT MADISON REQUESTS DECLARATION OF WAR
AGAINST THE DEY AND REGENCY OF ALGIERS.
FEBRUARY 23, 1815.

To the Senate and House of Representatives of the United States:

Congress will have seen by the communication from the consul-general of the United States at Algiers [Tobias Lear] laid before them on the 17th of November, 1812, the hostile proceedings of the Dey [the title 'dey' signified a subordinate agent of the Ottoman Empire] against that functionary. These have been followed by acts of more overt and direct warfare against the citizens of the United States trading in the Mediterranean, some of whom are still detained in captivity, notwithstanding the attempts which have been made to ransom them, and are treated with the rigor usual on the coast of Barbary.

The considerations which rendered it unnecessary and unimportant to commence hostile operations on the part of the United States being now terminated by the peace with Great Britain, which opens the prospect of an active and valuable trade of their citizens within the range of the Algerine cruisers, I recommend to Congress the expediency of an act declaring the existence of a state of war between the United States and the Dey and Regency of Algiers, and of such provisions as may be requisite for a vigorous prosecution of it to a successful issue.

SOURCE: Richardson, *Messages and Papers of the Presidents*, 1:539.

4

ANDREW JACKSON

DOCUMENT 18
PRESIDENT ANDREW JACKSON'S THIRD ANNUAL ADDRESS NOTIFYING CONGRESS OF ATTACKS UPON AMERICAN MERCHANT SHIPS IN THE DUTCH EAST INDIES AND THE FALKLAND ISLANDS. DECEMBER 6, 1831.

Fellow-Citizens of the Senate and House of Representatives:

... To China and the East Indies our commerce continues in its usual extent, and with increased facilities which the credit and capital of our merchants afford by substituting bills for payments in specie. A daring outrage having been committed in those seas by the plunder of one of our merchantmen engaged in the pepper trade at a port in Sumatra [Quallah Battoo], and the piratical perpetrators belonging to tribes in such a state of society that the usual course of proceedings between civilized nations could not be pursued, I forthwith dispatched a frigate [*Potomac*] with orders to require immediate satisfaction for the injury and indemnity to the sufferers. ...

I should have placed Buenos Ayres in the list of South American powers in respect to which nothing of importance affecting us was to be communicated but for occurrences which have lately taken place at the Falkland Islands, in which the name of that Republic has been used to cover with a show of authority acts injurious to our commerce and to the property and liberty of our fellow-citizens. In the course of the present year one of our vessels, engaged in the pursuit of a trade which we have always enjoyed without molestation, has been captured by a band acting, as they pretend, under the authority of the Government of Buenos Ayres [Argentina]. I have therefore given orders for the dispatch of an armed vessel [*Lexington*] to join our squadron in those seas and aid in affording all lawful protection to our trade which shall be necessary, and shall without delay send a minister to inquire into the nature of the circumstances and also of the claim, if any, that is set up by that Government to those islands. In the meantime, I submit the case to the consideration of Congress, to the end that they may clothe the Executive with such authority and means as they may deem necessary for providing a force adequate to the complete protection of our fellow-citizens fishing and trading in those seas.

SOURCE: James D. Richardson, ed., *Messages and Papers of the Presidents*, 20 vols. (New York: Bureau of National Literature, 1912), 2:1114–16.

DOCUMENT 19
PRESIDENT JACKSON'S FOURTH ANNUAL ADDRESS CONCERNING THE ATTACKS UPON AMERICAN MERCHANT SHIPS. DECEMBER 4, 1832.

. . . I refrain from making any communication on the subject of our affairs with Buenos Ayres, because the negotiation communicated to you in my last annual message was at the date of our last advices still pending and in a state that would render a publication of the details inexpedient. . . .

An act of atrocious piracy having been committed on one of our trading ships by the inhabitants of a settlement on the west coast of Sumatra, a frigate was dispatched with orders to demand satisfaction for the injury if those who committed it should be found to be members of a regular government, capable of maintaining the usual relations with foreign nations; but if, as it was supposed and as they proved to be, they were a band of lawless pirates, to inflict such a chastisement as would deter them and others from like aggressions. This last was done, and the effect has been an increased respect for our flag in those distant seas and additional security for our commerce.

SOURCE: Richardson, *Messages and Papers of the Presidents*, 2:1158–59.

5

JAMES K. POLK

DOCUMENT 20
PRESIDENT JAMES POLK REQUESTS DECLARATION OF WAR AGAINST MEXICO. MAY 11, 1846.

To the Senate and House of Representatives of the United States:

The existing state of the relations between the United States and Mexico renders it proper that I should bring the subject to the consideration of Congress. In my message at the commencement of your present session the state of these relations, the causes which led to the suspension of diplomatic intercourse between the two countries in March, 1845, and the long-continued and unredressed wrongs and injuries committed by the Mexican Government on citizens of the United States in their persons and property were briefly set forth.

As the facts and opinions which were then laid before you were carefully considered, I can not better express my present convictions of the condition of affairs up to that time than by referring you to that communication.

The strong desire to establish peace with Mexico on liberal and honorable terms, and the readiness of this Government to regulate and adjust our boundary and other causes of difference with that power on such fair and equitable principles as would lead to permanent relations of the most friendly nature, induced me in September last [1845] to seek the reopening of diplomatic relations between the two countries. Every measure adopted on our part had for its object the furtherance of these desired results. In communicating to Congress a succinct statement of the injuries which we had suffered from Mexico, and which have been accumulating during a period of more than twenty years, every expression that could tend to inflame the people of Mexico or defeat or delay a pacific result was carefully avoided. An envoy of the United States [John Slidell] repaired to Mexico with full powers to adjust every existing difference. But though present on the Mexican soil by agreement between the two Governments, invested with full powers, and bearing evidence of the most friendly dispositions, his mission has been unavailing. The Mexican Government not only refused to receive him or listen to his propositions, but after a long-continued series of menaces have at last invaded our territory and shed the blood of our fellow-citizens on our own soil.

It now becomes my duty to state more in detail the origin, progress, and failure of that mission. In pursuance of the instructions given in September last, an inquiry was made on the 13th of October, 1845, in the most friendly terms, through our consul in Mexico [John Black], of the minister for foreign affairs [Manuel de la Peña y Peña], whether the Mexican Government "would receive an envoy from the United States intrusted with full powers to adjust all the questions in dispute between the two Governments," with the assurance that "should the answer be in the affirmative such an envoy would be immediately dispatched to Mexico." The Mexican minister on the 15th of October gave an affirmative answer to this inquiry, requesting at the same time that our naval force at Vera Cruz might be withdrawn, lest its continued presence might assume the appearance of menace and coercion pending the negotiations. This force was immediately withdrawn. On the 10th of November, 1845, Mr. John Slidell, of Louisiana, was commissioned by me an envoy extraordinary and minister plenipotentiary of the United States to Mexico, and was intrusted with full powers to adjust both the questions of the Texas boundary and of indemnification to our citizens.* The redress of the wrongs of our citizens naturally and inseparably blended itself with the question of boundary. The settlement of the one question in any correct view of the subject involves that of the other. I could not for a moment entertain the idea that the claims of our much-injured and long-suffering citizens, many of which had existed for more than twenty years, should be postponed or separated from the settlement of the boundary question.

Mr. Slidell arrived at Vera Cruz on the 30th of November, and was courteously received by the authorities of that city. But the Government of General [José Joaquín de] Herrera was then tottering to its fall. The revolutionary party had seized upon the Texas question to effect or hasten its overthrow. Its determination to restore friendly relations with the United States, and to receive our minister to negotiate for the settlement of this question, was violently assailed, and was made the great theme of denunciation against it. The Government of General Herrera, there is good reason

---

*John Slidell, 1793–1871; born in New York City, graduate of Columbia Law School, moved to New Orleans in 1819, member of Congress from Louisiana, Confederate commissioner to France (1862–1865).

to believe, was sincerely desirous to receive our minister; but it yielded to the storm raised by its enemies, and on the 21st of December refused to accredit Mr. Slidell upon the most frivolous pretexts. These are so fully and ably exposed in the note of Mr. Slidell of the 24th of December last to the Mexican minister of foreign relations, herewith transmitted, that I deem it unnecessary to enter into further detail on this portion of the subject.

Five days after the date of Mr. Slidell's note General Herrera yielded the Government to General [Mariano] Paredes without a struggle, and on the 30th of December resigned the Presidency. This revolution was accomplished solely by the army, the people having taken little part in the contest; and thus the supreme power in Mexico passed into the hands of a military leader.

Determined to leave no effort untried to effect an amicable adjustment with Mexico, I directed Mr. Slidell to present his credentials to the Government of General Paredes and ask to be officially received by him. There would have been less ground for taking this step had General Paredes come into power by a regular constitutional succession. In that event his administration would have been considered but a mere constitutional continuance of the Government of General Herrera, and the refusal of the latter to receive our minister would have been deemed conclusive unless an intimation had been given by General Paredes of his desire to reverse the decision of his predecessor. But the Government of General Paredes owes its existence to a military revolution, by which the subsisting constitutional authorities had been subverted. The form of government was entirely changed, as well as all the high functionaries by whom it was administered.

Under these circumstances, Mr. Slidell, in obedience to my direction, addressed a note to the Mexican minister of foreign relations [Don Joaquín de Castillo y Lanzas], under date of the 1st of March last, asking to be received by that Government in the diplomatic character to which he had been appointed. This minister in his reply, under date of the 12th of March, reiterated arguments of his predecessor [Peña y Peña], and in terms that may be considered as giving just rounds of offense to the Government and people of the United States denied the application of Mr. Slidell. Nothing therefore remained for our envoy but to demand his passports and return to his own country.

Thus the Government of Mexico, though solemnly pledged by official acts in October last to receive and accredit an American envoy, violated their plighted faith and refused the offer of a peaceful adjustment of our difficulties. Not only was the offer rejected, but the indignity of its rejection was enhanced by the manifest breach of faith in refusing to admit the envoy who came because they had bound themselves to receive him. Nor can it be said that the offer was fruitless from the want of opportunity of discussing it; our envoy was present on their own soil. Nor can it be ascribed to a want of sufficient powers; our envoy had full powers to adjust every question of difference. Nor was there room for complaint that our propositions for settlement were unreasonable; permission was not even given our envoy to make any proposition whatever. Nor can it be objected that we, on our part, would not listen to any reasonable terms of their suggestion; the Mexican Government refused all negotiation, and have made no proposition of any kind.

In my message at the commencement of the present session I informed you that upon the earnest appeal both of the Congress and convention of Texas I had ordered an efficient military force to take a position "between the Nueces and the Del Norte." This had become necessary to meet a threatened invasion of Texas by the Mexican forces, for which extensive military preparations had been made. The invasion was threatened solely because Texas had determined, in accordance with a solemn resolution of the Congress of the United States, to annex herself to our Union, and under these circumstances it was plainly our duty to extend our protection over her citizens and soil.

This force was concentrated at Corpus Christi, and remained there until after I had received such information from Mexico as rendered it probable, if not certain, that the Mexican Government would refuse to receive our envoy.

Meantime Texas, by the final action of our Congress, had become an integral part of our Union. The Congress of Texas, by its act of December 19, 1836, had declared the Rio del Norte to be the boundary of that Republic. Its jurisdiction had been extended and exercised beyond the Nueces. The country between that river and the Del Norte had been represented in the Congress and in the convention of Texas, had thus taken part in the act of annexation itself, and is now included within one of our Congressional districts. Our own Congress had, moreover, with great unanimity, by the act approved December 31, 1845, recognized the country beyond the Nueces as a part of our territory by including it within our own revenue system, and a revenue officer to reside within that district has been appointed by and with the advice and consent of the Senate. It became, therefore, of urgent necessity to provide for the defense of that portion of our country. Accordingly, on the 13th of January last instructions were issued to the general in command of these troops to occupy the left bank of the Del Norte. This river, which is the southwestern boundary of the State of Texas, is an exposed frontier. From this quarter invasion was threatened; upon it and in its immediate vicinity, in the judgment of high military experience, are the proper stations for the protecting forces of the Government. In addition to this important consideration, several others occurred to induce this movement. Among these are the facilities afforded by the ports at Brazos Santiago and the mouth of the Del Norte for the reception of supplies by sea, the stronger and more healthful military positions, the convenience for obtaining a ready and a more abundant supply of provisions, water, fuel, and forage, and the advantages which are afforded by the Del Norte in forwarding supplies to such posts as may be established in the interior and upon the Indian frontier.

The movement of the troops to the Del Norte was made by the commanding general under positive instructions to abstain from all aggressive acts toward Mexico or Mexican citizens and to regard the relations between that Republic and the United States as peaceful unless she should declare war or commit acts of hostility indicative of a state of war. He was specially directed to protect private property and respect personal rights.

The Army moved from Corpus Christi on the 11th of March, and on the 28th of that month arrived on the left bank of the Del Norte opposite to Matamoras, where it encamped on a commanding position, which has since been strengthened by the erection of fieldworks. A depot has also been established at Point Isabel, near the Brazos Santiago, 30 miles in [the] rear of the encampment. The selection of this position was necessarily confided to the judgment of the general in command. The Mexican forces at Matamoras assumed a belligerent attitude, and on the 12th of April General [Pedro de] Ampudia, then in command, notified General [Zachary] Taylor to break up his camp within twenty-four hours and to retire beyond the Nueces River, and in the event of his failure to comply with these demands announced that arms, and arms alone, must decide the question. But no open act of hostility was committed until the 24th of April. On that day General [Mariano] Arista, who had succeeded to the command of the Mexican forces, communicated to General Taylor that "he considered hostilities commenced and should prosecute them." A party of dragoons of 63 men and officers on the same day dispatched from the American camp up the Rio del Norte, on its left bank, to ascertain whether the Mexican troops had crossed or were preparing to cross the river, "became engaged with a large body of these troops, and after a short affair, in which some 16 were killed and wounded, appear to have been surrounded and compelled to surrender."

The grievous wrongs perpetrated by Mexico upon our citizens throughout a long period of years remain unredressed, and solemn treaties pledging her public faith for this redress have been disregarded. A Government either unable or unwilling to enforce the execution of such treaties fails to perform one of its plainest duties.

Our commerce with Mexico has been almost annihilated. It was formerly highly beneficial to both nations, but our merchants have been deterred from prosecuting it by the system of outrage and extortion which the Mexican authorities have pursued against them, whilst their appeals through their own Government for indemnity have been made in vain. Our forbearance has gone to such an extreme as to be mistaken in its character. Had we acted with vigor in repelling the insults and redressing the injuries inflicted by Mexico at the commencement, we should doubtless have escaped all the difficulties in which we are now involved.

Instead of this, however, we have been exerting our best efforts to propitiate her good will. Upon the pretext that Texas, a nation as independent as herself, thought proper to unite its destinies with our own she has affected to believe that we have severed her rightful territory, and in official proclamations and manifestoes has repeatedly threatened to make war upon us for the purpose of reconquering Texas. In the meantime we have tried every effort at reconciliation. The cup of forbearance had been exhausted even before the recent information from the frontier of the Del Norte. But now, after reiterated menaces, Mexico has passed the boundary of the United States, has invaded our territory and shed American blood upon American soil. She has proclaimed that hostilities have commenced, and that the two nations are now at war.

As war exists, and, notwithstanding all our efforts to avoid it, exists by the act of Mexico herself, we are called upon by every consideration of duty and patriotism to vindicate with decision the honor, the rights, and the interests of our country.

Anticipating the possibility of a crisis like that which has arrived, instructions were given in August last, "as a precautionary measure" against invasion or threatened invasion, authorizing General Taylor, if the emergency required, to accept volunteers, not from Texas only, but from the States of Louisiana, Alabama, Mississippi, Tennessee, and Kentucky, and corresponding letters were addressed to the respective governors of those States. These instructions were repeated, and in January last, soon after the incorporation of "Texas into our Union of States," General Taylor was further "authorized by the President to make a requisition upon the executive of that State for such of its militia force as may be needed to repel invasion or to secure the country against apprehended invasion." On the 2nd day of March he was again reminded, "in the event of the approach of any considerable Mexican force, promptly and efficiently to use the authority with which he was clothed to call to him such auxiliary force as he might need." War actually existing and our territory having been invaded, General Taylor, pursuant to authority vested in him by my direction, has called on the governor of Texas for four regiments of State troops, two to be mounted and two to serve on foot, and on the governor of Louisiana for four regiments of infantry to be sent to him as soon as practicable.

In further vindication of our rights and defense of our territory, I invoke the prompt action of Congress to recognize the existence of the war, and to place at the disposition of the Executive the means of prosecuting the war with vigor, and thus hastening the restoration of peace. To this end I recommend that authority should be given to call into the public service a large body of volunteers to serve for not less than six or twelve months unless sooner discharged. A volunteer force is beyond question more efficient than any other description of citizen soldiers, and it is not to be doubted that a number far beyond that required would readily rush to the field upon the call of their country. I further recommend that a liberal provision be made for sustaining our entire military force and furnishing it with supplies and munitions of war.

The most energetic and prompt measures and the immediate appearance in arms of a large and overpowering force are recommended to Congress as the most certain and efficient means of bringing the existing collision with Mexico to a speedy and successful termination.

In making these recommendations I deem it proper to declare that it is my anxious desire not only to terminate hostilities speedily, but to bring all matters in dispute between this Government and Mexico to an early and amicable adjustment; and in this view I shall be prepared to renew negotiations whenever Mexico shall be ready to receive propositions or to make propositions of her own.

I transmit herewith a copy of the correspondence between our envoy to Mexico [Slidell] and the Mexican minister for foreign affairs [Castillo y Lanzas], and so much of the correspondence between that envoy and the Secretary of State and between the Secretary of War and the general in command on the Del Norte as is necessary to a full understanding of the subject.

SOURCE: James D. Richardson, ed., *Messages and Papers of the Presidents*, 20 vols. (New York: Bureau of National Literature, 1912), 3:2287–93.

6

ABRAHAM LINCOLN

DOCUMENT 21
PRESIDENT ABRAHAM LINCOLN'S PROCLAMATION TO FEDERALIZE STATE MILITIAS AND TO CONVENE AN EXTRAORDINARY SESSION OF CONGRESS. APRIL 15, 1861.

Whereas the laws of the United States have been for some time past and now are opposed and the execution thereof obstructed in the States of South Carolina, Georgia, Alabama, Florida, Mississippi, Louisiana, and Texas by combinations too powerful to be suppressed by the ordinary course of judicial proceedings or by the powers vested in the marshals by law:

Now, therefore, I, Abraham Lincoln, President of the United States, in virtue of the power in me vested by the Constitution and the laws, have thought fit to call forth, and hereby do call forth, the militia of the several States of the Union to the aggregate number of 75,000, in order to suppress said combinations and to cause the laws to be duly executed.

The details for this object will be immediately communicated to the State authorities through the War Department.

I appeal to all loyal citizens to favor, facilitate, and aid this effort to maintain the honor, the integrity, and the existence of our National Union and the perpetuity of popular government and to redress wrongs already long enough endured.

I deem it proper to say that the first service assigned to the forces hereby called forth will probably be to repossess the forts, places, and property which have been seized from the Union; and in every event the utmost care will be observed, consistently with the objects aforesaid, to avoid any devastation, any destruction of or interference with property, or any disturbance of peaceful citizens in any part of the country.

And I hereby command the persons composing the combinations aforesaid to disperse and retire peaceably to their respective abodes within twenty days from this date.

Deeming that the present condition of public affairs presents an extraordinary occasion, I do hereby, by virtue of the power in me vested by the Constitution, convene both Houses of Congress. Senators and Representatives are therefore summoned to assemble at their respective chambers at 12 o'clock noon on Thursday, the 4th day of July next, then and there to consider and determine such measures as, in their wisdom, the public safety and interest may seem to demand.

In witness whereof I have hereunto set my hand and caused the seal of the United States to be affixed. Done at the city of Washington, this 15th day of April, [SEAL] A.D.,1861, and of the Independence of the United States the eighty-fifth.

SOURCE: James D. Richardson, ed., *Messages and Papers of the Presidents*, 20 vols. (New York: Bureau of National Literature, 1912), 4:3215–16.

DOCUMENT 22
PRESIDENT LINCOLN'S MESSAGE TO SPECIAL SESSION OF CONGRESS. JULY 4, 1861.

Fellow-Citizens of the Senate and House of Representatives:

Having been convened on an extraordinary occasion, as authorized by the Constitution, your attention is not called to any ordinary subject of legislation.

At the beginning of the present Presidential term, four months ago, the functions of the Federal Government were found to be generally suspended within the several States of South Carolina, Georgia, Alabama, Mississippi, Louisiana, and Florida, excepting only those of the Post-Office Department.

Within these States all the forts, arsenals, dockyards, custom-houses, and the like, including the movable and stationary property in and about them, had been seized and were held in open hostility to this Government, excepting only Forts Pickens, Taylor, and Jefferson, on and near the Florida coast, and Fort Sumter, in Charleston Harbor, South Carolina. The forts thus seized had been put in improved condition, new ones had been built, and armed forces had been organized and were organizing, all avowedly with the same hostile purpose.

The forts remaining in the possession of the Federal Government in and near these States were either besieged or menaced by warlike preparations, and especially Fort Sumter was nearly surrounded by well-protected hostile batteries, with guns equal in quality to the best of its own and outnumbering the latter as perhaps ten to one. A disproportionate share of the Federal muskets and rifles had somehow found their way into these States, and had been seized to be used against the Government. Accumulations of the public revenue lying within them had been seized for the same object. The Navy was scattered in distant seas, leaving but a very small part of it within the immediate reach of the Government. Officers of the Federal Army and Navy had resigned in great numbers, and of those resigning a large proportion had taken up arms against the Government. Simultaneously and in connection with all this the purpose to sever the Federal Union was openly avowed. In accordance with this purpose, an ordinance had been adopted in each of these States declaring the States respectively to be separated from the National Union. A formula for instituting a combined government of these States had been promulgated, and this illegal organization, in the character of Confederate States, was already invoking recognition, aid, and intervention from foreign powers.

Finding this condition of things and believing it to be an imperative duty upon the incoming Executive to prevent, if possible, the consummation of such attempt to destroy the Federal Union, a choice of means to that end became indispensable. This choice was made, and was declared in the inaugural address [March 4, 1861]. The policy chosen looked to the exhaustion of all peaceful measures before a resort to any stronger ones. It sought only to hold the public places and property not already wrested from the Government and to collect the revenue, relying for the rest on time, discussion, and the ballot box. It promised a continuance of the mails at Government expense to the very people who were resisting the Government, and it gave repeated pledges against any disturbance to any of the people or any of their rights. Of all that which a President might constitutionally and justifiably do in such a case, everything was forborne without which it was believed possible to keep the Government on foot.

On the 5th of March, the present incumbent's first full day in office, a letter of Major [Robert] Anderson, commanding at Fort Sumter, written on the 28th of February and received at the War Department on the 4th of March, was by that Department placed in his hands. This letter expressed the professional opinion of the writer that reenforcements could not be thrown into that fort within the time for his relief rendered necessary by the limited supply of provisions, and with a view of holding possession of the same, with a force of less than 20,000 good and well-disciplined men. This opinion was concurred in by all the officers of his command, and their memoranda on the subject were made inclosures of Major Anderson's letter. The whole was immediately laid before Lieutenant-General [Winfield] Scott, who at once concurred with Major Anderson in opinion. On reflection, however, he took full time, consulting with other officers, both of the army and the navy, and at the end of four days came reluctantly, but decidedly, to the same conclusion as before. He also stated at the same time that no such sufficient force was then at the control of the Government or could be raised and brought to the ground within the time when the provisions in the fort would be exhausted. In a purely military point of view this reduced the duty of the Administration in the case to the mere matter of getting the garrison safely out of the fort.

It was believed, however, that to so abandon that position under the circumstances would be utterly ruinous; that the *necessity* under which it was to be done would not be fully understood; that by many it would be construed as a part of a *voluntary* policy; that at home it would discourage the friends of the Union, embolden its adversaries, and go far to insure to the latter a recognition abroad; that, in fact, it would be our national destruction consummated. This could not be allowed. Starvation was not yet upon the garrison, and ere it would be reached *Fort Pickens* might be reenforced. This last would be a clear indication of *policy*, and would better enable the country to accept the evacuation of Fort Sumter as a military *necessity*. An order was at once directed to be sent for the landing of the troops from the steamship *Brooklyn* into Fort Pickens. This order could not go by land, but must take the longer and slower route by sea. The first return news from the order was received just one week before the fall of Fort Sumter. The news itself was that the officer commanding the *Sabine*, to which vessel the troops had been transferred from the *Brooklyn*, acting upon some *quasi* armistice of the late Administration (and of the existence of which the present Administration, up to the time the order was dispatched, had only too vague and uncertain rumors to fix attention), had refused to land the troops. To now reenforce Fort Pickens before a crisis would be reached at Fort Sumter was impossible, rendered so by the near exhaustion of provisions in the latter-named fort. In precaution against such a conjuncture the Government had a few days before commenced preparing an expedition, as well adapted as might be, to relieve Fort Sumter, which expedition was intended to be ultimately used or not, according to circumstances. The strongest anticipated case for using it was now presented, and it was resolved to send it forward. As had been intended in this contingency, it was also resolved to notify the governor of South Carolina that he might expect an attempt would be made to provision the fort, and that if the attempt should not be resisted there would be no effort to throw in men, arms, or ammunition without further notice, or in case of an attack upon the fort. This notice was accordingly given, whereupon the fort was attacked and bombarded to its fall, without even awaiting the arrival of the provisioning expedition.

It is thus seen that the assault upon and reduction of Fort Sumter was in no sense a matter of self-defense on the part of the assailants. They well knew that the garrison in the fort could by no possibility commit aggression upon them. They knew—they were expressly notified—that the giving of bread to the few brave and hungry men of the garrison was all which would on that occasion be attempted, unless themselves, by resisting so much, should provoke more. They knew that this Government desired to keep the garrison in the fort, not to assail them, but merely to maintain visible possession, and thus to preserve the Union from actual and immediate dissolution, trusting, as hereinbefore stated, to time, discussion, and the ballot box for final adjustment; and they assailed and reduced the fort for precisely the reverse object—to drive out the visible authority of the Federal Union, and thus force it to immediate dissolution. That this was their object the Executive well understood; and having said to them in the inaugural address, "You can have no conflict without being yourselves the aggressors," he took pains not only to keep this declaration good, but also to keep the case so free from the power of ingenious sophistry as that the world should not be able to misunderstand it. By the affair at Fort Sumter, with its surrounding circumstances, that point was reached. Then and thereby the assailants of the Government began the conflict of arms, without a gun in sight or in expectancy to return their fire, save only the few in the fort, sent to that harbor years before for their own protection, and still ready to give that protection in whatever was lawful. In this act, discarding all else, they have forced upon the country the distinct issue, "Immediate dissolution or blood."

And this issue embraces more than the fate of these United States. It presents to the whole family of man the question whether a constitutional republic, or democracy—a government of the people by the same people—can or can not maintain its territorial integrity against its own domestic foes. It presents the question whether discontented individuals, too few in numbers to control administration according to organic law in any case, can always, upon the pretenses made in this case, or on any other pretenses, or arbitrarily without any pretense, break up their government, and thus practically put an end to free government upon the earth. It forces us to ask, Is there in all republics this inherent and fatal weakness? Must a government of necessity be too *strong* for the liberties of its own people, or too *weak* to maintain its own existence?

So viewing the issue, no choice was left but to call out the war power of the Government and so to resist force employed for its destruction by force for its preservation.

The call was made, and the response of the country was most gratifying, surpassing in unanimity and spirit the most sanguine expectation. Yet none of the States commonly called slave States, except Delaware, gave a regiment through regular State organization. A few regiments have been organized within some others of those States by individual enterprise and received into the Government service. Of course the seceded States, so called (and to which Texas had been joined about the time of the inauguration), gave no troops to the cause of the Union. The border States, so called, were not uniform in their action, some of them being almost *for* the Union, while in others, as Virginia, North Carolina, Tennessee, and Arkansas, the Union sentiment was nearly repressed and silenced. The course taken in Virginia was the most remarkable, perhaps the most important. A convention elected by the people of that State to consider this very question of disrupting the Federal Union was in session at the capital of Virginia when Fort Sumter fell. To this body the people had chosen a large majority of *professed* Union men. Almost immediately after the fall of Sumter many members of that majority went over to the original disunion minority and with them adopted an ordinance for withdrawing the State from the Union. Whether this change was wrought by their great approval of the assault upon Sumter or their great resentment at the Government's resistance to that assault is not definitely known. Although they submitted the ordinance for ratification to a vote of the people, to be taken on a day then somewhat more than a month distant, the convention and the legislature (which was also in session at the same time and place), with leading men of the State not members of either, immediately commenced acting as if the State were already out of the Union. They pushed military preparations vigorously forward all over the State. They seized the United States armory at Harpers Ferry and the navy-yard at Gosport, near Norfolk. They received—perhaps invited—into their State large bodies of troops, with their warlike appointments, from the so-called seceded States. They formally entered into a treaty of temporary alliance and cooperation with the so-called "Confederate States," and sent members to their congress at Montgomery; and, finally, they permitted the insurrectionary government to be transferred to their capital at Richmond.

The people of Virginia have thus allowed this giant insurrection to make its nest within her borders, and this Government has no choice left but to deal with it *where* it finds it; and it has the less regret, as the loyal citizens have in due form claimed its protection. Those loyal citizens this Government is bound to recognize and protect, as being Virginia.

In the border States, so called—in fact, the Middle States—there are those who favor a policy which they call "armed neutrality"; that is, an arming of those States to prevent the Union forces passing one way or the disunion the other over their soil. This would be disunion completed. Figuratively speaking, it would be the building of an impassable wall along the line of separation, and yet not quite an impassable one, for, under the guise of neutrality, it would tie the hands of the Union men and freely pass supplies from among them to the insurrectionists, which it could not do as an open enemy. At a stroke it would take all the trouble off the hands of secession, except only what proceeds from the external blockade. It would do for the disunionists that which of all things they most desire—feed them well and give them disunion without a struggle of their own. It recognizes no fidelity to the Constitution, no obligation to maintain the Union; and while very many who have favored it are doubtless loyal citizens, it is, nevertheless, very injurious in effect.

Recurring to the action of the Government, it may be stated that at first a call was made for 75,000 militia, and rapidly following this a proclamation was issued for closing the ports of the insurrectionary districts by proceeding in the nature of blockade. So far all was believed to be strictly legal. At this point the insurrectionists announced their purpose to enter upon the practice of privateering.

Other calls were made for volunteers to serve three years unless sooner discharged, and also for large additions to the Regular Army and Navy. These measures, whether strictly legal or not, were ventured upon under what appeared to be a popular demand and a public necessity, trusting then, as now, that Congress would readily ratify them. It is believed that nothing has been done beyond the constitutional competency of Congress.

Soon after the first call for militia it was considered a duty to authorize the Commanding General in proper cases, according to his discretion, to suspend the privilege of the writ of *habeas corpus*, or, in other words, to arrest and detain without resort to the ordinary processes and forms of law such individuals as he might deem dangerous to the public safety. This authority has purposely been exercised but very sparingly. Nevertheless, the legality and propriety of what has been done under it are questioned, and the attention of the country has been called to the proposition that one who is sworn to "take care that the laws be faithfully executed" should not himself violate them. Of course some consideration was given to the questions of power and propriety before this matter was acted upon. The whole of the laws which were required to be faithfully executed were being resisted and failing of execution in nearly one-third of the States. Must they be allowed to finally fail of execution, even had it been perfectly clear that by the use of the means necessary to their execution some single law, made in such extreme tenderness of the citizen's liberty that practically it relieves more of the guilty than of the innocent, should to a very limited extent be violated? To state the question more directly, Are all the laws *but one* to go unexecuted, and the Government itself go to pieces lest that one be violated? Even in such a case, would not the official oath be broken if the Government should be overthrown when it was believed that disregarding the single law would tend to preserve it? But it was not believed that this question was presented. It was not believed that any law was violated. The provision of the Constitution that "the privilege of the writ of *habeas corpus* shall not be suspended unless when, in cases of rebellion or invasion, the public safety may require it" is equivalent to a provision—*is* a provision—that such privilege may be suspended when, in cases of rebellion or invasion, the public safety *does* require it. It was decided that we have a case of rebellion and that the public safety does require the qualified suspension of the privilege of the writ which was authorized to be made. Now it is insisted that Congress, and not the Executive, is vested with this power; but the Constitution itself is silent as to which or who is to exercise the power; and as the provision was plainly made for a dangerous emergency, it can not be believed the framers of the instrument intended that in every case the danger should run its course until Congress could be called together, the very assembling of which might be prevented, as was intended in this case, by the rebellion.

No more extended argument is now offered, as an opinion at some length will probably be presented by the Attorney-General. Whether there shall be any legislation upon the subject, and, if any, what, is submitted entirely to the better judgment of Congress.

The forbearance of this Government had been so extraordinary and so long continued as to lead some foreign nations to shape their action as if they supposed the early destruction of our National Union was probable. While this on discovery gave the Executive some concern, he is now happy to say that the sovereignty and rights of the United States are now everywhere practically respected by foreign powers, and a general sympathy with the country is manifested throughout the world.

The reports of the Secretaries of the Treasury [Salmon P. Chase], War [Simon Cameron], and the Navy [Gideon Welles] will give the information in detail deemed necessary and convenient for your deliberation and action, while the Executive and all the Departments will stand ready to supply omissions or to communicate new facts considered important for you to know.

It is now recommended that you give the legal means for making this contest a short and a decisive one; that you place at the control of the Government for the work at least 400,000 men and $400,000,000. That number of men is about one-tenth of those of proper ages within the regions where apparently *all* are willing to engage, and the sum is less than a twenty-third part of the money value owned by the men who seem ready to devote the whole. A debt of $600,000,000 *now* is a less sum per head than was the debt of our Revolution when we came out of that struggle, and the money value in the country now bears even a greater proportion to what it was then than does the population. Surely each man has as strong a motive *now* to *preserve* our liberties as each had *then* to *establish* them.

A right result at this time will be worth more to the world than ten times the men and ten times the money. The evidence reaching us from the country leaves no doubt that the material for the work is abundant, and that it needs only the hand of legislation to give it legal sanction and the hand of the Executive to give it practical shape and efficiency. One of the greatest perplexities of the Government is to avoid receiving troops faster than it can provide for them. In a word, the people will save their Government if the Government itself will do its part only indifferently well.

It might seem at first thought to be of little difference whether the present movement at the South be called "secession" or "rebellion." The movers, however, well understand the difference. At the beginning they knew they could never raise their treason to any respectable magnitude by any name which implies violation of law. They knew their people possessed as much of moral sense, as much of devotion to law and order, and as much pride in and reverence for the history and Government of their common country as any other civilized and patriotic people. They knew they could make no advancement directly in the teeth of these strong and noble sentiments. Accordingly, they commenced by an insidious debauching of the public mind. They invented an ingenious sophism, which, if conceded, was followed by perfectly logical steps through all the incidents to the complete destruction of the Union. The sophism itself is that any State of the Union may *consistently* with the National Constitution, and therefore *lawfully* and *peacefully*, withdraw from the Union without the consent of the Union or of any other State. The little disguise that the supposed right is to be exercised only for just cause, themselves to be the sole judge of its justice, is too thin to merit any notice.

With rebellion thus sugar coated they have been drugging the public mind of their section for more than thirty years, and until at length they have brought many good men to a willingness to take up arms against the Government the day *after* some assembly of men have enacted the farcical pretense of taking their State out of the Union who could have been brought to no such thing the day *before*.

This sophism derives much, perhaps the whole, of its currency from the assumption that there is some omnipotent and sacred supremacy pertaining to a *State*—to each State of our Federal Union. Our States have neither more nor less power than they reserved to them in the Union by the Constitution, no one of them ever having been a State *out* of the Union. The original ones passed into the Union even *before* they cast off their British colonial dependence, and the new ones each came into the Union directly from a condition of dependence, excepting Texas; and even Texas, in its temporary independence, was never designated a State. The new ones only took the designation of States on coming into the Union, while that name was first adopted for the old ones in and by the Declaration of Independence. Therein the "United Colonies" were declared to be "free and independent States"; but even then the object plainly was not to declare their independence of *one another* or of the *Union*, but directly the contrary, as their mutual pledge and their mutual action before, at the time, and afterwards abundantly show. The express plighting of faith by each and all of the original thirteen in the Articles of Confederation, two years later, that the Union shall be perpetual is most conclusive. Having never been States, either in substance or in name, *outside* of the Union, whence this magical omnipotence of "State rights," asserting a claim of power to lawfully destroy the Union itself? Much is said about the "sovereignty" of the States, but the word even is not in the National Constitution, nor, as is believed, in any of the State constitutions. What is a "sovereignty" in the political sense of the term? Would it be far wrong to define it "a political community without a political superior"? Tested by this, no one of our States, except Texas, ever was a sovereignty; and even Texas gave up the character on coming into the Union, by which act she acknowledged the Constitution of the United States and the laws and treaties of the United States made in pursuance of the Constitution to be for her the supreme law of the land. The States have their status in the Union, and they have no other legal status. If they break from this, they can only do so against law and by revolution. The Union, and not themselves separately, procured their independence and their liberty. By conquest or purchase the Union gave each of them whatever of independence and liberty it has. The Union is older than any of the States, and, in fact, it created them as States. Originally some dependent colonies made the Union, and in turn the Union threw off their old dependence for them and made them States, such as they are. Not one of them ever had a State constitution independent of the Union. Of course it is not forgotten that all the new States framed their constitutions before they entered the Union, nevertheless dependent upon and preparatory to coming into the Union.

Unquestionably the States have the powers and rights reserved to them in and by the National Constitution; but among these surely are not included all conceivable powers, however mischievous or destructive, but at most such only as were known in the world at the time as governmental powers; and certainly a power to destroy the Government itself had never been known as a governmental—as a merely administrative—power. This relative matter of national power and State rights, as a principle, is no other than the principle of *generality* and *locality*. Whatever concerns the whole should be confided to the whole—to the General Government—while whatever concerns *only* the State should be left exclusively to the State. This is all there is of original principle about it. Whether the National Constitution in defining boundaries between the two has applied the principle with exact accuracy is not to be questioned. We are all bound by that defining without question.

What is now combated is the position that secession is consistent with the Constitution—is *lawful* and *peaceful*. It is not contended that there is any express law for it, and nothing should ever be implied as law which leads to unjust or absurd consequences. The nation purchased with money the countries out of which several of these States were formed. Is it just that they shall go off without leave and without refunding? The nation paid very large sums (in the aggregate, I believe, nearly a hundred millions) to relieve Florida of the aboriginal tribes. Is it just that she shall now be off without consent or without making any return? The nation is now in debt for money applied to the benefit of these so-called seceding States in common with the rest. Is it just either that creditors shall go unpaid or the remaining States pay the whole? A part of the present national debt was contracted to pay the old debts of Texas. Is it just that she shall leave and pay no part of this herself?

Again: If one State may secede, so may another; and when all shall have seceded none is left to pay the debts. Is this quite just to creditors? Did we notify them of this sage view of ours when we borrowed their money? If we now recognize this doctrine by allowing the seceders to go in peace, it is difficult to see what we can do if others choose to go or to extort terms upon which they will promise to remain.

The seceders insist that our Constitution admits of secession. They have assumed to make a national constitution of their own, in which of necessity they have either *discarded* or *retained* the right of secession, as they insist it exists in ours. If they have discarded it, they thereby admit that on principle it ought not to be in ours. If they have retained it, by their own construction of ours they show that to be consistent they must secede from one another whenever they shall find it the easiest way of settling their debts or effecting any other selfish or unjust object. The principle itself is one of disintegration, and upon which no government can possibly endure.

If all the States save one should assert the power to *drive* that one out of the Union, it is presumed the whole class of seceder politicians would at once deny the power and denounce the act as the greatest outrage upon State rights. But suppose that precisely the same act, instead of being called "driving the one out," should be called "the seceding of the others from that one," it would be exactly what the seceders claim to do, unless, indeed, they make the point that the one, because it is a minority, may rightfully do what the others, because they are a majority, may not rightfully do. These politicians are subtle and profound on the rights of minorities. They are not partial to that power which made the Constitution and speaks from the preamble, calling itself "we, the people."

It may well be questioned whether there is today a majority of the legally qualified voters of any State, except, perhaps, South Carolina, in favor of disunion. There is much reason to believe that the Union men are the majority in many, if not in every other one, of the so-called seceded States. The contrary has not been demonstrated in any one of them. It is ventured to affirm this even of Virginia and Tennessee; for the result of an election held in military camps, where the bayonets are all on one side of the question voted upon, can scarcely be considered as demonstrating popular sentiment. At such an election all that large class who are at once *for* the Union and *against* coercion would be coerced to vote against the Union.

It may be affirmed without extravagance that the free institutions we enjoy have developed the powers and improved the condition of our whole people beyond any example in the world. Of this we now have a striking and an impressive illustration. So large an army as the Government has now on foot was never before known without a soldier in it but who had taken his place there of his own free choice. But more than this, there are many single regiments whose members, one and another, possess full practical knowledge of all the arts, sciences, professions, and whatever else, whether useful or elegant, is known in the world; and there is scarcely one from which there could not be selected a President, a Cabinet, a Congress, and perhaps a court, abundantly competent to administer the Government itself. Nor do I say this is not true also in the army of our late friends, now adversaries in this contest, but if it is, so much better the reason why the Government which has conferred such benefits on both them and us should not be broken up. Whoever in any section proposes to abandon such a government would do well to consider in deference to what principle it is that he does it; what better he is likely to get in its stead; whether the substitute will give, or be intended to give, so much of good to the people. There are some foreshadowing on this subject. Our adversaries have adopted some declarations of independence in which, unlike the good old one penned by Jefferson, they omit the words "all men are created equal." Why? They have adopted a temporary national constitution, in the preamble of which, unlike our good old one signed by Washington, they omit "We, the people," and substitute "We, the deputies of the sovereign and independent States." Why? Why this deliberate pressing out of view the rights of men and the authority of the people?

This is essentially a people's contest. On the side of the Union it is a struggle for maintaining in the world that form and substance of government whose leading object is to elevate the condition of men; to lift artificial weights from all shoulders; to clear the paths of laudable pursuit for all; to afford all an unfettered start and a fair chance in the race of life. Yielding to partial and temporary departures, from necessity, this is the leading object of the Government for whose existence we contend.

I am most happy to believe that the plain people understand and appreciate this. It is worthy of note that while in this the Government's hour of trial large numbers of those in the Army and Navy who have been favored with the offices have resigned and proved false to the hand which had pampered them, not one common soldier or common sailor is known to have deserted his flag.

Great honor is due to those officers who remained true despite the example of their treacherous associates; but the greatest honor and most important fact of all is the unanimous firmness of the common soldiers and common sailors. To the last man, so far as known, they have successfully resisted the traitorous efforts of those whose commands but an hour before they obeyed as absolute law. This is the patriotic instinct of plain people. They understand without an argument that destroying the Government which was made by Washington means no good to them.

Our popular Government has often been called an experiment. Two points in it our people have already settled—the successful *establishing* and the successful *administering* of it. One still remains—its successful *maintenance* against a formidable internal attempt to overthrow it. It is now for them to demonstrate to the world that those who can fairly carry an election can also suppress a rebellion; that ballots are the rightful and peaceful successors of bullets, and that when ballots have fairly and constitutionally decided there can be no successful appeal back to bullets; that there can be no successful appeal except to ballots themselves at succeeding elections. Such will be a great lesson of peace, teaching men that what they can not take by an election neither can they take it by a war; teaching all the folly of being the beginners of a war.

Lest there be some uneasiness in the minds of candid men as to what is to be the course of the Government toward the Southern States *after* the rebellion shall have been suppressed, the Executive deems it proper to say it will be his purpose then, as ever, to be guided by the Constitution and the laws, and that he probably will have no different understanding of the powers and duties of the Federal Government relative to the rights of the States and the people under the Constitution than that expressed in the inaugural address.

He desires to preserve the Government, that it may be administered for all as it was administered by the men who made it. Loyal citizens everywhere have the right to claim this of their government, and the government has no right to withhold or neglect it. It is not perceived that in giving it there is any coercion, any conquest, or any subjugation in any just sense of those terms.

The Constitution provides, and all the States have accepted the provision, that "the United States shall guarantee to every State in this Union a republican form of government." But if a State may lawfully go out of the Union, having done so it may also discard the republican form of government; so that to prevent its going out is an indispensable *means* to the *end* of maintaining the guaranty mentioned; and when an end is lawful and obligatory the indispensable means to it are also lawful and obligatory.

It was with the deepest regret that the Executive found the duty of employing the war power in defense of the Government forced upon him. He could but perform this duty or surrender the existence of the Government. No compromise by public servants could in this case be a cure; not that compromises are not often proper, but that no popular government can long survive a marked precedent that those who carry an election can only save the government from immediate destruction by giving up the main point upon which the people gave the election. The people themselves, and not their servants, can safely reverse their own deliberate decisions.

As a private citizen the Executive could not have consented that these institutions shall perish; much less could he [act] in betrayal of so vast and so sacred a trust as these free people had confided to him. He felt that he had no moral right to shrink, nor even to count the chances of his own life, in what might follow. In full view of his great responsibility he has so far done what he has deemed his duty. You will now, according to your own judgment, perform yours. He sincerely hopes that your views and your action may so accord with his as to assure all faithful citizens who have been disturbed in their rights of a certain and speedy restoration to them under the Constitution and the laws.

And having thus chosen our course, without guile and with pure purpose, let us renew our trust in God and go forward without fear and with manly hearts.

SOURCE: Richardson, *Messages and Papers of the Presidents*, 7:3221–32.

DOCUMENT 23
PRESIDENT LINCOLN'S PROCLAMATION OF INSURRECTION IN THE SO-CALLED CONFEDERATE STATES. AUGUST 16, 1861.

Whereas on the 15th day of April, 1861, the President of the United States, in view of an insurrection against the laws, Constitution, and Government of the United States which had broken out within the States of South Carolina, Georgia, Alabama, Florida, Mississippi, Louisiana, and Texas, and in pursuance of the provisions of the act entitled "An act to provide for calling forth the militia to execute the laws of the Union, suppress insurrections, and repel invasions, and to repeal the act now in force for that purpose," approved February 28, 1795, did call forth the militia to suppress said insurrection and to cause the laws of the Union to be duly executed, and the insurgents have failed to disperse by the time directed by the President; and

Whereas such insurrection has since broken out, and yet exists, within the States of Virginia, North Carolina, Tennessee, and Arkansas; and

Whereas the insurgents in all the said States claim to act under the authority thereof, and such claim is not disclaimed or repudiated by the persons exercising the functions of government in such State or States or in the part or parts thereof in which such combinations exist, nor has such insurrection been suppressed by said States:

Now, therefore, I, Abraham Lincoln, President of the United States, in pursuance of an act of Congress approved July 13, 1861, do hereby declare that the inhabitants of the said States of Georgia, South Carolina, Virginia, North Carolina, Tennessee, Alabama, Louisiana, Texas, Arkansas, Mississippi, and Florida (except the inhabitants of that part of the State of Virginia lying west of the Alleghany Mountains and of such other parts of that State and the other States hereinbefore named as may maintain a loyal adhesion to the Union and the Constitution or may be from time to time occupied and controlled by forces of the United States engaged in the dispersion of said insurgents) are in a state of insurrection against the United States, and that all commercial intercourse between the same and the inhabitants thereof, with the exceptions aforesaid, and the citizens of other States and other parts of the United States is unlawful, and will remain unlawful until such insurrection shall cease or has been suppressed; that all goods and chattels, wares and merchandise, coming from any of said States, with the exceptions aforesaid, into other parts of the United States without the special license and permission of the President, through the Secretary of the Treasury, or proceeding to any of said States, with the exceptions aforesaid, by land or water, together with the vessel or vehicle conveying the same or conveying persons to or from said States, with said exceptions, will be forfeited to the United States; and that from and after fifteen days from the issuing of this proclamation all ships and vessels belonging in whole or in part to any citizen or inhabitant of any of said States, with said exceptions, found at sea or in any port of the United States will be forfeited to the United States: and I hereby enjoin upon all district attorneys, marshals, and officers of the revenue and of the military and naval forces of the United States to be vigilant in the execution of said act and in the enforcement of the penalties and forfeitures imposed or declared by it, leaving any party who may think himself aggrieved thereby to his application to the Secretary of the Treasury for the remission of any penalty or forfeiture which the said Secretary is authorized by law to grant if in his judgment the special circumstances of any case shall require such remission.

SOURCE: Richardson, *Messages and Papers of the Presidents*, 4:3238–39.

7

ULYSSES S. GRANT

DOCUMENT 24
PRESIDENT ULYSSES GRANT'S STATE OF THE UNION
MESSAGE CONCERNING THE LANDING OF MARINES
IN KOREA. DECEMBER 4, 1871.

. . . Prompted by a desire to put an end to the barbarous treatment of our shipwrecked sailors on the Corean [*sic*] coast, I instructed our minister at Peking to endeavor to conclude a convention with Corea for securing the safety and humane treatment of such mariners.*

Admiral John Rodgers was instructed to accompany him, with a sufficient force to protect him in case of need.

A small surveying party sent out, on reaching the coast, was treacherously attacked at a disadvantage. Ample opportunity was given for explanation and apology for the insult. Neither came. A force was then landed. After an arduous march over a rugged and difficult country, the forts from which the outrages had been committed were reduced by a gallant assault and were destroyed. Having thus punished the criminals, and having vindicated the

---

* In 1869 the American vessel *General Sherman* ran aground along the Han River in Korea. The Koreans torched the ship and massacred the crew. In an effort to protect American missionaries and merchants on the Korean peninsula, the Grant administration sent Frederick Low, U.S. minister to China, to the region to gain assurances that Americans would be protected. In May 1871, Low arrived aboard the flagship *Colorado*, along with four other warships of the Asiatic Fleet. The fleet commander, Rear Admiral John Rodgers, anchored near the mouth of the Han River and sent a survey team to inspect the tributary approaches to Seoul. On June 1 this survey team was fired upon by one of five forts protecting the Han River. Ten days later Rodgers and Low decided to respond with a punitive Marine expedition against the forts. The "Citadel" battle, as it became known, killed two hundred Koreans and earned for six marines the Medal of Honor. Although Low and Rodgers failed to negotiate any formal treaty with the Koreans as a result of this battle, the Koreans no longer fired upon American vessels, whether merchantmen or warships.

honor of the flag, the expedition returned, finding it impracticable, under the circumstances, to conclude the desired convention. I respectfully refer to the correspondence relating thereto, herewith submitted, and leave the subject for such action as Congress may see fit to take.

SOURCE: U.S. State Department, *Foreign Relations of the United States, 1871* (Washington, DC: Government Printing Office, 1875), vi.

8

WILLIAM McKINLEY

DOCUMENT 25
PRESIDENT WILLIAM McKINLEY ASKS FOR WAR
AGAINST SPAIN. APRIL 11, 1898.

———✦———

To the Congress of the United States:

Obedient to that precept of the Constitution [Article 2, Section 3] which commands the President to give from time to time to the Congress information of the state of the Union and to recommend to their consideration such measures as he shall judge necessary and expedient, it becomes my duty to now address your body with regard to the grave crisis that has arisen in the relations of the United States to Spain by reason of the warfare that for more than three years has raged in the neighboring island of Cuba.[1]

I do so because of the intimate connection of the Cuban question with the state of our own Union and the grave relation the course which it is now incumbent upon the nation to adopt must bear to the traditional policy of our Government if it is to accord with the precepts laid down by the founders of the Republic and religiously observed by succeeding Administrations to the present day.

The present revolution is but the successor of other similar insurrections which have occurred in Cuba against the dominion of Spain, extending over a period of nearly half a century, each of which during its progress has subjected the United States to great effort and expense in enforcing its neutrality laws, caused enormous losses to American trade and commerce, caused irritation, annoyance, and disturbance among our citizens, and, by the exercise of cruel, barbarous, and uncivilized practices of warfare, shocked the sensibilities and offended the humane sympathies of our people.

---

[1]Since 1895, Spanish troops had been fighting Cuban nationalists in a savage guerrilla conflict chiefly in the unsettled eastern end of the island.

Since the present revolution began, in February, 1895, this country has seen the fertile domain at our threshold ravaged by fire and sword in the course of a struggle unequaled in the history of the island and rarely paralleled as to the numbers of the combatants and the bitterness of the contest by any revolution of modern times where a dependent people striving to be free have been opposed by the power of the sovereign state.

Our people have beheld a once prosperous community reduced to comparative want, its lucrative commerce virtually paralyzed, its exceptional productiveness diminished, its fields laid waste, its mills in ruins, and its people perishing by tens of thousands from hunger and destitution. We have found ourselves constrained, in the observance of that strict neutrality which our laws enjoin and which the law of nations commands, to police our own waters and watch our own seaports in prevention of any unlawful act in aid of the Cubans.

Our trade has suffered, the capital invested by our citizens in Cuba has been largely lost, and the temper and forbearance of our people have been so sorely tried as to beget a perilous unrest among our own citizens, which has inevitably found its expression from time to time in the National Legislature [U.S. Congress], so that issues wholly external to our own body politic engross attention and stand in the way of that close devotion to domestic advancement that becomes a self-contained commonwealth whose primal maxim has been the avoidance of all foreign entanglements. All this must awaken, and has, indeed, aroused, the utmost concern on the part of this Government, as well during my predecessor's term as in my own.

In April, 1896, the evils from which our country suffered through the Cuban war became so onerous that my predecessor made an effort to bring about a peace through the mediation of this Government in any way that might tend to an honorable adjustment of the contest between Spain and her revolted colony, on the basis of some effective scheme of self-government for Cuba under the flag and sovereignty of Spain. It failed through the refusal of the Spanish government then in power to consider any form of mediation or, indeed, any plan of settlement which did not begin with the actual submission of the insurgents to the mother country, and then only on such terms as Spain herself might see fit to grant. The war continued unabated. The resistance of the insurgents was in no wise diminished.

The efforts of Spain were increased, both by the dispatch of fresh levies [troops] to Cuba and by the addition to the horrors of the strife of a new and inhuman phase happily unprecedented in the modern history of civilized Christian peoples. The policy of devastation and concentration, inaugurated by the Captain-General's *bando*[2] of October 21, 1896, in the Province of Pinar del Rio was thence extended to embrace all of the island to which the power of the Spanish arms was able to reach by occupation or by military operations. The peasantry, including all dwelling in the open agricultural interior, were driven into the garrison towns or isolated places held by the troops.

The raising and movement of provisions of all kinds were interdicted. The fields were laid waste, dwellings unroofed and fired, mills destroyed, and, in short, everything that could desolate the land and render it unfit for human habitation or support was commanded by one or the other of the contending parties and executed by all the powers at their disposal.

By the time the present Administration took office, a year ago, reconcentration (so called) had been made effective over the better part of the four central and western provinces—Santa Clara, Matanzas, Havana, and Pinar del Rio.

The agricultural population to the estimated number of 300,000 or more was herded within the towns and their immediate vicinage, deprived of the means of support, rendered destitute of shelter, left poorly clad, and exposed to the most unsanitary conditions. As the scarcity of food increased with the devastation of the depopulated areas of production, destitution and want became misery and starvation. Month by month the death rate increased in an alarming ratio. By March, 1897, according to conservative estimates from official Spanish sources, the mortality among the reconcentrados from starvation and the diseases thereto incident exceeded 50 percent of their total number.

No practical relief was accorded to the destitute. The overburdened towns, already suffering from the general dearth, could give no aid. So-called "zones of cultivation" established within the immediate areas of effective military control about the cities and fortified camps proved illusory as a remedy for the suffering. The unfortunates, being for the most part women and children, with aged and helpless men, enfeebled by disease and hunger, could not have tilled the soil without tools, seed, or shelter for their own support or for the supply of the cities. Reconcentration, adopted avowedly as a war measure in order to cut off the resources of the insurgents, worked its predestined result. As I said in my message of last

---

[2]Spain's military governor to Cuba, General Valeriano Weyler, began a policy of forcing the rural populace into concentration camps, thereby separating the rural population from the revolutionary insurgents. This martial policy was called reconcentration.

December, it was not civilized warfare; it was extermination. The only peace it could beget was that of the wilderness and the grave.

Meanwhile the military situation in the island had undergone a noticeable change. The extraordinary activity that characterized the second year of the war, when the insurgents invaded even the thitherto unharmed fields of Pinar del Rio and carried havoc and destruction up to the walls of the city of Havana itself, had relapsed into a dogged struggle in the central and eastern provinces. The Spanish arms regained a measure of control in Pinar del Rio and parts of Havana, but, under the existing conditions of the rural country, without immediate improvement of their productive situation. Even thus partially restricted, the revolutionists held their own, and their conquest and submission, put forward by Spain as the essential and sole basis of peace, seemed as far distant as at the outset.

In this state of affairs my Administration found itself confronted with the grave problem of its duty. My message of last December reviewed the situation and narrated the steps taken with a view to relieving its acuteness and opening the way to some form of honorable settlement. The assassination of the prime minister, [Enrique] Canovas, led to a change of government in Spain. The former administration, pledged to subjugation without concession, gave place to that of a more liberal party, committed long in advance to a policy of reform involving the wider principle of home rule for Cuba and Puerto Rico.

The overtures of this Government made through its new envoy, General [Stewart] Woodford, and looking to an immediate and effective amelioration of the condition of the island, although not accepted to the extent of admitted mediation in any shape, were met by assurances that home rule in an advanced phase would be forthwith offered to Cuba, without waiting for the war to end, and that more humane methods should thenceforth prevail in the conduct of hostilities. Coincidentally with these declarations the new government of Spain continued and completed the policy, already begun by its predecessor, of testifying friendly regard for this nation by releasing American citizens held under one charge or another connected with the insurrection, so that by the end of November not a single person entitled in any way to our national protection remained in a Spanish prison.

While these negotiations were in progress the increasing destitution of the unfortunate reconcentrados and the alarming mortality among them claimed earnest attention. The success which had attended the limited measure of relief extended to the suffering American citizens among them by the judicious expenditure through the consular agencies of the money appropriated expressly for their succor by the joint resolution approved

May 24, 1897, prompted the humane extension of a similar scheme of aid to the great body of sufferers. A suggestion to this end was acquiesced in by the Spanish authorities.

On the 24th of December last I caused to be issued an appeal to the American people inviting contributions in money or in kind for the succor of the starving sufferers in Cuba, following this on the 8th of January by a similar public announcement of the formation of a central Cuban relief committee, with headquarters in New York City, composed of three members representing the American National Red Cross and the religious and business elements of the community.

The efforts of that committee have been untiring and have accomplished much. Arrangements for free transportation to Cuba have greatly aided the charitable work. The president of the American Red Cross and representatives of other contributory organizations have generously visited Cuba and cooperated with the consul-general and the local authorities to make effective distribution of the relief collected through the efforts of the central committee. Nearly $200,000 in money and supplies has already reached the sufferers, and more is forthcoming. The supplies are admitted duty free, and transportation to the interior has been arranged, so that the relief, at first necessarily confined to Havana and the larger cities, is now extended through most, if not all, of the towns where suffering exists.

Thousands of lives have already been saved. The necessity for a change in the condition of the reconcentrados is recognized by the Spanish Government. Within a few days past the orders of General Weyler have been revoked. The reconcentrados, it is said, are to be permitted to return to their homes and aided to resume the self-supporting pursuits of peace. Public works have been ordered to give them employment and a sum of $600,000 has been appropriated for their relief.

The war in Cuba is of such a nature that, short of subjugation or extermination, a final military victory for either side seems impracticable. The alternative lies in the physical exhaustion of the one or the other party, or perhaps of both—a condition which in effect ended the ten years' war by the truce of Zanjón.[3] The prospect of such a protraction and conclusion of the present strife is a contingency hardly to be contemplated with equanimity by the civilized world, and least of all by the United States, affected and injured as we are, deeply and intimately, by its very existence.

---

[3] Following ten years of a colonial war with Cuban nationalists, Spain agreed in February 1878 at Zanjón to a cease-fire with the insurgents while granting them amnesty and limited local self-autonomy.

Realizing this, it appeared to be my duty, in a spirit of true friendliness, no less to Spain than to the Cubans, who have so much to lose by the prolongation of the struggle, to seek to bring about an immediate termination of the war. To this end I submitted on the 27th ultimo, as a result of much representation and correspondence, through the United States minister at Madrid, propositions to the Spanish Government looking to an armistice until October 1 for the negotiation of peace with the good offices of the President.

In addition I asked the immediate revocation of the order of reconcentration, so as to permit the people to return to their farms and the needy to be relieved with provisions and supplies from the United States, cooperating with the Spanish authorities, so as to afford full relief.

The reply of the Spanish cabinet was received on the night of the 31st ultimo. It offered, as the means to bring about peace in Cuba, to confide the preparation thereof to the insular parliament, inasmuch as the concurrence of that body would be necessary to reach a final result, it being, however, understood that the powers reserved by the constitution to the central Government are not lessened or diminished. As the Cuban parliament does not meet until the 4th of May next, the Spanish Government would not object for its part to accept at once a suspension of hostilities if asked for by the insurgents from the general-in-chief, to whom it would pertain in such case to determine the duration and conditions of the armistice.

The propositions submitted by General Woodford and the reply of the Spanish Government were both in the form of brief memoranda, the texts of which are before me and are substantially in the language above given. The function of the Cuban parliament in the matter of "preparing" peace and the manner of its doing so are not expressed in the Spanish memorandum, but from General Woodford's explanatory reports of preliminary discussions preceding the final conference it is understood that the Spanish Government stands ready to give the insular congress full powers to settle the terms of peace with the insurgents, whether by direct negotiation or indirectly by means of legislation does not appear.

With this last overture in the direction of immediate peace, and its disappointing reception by Spain, the Executive is brought to the end of his effort.

In my annual message of December last I said:

Of the untried measures there remain only: Recognition of the insurgents as belligerents; recognition of the independence of Cuba; neutral intervention to end the war by imposing a rational compromise between the contestants, and intervention in favor of one or the other party. I speak not of forcible annexation for that can not be thought of. That, by our code of morality, would be criminal aggression.

Thereupon I reviewed these alternatives in the light of President [Ulysses] Grant's measured words, uttered in 1875, when, after seven years of sanguinary, destructive, and cruel hostilities in Cuba, he reached the conclusion that the recognition of the independence of Cuba was impracticable and indefensible and that the recognition of belligerence was not warranted by the facts according to the tests of public law. I commented especially upon the latter aspect of the question, pointing out the inconveniences and positive dangers of a recognition of belligerence, which, while adding to the already onerous burdens of neutrality within our own jurisdiction, could not in any way extend our influence or effective offices in the territory of hostilities.

Nothing has since occurred to change my view in this regard, and I recognize as fully now as then that the issuance of a proclamation of neutrality, by which process the so-called recognition of belligerents is published, could of itself and unattended by other action accomplish nothing toward the one end for which we labor—the instant pacification of Cuba and the cessation of the misery that afflicts the island.

Turning to the question of recognizing at this time the independence of the present insurgent government in Cuba, we find safe precedents in our history from an early day. They are well summed up in President [Andrew] Jackson's message to Congress, December 21, 1836, on the subject of the recognition of the independence of Texas. He said:

In all the contests that have arisen out of the revolutions of France, out of the disputes relating to the crowns of Portugal and Spain, out of the revolutionary movements of those Kingdoms, out of the separation of the American possessions of both from the European Governments, and out of the numerous and constantly occurring struggles for dominion in Spanish America, so wisely consistent with our just principles has been the action of our Government that we have under the most critical circumstances avoided all censure and encountered no other evil than that produced by a transient estrangement of good will in those against whom we have been by force of evidence compelled to decide.

It has thus been made known to the world that the uniform policy and practice of the United States is to avoid all interference in disputes which merely relate to the internal government of other nations, and eventually to recognize the authority of the prevailing party, without reference to our particular interests and views or to the merits of the original controversy. . . .

. . . But on this as on every trying occasion safety is to be found in a rigid adherence to principle.

In the contest between Spain and her revolted colonies we stood aloof and waited, not only until the ability of the new States to protect themselves was fully established, but until the danger of their being again subjugated had entirely passed away. Then, and not till then, were they recognized. Such was our course in regard to Mexico herself. . . . It is true that, with regard to Texas, the civil authority of Mexico has been expelled, its invading army defeated, the chief of the Republic himself captured, and all present power to control the government of Texas annihilated within its confines. But, on the other hand, there is, in appearance at least, an immense disparity of physical force on the side of Mexico. The Mexican Republic under another Executive is rallying its forces under a new leader and menacing a fresh invasion to recover its lost dominion.

Upon the issue of this threatened invasion the independence of Texas may be considered as suspended, and were there nothing peculiar in the relative situation of the United States and Texas our acknowledgement of its independence at such a crisis could scarcely be regarded as consistent with that prudent reserve with which we have heretofore held ourselves bound to treat all similar questions.

Thereupon Andrew Jackson proceeded to consider the risk that there might be imputed to the United States motives of selfish interest in view of the former claim on our part to the territory of Texas and of the avowed purpose of the Texans in seeking recognition of independence as an incident to the incorporation of Texas in the Union, concluding thus:

Prudence, therefore, seems to dictate that we should still stand aloof and maintain our present attitude, if not until Mexico itself or one of the great foreign powers shall recognize the independence of the new Government, at least until the lapse of time or the course of events shall have proved beyond cavil or dispute the ability of the people of that country to maintain their separate sovereignty and to uphold the Government constituted by them. Neither of the contending parties can justly complain of this course. By pursuing it we are but carrying out the long-established policy of our Government—a policy which has secured to us respect and influence abroad and inspired confidence at home.

These are the words of the resolute and patriotic Jackson. They are evidence that the United States, in addition to the test imposed by public law as the condition of the recognition of independence by a neutral state (to wit, that the revolted state shall "constitute in fact a body politic, having a government in substance as well as in name, possessed of the elements of stability," and forming de facto, "if left to itself, a state among the nations, reasonably capable of discharging the duties of a state"), has imposed for its own governance in dealing with cases like these the further condition that recognition of independent statehood is not due to a revolted dependency until the danger of its being again subjugated by the parent state has entirely passed away.

This extreme test was, in fact, applied in the case of Texas. The Congress to whom President Jackson referred the question as one "probably leading to war," and therefore a proper subject for "a previous understanding with that body by whom war can alone be declared and by whom all the provisions for sustaining its perils must be furnished," left the matter of the recognition of Texas to the discretion of the Executive, providing merely for the sending of a diplomatic agent when the President should be satisfied that the Republic of Texas had become "an independent state." It was so recognized by President [Martin] Van Buren, who commissioned a chargé d'affaires March 7, 1837, after Mexico had abandoned an attempt to reconquer the Texas territory, and when there was at the time no bona fide contest going on between the insurgent province and its former sovereign.

I said in my message of December last:

> It is to be seriously considered whether the Cuban insurrection possesses beyond dispute the attributes of statehood, which alone can demand the recognition of belligerency in its favor.

The same requirement must certainly be no less seriously considered when the graver issue of recognizing independence is in question, for no less positive test can be applied to the greater act than to the lesser, while, on the other hand, the influences and consequences of the struggle upon the internal policy of the recognizing state, which form important factors when the recognition of belligerency is concerned, are secondary, if not rightly eliminable, factors when the real question is whether the community claiming recognition is or is not independent beyond peradventure.

Nor from the standpoint of expediency do I think it would be wise or prudent for this Government to recognize at the present time the independence of the so-called Cuban Republic. Such recognition is not necessary in order to enable the United States to intervene and pacify the island. To commit this country now to the recognition of any particular government in Cuba might subject us to embarrassing conditions of international obligation toward the organization so recognized. In case of intervention our conduct would be subject to the approval or disapproval of such government. We would be required to submit to its direction and to assume to it the mere relation of a friendly ally.

When it shall appear hereafter that there is within the island a government capable of performing the duties and discharging the functions of a separate nation, and having as a matter of fact the proper forms and attributes of nationality, such government can be promptly and readily recognized and the relations and interests of the United States with such nation adjusted.

There remain the alternative forms of intervention to end the war, either as an impartial neutral, by imposing a rational compromise between the contestants, or as the active ally of the one party or the other.

As to the first, it is not to be forgotten that during the last few months the relation of the United States has virtually been one of friendly intervention in many ways, each not of itself conclusive, but all tending to the exertion of a potential influence toward an ultimate pacific result, just and honorable to all interests concerned. The spirit of all our acts hitherto has been an earnest, unselfish desire for peace and prosperity in Cuba, untarnished by differences between us and Spain and unstained by the blood of American citizens.

The forcible intervention of the United States as a neutral to stop the war, according to the large dictates of humanity and following many historical precedents where neighboring states have interfered to check the hopeless sacrifices of life by internecine conflicts beyond their borders, is justifiable on rational grounds. It involves, however, a hostile constraint upon both the parties to the contest, as well as to enforce a truce as to guide the eventual settlement.

The grounds for such intervention may be briefly summarized as follows:

FIRST. In the cause of humanity and to put an end to the barbarities, bloodshed, starvation, and horrible miseries now existing there, and which the parties to the conflict are either unable or unwilling to stop or mitigate. It is no answer to say this is all in another country, belonging to another nation, and is therefore none of our business. It is specially our duty, for it is right at our door.

SECOND. We owe it to our citizens in Cuba to afford them that protection and indemnity for life and property which no government there can or will afford, and to that end to terminate the conditions that deprive them of legal protection.

THIRD. The right to intervene may be justified by the very serious injury to the commerce, trade, and business of our people and by the wanton destruction of property and devastation of the island.

FOURTH, and which is of the utmost importance. The present condition of affairs in Cuba is a constant menace to our peace and entails upon this Government an enormous expense. With such a conflict waged for years in an island so near us and with which our people have such trade and business relations; when the lives and liberty of our citizens are in constant danger and their property destroyed and themselves ruined; where our trading vessels are liable to seizure and are seized at our very door by warships of a foreign nation; the expeditions of filibustering that we are powerless to prevent altogether, and the irritating questions and entanglements thus arising—all these and others that I need not mention, with the resulting strained relations, are a constant menace to our peace and compel us to keep on a semi-war footing with a nation with which we are at peace.

These elements of danger and disorder already pointed out have been strikingly illustrated by a tragic event which has deeply and justly moved the American people. I have already transmitted to Congress the report of the naval court of inquiry on the destruction of the battleship *Maine* in the harbor of Havana during the night of the 15th of February. The destruction of that noble vessel has filled the national heart with inexpressible horror. Two hundred and fifty-eight brave sailors and marines and two officers of our Navy, reposing in the fancied security of a friendly harbor, have been hurled to death, grief and want brought to their homes, and sorrow to the nation.

The naval court of inquiry, which, it is needless to say, commands the unqualified confidence of the Government, was unanimous in its conclusion that the destruction of the *Maine* was caused by an exterior explosion —that of a submarine mine. It did not assume to place the responsibility. That remains to be fixed.[4]

In any event, the destruction of the *Maine*, by whatever exterior cause, is a patent and impressive proof of a state of things in Cuba that is intolerable. That condition is thus shown to be such that the Spanish Government can not assure safety and security to a vessel of the American Navy in the harbor of Havana on a mission of peace, and rightfully there.

Further referring in this connection to recent diplomatic correspondence, a dispatch from our minister to Spain of the 26th ultimo contained the statement that the Spanish minister for foreign affairs assured him positively that Spain will do all that the highest honor and justice require in

---

[4]On February 15, 1898, the U.S. battleship *Maine* exploded and sank in Havana harbor, killing 260 American sailors. American public opinion held Spain responsible, thus precipitating war. Later investigations have suggested that the explosion was probably caused by poor ventilation in the warship's gunpowder storage areas, leading to overheating and spontaneous combustion.

the matter of the *Maine*. The reply above referred to, of the 31st ultimo, also contained an expression of the readiness of Spain to submit to an arbitration all the differences which can arise in this matter, which is subsequently explained by the note of the Spanish minister at Washington of the 10th instant, as follows:

> As to the question of fact which springs from the diversity of views between the reports of the American and Spanish boards, Spain proposes that the facts be ascertained by an impartial investigation by experts, whose decision Spain accepts in advance.

To this I have made no reply.

President Grant, in 1875, after discussing the phases of the contest as it then appeared and its hopeless and apparent indefinite prolongation, said:

> In such event I am of opinion that other nations will be compelled to assume the responsibility which devolves upon them, and to seriously consider the only remaining measures possible—mediation and intervention. Owing, perhaps, to the large expanse of water separating the island from the peninsula, . . . the contending parties appear to have within themselves no depository of common confidence to suggest wisdom when passion and excitement have their sway and to assume the part of peacemaker. In this view in the earlier days of the contest the good offices of the United States as a mediator were tendered in good faith, without any selfish purpose, in the interest of humanity, and in sincere friendship for both parties, but were at the time declined by Spain, with the declaration, nevertheless, that at a future time they would be indispensable. No intimation has been received that in the opinion of Spain that time has been reached. And yet the strife continues, with all its dread horrors and all its injuries to the interests of the United States and of other nations. Each party seems quite capable of working great injury and damage to the other, as well as to all the relations and interests dependent on the existence of peace in the island; but they seem incapable of reaching any adjustment, and both have thus far failed of achieving any success whereby one party shall possess and control the island to the exclusion of the other. Under these circumstances the agency of others, either by mediation or by intervention, seems to be the only alternative which must, sooner or later, be invoked for the termination of the strife.

In the last annual message of my immediate predecessor [President Grover Cleveland], during the pending struggle, it was said:

> When the inability of Spain to deal successfully with the insurrection has become manifest and it is demonstrated that her sovereignty is extinct in Cuba for all purposes of its rightful existence, and when a hopeless struggle

for its reestablishment has degenerated into a strife which means nothing more than the useless sacrifice of human life and the utter destruction of the very subject-matter of the conflict, a situation will be presented in which our obligations to the sovereignty of Spain will be superseded by higher obligations, which we can hardly hesitate to recognize and discharge.

In my annual message to Congress December last, speaking to this question, I said:

> The near future will demonstrate whether the indispensable condition of a righteous peace, just alike to the Cubans and to Spain, as well as equitable to all our interests so intimately involved in the welfare of Cuba, is likely to be attained. If not, the exigency of further and other action by the United States will remain to be taken. When that time comes, that action will be determined in the line of indisputable right and duty. It will be faced, without misgiving or hesitancy, in the light of the obligation this Government owes to itself, to the people who have confided to it the protection of their interests and honor, and to humanity.
>
> Sure of the right, keeping free from all offense ourselves, actuated only by upright and patriotic considerations, moved neither by passion nor selfishness, the Government will continue its watchful care over the rights and property of American citizens and will abate none of its efforts to bring about by peaceful agencies a peace which shall be honorable and enduring. If it shall hereafter appear to be a duty imposed by our obligations to ourselves, to civilization, and to humanity to intervene with force, it shall be without fault on our part and only because the necessity for such action will be so clear as to command the support and approval of the civilized world.

The long trial has proved that the object for which Spain has waged the war can not be attained. The fire of insurrection may flame or may smolder with varying seasons, but it has not been and it is plain that it can not be extinguished by present methods. The only hope of relief and repose from a condition which can no longer be endured is the enforced pacification of Cuba. In the name of humanity, in the name of civilization, in behalf of endangered American interests which give us the right and the duty to speak and to act, the war in Cuba must stop.

In view of these facts and of these considerations I ask the Congress to authorize and empower the President to take measures to secure a full and final termination of hostilities between the Government of Spain and the people of Cuba, and to secure in the island the establishment of a stable government, capable of maintaining order and observing its international obligations, insuring peace and tranquillity and the security of its citizens as well as our own, and to use the military and naval forces of the United States as may be necessary for these purposes.

And in the interest of humanity and to aid in preserving the lives of the starving people of the island I recommend that the distribution of food and supplies be continued and that an appropriation be made out of the public Treasury to supplement the charity of our citizens.

The issue is now with the Congress. It is a solemn responsibility. I have exhausted every effort to relieve the intolerable condition of affairs which is at our doors. Prepared to execute every obligation imposed upon me by the Constitution and the law, I await your action.

Yesterday, and since the preparation of the foregoing message, official information was received by me that the latest decree of Spain directs . . . a suspension of hostilities, the duration and details of which have not yet been communicated to me.

This fact, with every other pertinent consideration, will, I am sure, have your just and careful attention in the solemn deliberations upon which you are about to enter. If this measure attains a successful result, then our aspirations as a Christian, peace-loving people will be realized. If it fails, it will be only another justification for our contemplated action.[5]

SOURCE: James D. Richardson, ed., *Messages and Papers of the Presidents*, 20 vols. (New York: Bureau of National Literature, 1912), 8:6281–92.

DOCUMENT 26
PRESIDENT McKINLEY ACKNOWLEDGES THE CONGRESSIONAL RESOLUTION AUTHORIZING WAR AGAINST SPAIN. APRIL 25, 1898.

I transmit to the Congress, for its consideration and appropriate action, copies of correspondence recently had with the representative of Spain in the United States, with the United States minister at Madrid, and through the latter with the Government of Spain, showing the action taken under the joint resolution [Declaration of War against Spain] approved April 20, 1898, "for the recognition of the independence of the people of Cuba, demanding that the Government of Spain relinquish its authority and gov-

---

[5]On April 20 a joint session of Congress authorized President McKinley to dispatch U.S. land and naval forces to Cuba.

ernment in the island of Cuba, and to withdraw its land and naval forces from Cuba and Cuban waters, and directing the President of the United States to use the land and naval forces of the United States to carry these resolutions into effect."

Upon communicating to the Spanish minister in Washington [Luis Polo de Bernabé] the demand which it became the duty of the Executive to address to the Government of Spain in obedience to said resolution, the minister asked for his passports and withdrew. The United States minister at Madrid [Stewart L. Woodford] was in turn notified by the Spanish minister for foreign affairs [Don Pio Gullon y Iglesias] that the withdrawal of the Spanish representative from the United States had terminated diplomatic relations between the two countries, and that all official communications between their respective representatives ceased therewith.

I commend to your especial attention the note addressed to the United States minister at Madrid by the Spanish minister for foreign affairs on the 21st instant, whereby the foregoing notification was conveyed. It will be perceived therefrom that the Government of Spain, having cognizance of the joint resolution of the United States Congress, and in view of the things which the President is thereby required and authorized to do, responds by treating the reasonable demands of this Government as measures of hostility, following with that instant and complete severance of relations by its action which by the usage of nations accompanies an existent state of war between sovereign powers.

The position of Spain being thus made known, and the demands of the United States being denied, with a complete rupture of intercourse, by the act of Spain, I have been constrained, in exercise of the power and authority conferred upon me by the joint resolution aforesaid, to proclaim, under date of April 22, 1898, a blockade of certain ports of the north coast of Cuba, lying between Cardenas and Bahia Honda, and of the port of Cienfuegos, on the south coast of Cuba, and further in exercise of my constitutional powers and using the authority conferred upon me by the act of Congress approved April 22, 1898, to issue my proclamation dated April 23, 1898, calling forth volunteers in order to carry into effect the said resolution of April 20, 1898. Copies of these proclamations are hereto appended.

In view of the measures so taken, and with a view to the adoption of such other measures as may be necessary to enable me to carry out the expressed will of the Congress of the United States in the premises, I now recommend to your honorable body the adoption of a joint resolution declaring that a state of war exists between the United States of America and the Kingdom of Spain, and I urge speedy action thereon, to the end that the definition of the international status of the United States as a belligerent power may be made known and the assertion of all its rights and the maintenance of all its duties in the conduct of a public war may be assured.

SOURCE: Richardson, *Messages and Papers of the Presidents*, 8:6296–98.

DOCUMENT 27
PRESIDENT McKINLEY'S EXECUTIVE ORDERS FOR THE OCCUPATION OF THE PHILIPPINES AFTER THE AMERICAN NAVAL VICTORY AT MANILA. MAY 19, 1898.

The SECRETARY OF WAR.

SIR: The destruction of the Spanish fleet at Manila, followed by the taking of the naval station at Cavite, the paroling of the garrisons, and the acquisition of the control of the bay, has rendered it necessary, in the further prosecution of the measures adopted by this Government for the purpose of bringing about an honorable and durable peace with Spain, to send an army of occupation to the Philippines for the twofold purpose of completing the reduction of the Spanish power in that quarter and of giving order and security to the islands while in the possession of the United States. For the command of this expedition I have designated Major-General Wesley Merritt, and it now becomes my duty to give instructions as to the manner in which the movement shall be conducted.*

The first effect of the military occupation of the enemy's territory is the severance of the former political relations of the inhabitants and the establishment of a new political power. Under this changed condition of things the inhabitants, so long as they perform their duties, are entitled to security in their persons and property and in all their private rights and relations. It is my desire that the people of the Philippines should be acquainted with the purpose of the United States to discharge to the fullest extent its obligations in this regard. It will therefore be the duty of the commander of

*President McKinley presented a set of executive orders to Secretary of War Russell A. Alger, Secretary of the Treasury Lyman J. Gage, and Secretary of the Navy John D. Long. These orders became the basis of the U.S. military occupation of the Philippines, under the command of Major General Wesley Merritt.

the expedition, immediately upon his arrival in the islands, to publish a proclamation declaring that we come not to make war upon the people of the Philippines, nor upon any party or faction among them, but to protect them in their homes, in their employments, and in their personal and religious rights. All persons who, either by active aid or by honest submission, co-operate with the United States in its efforts to give effect to this beneficent purpose will receive the reward of its support and protection. Our occupation should be as free from severity as possible.

Though the powers of the military occupant are absolute and supreme and immediately operate upon the political condition of the inhabitants, the municipal laws of the conquered territory, such as affect private rights of person and property and provide for the punishment of crime, are considered as continuing in force, so far as they are compatible with the new order of things, until they are suspended or superseded by the occupying belligerent; and in practice they are not usually abrogated, but are allowed to remain in force and to be administered by the ordinary tribunals substantially as they were before the occupation. This enlightened practice is, so far as possible, to be adhered to on the present occasion. The judges and the other officials connected with the administration of justice may, if they accept the authority of the United States, continue to administer the ordinary law of the land as between man and man under the supervision of the American commander-in-chief. The native constabulary will, so far as may be practicable, be preserved. The freedom of the people to pursue their accustomed occupations will be abridged only when it may be necessary to do so.

While the rule of conduct of the American commander-in-chief will be such as has just been defined, it will be his duty to adopt measures of a different kind if, unfortunately, the course of the people should render such measures indispensable to the maintenance of law and order. He will then possess the power to replace or expel the native officials in part or altogether, to substitute new courts of his own constitution for those that now exist, or to create such new or supplementary tribunals as may be necessary. In the exercise of these high powers the commander must be guided by his judgment and his experience and a high sense of justice.

One of the most important and most practical problems with which the commander of the expedition will have to deal is that of the treatment of property and the collection and administration of the revenues. It is conceded that all public funds and securities belonging to the government of the country in its own right and all arms and supplies and other movable property of such government may be seized by the military occupant and converted to the use of this Government. The real property of the state he may hold and administer, at the same time enjoying the revenues thereof; but he is not to destroy it save in the case of military necessity. All public means of transportation, such as telegraph lines, cables, railways, and boats belonging to the state may be appropriated to his use, but unless in case of military necessity they are not to be destroyed. All churches and buildings devoted to religious worship and to the arts and sciences, all schoolhouses, are, so far as possible, to be protected, and all destruction or intentional defacement of such places, of historical monuments or archives, or of works of science or art is prohibited save when required by urgent military necessity.

Private property, whether belonging to individuals or corporations, is to be respected, and can be confiscated only as hereafter indicated. Means of transportation, such as telegraph lines and cables, railways, and boats, may, although they belong to private individuals or corporations, be seized by the military occupant, but unless destroyed under military necessity, are not to be retained.

While it is held to be the right of a conqueror to levy contributions upon the enemy in their seaports, towns, or provinces which may be in his military possession by conquest, and to apply the proceeds to defray the expenses of the war, this right is to be exercised within such limitations that it may not savor of confiscation. As the result of military occupation the taxes and duties payable by the inhabitants to the former government become payable to the military occupant, unless he sees fit to substitute for them other rates or modes of contribution to the expenses of the government. The moneys so collected are to be used for the purpose of paying expenses of government under the military occupation, such as the salaries of the judges and the police, and for the payment of the expenses of the army.

Private property taken for the use of the army is to be paid for when possible in cash at a fair valuation, and when payment in cash is not possible receipts are to be given.

In order that there may be no conflict of authority between the army and the navy in the administration of affairs in the Philippines you are instructed to confer with the Secretary of the Navy so far as necessary for the purpose of devising measures to secure the harmonious action of those two branches of the public service.

I will give instructions to the Secretary of the Treasury to make a report to me upon the subject of the revenues of the Philippines, with a view to the formulation of such revenue measures as may seem expedient. All ports and places in the Philippines which may be in the actual possession of our land and naval forces will be opened, while our military occupation may continue, to the commerce of all neutral nations, as well as our own, in articles not contrabrand of war, and upon payment of the prescribed rates of duty which may be in force at the time of the importation.

The SECRETARY OF THE TREASURY.

SIR: . . . It is held to be the right to levy contributions upon the enemy in all places which may be in military possession by conquest, and to apply the proceeds to defray the cost of the war, including the expenses of government during the military occupation. It is desirable, however, and in accordance with the views of modern civilization, to confine the exercise of this power, so far as possible, to the collection of such contributions as are equivalent to the duties and taxes already established in the territory. I have determined to order that all ports or places in the Philippines which may be in the actual possession of our land and naval forces by conquest shall be opened, while our military occupation may continue, to the commerce of all neutral nations, as well as our own, in articles not contrabrand of war, upon payment of the rates of duty which may be in force at the time when the goods are imported. In the execution of this policy it may be advisable to substitute new rates of duty and new taxes for those now levied in the Philippines. You are therefore instructed to examine the existing Spanish laws in relation to duties and taxes, and to report to me such recommendations as you may deem it proper to make with respect either to the rates of duties and taxes or to the regulations which should be adopted for their imposition and collection.

As the levy of all contributions in territory occupied by a belligerent is a military right derived from the law of nations, the collection and distribution of duties and taxes in the Philippines during the military occupation of the United States will be made, under the orders of the Secretary of War and the Secretary of the Navy, by the military or naval commanders, as the case may be, of the ports or places which may be in the possession of our forces. Your report is desired in order that I may be able to give the proper directions to the Departments of War and of the Navy.

The SECRETARY OF THE NAVY.

SIR: . . . I inclose herewith a copy of an order which I have this day addressed to the Secretary of War, setting forth the principles on which the occupation of the Philippines is to be carried out. You are instructed to confer with the Secretary of War in order that measures may be devised by which any conflict of authority between the officers of our army and navy in the Philippines may be avoided.

I have given instructions to the Secretary of the Treasury to examine the subject of the duties and taxes imposed by Spain in the Philippines and to report to me any recommendations which he may deem it proper to make in regard to the revenues of the islands. I have informed him, however, that the collection and disbursement of the duties and taxes collected there will, as a measure of military right derived from the law of nations, be made, under the orders of the Secretary of War and the Secretary of the Navy, by our military or naval commanders, as the case may be, at the ports or places which may be in possession of our forces.

SOURCE: Richardson, *Messages and Papers of the Presidents* (1913), 10:208–12.

DOCUMENT 28
PRESIDENT McKINLEY'S STATE OF THE UNION ADDRESS DESCRIBING THE INSURRECTION IN THE PHILIPPINES. DECEMBER 5, 1899.

. . . On the 10th of December, 1898, the treaty of peace between the United States and Spain was signed. It provided, among other things, that Spain should cede to the United States the archipelago known as the Philippine Islands, that the United States should pay to Spain the sum of twenty millions of dollars, and that the civil rights and political status of the native inhabitants of the territories thus ceded to the United States should be determined by the Congress. The treaty was ratified by the Senate on the 6th of February, 1899, and by the Government of Spain on the 19th of March following. The ratifications were exchanged on the 11th of April and the treaty publicly proclaimed. On the 2d of March the Congress voted the sum contemplated by the treaty, and the amount was paid over to the Spanish Government on the 1st of May.

In this manner the Philippines came to the United States. The islands were ceded by the Government of Spain, which had been in undisputed possession of them for centuries. They were accepted not merely by our authorized commissioners in Paris [William Day, Whitelaw Reid, Cushman Davis, William Frye, and George Gray] under the direction of the Executive, but by the constitutional and well-considered action of the representatives of the people of the United States in both Houses of Congress.

I had every reason to believe, and I still believe that this transfer of sovereignty was in accordance with the wishes and the aspirations of the great mass of the Filipino people.

From the earliest moment no opportunity was lost of assuring the people of the islands of our ardent desire for their welfare and of the intention of this Government to do everything possible to advance their interests. In my order of the 19th of May, 1898, the commander of the military expedition dispatched to the Philippines was instructed to declare that we came not to make war upon the people of that country, "nor upon any party or faction among them, but to protect them in their homes, in their employments, and in their personal and religious rights." That there should be no doubt as to the paramount authority there, on the 17th of August it was directed that "there must be no joint occupation with the insurgents"; that the United States must preserve the peace and protect persons and property within the territory occupied by their military and naval forces; that the insurgents and all others must recognize the military occupation and authority of the United States. As early as December 4, before the cession, and in anticipation of that event, the commander in Manila was urged to restore peace and tranquillity and to undertake the establishment of a beneficent government, which should afford the fullest security for life and property.

On the 21st of December, after the treaty was signed, the commander of the forces of occupation was instructed "to announce and proclaim in the most public manner that we come not as invaders and conquerors, but as friends to protect the natives in their homes, in their employments, and in their personal and religious rights." On the same day, while ordering General [Elwell] Otis to see that the peace should be preserved in Iloilo, he was admonished that: "It is most important that there should be no conflict with the insurgents." On the 1st day of January, 1899, urgent orders were reiterated that the kindly intentions of this Government should be in every possible way communicated to the insurgents.

On the 21st of January I announced my intention of dispatching to Manila a commission composed of three gentlemen of the highest character and distinction, thoroughly acquainted with the Orient, who, in association with Admiral [George] Dewey and Major-General Otis, were instructed "to facilitate the most humane and effective extension of authority throughout the islands, and to secure with the least possible delay the benefits of a wise and generous protection of life and property to the inhabitants." These gentlemen were Dr. Jacob Gould Schurman, president of Cornell University; the Hon. Charles Denby, for many years minister to

China; and Prof. Dean C. Worcester, of the University of Michigan, who had made a most careful study of life in the Philippines. While the treaty of peace was under consideration in the Senate, these Commissioners set out on their mission of good will and liberation. Their character was a sufficient guaranty of the beneficent purpose with which they went, even if they had not borne the positive instructions of this Government, which made their errand pre-eminently one of peace and friendship.

But before their arrival at Manila the sinister ambition of a few leaders of the Filipinos had created a situation full of embarrassment for us and most grievous in its consequences to themselves. The clear and impartial preliminary report of the Commissioners, which I transmit herewith, gives so lucid and comprehensive a history of the present insurrectionary movement that the story need not be here repeated. It is enough to say that the claim of the rebel leader [Emilio Aguinaldo] that he was promised independence by an officer of the United States in return for his assistance has no foundation in fact and is categorically denied by the very witnesses who were called to prove it. The most the insurgent leader hoped for when he came back to Manila was the liberation of the islands from the Spanish control, which they had been laboring for years without success to throw off.

The prompt accomplishment of this work by the American Army and Navy gave him other ideas and ambitions, and insidious suggestions from various quarters perverted the purposes and intentions with which he had taken up arms. No sooner had our army captured Manila than the Filipino forces began to assume an attitude of suspicion and hostility which the utmost efforts of our officers and troops were unable to disarm or modify. Their kindness and forbearance were taken as a proof of cowardice. The aggressions of the Filipinos continually increased until finally, just before the time set by the Senate of the United States for a vote upon the treaty, an attack, evidently prepared in advance, was made all along the American lines, which resulted in a terribly destructive and sanguinary repulse of the insurgents.

Ten days later an order of the insurgent government was issued to its adherents who had remained in Manila, of which General Otis justly observes that "for barbarous intent it is unequaled in modern times." It directs that at 8 o'clock on the night of the 15th of February the "territorial militia" shall come together in the streets of San Pedro armed with their *bolos*, with guns and ammunition where convenient; that Filipino families only shall be respected; but that all other individuals, of whatever race they may be, shall be exterminated without any compassion, after the extermination of the army of occupation, and adds: "Brothers, we must avenge ourselves on the Americans and exterminate them, that we may take our revenge for the infamies and treacheries which they have committed upon us. Have no compassion upon them; attack with vigor." A copy of this fell by good fortune into the hands of our officers and they were able to take measures to control the rising, which was actually attempted on the night of February 22, a week later than was originally contemplated. Considerable numbers of armed insurgents entered the city by waterways and swamps and in concert with confederates inside attempted to destroy Manila by fire. They were kept in check during the night and the next day driven out of the city with heavy loss.

This was the unhappy condition of affairs which confronted our Commissioners on their arrival in Manila. They had come with the hope and intention of co-operating with Admiral Dewey and Major-General Otis in establishing peace and order in the archipelago and the largest measure of self-government compatible with the true welfare of the people. What they actually found can best be set forth in their own words:

> Deplorable as war is, the one in which we are now engaged was unavoidable by us. We were attacked by a bold, adventurous, and enthusiastic army. No alternative was left to us except ignominious retreat.
>
> It is not to be conceived of that any American would have sanctioned the surrender of Manila to the insurgents. Our obligations to other nations and to the friendly Filipinos and to ourselves and our flag demanded that force should be met by force. Whatever the future of the Philippines may be, there is no course open to us now except the prosecution of the war until the insurgents are reduced to submission. The Commission is of the opinion that there has been no time since the destruction of the Spanish squadron by Admiral Dewey when it was possible to withdraw our forces from the island either with honor to ourselves or with safety to the inhabitants.

The course thus clearly indicated has been unflinchingly pursued. The rebellion must be put down. Civil government cannot be thoroughly established until order is restored. With a devotion and gallantry worthy of its most brilliant history, the Army, ably and loyally assisted by the Navy, has carried on this unwelcome but most righteous campaign with richly deserved success. The noble self-sacrifice with which our soldiers and sailors whose terms of service had expired refused to avail themselves of their right to return home as long as they were needed at the front forms one of the brightest pages in our annals. Although their operations have been somewhat interrupted and checked by a rainy season of unusual violence and duration, they have gained ground steadily in every direction, and now look forward confidently to a speedy completion of their task.

The unfavorable circumstances connected with an active campaign have not been permitted to interfere with the equally important work of reconstruction. Again I invite your attention to the report of the Commissioners for the interesting and encouraging details of the work already accomplished in the establishment of peace and order and the inauguration of self-governing municipal life in many portions of the archipelago. A notable beginning has been made in the establishment of a government in the island of Negros which is deserving of special consideration. This was the first island to accept American sovereignty. Its people unreservedly proclaimed allegiance to the United States and adopted a constitution looking to the establishment of a popular government. It was impossible to guarantee to the people of Negros that the constitution so adopted should be the ultimate form of government. Such a question, under the treaty with Spain and in accordance with our own Constitution and laws, came exclusively within the jurisdiction of the Congress. The government actually set up by the inhabitants of Negros eventually proved unsatisfactory to the natives themselves. A new system was put into force by order of the Major-General Commanding the Department, of which the following are the most important elements:

It was ordered that the government of the island of Negros should consist of a military governor appointed by the United States military governor of the Philippines, and a civil governor and an advisory council elected by the people. The military governor was authorized to appoint secretaries of the treasury, interior, agriculture, public instruction, an attorney-general, and an auditor. The seat of government was fixed at Bacolod. The military governor exercises the supreme executive power. He is to see that the laws are executed, appoint to office, and fill all vacancies in office not otherwise provided for, and may, with the approval of the military governor of the Philippines, remove any officer from office. The civil governor advises the military governor on all public civil questions and presides over the advisory council. He, in general, performs the duties which are performed by secretaries of state in our own system of government.

The advisory council consists of eight members elected by the people within territorial limits which are defined in the order of the commanding general.

The times and places of holding elections are to be fixed by the military governor of the island of Negros. The qualifications of voters are as follows: (1) A voter must be a male citizen of the island of Negros. (2) Of the age of 21 years. (3) He shall be able to speak, read, and write the English, Spanish, or Visayan language, or he must own real property worth $500, or pay a rental on real property of the value of $1,000. (4) He must have resided in the island not less than one year preceding, and in the district in which he offers to register as a voter not less than three months immediately preceding the time he offers to register. (5) He must register at a time fixed by law before voting. (6) Prior to such registration he shall have paid all taxes due by him to the Government. Provided, that no insane person shall be allowed to register or vote.

The military governor [of the island of Negros] has the right to veto all bills or resolutions adopted by the advisory council, and his veto is final if not disapproved by the military governor of the Philippines.

The advisory council discharges all the ordinary duties of a legislature. The usual duties pertaining to said offices are to be performed by the secretaries of the treasury, interior, agriculture, public instruction, the attorney-general, and the auditor.

The judicial power is vested in three judges, who are to be appointed by the military governor of the island. Inferior courts are to be established.

Free public schools are to be established throughout the populous districts of the island, in which the English language shall be taught, and this subject will receive the careful consideration of the advisory council.

The burden of government must be distributed equally and equitably among the people. The military authorities will collect and receive the customs revenue, and will control postal matters and Philippine inter-island trade and commerce.

The military governor, subject to the approval of the military governor of the Philippines, determines all questions not specifically provided for and which do not come under the jurisdiction of the advisory council.

The authorities of the Sulu Islands [chain of islands in the southwestern Philippine archipelago, barely under Spanish control prior to 1898] have accepted the succession of the United States to the rights of Spain, and our flag floats over that territory. On the 10th of August, 1899, Brigadier Gen. J. C. Bates, United States Volunteers, negotiated an agreement with the Sultan and his principal chiefs, which I transmit herewith. By Article I the sovereignty of the United States over the whole archipelago of Jolo and its dependencies is declared and acknowledged.

The United States flag will be used in the archipelago and its dependencies, on land and sea. Piracy is to be suppressed, and the Sultan agrees to co-operate heartily with the United States authorities to that end and to make every possible effort to arrest and bring to justice all persons engaged in piracy. All trade in domestic products of the archipelago of Jolo when carried on with any part of the Philippine Islands and under the American flag shall be free, unlimited, and undutiable. The United States will give full protection to the Sultan in case any foreign nation should attempt to impose upon him. The United States will not sell the island of Jolo or any other island of the Jolo archipelago to any foreign nation—without the consent of the Sultan. Salaries for the Sultan and his associates in the administration of the islands have been agreed upon to the amount of $760 monthly.

Article X provides that any slave in the archipelago of Jolo shall have the right to purchase freedom by paying to the master the usual market value. The agreement by General Bates was made subject to confirmation by the President and to future modifications by the consent of the parties in interest. I have confirmed said agreement, subject to the action of the Congress, and with the reservation, which I have directed shall be communicated to the Sultan of Jolo, that this agreement is not to be deemed in any way to authorize or give the consent of the United States to the existence of slavery in the Sulu archipelago. I communicate these facts to the Congress for its information and action.

Everything indicates that with the speedy suppression of the Tagalo rebellion life in the archipelago will soon resume its ordinary course under the protection of our sovereignty, and the people of those favored islands will enjoy a prosperity and a freedom which they have never before known. Already hundreds of schools are open and filled with children. Religious freedom is sacredly assured and enjoyed. The courts are dispensing justice. Business is beginning to circulate in its accustomed channels. Manila, whose inhabitants were fleeing to the country a few months ago, is now a populous and thriving mart of commerce. The earnest and unremitting endeavors of the Commission and the Admiral and Major-General Commanding the Department of the Pacific to assure the people of the beneficent intentions of this Government have had their legitimate effect in convincing the great mass of them that peace and safety and prosperity and stable government can only be found in a loyal acceptance of the authority of the United States.

The future government of the Philippines rests with the Congress of the United States. Few graver responsibilities have ever been confided to us. If we accept them in a spirit worthy of our race and our traditions [McKinley is referring to the popularly accepted notion of the political, economic, and social superiority of states inhabited by Anglo-Saxon ethnic groups], a great opportunity comes with them. The islands lie under the shelter of our flag.

They are ours by every title of law and equity. They cannot be abandoned. If we desert them we leave them at once to anarchy and finally to barbarism. We fling them, a golden apple of discord, among the rival powers, no one of which could permit another to seize them unquestioned. Their rich plains and valleys would be the scene of endless strife and bloodshed. The advent of Dewey's fleet in Manila Bay instead of being, as we hope, the dawn of a new day of freedom and progress, will have been the beginning of an era of misery and violence worse than any which has darkened their unhappy past. The suggestion has been made that we could renounce our authority over the islands and, giving them independence, could retain a protectorate over them. This proposition will not be found, I am sure, worthy of your serious attention. Such an arrangement would involve at the outset a cruel breach of faith. It would place the peaceable and loyal majority, who ask nothing better than to accept our authority, at the mercy of the minority of armed insurgents. It would make us responsible for the acts of the insurgent leaders and give us no power to control them. It would charge us with the task of protecting them against each other and defending them against any foreign power with which they chose to quarrel. In short, it would take from the Congress of the United States the power of declaring war and vest that tremendous prerogative in the Tagal leader of the hour.

It does not seem desirable that I should recommend at this time a specific and final form of government for these islands. When peace shall be restored it will be the duty of Congress to construct a plan of government which shall establish and maintain freedom and order and peace in the Philippines. The insurrection is still existing, and when it terminates further information will be required as to the actual condition of affairs before inaugurating a permanent scheme of civil government. The full report of the Commission, now in preparation, will contain information and suggestions which will be of value to Congress, and which I will transmit as soon as it is completed. As long as the insurrection continues the military arm must necessarily be supreme. But there is no reason why steps should not be taken from time to time to inaugurate governments essentially popular in their form as fast as territory is held and controlled by our troops. To this end I am considering the advisability of the return of the Commission, or such of the members thereof as can be secured, to aid the existing authorities and facilitate this work throughout the islands. I have believed that reconstruction should not begin by the establishment of one central civil government for all the islands, with its seat at Manila, but rather that the work should be commenced by building up from the bottom, first establishing municipal governments and then provincial governments, a central government at last to follow.

Until Congress shall have made known the formal expression of its will I shall use the authority vested in me by the Constitution and the statutes to uphold the sovereignty of the United States in those distant islands as in all other places where our flag rightfully floats. I shall put at the disposal of the Army and Navy all the means which the liberality of Congress and the people have provided to cause this unprovoked and wasteful insurrection to cease. If any orders of mine were required to insure the merciful conduct of military and naval operations, they would not be lacking; but every step of the progress of our troops has been marked by a humanity which has surprised even the misguided insurgents. The truest kindness to them will be a swift and effective defeat of their present leader. The hour of victory will be the hour of clemency and reconstruction.

No effort will be spared to build up the waste places desolated by war and by long years of misgovernment. We shall not wait for the end of strife to begin the beneficent work. We shall continue, as we have begun, to open the schools and the churches, to set the courts in operation, to foster industry and trade and agriculture, and in every way in our power to make these people whom Providence has brought within our jurisdiction feel that it is their liberty and not our power, their welfare and not our gain, we are seeking to enhance. Our flag has never waved over any community but in blessing. I believe the Filipinos will soon recognize the fact that it has not lost its gift of benediction in its world-wide journey to their shores.

SOURCE: Richardson, *Messages and Papers of the Presidents* (1903), 13:6391–99.

DOCUMENT 29

PRESIDENT McKINLEY'S STATE OF THE UNION ADDRESS CONCERNING THE FILIPINO INSURRECTION. DECEMBER 3, 1900.

... In my last annual message I dwelt at some length upon the condition of affairs in the Philippines. While seeking to impress upon you that the grave responsibility of the future government of those islands rests with the Congress of the United States, I abstained from recommending at that time a specific and final form of government for the territory actually held by the United States forces and in which as long as insurrection continues the military arm must necessarily be supreme. I stated my purpose, until the

Congress shall have made the formal expression of its will, to use the authority vested in me by the Constitution and the statutes to uphold the sovereignty of the United States in those distant islands as in all other places where our flag rightfully floats, placing, to that end, at the disposal of the army and navy all the means which the liberality of the Congress and the people have provided. No contrary expression of the will of the Congress having been made, I have steadfastly pursued the purpose so declared, employing the civil arm as well toward the accomplishment of pacification and the institution of local governments within the lines of authority and law.

Progress in the hoped-for direction has been favorable. Our forces have successfully controlled the greater part of the islands, overcoming the organized forces of the insurgents and carrying order and administrative regularity to all quarters. What opposition remains is for the most part scattered, obeying no concerted plan of strategic action, operating only by the methods common to the traditions of guerrilla warfare, which, while ineffective to alter the general control now established, are still sufficient to beget insecurity among the populations that have felt the good results of our control and thus delay the conferment upon them of the fuller measures of local self-government, of education, and of industrial and agricultural development which we stand ready to give to them.

By the spring of this year the effective opposition of the dissatisfied Tagals to the authority of the United States was virtually ended, thus opening the door for the extension of a stable administration over much of the territory of the Archipelago. Desiring to bring this about, I appointed in March last a civil Commission composed of the Hon. William H. Taft, of Ohio; Prof. Dean C. Worcester, of Michigan; the Hon. Luke I. Wright, of Tennessee; the Hon. Henry C. Ide, of Vermont, and Prof. Bernard Moses, of California. The aims of their mission and the scope of their authority are clearly set forth in my instructions of April 7, 1900, addressed to the Secretary of War [Elihu Root] to be transmitted to them:

> In the message transmitted to the Congress on the 5th of December, 1899, I said speaking of the Philippine Islands: "As long as the insurrection continues the military arm must necessarily be supreme. But there is no reason why steps should not be taken from time to time to inaugurate governments essentially popular in their form as fast as territory is held and controlled by our troops. To this end I am considering the advisability of the return of the Commission, or such of the members thereof as can be secured, to aid the existing authorities and facilitate this work throughout the islands."

To give effect to the intention thus expressed, I have appointed the Hon. William H. Taft, of Ohio; Prof. Dean C. Worcester, of Michigan; Hon. Luke I. Wright, of Tennessee; Hon. Henry C. Ide, of Vermont, and Prof. Bernard Moses, of California, Commissioners to the Philippine Islands to continue and perfect the work of organizing and establishing civil government already commenced by the military authorities, subject in all respects to any laws which Congress may hereafter enact.

The Commissioners named will meet and act as a board, and the Hon. William H. Taft is designated as president of the board. It is probable that the transfer of authority from military commanders to civil officers will be gradual and will occupy a considerable period. Its successful accomplishment and the maintenance of peace and order in the meantime will require the most perfect co-operation between the civil and military authorities in the islands, and both should be directed during the transition period by the same Executive Department. The Commission will therefore report to the Secretary of War, and all their action will be subject to your approval and control.

You will instruct the Commission to proceed to the city of Manila, where they will make their principal office, and to communicate with the Military Governor of the Philippine Islands, whom you will at the same time direct to render to them every assistance within his power in the performance of their duties. Without hampering them by too specific instructions, they should in general be enjoined, after making themselves familiar with the conditions and needs of the country, to devote their attention in the first instance to the establishment of municipal governments, in which the natives of the islands, both in the cities and in the rural communities, shall be afforded the opportunity to manage their own local affairs to the fullest extent of which they are capable and subject to the least degree of supervision and control which a careful study of their capacities and observation of the workings of native control show to be consistent with the maintenance of law, order, and loyalty.

The next subject in order of importance should be the organization of government in the larger administrative divisions corresponding to counties, departments, or provinces, in which the common interests of many or several municipalities falling within the same tribal lines, or the same natural geographical limits, may best be subserved by a common administration. Whenever the Commission is of the opinion that the condition of affairs in the islands is such that the central administration may safely be transferred from military to civil control they will report that conclusion to you, with their recommendations as to the form of central government to be established for the purpose of taking over the control.

Beginning with the 1st day of September, 1900, the authority to exercise, subject to my approval, through the Secretary of War, that part of the power of government in the Philippine Islands which is of a legislative nature is to be transferred from the Military Governor of the islands to this Commission, to be thereafter exercised by them in the place and stead of the Military Governor, under such rules and regulations as you shall prescribe, until the establishment of the civil central government for the islands contemplated in the last foregoing paragraph, or until Congress shall otherwise provide. Exercise of this legislative authority will include the making of rules and orders, having the effect of law, for the raising of revenue by taxes, customs duties, and imposts; the appropriation and expenditure of public funds of the islands; the establishment of an educational system throughout the islands; the establishment of a system to secure an efficient civil service; the organization and establishment of courts; the organization and establishment of municipal and departmental governments, and all other matters of a civil nature for which the Military Governor is now competent to provide by rules or orders of a legislative character.

The Commission will also have power during the same period to appoint to office such officers under the judicial, educational, and civil-service systems and in the municipal and departmental governments as shall be provided for. Until the complete transfer of control the Military Governor will remain the chief executive head of the government of the islands, and will exercise the executive authority now possessed by him and not herein expressly assigned to the Commission, subject, however, to the rules and orders enacted by the Commission in the exercise of the legislative powers conferred upon them. In the meantime the municipal and departmental governments will continue to report to the Military Governor and be subject to his administrative supervision and control, under your direction, but that supervision and control will be confined within the narrowest limits consistent with the requirement that the powers of government in the municipalities and departments shall be honestly and effectively exercised and that law and order and individual freedom shall be maintained.

All legislative rules and orders, establishments of government, and appointments to office by the Commission will take effect immediately, or at such times as they shall designate, subject to your approval and action upon the coming in of the Commission's reports, which are to be made from time to time as their action is taken. Wherever civil governments are constituted under the direction of the Commission such military posts, garrisons, and forces will be continued for the suppression of insurrection and brigandage and the maintenance of law and order as the Military Commander shall deem requisite, and the military forces shall be at all times subject, under his orders, to the call of the civil authorities for the maintenance of law and order and the enforcement of their authority.

In the establishment of municipal governments the Commission will take as the basis of their work the governments established by the Military Governor under his order of August 8, 1899, and under the report of the board constituted by the Military Governor by his order of January 29, 1900, to formulate and report a plan of municipal government, of which His Honor Cayetano Arellano, President of the Audiencia, was chairman, and they will give to the conclusions of that board the weight and consideration which the high character and distinguished abilities of its members justify.

In the constitution of departmental or provincial governments they will give especial attention to the existing government of the island of Negros, constituted, with the approval of the people of that island, under the order of the Military Governor of July 22, 1899, and after verifying, so far as may be practicable, the reports of the successful working of that government they will be guided by the experience thus acquired so far as it may be applicable to the condition existing in other portions of the Philippines. They will avail themselves, to the fullest degree practicable, of the conclusions reached by the previous Commission to the Philippines.

In the distribution of powers among the governments organized by the Commission, the presumption is always to be in favor of the smaller subdivision, so that all the powers which can properly be exercised by the municipal government shall be vested in that government, and all the powers of a more general character which can be exercised by the departmental government shall be vested in that government, and so that in the governmental system, which is the result of the process, the central government of the islands, following the example of the distribution of the powers between the States and the National Government of the United States, shall have no direct administration except of matters of purely general concern, and shall have only such supervision and control over local governments as may be necessary to secure and enforce faithful and efficient administration by local officers.

The many different degrees of civilization and varieties of custom and capacity among the people of the different islands preclude very definite instruction as to the part which the people shall take in the selection of their own officers; but these general rules are to be observed: That in all cases the municipal officers, who administer the local affairs of the people, are to be selected by the people, and that wherever officers of more extended jurisdiction are to be selected in any way, natives of the islands are to be preferred, and if they can be found competent and willing to perform the duties, they are to receive the offices in preference to any others.

It will be necessary to fill some offices for the present with Americans which after a time may well be filled by natives of the islands. As soon as practicable a system for ascertaining the merit and fitness of candidates for civil office should be put in force. An indispensable qualification for all offices and positions of trust and authority in the islands must be absolute and unconditional loyalty to the United States, and absolute and unhampered authority and power to remove and punish any officer deviating from that standard must at all times be retained in the hands of the central authority of the islands.

In all the forms of government and administrative provisions which they are authorized to prescribe the Commission should bear in mind that the government which they are establishing is designed not for our satisfaction, or for the expression of our theoretical views, but for the happiness, peace, and prosperity of the people of the Philippine Islands, and the measures adopted should be made to conform to their customs, their habits, and even their prejudices, to the fullest extent consistent with the accomplishment of the indispensable requisites of just and effective government.

At the same time the Commission should bear in mind, and the people of the islands should be made plainly to understand, that there are certain great principles of government which have been made the basis of our governmental system which we deem essential to the rule of law and the maintenance of individual freedom, and of which they have, unfortunately, been denied the experience possessed by us; that there are also certain practical rules of government which we have found to be essential to the preservation of these great principles of liberty and law, and that these principles and these rules of government must be established and maintained in their islands for the sake of their liberty and happiness, however much they may conflict with the customs or laws of procedure with which they are familiar.

It is evident that the most enlightened thought of the Philippine Islands fully appreciates the importance of these principles and rules, and they will inevitably within a short time command universal assent.

Upon every division and branch of the government of the Philippines, therefore, must be imposed these inviolable rules:

That no person shall be deprived of life, liberty, or property without due process of law; that private property shall not be taken for public use without just compensation; that in all criminal prosecutions the accused shall enjoy the right to a speedy and public trial, to be informed of the nature and cause of the accusation, to be confronted with the witnesses against him, to have compulsory process for obtaining witnesses in his favor, and to have the assistance of counsel for his defense; that excessive bail shall not be required, nor excessive fines imposed, nor cruel and unusual punishment inflicted; that no person shall be put twice in jeopardy for the same offense, or be compelled in any criminal case to be a witness against himself; that the right to be secure against unreasonable searches and seizures shall not be violated; that neither slavery nor involuntary servitude shall exist except as a punishment for crime; that no bill of attainder or *ex-post-facto* law shall be passed; that no law shall be passed abridging the freedom of speech or of the press, or the rights of the people to peaceably assemble and petition the Government for a redress of grievances; that no law shall be made respecting an establishment of religion, or prohibiting the free exercise thereof, and that the free exercise and enjoyment of religious profession and worship without discrimination or preference shall forever be allowed.

It will be the duty of the Commission to make a thorough investigation into the titles to the large tracts of land held or claimed by individuals or by religious orders; into the justice of the claims and complaints made against such landholders by the people of the island or any part of the people, and to seek by wise and peaceable measures a just settlement of the controversies and redress of wrongs which have caused strife and bloodshed in the past. In the performance of this duty the Commission is enjoined to see that no injustice is done; to have regard for substantial rights and equity, disregarding technicalities so far as substantial right permits, and to observe the following rules:

That the provision of the Treaty of Paris* pledging the United States to the protection of all rights of property in the islands, and as well the principle of our own Government which prohibits the taking of private property without due process of law, shall not be violated; that

---

*The Treaty of Paris, signed on December 10, 1898, ended the Spanish-American War. It transferred Puerto Rico and the Philippine Islands to the United States in exchange for $20 million.

the welfare of the people of the islands, which should be a paramount consideration, shall be attained consistently with this rule of property rights; that if it becomes necessary for the public interest of the people of the islands to dispose of claims to property which the Commission finds to be not lawfully acquired and held, disposition shall be made thereof by due legal procedure, in which there shall be full opportunity for fair and impartial hearing and judgment; that if the same public interests require the extinguishment of property rights lawfully acquired and held, due compensation shall be made out of the public treasury therefor; that no form of religion and no minister of religion shall be forced upon any community or upon any citizen of the islands; that, upon the other hand, no minister of religion shall be interfered with or molested in following his calling, and that the separation between State and Church shall be real, entire, and absolute.

It will be the duty of the Commission to promote and extend, and, as they find occasion, to improve the system of education already inaugurated by the military authorities. In doing this they should regard as of first importance the extension of a system of primary education which shall be free to all, and which shall tend to fit the people for the duties of citizenship and for the ordinary avocations of a civilized community. This instruction should be given in the first instance in every part of the islands in the language of the people. In view of the great number of languages spoken by the different tribes, it is especially important to the prosperity of the islands that a common medium of communication may be established, and it is obviously desirable that this medium should be the English language. Especial attention should be at once given to affording full opportunity to all the people of the islands to acquire the use of the English language.

It may be well that the main changes which should be made in the system of taxation and in the body of the laws under which the people are governed, except such changes as have already been made by the military government, should be relegated to the civil government which is to be established under the auspices of the Commission. It will, however, be the duty of the Commission to inquire diligently as to whether there are any further changes which ought not to be delayed, and if so, they are authorized to make such changes subject to your approval. In doing so they are to bear in mind that taxes which tend to penalize or repress industry and enterprise are to be avoided; that provisions for taxation should be simple, so that they may be understood by the people; that they should affect the fewest practicable subjects of taxation which will serve for the general distribution of the burden.

The main body of the laws which regulate the rights and obligations of the people should be maintained with as little interference as possible. Changes made should be mainly in procedure, and in the criminal laws to secure speedy and impartial trials, and at the same time effective administration and respect for individual rights.

In dealing with the uncivilized tribes of the islands the Commission should adopt the same course followed by Congress in permitting the tribes of our North American Indians to maintain their tribal organization and government, and under which many of those tribes are now living in peace and contentment, surrounded by a civilization to which they are unable or unwilling to conform. Such tribal governments should, however, be subjected to wise and firm regulation, and, without undue or petty interference, constant and active effort should be exercised to prevent barbarous practices and introduce civilized customs.

Upon all officers and employees of the United States, both civil and military, should be impressed a sense of the duty to observe not merely the material but the personal and social rights of the people of the islands, and to treat them with the same courtesy and respect for their personal dignity which the people of the United States are accustomed to require from each other.

The articles of capitulation of the city of Manila on the 13th of August, 1898, concluded with these words:

"This city, its inhabitants, its churches and religious worship, its educational establishments, and its private property of all descriptions, are placed under the special safeguard of the faith and honor of the American Army."

I believe that this pledge has been faithfully kept. As high and sacred an obligation rests upon the Government of the United States to give protection for property and life, civil and religious freedom, and wise, firm, and unselfish guidance in the paths of peace and prosperity to all the people of the Philippine Islands. I charge this Commission to labor for the full performance of this obligation, which concerns the honor and conscience of their country, in the firm hope that through their labors all the inhabitants of the Philippine Islands may come to look back with gratitude to the day when God gave victory to American arms at Manila and set their land under the sovereignty and the protection of the people of the United States.

Coincidently with the entrance of the Commission upon its labors I caused to be issued by General [Arthur] MacArthur, the Military Governor of the Philippines, on June 21, 1900, a proclamation of amnesty in generous terms, of which many of the insurgents took advantage, among them a number of important leaders.

This Commission, composed of eminent citizens representing the diverse geographical and political interests of the country, and bringing to their task the ripe fruits of long and intelligent service in educational, administrative, and judicial careers, made great progress from the outset. As early as August 21, 1900, it submitted a preliminary report, which will be laid before the Congress, and from which it appears that already the good effects of returning order are felt; that business, interrupted by hostilities, is improving as peace extends; that a larger area is under sugar cultivation than ever before; that the customs revenues are greater than at any time during the Spanish rule; that economy and efficiency in the military administration have created a surplus fund of $6,000,000, available for needed public improvements; that a stringent civil-service law is in preparation; that railroad communications are expanding, opening up rich districts, and that a comprehensive scheme of education is being organized.

Later reports from the Commission show yet more encouraging advance toward insuring the benefits of liberty and good government to the Filipinos, in the interest of humanity and with the aim of building up an enduring, self-supporting, and self-administering community in those Far Eastern seas. I would impress upon the Congress that whatever legislation may be enacted in respect to the Philippine Islands should be along these generous lines. The fortune of war has thrown upon this nation an unsought trust which should be unselfishly discharged, and devolved upon this Government a moral as well as material responsibility toward these millions whom we have freed from an oppressive yoke.

I have on another occasion called the Filipinos "the wards of the nation." Our obligation as guardian was not lightly assumed; it must not be otherwise than honestly fulfilled, aiming first of all to benefit those who have come under our fostering care. It is our duty so to treat them that our flag may be no less beloved in the mountains of Luzon and the fertile zones of Mindanao and Negros than it is at home, that there as here it shall be the revered symbol of liberty, enlightenment, and progress in every avenue of development.

The Filipinos are a race quick to learn and to profit by knowledge. He would be rash who, with the teachings of contemporaneous history in view, would fix a limit to the degree of culture and advancement yet within the reach of these people if our duty toward them be faithfully performed.

SOURCE: Richardson, *Messages and Papers of the Presidents* (1913), 14:6441–47.

DOCUMENT 30

PRESIDENT McKINLEY'S STATE OF THE UNION ADDRESS JUSTIFYING INTERVENTION IN CHINA'S BOXER REBELLION. DECEMBER 3, 1900.

... In our foreign intercourse the dominant question has been the treatment of the Chinese problem. Apart from this our relations with the powers have been happy.

The recent troubles in China spring from the anti-foreign agitation which for the past three years has gained strength in the northern provinces.[1] Their origin lies deep in the character of the Chinese races and in the traditions of their Government. The Taiping rebellion and the opening of Chinese ports to foreign trade and settlement disturbed alike the homogeneity and the seclusion of China.

Meanwhile foreign activity made itself felt in all quarters, not alone on the coast, but along the great river arteries and in the remoter districts, carrying new ideas and introducing new associations among a primitive people which had pursued for centuries a national policy of isolation.

The telegraph and the railway spreading over their land, the steamers plying on their waterways, the merchant and the missionary penetrating year by year farther to the interior, became to the Chinese mind types of an alien invasion, changing the course of their national life and fraught with vague forebodings of disaster to their beliefs and their self-control.

For several years before the present troubles all the resources of foreign diplomacy, backed by moral demonstrations of the physical force of fleets and arms, having been needed to secure due respect for the treaty rights of foreigners and to obtain satisfaction from the responsible authorities for the sporadic outrages upon the persons and property of unoffending sojourners, which from time to time occurred at widely separated points in the northern provinces, as in the case of the outbreaks in Sze-chuen [Sichuan] and Shan-tung [Shandong].

Posting of anti-foreign placards became a daily occurrence, which the repeated reprobation of the Imperial power failed to check or punish.

---

[1] In the winter of 1900 a Chinese secret society took up arms to expel foreigners and foreign influence from China. Because the rebels used a clenched fist as their symbol, Westerners called them Boxers. After attacking missionaries the Boxers laid siege to the section of Peking (Beijing), the Chinese capital, where the foreign diplomatic and commercial legations were housed. The United States joined an international military expedition in the summer of 1900 to rescue the Western legations and crush the Boxer Rebellion.

These inflammatory appeals to the ignorance and superstition of the masses, mendacious and absurd in their accusations and deeply hostile in their spirit, could not but work cumulative harm. They aimed at no particular class of foreigners; they were impartial in attacking everything foreign.

An outbreak in Shan-tung, in which German missionaries were slain, was the too natural result of these malevolent teachings. The posting of seditious placards, exhorting to the utter destruction of foreigners and of every foreign thing, continued unrebuked. Hostile demonstrations toward the stranger gained strength by organization.

The sect, commonly styled the Boxers, developed greatly in the provinces north of the Yang-Tse, and with the collusion of many notable officials, including some in the immediate councils of the Throne itself, became alarmingly aggressive. No foreigner's life, outside of the protected treaty ports, was safe. No foreign interest was secure from spoliation.

The diplomatic representatives of the powers in Peking strove in vain to check this movement. Protest was followed by demand and demand by renewed protest, to be met with perfunctory edicts from the Palace and evasive and futile assurances from the Tsung-li Yamen [China's Ministry of Foreign Affairs]. The circle of the Boxer influence narrowed about Peking, and while nominally stigmatized as seditious, it was felt that its spirit pervaded the capital itself, that the Imperial forces were imbued with its doctrines, and that the immediate counselors of the Empress Dowager [Tzü Hsi] were in full sympathy with the anti-foreign movement.

The increasing gravity of the conditions in China and the imminence of peril to our own diversified interests in the Empire, as well as to those of all the other treaty governments, were soon appreciated by this Government, causing it profound solicitude. The United States from the earliest days of foreign intercourse with China had followed a policy of peace, omitting no occasions to testify good will, to further the extension of lawful trade, to respect the sovereignty of its Government, and to insure by all legitimate and kindly but earnest means the fullest measure of protection for the lives and property of our law-abiding citizens and for the exercise of their beneficent callings among the Chinese people.

Mindful of this, it was felt to be appropriate that our purposes should be pronounced in favor of such course as would hasten united action of the powers at Peking to promote the administrative reforms so greatly needed for strengthening the Imperial Government and maintaining the integrity of China, in which we believed the whole western world to be alike concerned. To these ends I caused to be addressed to the several powers occupying territory and maintaining spheres of influence in China the circular proposals of 1899, inviting from them declarations of their intentions and views as to the desirability of the adoption of measures insuring the benefits of equality of treatment of all foreign trade throughout China.

With gratifying unanimity the responses coincided in this common policy, enabling me to see in the successful termination of these negotiations proof of the friendly spirit which animates the various powers interested in the untrammeled development of commerce and industry in the Chinese Empire as a source of vast benefit to the whole commercial world.

In this conclusion, which I had the gratification to announce as a completed engagement to the interested powers on March 20, 1900, I hopefully discerned a potential factor for the abatement of the distrust of foreign purposes which for a year past had appeared to inspire the policy of the Imperial Government, and for the effective exertion by it of power and authority to quell the critical anti-foreign movement in the northern provinces most immediately influenced by the Manchu sentiment.

Seeking to testify confidence in the willingness and ability of the Imperial administration to redress the wrongs and prevent the evils we suffered and feared, the marine guard, which had been sent to Peking in the autumn of 1899 for the protection of the legation, was withdrawn at the earliest practicable moment, and all pending questions were remitted, as far as we were concerned, to the ordinary resorts of diplomatic intercourse.

The Chinese Government proved, however, unable to check the rising strength of the Boxers and appeared to be a prey to internal dissensions. In the unequal contest the anti-foreign influences soon gained the ascendancy under the leadership of Prince Tuan. Organized armies of Boxers, with which the Imperial forces affiliated, held the country between Peking and the coast, penetrated into Manchuria up to the Russian borders, and through their emissaries threatened a like rising throughout northern China.

Attacks upon foreigners, destruction of their property, and slaughter of native converts were reported from all sides. The Tsung-li Yamen, already permeated with hostile sympathies, could make no effective response to the appeals of the legations. At this critical juncture, in the early spring of this year, a proposal was made by the other powers that a combined fleet should be assembled in Chinese waters as a moral demonstration, under cover of which to exact of the Chinese Government respect for foreign treaty rights and the suppression of the Boxers.

The United States, while not participating in the joint demonstration, promptly sent from the Philippines all ships that could be spared for service on the Chinese coast. A small force of marines was landed at Taku and sent to Peking for the protection of the American legation. Other powers took similar action, until some four hundred men were assembled in the capital as legation guards.

Still the peril increased. The legations reported the development of the seditious movement in Peking and the need of increased provision for defense against it. While preparations were in progress for a larger expedition, to strengthen the legation guards and keep the railway open, an attempt of the foreign ships to make a landing at Taku was met by fire from the Chinese forts. The forts were thereupon shelled by the foreign vessels, the American admiral taking no part in the attack, on the ground that we were not at war with China and that a hostile demonstration might consolidate the anti-foreign elements and strengthen the Boxers to oppose the relieving column.

Two days later the Taku forts were captured after a sanguinary conflict. Severance of communication with Peking followed, and a combined force of additional guards, which was advancing to Peking by the Pei-Ho, was checked at Langfang. The isolation of the legations was complete.

The siege and the relief of the legations has passed into undying history. In all the stirring chapter which records the heroism of the devoted band, clinging to hope in the face of despair, and the undaunted spirit that led their relievers through battle and suffering to the goal, it is a memory of which my countrymen may be justly proud that the honor of our flag was maintained alike in the siege and the rescue, and that stout American hearts have again set high, in fervent emulation with true men of other race and language, the indomitable courage that ever strives for the cause of right and justice.

By June 19 the legations were cut off. An identical note from the Yamen ordered each minister to leave Peking, under a promised escort, within twenty-four hours. To gain time they replied, asking prolongation of the time, which was afterwards granted, and requesting an interview with the Tsung-li Yamen on the following day. No reply being received, on the morning of the 20th the German minister, Baron [Klemens] von Ketteler, set out for the Yamen to obtain a response, and on the way was murdered.

An attempt by the legation guard to recover his body was foiled by the Chinese. Armed forces turned out against the legations. Their quarters were surrounded and attacked. The mission compounds were abandoned, their inmates taking refuge in the British legation, where all the other legations and guards gathered for more effective defense. Four hundred persons were crowded in its narrow compass. Two thousand native converts were assembled in a nearby palace under protection of the foreigners. Lines of defense were strengthened, trenches dug, barricades raised, and preparations made to stand a siege, which at once began.

From June 20 until July 17, writes Minister [Edwin H.] Conger, "there was scarcely an hour during which there was not firing upon some part of our lines and into some of the legations, varying from a single shot to a general and continuous attack along the whole line." Artillery was placed around the legations and on the over-looking palace walls, and thousands of 3-inch shot and shell were fired, destroying some buildings and damaging all. So thickly did the balls rain, that, when the ammunition of the besieged ran low, five quarts of Chinese bullets were gathered in an hour in one compound and recast.

Attempts were made to burn the legations by setting neighboring houses on fire, but the flames were successfully fought off, although the Austrian, Belgian, Italian, and Dutch legations were then and subsequently burned. With the aid of the native converts, directed by the missionaries, to whose helpful co-operation Mr. Conger awards unstinted praise, the British legation was made a veritable fortress. The British minister, Sir Claude MacDonald, was chosen general commander of the defense, with the secretary of the American legation, Mr. E. G. Squiers, as chief of staff.

To save life and ammunition the besieged sparingly returned the incessant fire of the Chinese soldiery, fighting only to repel attack or make an occasional successful sortie for strategic advantage, such as that of fifty-five American, British, and Russian marines led by Captain [John Twiggs "Handsome Jack"] Myers, of the United States Marine Corps, which resulted in the capture of a formidable barricade on the wall that gravely menaced the American position. It was held to the last, and proved an invaluable acquisition, because commanding the water gate through which the relief column entered.

During the siege the defenders lost 65 killed, 1,135 wounded, and 7 by disease—the last all children.

On July 14 the besieged had their first communication with the Tsung-li Yamen, from whom a message came inviting them to a conference, which was declined. Correspondence, however, ensued and a sort of armistice was agreed upon, which stopped the bombardment and lessened the rifle fire for a time. Even then no protection whatever was afforded, nor any aid given, save to send to the legations a small supply of fruit and three sacks of flour.

Indeed, the only communication had with the Chinese Government related to the occasional delivery or dispatch of a telegram or to the demands of the Tsung-li Yamen for the withdrawal of the legations to the coast under escort. Not only are the protestations of the Chinese Government that it protected and succored the legations positively contradicted, but irresistible proof accumulates that the attacks upon them were made by Imperial troops, regularly uniformed, armed, and officered, belonging to the command of Jung Lu, the Imperial commander in chief. Decrees encouraging the Boxers, organizing them under prominent Imperial officers, provisioning them, and even granting them large sums in the name of the Empress Dowager, are known to exist. Members of the Tsung-li Yamen who counseled protection of the foreigners were beheaded. Even in the distant provinces men suspected of foreign sympathy were put to death, prominent among these being Chang Yen-hoon, formerly Chinese minister in Washington.

With the negotiation of the partial armistice of July 14, a proceeding which was doubtless promoted by the representations of the Chinese envoy in Washington, the way was opened for the conveyance to Mr. Conger of a test message sent by the Secretary of State through the kind offices of Minister Wu Ting-fang. Mr. Conger's reply, dispatched from Peking on July 18 through the same channel, afforded to the outside world the first tidings that the inmates of the legations were still alive and hoping for succor.

This news stimulated the preparations for a joint relief expedition in numbers sufficient to overcome the resistance which for a month had been organizing between Taku and the capital. Reinforcements sent by all the co-operating Governments were constantly arriving. The United States contingent, hastily assembled from the Philippines or dispatched from this country, amounted to some 5,000 men, under the able command first of the lamented Colonel [Emerson] Liscum and afterwards of General [Adna R.] Chaffee.

Toward the end of July the movement began. A severe conflict followed at Tientsin, in which Colonel Liscum was killed. The city was stormed and partly destroyed. Its capture afforded the base of operations from which to make the final advance, which began in the first days of August, the expedition being made up of Japanese, Russian, British, and American troops at the outset.

Another battle was fought and won at Yangtsun. Thereafter the disheartened Chinese troops offered little show of resistance. A few days later the important position of Ho-si-woo was taken. A rapid march brought the united forces to the populous city of Tung Chow, which capitulated without a contest.

On August 14 the capital was reached. After a brief conflict beneath the walls the relief column entered and the legations were saved. The United States soldiers, sailors, and marines, officers and men alike, in those distant climes and unusual surroundings, showed the same valor, discipline, and good conduct and gave proof of the same high degree of intelligence and efficiency which have distinguished them in every emergency.

The Imperial family and the Government had fled a few days before. The city was without visible control. The remaining Imperial soldiery had made on the night of the 13th a last attempt to exterminate the besieged, which was gallantly repelled. It fell to the occupying forces to restore order and organize a provisional administration.

Happily the acute disturbances were confined to the northern provinces. It is a relief to recall and a pleasure to record the loyal conduct of the viceroys and local authorities of the southern and eastern provinces. Their efforts were continuously directed to the pacific control of the vast populations under their rule and to the scrupulous observance of foreign treaty rights. At critical moments they did not hesitate to memorialize the Throne, urging the protection of the legations, the restoration of communication, and the assertion of the Imperial authority against the subversive elements. They maintained excellent relations with the official representatives of foreign powers. To their kindly disposition is largely due the success of the consuls in removing many of the missionaries from the interior to places of safety. In this relation the action of the consuls should be highly commended. In Shan-tung and eastern Chili the task was difficult, but, thanks to their energy and the cooperation of American and foreign naval commanders, hundreds of foreigners, including those of other nationalities than ours, were rescued from imminent peril.

The policy of the United States through all this trying period was clearly announced and scrupulously carried out. A circular note to the powers dated July 3 proclaimed our attitude. Treating the condition in the north as one of virtual anarchy, in which the great provinces of the south and southeast had no share, we regarded the local authorities in the latter quarters as representing the Chinese people with whom we sought to remain in peace and friendship. Our declared aims involved no war against the Chinese nation. We adhered to the legitimate office of rescuing the imperiled legation, obtaining redress for wrongs already suffered, securing wherever possible the safety of American life and property in China, and preventing a spread of the disorders or their recurrence.

As was then said, "The policy of the Government of the United States is to seek a solution which may bring about permanent safety and peace to China, preserve Chinese territorial and administrative entity, protect all rights guaranteed to friendly powers by treaty and international law, and safeguard for the world the principle of equal and impartial trade with all parts of the Chinese Empire."

Faithful to those professions which, as it proved, reflected the views and purposes of the other co-operating Governments, all our efforts have been directed toward ending the anomalous situation in China by negotiations for a settlement at the earliest possible moment. As soon as the sacred duty of relieving our legation and its dependents was accomplished we withdrew from active hostilities, leaving our legation under an adequate guard in Peking as a channel of negotiation and settlement—a course adopted by others of the interested powers. Overtures of the empowered representatives of the Chinese Emperor have been considerately entertained.

The Russian proposition looking to the restoration of the Imperial power in Peking has been accepted as in full consonance with our own desires, for we have held and hold that effective reparation for wrongs suffered and an enduring settlement that will make their recurrence impossible can best be brought about under an authority which the Chinese nation reverences and obeys. While so doing we forego no jot of our undoubted right to exact exemplary and deterrent punishment of the responsible authors and abettors of the criminal acts whereby we and other nations have suffered grievous injury.

For the real culprits, the evil counselors who have misled the Imperial judgment and diverted the sovereign authority to their own guilty ends, full expiation becomes imperative within the rational limits of retributive justice. Regarding this as the initial condition of an acceptable settlement between China and the powers, I said in my message of October 18 to the Chinese Emperor:

> I trust that negotiations may begin so soon as we and the other offended Governments shall be effectively satisfied of Your Majesty's ability and power to treat with just sternness the principal offenders, who are doubly culpable, not alone toward the foreigners, but toward Your Majesty, under whose rule the purpose of China to dwell in concord with the world had hitherto found expression in the welcome and protection assured to strangers.

Taking, as a point of departure, the Imperial edict appointing Earl Li Hung Chang and Prince Ching plenipotentiaries to arrange a settlement, and the edict of September 25, whereby certain high officials were designated for punishment, this Government has moved, in concert with the other powers, toward the opening of negotiations, which Mr. Conger, assisted by Mr. [William] Rockhill, has been authorized to conduct on behalf of the United States.[2]

General bases of negotiation formulated by the Government of the French Republic have been accepted with certain reservations as to details, made necessary by our own circumstances, but, like similar reservations by other powers, open to discussion in the progress of the negotiations. The disposition of the Emperor's Government to admit liability for wrongs done to foreign Governments and their nationals, and to act upon such

---

[2]**William Woodville Rockhill**, 1854–1914; U.S. diplomat to China and Korea (1888–1892), appointed third assistant secretary of state in 1894, served as U.S. special agent to China from 1900–1901.

additional designation of the guilty persons as the foreign ministers at Peking may be in a position to make, gives hope of a complete settlement of all questions involved, assuring foreign rights of residence and intercourse on terms of equality for all the world.

I regard as one of the essential factors of a durable adjustment the securement of adequate guarantees for liberty of faith, since insecurity of those natives who may embrace alien creeds is a scarcely less effectual assault upon the rights of foreign worship and teaching than would be the direct invasion thereof.

The matter of indemnity for our wronged citizens is a question of grave concern. Measured in money alone, a sufficient reparation may prove to be beyond the ability of China to meet. All the powers concur in emphatic disclaimers of any purpose of aggrandizement through the dismemberment of the Empire. I am disposed to think that due compensation may be made in part by increased guarantees of security for foreign rights and immunities, and, most important of all, by the opening of China to the equal commerce of all the world.[3] These views have been and will be earnestly advocated by our representatives.

The Government of Russia has put forward a suggestion, that in the event of protracted divergence of views in regard to indemnities the matter may be relegated to the Court of Arbitration at The Hague. I favorably incline to this, believing that high tribunal could not fail to reach a solution no less conducive to the stability and enlarged prosperity of China itself than immediately beneficial to the powers.

SOURCE: Richardson, *Messages and Papers of the Presidents* (1913), 14:6417–25.

---

[3]In 1899, President McKinley's secretary of state, John Hay, circulated a letter to Germany, Russia, Britain, France, Italy, and Japan, suggesting that these foreign powers permit Chinese authorities to collect tariff duties within their respective commercial zones, or spheres of influence, in China. Hay hoped to preserve some semblance of Chinese sovereignty by preventing other nations from carving up China and, at the same time, to give an "Open Door" to American trade throughout that country.

9

THEODORE ROOSEVELT

DOCUMENT 31
PRESIDENT THEODORE ROOSEVELT'S STATE OF THE UNION ADDRESS ON THE TURMOIL IN THE ISTHMUS OF PANAMA. DECEMBER 7, 1903.

. . . By the act of June 28, 1902, the Congress authorized the President to enter into treaty with Colombia for the building of the canal across the Isthmus of Panama; it being provided that in the event of failure to secure such treaty after the lapse of a reasonable time recourse should be had to building a canal through Nicaragua. It has not been necessary to consider this alternative, as I am enabled to lay before the Senate a treaty providing for the building of the canal across the Isthmus of Panama. This was the route which commended itself to the deliberate judgment of the Congress, and we can now acquire by treaty the right to construct the canal over this route. The question now, therefore, is not by which route the isthmian canal shall be built, for that question has been definitely and irrevocably decided. The question is simply whether or not we shall have an isthmian canal.

When the Congress directed that we should take the Panama route under treaty with Colombia, the essence of the condition, of course, referred not to the Government which controlled that route, but to the route itself; to the territory across which the route lay, not to the name which for the moment the territory bore on the map. The purpose of the law was to authorize the President to make a treaty with the power in actual control of the Isthmus of Panama. This purpose has been fulfilled.

In the year 1846 this Government entered into a treaty with New Granada, the predecessor upon the Isthmus of the Republic of Colombia and of the present Republic of Panama, by which treaty it was provided that the Government and citizens of the United States should always have free and open right of way or transit across the Isthmus of Panama by any modes of communication that might be constructed, while in turn our

Government guaranteed the perfect neutrality of the above-mentioned Isthmus with the view that the free transit from the one to the other sea might not be interrupted or embarrassed. The treaty vested in the United States a substantial property right carved out of the rights of sovereignty and property which New Granada then had and possessed over the said territory. The name of New Granada has passed away and its territory has been divided. Its successor, the Government of Colombia, has ceased to own any property in the Isthmus. A new Republic, that of Panama, which was at one time a sovereign state, and at another time a mere department of the successive confederations known as New Granada and Colombia, has now succeeded to the rights which first one and then the other formerly exercised over the Isthmus. But as long as the Isthmus endures, the mere geographical fact of its existence, and the peculiar interest therein which is required by our position, perpetuate the solemn contract which binds the holders of the territory to respect our right to freedom of transit across it, and binds us in return to safeguard for the Isthmus and the world the exercise of that inestimable privilege. The true interpretation of the obligations upon which the United States entered in this treaty of 1846 has been given repeatedly in the utterances of Presidents and Secretaries of State. Secretary [of State Lewis] Cass in 1858 officially stated the position of this Government as follows:

> "The progress of events has rendered the interoceanic route across the narrow portion of Central America vastly important to the commercial world, and especially to the United States, whose possessions extend along the Atlantic and Pacific coasts, and demand the speediest and easiest modes of communication. While the rights of sovereignty of the states occupying this region should always be respected, we shall expect that these rights be exercised in a spirit befitting the occasion and the wants and circumstances that have arisen. Sovereignty has its duties as well as its rights, and none of these local governments, even if administered with more regard to the just demands of other nations than they have been, would be permitted, in a spirit of Eastern isolation, to close the gates of intercourse on the great highways of the world, and justify the act by the pretension that these avenues of trade and travel belong to them and that they choose to shut them, or, what is almost equivalent, to encumber them with such unjust relations as would prevent their general use."

Seven years later, in 1865, Mr. [Secretary of State William] Seward in different communications took the following position:

> "The United States have taken and will take no interest in any question of internal revolution in the State of Panama, or any State of the United States

of Colombia, but will maintain a perfect neutrality in connection with such domestic altercations. The United States will, nevertheless, hold themselves ready to protect the transit trade across the Isthmus against invasion of either domestic or foreign disturbers of the peace of the State of Panama. . . . Neither the text nor the spirit of the stipulation in that article by which the United States engages to preserve the neutrality of the Isthmus of Panama, imposes an obligation on this Government to comply with the requisition [of the President of the United States of Colombia for a force to protect the Isthmus of Panama from a body of insurgents of that country]. The purpose of the stipulation was to guarantee the Isthmus against seizure or invasion by a foreign power only."

Attorney-General [James] Speed, under date of November 7, 1865, advised Secretary Seward as follows:

"From this treaty it can not be supposed that New Granada invited the United States to become a party to the intestine troubles of that Government, nor did the United States become bound to take sides in the domestic broils of New Granada. The United States did guarantee New Granada in the sovereignty and property over the territory. This was as against other and foreign governments."

For four hundred years, ever since shortly after the discovery of this hemisphere, the canal across the Isthmus has been planned. For two score years it has been worked at. When made it is to last for the ages. It is to alter the geography of a continent and the trade routes of the world. We have shown by every treaty we have negotiated or attempted to negotiate with the peoples in control of the Isthmus and with foreign nations in reference thereto our consistent good faith in observing our obligations; on the one hand to the peoples of the Isthmus, and on the other hand to the civilized world whose commercial rights we are safeguarding and guaranteeing by our action. We have done our duty to others in letter and in spirit, and we have shown the utmost forbearance in exacting our own rights.

Last spring, under the act above referred to [Public Law 57-183, 32 Stat. 481, passed June 28, 1902], a treaty concluded between the representatives of the Republic of Colombia and of our Government was ratified by the Senate. This treaty was entered into at the urgent solicitation of the people of Colombia and after a body of experts appointed by our Government especially to go into the matter of the routes across the Isthmus had pronounced unanimously in favor of the Panama route. In drawing up this treaty every concession was made to the people and to the Government of Colombia. We were more than just in dealing with them.

Our generosity was such as to make it a serious question whether we had not gone too far in their interest at the expense of our own; for in our scrupulous desire to pay all possible heed, not merely to the real but even to the fancied rights of our weaker neighbor, who already owed so much to our protection and forbearance, we yielded in all possible ways to her desires in drawing up the treaty. Nevertheless the Government of Colombia not merely repudiated the treaty, but repudiated it in such manner as to make it evident by the time the Colombian Congress adjourned that not the scantiest hope remained of ever getting a satisfactory treaty from them. The Government of Colombia made the treaty, and yet when the Colombian Congress was called to ratify it the vote against ratification was unanimous. It does not appear that the Government made any real effort to secure ratification.

Immediately after the adjournment of the Congress a revolution broke out in Panama. The people of Panama had long been discontented with the Republic of Colombia, and they had been kept quiet only by the prospect of the conclusion of the treaty, which was to them a matter of vital concern. When it became evident that the treaty was hopelessly lost, the people of Panama rose literally as one man. Not a shot was fired by a single man on the Isthmus in the interest of the Colombian Government. Not a life was lost in the accomplishment of the revolution. The Colombian troops stationed on the Isthmus, who had long been unpaid, made common cause with the people of Panama, and with astonishing unanimity the new Republic was started. The duty of the United States in the premises was clear. In strict accordance with the principles laid down by Secretaries Cass and Seward in the official documents above quoted, the United States gave notice that it would permit the landing of no expeditionary force, the arrival of which would mean chaos and destruction along the line of the railroad and of the proposed canal, and an interruption of transit as an inevitable consequence. The de facto Government of Panama was recognized in the following telegram:

> "The people of Panama have, by apparently unanimous movement, dissolved their political connection with the Republic of Colombia and resumed their independence. When you are satisfied that a de facto government, republican in form and without substantial opposition from its own people, has been established in the State of Panama, you will enter into relations with it as the responsible government of the territory and look to it for all due action to protect the persons and property of citizens of the United States and to keep open the isthmian transit, in accordance with the obliga-

tions of existing treaties governing the relations of the United States to that Territory."

The Government of Colombia was notified of our action by the following telegram:

"The people of Panama having, by an apparently unanimous movement, dissolved their political connection with the Republic of Colombia and resumed their independence, and having adopted a Government of their own, republican in form, with which the Government of the United States of America has entered into relations, the President of the United States, in accordance with the ties of friendship which have so long and so happily existed between the respective nations, most earnestly commends to the Governments of Colombia and of Panama the peaceful and equitable settlement of all questions at issue between them. He holds that he is bound not merely by treaty obligations, but by the interests of civilization, to see that the peaceful traffic of the world across the Isthmus of Panama shall not longer be disturbed by a constant succession of unnecessary and wasteful civil wars."

When these events happened, fifty-seven years had elapsed since the United States had entered into its treaty with New Granada. During that time the Governments of New Granada and of its successor, Colombia, have been in a constant state of flux. The following is a partial list [deleted here] of the disturbances on the Isthmus of Panama during the period in question as reported to us by our consuls. It is not possible to give a complete list, and some of the reports that speak of "revolutions" must mean unsuccessful revolutions.

. . . The revolutions, rebellions, insurrections, riots, and other outbreaks that have occurred during the period in question . . . number 53 for the 57 years. It will be noted that one of them lasted for nearly three years before it was quelled; another for nearly a year. In short, the experience of over half a century has shown Colombia to be utterly incapable of keeping order on the Isthmus. Only the active interference of the United States has enabled her to preserve so much as a semblance of sovereignty. Had it not been for the exercise by the United States of the police power in her interest, her connection with the Isthmus would have been sundered long ago. In 1856, in 1860, in 1873, in 1885, in 1901, and again in 1902, sailors and marines from United States warships were forced to land in order to patrol the Isthmus, to protect life and property, and to see that the transit across the Isthmus was kept open. In 1861, in 1862, in 1885, and in 1900, the Colombian Government asked that the United States Government would land troops to protect its interests and maintain order on the Isthmus. Perhaps the most extraordinary request is that which has just been received and which runs as follows:

> "Knowing that revolution has already commenced in Panama [an eminent Colombian] says that if the Government of the United States will land troops to preserve Colombian sovereignty, and the transit, if requested by Colombian chargé d'affaires, this Government will declare martial law; and, by virtue of vested constitutional authority, when public order is disturbed, will approve by decree ratification of the canal treaty as signed; or, if the Government of the United States prefers, will call extra session of the Congress—with new and friendly members—next May to approve the treaty. [An eminent Colombian] has the perfect confidence of vicepresident, he says, and if it became necessary will go to the Isthmus or send representatives there to adjust matters along above lines to the satisfaction of the people there."

This dispatch is noteworthy from two standpoints. Its offer of immediately guaranteeing the treaty to us is in sharp contrast with the positive and contemptuous refusal of the Congress which has just closed its sessions to consider favorably such a treaty; it shows that the Government which made the treaty really had absolute control over the situation, but did not choose to exercise this control. The dispatch further calls on us to restore order and secure Colombian supremacy in the Isthmus from which the Colombian Government has just by its action decided to bar us by preventing the construction of the canal.

The control, in the interest of the commerce and traffic of the whole civilized world, of the means of undisturbed transit across the Isthmus of Panama has become of transcendent importance to the United States. We have repeatedly exercised this control by intervening in the course of domestic dissension, and by protecting the territory from foreign invasion. In 1853 Mr. [Edward] Everett assured the Peruvian minister [Juan I. de Osma] that we should not hesitate to maintain the neutrality of the Isthmus in the case of war between Peru and Colombia. In 1864 Colombia, which has always been vigilant to avail itself of its privileges conferred by the treaty, expressed its expectation that in the event of war between Peru and Spain the United States would carry into effect the guaranty of neutrality. There have been few administrations of the State Department in which this treaty has not, either by the one side or the other, been used as a basis of more or less important demands. It was said by Mr. [Secretary of State Hamilton] Fish in 1871 that the Department of State had reason to believe that an attack upon Colombian sovereignty on the Isthmus had, on several occasions, been averted by warning from this Government. In 1886, when Colombia was under the menace of hostilities from Italy in the Cerruti case,[1] Mr. [Secretary of State Thomas F.] Bayard expressed the serious concern that the United States could not but feel, that a European power should resort to force against a sister republic of this hemisphere, as to the sovereign and uninterrupted use of a part of whose territory we are guarantors under the solemn faith of a treaty.

The above recital of facts establishes beyond question: First, that the United States has for over half a century patiently and in good faith carried out its obligations under the treaty of 1846; second, that when for the first time it became possible for Colombia to do anything in requital of the services thus repeatedly rendered to it for fifty-seven years by the United States, the Colombian Government peremptorily and offensively refused thus to do its part, even though to do so would have been to its advantage and immeasurably to the advantage of the State of Panama, at that time under its jurisdiction; third, that throughout this period revolutions, riots, and factional disturbances of every kind have occurred one after the other in almost uninterrupted succession, some of them lasting for months and even for years, while the central government was unable to put them down or to make peace with the rebels; fourth, that these disturbances instead of showing any sign of abating have tended to grow more numerous and more serious in the immediate past; fifth, that the control of Colombia over the Isthmus of Panama could not be maintained without the armed intervention and assistance of the United States. In other words, the Government of Colombia, though wholly unable to maintain order on the Isthmus, has nevertheless declined to ratify a treaty the conclusion of which opened the only chance to secure its own stability and to guarantee permanent peace on, and the construction of a canal across, the Isthmus.

Under such circumstances the Government of the United States would have been guilty of folly and weakness, amounting in their sum to a crime against the Nation, had it acted otherwise than it did when the revolution of November 3 last took place in Panama. This great enterprise of building the interoceanic canal can not be held up to gratify the whims, or out of respect to the governmental impotence, or to the even more sinister and evil political peculiarities, of people who, though they dwell afar off, yet,

---

[1]During the Colombian civil war of 1884, the property of Italian businessman Ernesto Cerruti was destroyed. The Bogotá government rejected Cerruti's claims, thereby causing Italy to threaten Colombia with military action. The case was finally settled in 1898 through U.S. arbitration.

against the wish of the actual dwellers on the Isthmus, assert an unreal supremacy over the territory. The possession of a territory fraught with such peculiar capacities as the Isthmus in question carries with it obligations to mankind. The course of events has shown that this canal can not be built by private enterprise, or by any other nation than our own; therefore it must be built by the United States.

Every effort has been made by the Government of the United States to persuade Colombia to follow a course which was essentially not only to our interests and to the interests of the world, but to the interests of Colombia itself. These efforts have failed; and Colombia, by her persistence in repulsing the advances that have been made, has forced us, for the sake of our own honor, and of the interest and well-being, not merely of our own people, but of the people of the Isthmus of Panama and the people of the civilized countries of the world, to take decisive steps to bring to an end a condition of affairs which had become intolerable. The new Republic of Panama immediately offered to negotiate a treaty with us. This treaty [Hay-Bunau-Varilla Treaty] I herewith submit. By it our interests are better safeguarded than in the treaty with Colombia which was ratified by the Senate at its last session. It is better in its terms than the treaties offered to us by the Republics of Nicaragua and Costa Rica. At last the right to begin this great undertaking is made available. Panama has done her part. All that remains is for the American Congress to do its part, and forthwith this Republic will enter upon the execution of a project colossal in its size and of well-nigh incalculable possibilities for the good of this country and the nations of mankind.

By the provisions of the treaty the United States guarantees and will maintain the independence of the Republic of Panama. There is granted to the United States in perpetuity the use, occupation, and control of a strip ten miles wide and extending three nautical miles into the sea at either terminal, with all lands lying outside of the zone necessary for the construction of the canal or for its auxiliary works, and with the islands in the Bay of Panama. The cities of Panama and Colón are not embraced in the canal zone, but the United States assumes their sanitation and, in case of need, the maintenance of order therein; the United States enjoys within the granted limits all the rights, power, and authority which it would possess were it the sovereign of the territory to the exclusion of the exercise of sovereign rights by the Republic. All railway and canal property rights belonging to Panama and needed for the canal pass to the United States, including any property of the respective companies in the cities of Panama and Colón; the works, property, and personnel of the canal and railways are exempted from taxation as well in the cities of Panama and Colón as in the canal zone and its dependencies. Free immigration of the personnel and importation of supplies for the construction and operation of the canal are granted. Provision is made for the use of military force and the building of fortifications by the United States for the protection of the transit. In other details, particularly as to the acquisition of the interests of the New Panama Canal Company and the Panama Railway by the United States and the condemnation of private property for the uses of the canal, the stipulations of the Hay-Herran treaty[2] are closely followed, while the compensation to be given for these enlarged grants remains the same, being ten millions of dollars payable on exchange of ratifications; and, beginning nine years from that date, an annual payment of $250,000 during the life of the convention.

SOURCE: James D.Richardson, ed., *Messages and Papers of the Presidents: Theodore Roosevelt* (1912), 14:6784–6815.

DOCUMENT 32
PRESIDENT ROOSEVELT'S STATE OF THE UNION ADDRESS CONCERNING AN INCREASE IN U.S. ARMED FORCES. DECEMBER 6, 1904.

. . . In treating of our foreign policy and of the attitude that this great nation should assume in the world at large, it is absolutely necessary to consider the army and the navy, and the Congress, through which the thought of the nation finds its expression, should keep ever vividly in mind the fundamental fact that it is impossible to treat our foreign policy, whether this policy takes shape in the effort to secure justice for others or justice for ourselves, save as conditioned upon the attitude we are willing to take toward our army, and especially toward our navy. It is not merely

[2]Treaty signed in 1903 under which the United States agreed to pay Colombia $10 million and an annual fee of $250,000 for a canal through Panama. The United States also agreed to guarantee the independence of Panama. After the Colombian government was unable to win ratification of this treaty, however, President Theodore Roosevelt recognized a new government in an independent Panama. Instead of payment to Colombia the United States, under the terms of the Hay-Bunau-Varilla Treaty of November 1903, agreed to pay the same fee to the new Panamanian government in return for granting to the United States in perpetuity the use and control of a canal zone ten miles wide across the Isthmus of Panama. This later treaty was greatly revised by the Panama Canal Treaty of 1977.

unwise, it is contemptible, for a nation, as for an individual, to use high-sounding language to proclaim its purposes, or to take positions which are ridiculous if unsupported by potential force, and then to refuse to provide this force. If there is no intention of providing and of keeping the force necessary to back up a strong attitude, then it is far better not to assume such an attitude.

The steady aim of this nation, as of all enlightened nations, should be to strive to bring ever nearer the day when there shall prevail throughout the world the peace of justice. There are kinds of peace which are highly undesirable, which are in the long run as destructive as any war. Tyrants and oppressors have many times made a wilderness and called it peace. Many times peoples who were slothful or timid or shortsighted, who had been enervated by ease or by luxury, or misled by false teachings, have shrunk in unmanly fashion from doing duty that was stern and that needed self-sacrifice, and have sought to hide from their own minds their short-comings, their ignoble motives by calling them love of peace. The peace of tyrannous terror, the peace of craven weakness, the peace of injustice, all these should be shunned as we shun unrighteous war. The goal to set before us as a nation, the goal which should be set before all mankind, is the attainment of the peace of justice, of the peace which comes when each nation is not merely safe-guarded in its own rights, but scrupulously recognizes and performs its duty toward others. Generally peace tells for righteousness; but if there is conflict between the two, then our fealty is due first to the cause of righteousness. Unrighteous wars are common, and unrighteous peace is rare; but both should be shunned. The right to freedom and the responsibility for the exercise of that right can not be divorced. One of our great poets has well and finely said that freedom is not a gift that tarries long in the hands of cowards. Neither does it tarry long in the hands of those too slothful, too dishonest, or too unintelligent to exercise it. The eternal vigilance which is the price of liberty must be exercised, sometimes to guard against outside foes; although of course far more often to guard against our own selfish or thoughtless shortcomings.

If these self-evident truths are kept before us, and only if they are so kept before us, we shall have a clear idea of what our foreign policy in its larger aspects should be. It is our duty to remember that a nation has no more right to do injustice to another nation, strong or weak, than an individual has to do injustice to another individual; that the same moral law applies in one case as in the other. But we must also remember that it is as much the duty of the nation to guard its own rights and its own interests as it is the duty of the individual so to do. Within the nation the individual has now delegated this right to the state, that is, to the representative of all the individuals, and it is a maxim of the law that for every wrong there is remedy. But in international law we have not advanced by any means as far as we have advanced in municipal law. There is as yet no judicial way of enforcing a right in international law. When one nation wrongs another or wrongs many others, there is no tribunal before which the wrongdoer can be brought. Either it is necessary supinely to acquiesce in the wrong, and thus put a premium upon brutality and aggression, or else it is necessary for the aggrieved nation valiantly to stand up for its rights. Until some method is devised by which there shall be a degree of international control over offending nations, it would be a wicked thing for the most civilized powers, for those with the most sense of international obligations and with the keenest and most generous appreciation of the difference between right and wrong, to disarm. If the great civilized nations of the present day should completely disarm, the result would mean an immediate recrudescence of barbarism in one form or another. Under any circumstances, a sufficient armament would have to be kept up to serve the purposes of international police; and until international cohesion and the sense of international duties and rights are far more advanced than at present, a nation desirous both of securing respect for itself and of doing good to others must have a force adequate for the work which it feels is allotted to it as its part of the general world duty. Therefore it follows that a self-respecting, just, and far-seeing nation should on the one hand endeavor by every means to aid in the development of the various movements which tend to provide substitutes for war, which tend to render nations in their actions toward one another, and indeed toward their own peoples, more responsive to the general sentiment of humane and civilized mankind; and on the other hand that it should keep prepared while scrupulously avoiding wrongdoing itself, to repel any wrong, and in exceptional cases to take action which in a more advanced stage of international relations would come under the head of the exercise of the international police. A great free people owes it to itself and to all mankind not to sink into helplessness before the powers of evil.

We are in every way endeavoring to help on, with cordial good will, every movement which will tend to bring us into more friendly relations with the rest of mankind. In pursuance of this policy I shall shortly lay before the Senate treaties of arbitration with all powers which are willing to enter into these treaties with us. It is not possible at this period of the world's development to agree to arbitrate all matters, but there are many matters of possible difference between us and other nations which can be thus arbitrated. Furthermore, at the request of the Interparliamentary

Union, an eminent body composed of practical statesmen from all countries, I have asked the powers to join with this government in a second Hague conference, at which it is hoped that the work already so happily begun at The Hague may be carried some steps further toward completion. This carries out the desire expressed by the first Hague conference itself.

It is not true that the United States feels any land hunger or entertains any projects as regards the other nations of the Western Hemisphere save such as are for their welfare. All that this country desires is to see the neighboring countries stable, orderly, and prosperous. Any country whose people conduct themselves well can count upon our hearty friendship. If a nation shows that it knows how to act with reasonable efficiency and decency in social and political matters, if it keeps order and pays its obligations, it need fear no interference from the United States. Chronic wrongdoing, or an impotence which results in a general loosening of the ties of civilized society, may in America, as elsewhere, ultimately require intervention by some civilized nation, and in the Western Hemisphere the adherence of the United States to the Monroe Doctrine may force the United States, however reluctantly, in flagrant cases of such wrongdoing or impotence, to the exercise of an international police power. If every country washed by the Caribbean Sea would show the progress in stable and just civilization which with the aid of the Platt amendment* Cuba has shown since our troops left the island, and which so many of the republics in both Americas are constantly and brilliantly showing, all question of interference by this nation with their affairs would be at an end. Our interests and those of our southern neighbors are in reality identical. They have great natural riches, and if within their borders the reign of law and justice obtains, prosperity is sure to come to them. While they thus obey the primary laws of civilized society they may rest assured that they will be treated by us in a spirit of cordial and helpful sympathy. We would interfere with them only in the last resort, and then only if it became evident that their inability or unwilling-

---

* The amendment to the 1903 Cuban constitution granted the United States the authority to intervene militarily in Cuba to preserve the island's independence and maintain law and order; the amendment also granted the U.S. Navy a coaling station at Guantánamo Bay. The amendment was requested by Secretary of War Elihu Root in 1901 and was added as a proviso in the army appropriation bill of that year by Senator Orville Platt of Connecticut. In what became an important element of President Franklin D. Roosevelt's Good Neighbor policy toward Latin America, the United States and Cuba agreed to rescind the amendment in 1934.

ness to do justice at home and abroad had violated the rights of the United States or had invited foreign aggression to the detriment of the entire body of American nations. It is a mere truism to say that every nation, whether in America or anywhere else, which desires to maintain its freedom, its independence, must ultimately realize that the right of such independence can not be separated from the responsibility of making good use of it.

In asserting the Monroe Doctrine, in taking such steps as we have taken in regard to Cuba, Venezuela, and Panama, and in endeavoring to circumscribe the theater of war in the Far East, and to secure the Open Door in China, we have acted in our own interest as well as in the interest of humanity at large. There are however, cases in which, while our own interests are not greatly involved, strong appeal is made to our sympathies. Ordinarily it is very much wiser and more useful for us to concern ourselves with striving for our own moral and material betterment here at home than to concern ourselves with trying to better the conditions of things in other countries. We have plenty of sins of our own to war against.

SOURCE: U.S. State Department, *Foreign Relations of the United States, 1904* (Washington, DC: Government Printing Office, 1905), xxxix–xlii.

DOCUMENT 33
PRESIDENT ROOSEVELT'S COROLLARY TO THE MONROE DOCTRINE AND INTERVENTION IN THE DOMINICAN REPUBLIC. DECEMBER 5, 1905.

———◆———

. . . One of the most effective instruments for peace is the Monroe Doctrine as it has been and is being gradually developed by this nation and accepted by other nations. No other policy could have been as efficient in promoting peace in the Western Hemisphere and in giving to each nation thereon the chance to develop along its own lines. If we had refused to apply the doctrine to changing conditions it would now be completely outworn, would not meet any of the needs of the present day, and, indeed, would probably by this time have sunk into complete oblivion. It is useful at home, and is meeting with recognition abroad because we have adapted our application of it to meet the growing and changing needs of the hemisphere. When we announce a policy such as the Monroe Doctrine we thereby commit ourselves to the consequences of the policy, and those consequences from time to time alter. It is out of the question to claim a right and yet shirk the responsibility for its exercise. Not only we, but all American republics who are benefited by the existence of the doctrine, must recognize the obligations each nation is under as regards foreign peoples no less than its duty to insist upon its own rights.

That our rights and interests are deeply concerned in the maintenance of the doctrine is so clear as hardly to need argument. This is especially true in view of the construction of the Panama Canal. As a mere matter of self–defense we must exercise a close watch over the approaches to this canal; and this means that we must be thoroughly alive to our interests in the Caribbean Sea.

There are certain essential points which must never be forgotten as regards the Monroe Doctrine. In the first place we must as a nation make it evident that we do not intend to treat it in any shape or way as an excuse for aggrandizement on our part at the expense of the republics to the south. We must recognize the fact that in some South American countries there has been much suspicion lest we should interpret the Monroe Doctrine as in some way inimical to their interests, and we must try to convince all the other nations of this continent once and for all that no just and orderly government has anything to fear from us. There are certain republics to the south of us which have already reached such a point of stability, order, and prosperity that they themselves, though as yet hardly consciously, are among the guarantors of this doctrine. These republics we now meet not only on a basis of entire equality, but in a spirit of frank and respectful friendship, which we hope is mutual. If all of the republics to the south of us will only grow as those to which I allude have already grown, all need for us to be the especial champions of the doctrine will disappear, for no stable and growing American republic wishes to see some great non–American military power acquire territory in its neighborhood. All that this country desires is that the other republics on this continent shall be happy and prosperous; and they cannot be happy and prosperous unless they maintain order within their boundaries and behave with a just regard for their obligations toward outsiders. It must be understood that under no circumstances will the United States use the Monroe Doctrine as a cloak for territorial aggression. We desire peace with all the world, but perhaps most of all with the other peoples of the American continent. There are, of course, limits to the wrongs which any self-respecting nation can endure. It is always possible that wrong actions toward this nation, or toward citizens of this nation, in some state unable to keep order among its own people, unable to secure justice from outsiders, and unwilling to do justice to those outsiders who treat it well, may result in our having to take action to protect our rights; but such action will not be taken with a view to territorial aggression, and it will be taken at all only with extreme reluctance and when it has become evident that every other resource has been exhausted.

Moreover, we must make it evident that we do not intend to permit the Monroe Doctrine to be used by any nation on this continent as a shield to protect it from the consequences of its own misdeeds against foreign nations. If a republic to the south of us commits a tort against a foreign nation, such as an outrage against a citizen of that nation, then the Monroe Doctrine does not force us to interfere to prevent punishment of the tort, save to see that the punishment does not assume the form of territorial occupation in any shape. The case is more difficult when it refers to a contractual obligation. Our own government has always refused to enforce such contractual obligations on behalf of its citizens by an appeal to arms. It is much to be wished that all foreign governments would take the same view. But they do not; and in consequence we are liable at any time to be brought face to face with disagreeable alternatives. On the one hand, this country would certainly decline to go to war to prevent a foreign government from collecting a just debt; on the other hand, it is very inadvisable to permit any foreign power to take possession, even temporarily, of the custom-houses of an American republic in order to enforce the payment of its obligations; for such temporary occupation might turn into a permanent occupation. The only escape from these alternatives may at any time be that we must ourselves undertake to bring about some arrangement by which so much as possible of a just obligation shall be paid. It is far better that this country should put through such an arrangement, rather than allow any foreign country to undertake it. To do so insures the defaulting republic from having to pay debt of an improper character under duress, while it also insures honest creditors of the republic from being passed by in the interest of dishonest or grasping creditors. Moreover, for the United States to take such a position offers the only possible way of insuring us against a clash with some foreign power. The position is, therefore, in the interest of peace as well as in the interest of justice. It is of benefit to our people; it is of benefit to foreign peoples; and most of all it is really of benefit to the people of the country concerned.

This brings me to what should be one of the fundamental objects of the Monroe Doctrine. We must ourselves in good faith try to help upward toward peace and order those of our sister republics which need such help. Just as there has been a gradual growth of the ethical element in the relations of one individual to another, so we are, even though slowly, more and more coming to recognize the duty of bearing one another's burdens, not only as among individuals, but also as among nations.

SANTO DOMINGO

Santo Domingo, in her turn, has now made an appeal to us to help her, and not only every principle of wisdom but every generous instinct within us bids us respond to the appeal. It is not of the slightest consequence whether we grant the aid needed by Santo Domingo as an incident to the wise development of the Monroe Doctrine or because we regard the case of Santo Domingo as standing wholly by itself, and to be treated as such, and not on general principles or with any reference to the Monroe Doctrine. The important point is to give the needed aid, and the case is certainly sufficiently peculiar to deserve to be judged purely on its own merits. The conditions in Santo Domingo have for a number of years grown from bad to worse until a year ago all society was on the verge of dissolution. Fortunately, just at this time a ruler sprang up in Santo Domingo, who, with his colleagues, saw the dangers threatening their country and appealed to the friendship of the only great and powerful neighbor who possessed the power, and as they hoped also the will to help them. There was imminent danger of foreign intervention. The previous rulers of Santo Domingo had recklessly incurred debts, and owing to her internal disorders she had ceased to be able to provide means of paying the debts. The patience of her foreign creditors had become exhausted, and at least two foreign nations were on the point of intervention, and were only prevented from intervening by the unofficial assurance of this government that it would itself strive to help Santo Domingo in her hour of need. In the case of one of these nations, only the actual opening of negotiations to this end by our government prevented the seizure of territory in Santo Domingo by a European power. Of the debts incurred some were just, while some were not of a character which really renders it obligatory on or proper for Santo Domingo to pay them in full. But she could not pay any of them unless some stability was assured her government and people.

Accordingly, the Executive Department of our government negotiated a treaty under which we are to try to help the Dominican people to straighten out their finances. This treaty is pending before the Senate. In the meantime a temporary arrangement has been made which will last until the Senate has had time to take action upon the treaty. Under this arrangement the Dominican Government has appointed Americans to all the important positions in the customs service, and they are seeing to the honest collection of the revenues, turning over forty-five per cent to the government for running expenses and putting the other fifty-five per cent into a safe depository for equitable division in case the treaty shall be ratified, among the various creditors, whether European or American.

The custom-houses offer well-nigh the only sources of revenue in Santo Domingo, and the different revolutions usually have as their real aim the obtaining of these custom-houses. The mere fact that the collectors of customs are Americans, that they are performing their duties with efficiency and honesty, and that the treaty is pending in the Senate gives a certain moral power to the government of Santo Domingo which it has not had before. This has completely discouraged all revolutionary movement, while it has already produced such an increase in the revenues that the government is actually getting more from the forty-five per cent that the American collectors turn over to it than it got formerly when it took the entire revenue. It is enabling the poor, harassed people of Santo Domingo once more to turn their attention to industry and to be free from the curse of interminable revolutionary disturbance. It offers to all bona-fide creditors, American and European, the only really good chance to obtain that to which they are justly entitled, while it in return gives to Santo Domingo the only opportunity of defense against claims which it ought not to pay, for now if it meets the views of the Senate we shall ourselves thoroughly examine all these claims, whether American or foreign, and see that none that are improper are paid. There is, of course, opposition to the treaty from dishonest creditors, foreign and American, and from the professional revolutionists of the island itself. We have already reason to believe that some of the creditors who do not dare expose their claims to honest scrutiny are endeavoring to stir up sedition in the island and opposition to the treaty. In the meantime, I have exercised the authority vested in me by the joint resolution of the Congress to prevent the introduction of arms into the island for revolutionary purposes.

Under the course taken, stability and order and all the benefits of peace are at last coming to Santo Domingo, danger of foreign intervention has been suspended, and there is at last a prospect that all creditors will get justice, no more and no less. If the arrangement is terminated by the failure of the treaty, chaos will follow; and if chaos follows, sooner or later this government may be involved in serious difficulties with foreign governments over the island, or else may be forced itself to intervene in the island in some unpleasant fashion. Under the proposed treaty the independence of the island is scrupulously respected, the danger of violation of the Monroe Doctrine by the intervention of foreign powers vanishes, and the interference of our government is minimized, so that we shall only act in conjunction with the Santo Domingo authorities to secure the proper administration of the customs, and therefore to secure the payment of just debts and to secure the Dominican Government against demands for unjust debts. The proposed method will give the people of Santo Domingo the same chance to move onward and upward which we have already given to the people of Cuba. It will be doubly to our discredit as a nation if we fail to take advantage of this chance; for it will be of damage to ourselves, and it will be of incalculable damage to Santo Domingo. Every consideration of wise policy, and, above all, every consideration of large generosity, bids us meet the request of Santo Domingo as we are now trying to meet it.

SOURCE: Richardson, *Messages and Papers of the Presidents* (1912), 10:7374–79.

DOCUMENT 34
PRESIDENT ROOSEVELT'S STATE OF THE UNION ADDRESS
CONCERNING U.S. INTERVENTION IN CUBA.
DECEMBER 3, 1906.

. . . Last August an insurrection broke out in Cuba which it speedily grew evident that the existing Cuban Government was powerless to quell. This Government was repeatedly asked by the then Cuban Government to intervene, and finally was notified by the President of Cuba that he intended to resign; that his decision was irrevocable; that none of the other constitutional officers would consent to carry on the Government, and that he was powerless to maintain order. It was evident that chaos was impending, and there was every probability that if steps were not immediately taken by this Government to try to restore order, the representatives of various European nations in the island would apply to their respective governments for armed intervention in order to protect the lives and property of their citizens. Thanks to the preparedness of our Navy, I was able immediately to send enough ships to Cuba to prevent the situation from becoming hopeless; and I furthermore dispatched to Cuba the Secretary of War [William Howard Taft] and the Assistant Secretary of State [Robert Bacon], in order that they might grapple with the situation on the ground. All efforts to secure an agreement between the contending factions, by which they should themselves come to an amicable understanding and settle upon some modus vivendi—some provisional government of their own—failed.

Finally the President of the Republic resigned. The quorum of Congress assembled failed by deliberate purpose of its members, so that there was no power to act on his resignation, and the Government came to a halt. In accordance with the so-called Platt amendment, which was embodied in the constitution of Cuba, I thereupon proclaimed a provisional government for the island, the Secretary of War acting as provisional governor until he could be replaced by Mr. [Charles E.] Magoon, the late minister to Panama and governor of the Canal Zone on the Isthmus; troops were sent to support them and relieve the Navy; the expedition being handled with most satisfactory speed and efficiency. The insurgent chiefs immediately agreed that their troops should lay down their arms and disband; and the agreement was carried out. The provisional government has left the personnel of the old government and the old laws, so far as might be, unchanged and will thus administer the island for a few months until tranquility can be restored, a new election properly held, and a new government inaugurated. Peace has come in the island; and the harvesting of the sugar-cane crop, the great crop of the island, is about to proceed.

When the election has been held and the new government inaugurated in peaceful and orderly fashion the provisional government will come to an end. I take this opportunity of expressing upon behalf of the American people, with all possible solemnity, our most earnest hope that the people of Cuba will realize the imperative need of preserving justice and keeping order in the Island. The United States wishes nothing of Cuba except that it shall prosper morally and materially, and wishes nothing of the Cubans save that they shall be able to preserve order among themselves and therefore to preserve their independence. If the elections become a farce, and if the insurrectionary habit becomes confirmed in the Island, it is absolutely out of the question that the Island should continue independent; and the United States, which has assumed the sponsorship before the civilized world for Cuba's career as a nation, would again have to intervene and to see that the government was managed in such orderly fashion as to secure the safety of life and property. The path to be trodden by those who exercise self-government is always hard, and we should have every charity and patience with the Cubans as they tread this difficult path. I have the utmost sympathy with, and regard for, them; but I most earnestly adjure them solemnly to weigh their responsibilities and to see that when their new government is started it shall run smoothly, and with freedom from flagrant denial of right on the one hand, and from insurrectionary disturbances on the other.

SOURCE: Richardson, *Messages and Papers of the Presidents* (1912), 15:7023–7070.

10

WILLIAM H. TAFT

DOCUMENT 35

PRESIDENT WILLIAM TAFT'S STATE OF THE UNION ADDRESS CONCERNING U.S. INTERVENTION IN CENTRAL AMERICA AND THE CARIBBEAN. DECEMBER 3, 1912.

. . . The foreign relations of the United States actually and potentially affect the state of the Union to a degree not widely realized and hardly surpassed by any other factor in the welfare of the whole nation. The position of the United States in the moral, intellectual, and material relations of the family of nations should be a matter of vital interest to every patriotic citizen. The national prosperity and power impose upon us duties which we can not shirk if we are to be true to our ideals. The tremendous growth of the export trade of the United States has already made that trade a very real factor in the industrial and commercial prosperity of the country. With the development of our industries the foreign commerce of the United States must rapidly become a still more essential factor in its economic welfare. Whether we have a farseeing and wise diplomacy and are not recklessly plunged into unnecessary wars, and whether our foreign policies are based upon an intelligent grasp of present-day world conditions and a clear view of the potentialities of the future, or are governed by a temporary and timid expediency or by narrow views befitting an infant nation, are questions in the alternative consideration of which must convince any thoughtful citizen that no department of national polity offers greater opportunity for promoting the interests of the whole people on the one hand, or greater chance on the other of permanent national injury, than that which deals with the foreign relations of the United States.

The fundamental foreign policies of the United States should be raised high above the conflict of partisanship and wholly dissociated from differences as to domestic policy. In its foreign affairs the United States should present to the world a united front. The intellectual, financial, and industrial interest of the country and the publicist, the wage earner, the farmer, and the citizen of whatever occupation must cooperate in a spirit of high patriotism to promote that national solidarity which is indispensable to national efficiency and to the attainment of national ideals.

The relations of the United States with all foreign powers remain upon a sound basis of peace, harmony, and friendship. A greater insistence upon justice to American citizens or interests wherever it may have been denied and a stronger emphasis of the need of mutuality in commercial and other relations have only served to strengthen our friendships with foreign countries by placing those friendships upon a firm foundation of realities as well as aspirations. . . .

The diplomacy of the present administration has sought to respond to modern ideas of commercial intercourse. This policy has been characterized as substituting dollars for bullets. It is one that appeals alike to idealistic humanitarian sentiments, to the dictates of sound policy and strategy, and to legitimate commercial aims. It is an effort frankly directed to the increase of American trade upon the axiomatic principle that the government of the United States shall extend all proper support to every legitimate and beneficial American enterprise abroad. How great have been the results of this diplomacy, coupled with the maximum and minimum provision of the tariff law, will be seen by some consideration of the wonderfiil increase in the export trade of the United States. Because modern diplomacy is commercial, there has been a disposition in some quarters to attribute to it none but materialistic aims. How strikingly erroneous is such an impression may be seen from a study of the results by which the diplomacy of the United States can be judged. . . .

In Central America the aim has been to help such countries as Nicaragua and Honduras to help themselves. They are the immediate beneficiaries. The national benefit to the United States is two-fold. First, it is obvious that the Monroe Doctrine is more vital in the neighborhood of the Panama Canal and the zone of the Caribbean than anywhere else. There, too, the maintenance of that doctrine falls most heavily upon the United States. It is therefore essential that the countries within that sphere shall be removed from the jeopardy involved by heavy foreign debt and chaotic national finances and from the ever-present danger of international complication due to disorder at home. Hence the United States has been glad to encourage and support American bankers who were willing to lend a helping hand to the financial rehabilitation of such countries because this financial rehabilitation and the protection of their customhouses from being the prey of would-be dictators would remove at one stroke the menace of foreign creditors and the menace of revolutionary disorder.

The second advantage of the United States is one affecting chiefly all the southern and Gulf ports and the business and industry of the South. The republics of Central America and the Caribbean possess great natural wealth. They need only a measure of stability and the means of financial regeneration to enter upon an era of peace and prosperity, bringing profit and happiness to themselves and at the same time creating conditions sure to lead to a flourishing interchange of trade with this country.

I wish to call your especial attention to the recent occurrences in Nicaragua, for I believe the terrible events recorded there during the revolution of the past summer—the useless loss of life, the devastation of property, the bombardment of defenseless cities, the killing and wounding of women and children, the torturing of noncombatants to exact contributions, and the suffering of thousands of human beings—might have been averted had the Department of State, through approval of the loan convention by the Senate, been permitted to carry out its now well-developed policy of encouraging the extending of financial aid to weak Central American states with the primary objects of avoiding just such revolutions by assisting those republics to rehabilitate their finances, to establish their currency on a stable basis, to remove the customhouses from the danger of revolutions by arranging for their secure administration, and to establish reliable banks.

During this last revolution in Nicaragua, the government of that republic having admitted its inability to protect American life and property against acts of sheer lawlessness on the part of the malcontents, and having requested this government to assume that office, it became necessary to land over 2,000 marines and bluejackets in Nicaragua. Owing to their presence the constituted government of Nicaragua was free to devote its attention wholly to its internal troubles, and was thus enabled to stamp out the rebellion in a short space of time. When the Red Cross supplies sent to Granada had been exhausted, 8,000 persons having been given food in one day upon the arrival of the American forces, our men supplied other unfortunate, needy Nicaraguans from their own haversacks. I wish to congratulate the officers and men of the United States Navy and Marine Corps who took part in reestablishing order in Nicaragua upon their splendid conduct, and to record with sorrow the death of seven American marines and bluejackets. Since the reestablishment of peace and order, elections have been held amid conditions of quiet and tranquility. Nearly all the American marines have now been withdrawn. The country should soon be on the road to recovery. The only apparent danger now threatening Nicaragua arises from the shortage of funds. Although American bankers have already rendered assistance, they may naturally be loath to advance a loan adequate to set the country upon its feet without the support of some such convention as that of June, 1911, upon which the Senate has not yet acted. . . .

During the past summer the revolution against the administration which followed the assassination of President Caceres a year ago last November brought the Dominican Republic to the verge of administrative chaos, without offering any guaranties of eventual stability in the ultimate success of either party. In pursuance of the treaty relations of the United States with the Dominican Republic, which were threatened by the necessity of suspending the operation under American administration of the customhouses on the Haitian frontier, it was found necessary to dispatch special commissioners to the island to reestablish the customhouses and with a guard sufficient to insure needed protection to the customs administration. The efforts which have been made appear to have resulted in the restoration of normal conditions throughout the republic. The good offices which the commissioners were able to exercise were instrumental in bringing the contending parties together and in furnishing a basis of adjustment which it is hoped will result in permanent benefit to the Dominican people.

Mindful of its treaty relations, and owing to the position of the government of the United States as mediator between the Dominican Republic and Haiti in their boundary dispute, and because of the further fact that the revolutionary activities on the Haitian-Dominican frontier had become so active as practically to obliterate the line of demarcation that had been heretofore recognized pending the definitive settlement of the boundary in controversy, it was found necessary to indicate to the two island governments a provisional de facto boundary line. This was done without prejudice to the rights or obligations of either country in a final settlement to be reached by arbitration. The tentative line chosen was one which, under the circumstances brought to the knowledge of this government, seemed to conform to the best interests of the disputants. The border patrol which it had been found necessary to reestablish for customs purposes between the two countries was instructed provisionally to observe this line.

The republic of Cuba last May was in the throes of a lawless uprising that for a time threatened the destruction of a great deal of valuable property—much of it owned by Americans and other foreigners—as well as the existence of the government itself. The armed forces of Cuba being inadequate to guard property from attack and at the same time properly to operate against the rebels, a force of American marines was dispatched from our naval station at Guantánamo into the province of Oriente for the protection of American and other foreign life and property. The Cuban government was thus able to use all its forces in putting down the outbreak, which it succeeded in doing in a period of six weeks. The presence of two American warships in the harbor of Habana during the most critical period of this disturbance contributed in great measure to allay the fears of the inhabitants, including a large foreign colony.

There has been under discussion with the government of Cuba for some time the question of the release by this government of its leasehold rights at Bahia Honda, on the northern coast of Cuba, and the enlargement, in exchange therefore, of the naval station which has been established at Guantánamo Bay, on the south. As the result of the negotiations thus carried on an agreement has been reached between the two governments providing for the suitable enlargement of the Guantánamo Bay station upon terms which are entirely fair and equitable to all parties concerned.

At the request alike of the government and both political parties in Panama, an American commission undertook supervision of the recent presidential election in that republic, where our treaty relations, and, indeed, every geographical consideration, make the maintenance of order and satisfactory conditions of peculiar interest to the government of the United States. The elections passed without disorder, and the new administration has entered upon its functions.

The government of Great Britain has asked the support of the United States for the protection of the interests of British holders of the foreign bonded debt of Guatemala. While this government is hopeful of an arrangement equitable to the British bondholders, it is naturally unable to view the question apart from its relation to the broad subject of financial stability in Central America, in which the policy of the United States does not permit it to escape a vital interest. Through a renewal of negotiations between the government of Guatemala and American bankers, the aim of which is a loan for the rehabilitation of Guatemalan finances, a way appears to be open by which the government of Guatemala could promptly satisfy any equitable and just British claims, and at the same time so improve its whole financial position as to contribute greatly to the increased prosperity of the republic and to redound to the benefit of foreign investments and foreign trade with that country. Failing such an arrangement, it may become impossible for the government of the United States to escape its obligations in connection with such measures as may become necessary to exact justice to legitimate foreign claims.

In the recent revolution in Nicaragua, which, it was generally admitted, might well have resulted in a general Central American conflict but for the

intervention of the United States, the government of Honduras was especially menaced; but fortunately peaceful conditions were maintained within
the borders of that republic. The financial condition of that country
remains unchanged, no means having been found for the final adjustment
of pressing outstanding foreign claims. This makes it the more regrettable
that the financial convention between the United States and Honduras has
thus far failed of ratification. The government of the United States continues to hold itself ready to cooperate with the government of Honduras,
which, it is believed, can not much longer delay the meeting of its foreign
obligations, and it is hoped at the proper time American bankers will be
willing to cooperate for this purpose.

It is not possible to make the Congress a communication upon the present foreign relations of the United States so detailed as to convey an adequate impression of the enormous increase in the importance and activities
of those relations. If this government is really to preserve to the American
people that free opportunity in foreign markets which will soon be indispensable to our prosperity, ever greater efforts must be made. Otherwise
the American merchant, manufacturer, and exporter will find many a field
in which American trade should logically predominate preempted through
the more energetic efforts of other governments and other commercial
nations.

There are many ways in which through hearty cooperation the Legislative and Executive branches of this government can do much. The absolute
essential is the spirit of united effort and singleness of purpose. I will allude
only to a very few specific examples of action which ought then to result.
America can not take its proper place in the most important fields for its
commercial activity and enterprise unless we have a merchant marine.
American commerce and enterprise can not be effectively fostered in those
fields unless we have good American banks in the countries referred to. We
need American newspapers in those countries and proper means for public information about them. We need to assure the permanency of a trained
foreign service. We need legislation enabling the members of the foreign
service to be systematically brought in direct contact with the industrial,
manufacturing, and exporting interests of this country in order that
American businessmen may enter the foreign field with a clear perception
of the exact conditions to be dealt with and the officers themselves may
prosecute their work with a clear idea of what American industrial and
manufacturing interests require.

Congress should fully realize the conditions which obtain in the world
as we find ourselves at the threshold of our middle age as a nation. We have

emerged full grown as a peer in the great concourse of nations. We have passed through various formative periods. We have been self-centered in the struggle to develop our domestic resources and deal with our domestic questions. The nation is now too matured to continue in its foreign relations those temporary expedients natural to a people to whom domestic affairs are the sole concern. In the past our diplomacy has often consisted, in normal times, in a mere assertion of the right to international existence. We are now in a larger relation with broader rights of our own and obligations to other than ourselves. A number of great guiding principles were laid down early in the history of this government. The recent task of our diplomacy has been to adjust those principles to the conditions of today, to develop their corollaries, to find practical applications of the old principles expanded to meet new situations. Thus are being evolved bases upon which can rest the superstructure of policies which must grow with the destined progress of this nation. The successful conduct of our foreign relations demands a broad and a modern view. We can not meet new questions nor build for the future if we confine ourselves to outworn dogmas of the past and to the perspective appropriate at our emergence from colonial times and conditions. The opening of the Panama Canal will mark a new era in our international life and create new and worldwide conditions which, with their vast correlations and consequences, will obtain for hundreds of years to come. We must not wait for events to overtake us unawares. With continuity of purpose we must deal with the problems of our external relations by a diplomacy modern, resourceful, magnanimous, and fittingly expressive of the high ideals of a great nation.

SOURCE: U.S. State Department, *Foreign Relations of the United States, 1912* (Washington, DC: Government Printing Office, 1919), vii–xxvii.

11

WOODROW WILSON

DOCUMENT 36
PRESIDENT WOODROW WILSON'S SPECIAL MESSAGE TO CONGRESS ON THE TAMPICO INCIDENT IN MEXICO. APRIL 20, 1914.

———◆———

Gentlemen of the Congress:

It is my duty to call your attention to a situation which has arisen in our dealings with Gen. Victoriano Huerta at Mexico City which calls for action, and to ask your advice and co-operation.

On April 9 a paymaster of the U.S.S. *Dolphin* landed at the Iturbide bridge landing at Tampico with a whaleboat and boat's crew to take off certain supplies for his ship, and while engaged in loading the boat was arrested by an officer and squad of men of the army of General Huerta. Neither the paymaster nor any one of the crew was armed. Two of the men were in the boat when the arrest was made, and were obliged to leave it and submit to be taken into custody, notwithstanding that the boat carried, both at her bow and her stern, the flag of the United States. The officer who made the arrest was proceeding up one of the streets of the town with his prisoners when met by an officer of higher authority, who ordered him to return to the landing and await orders, and within an hour and a half from the time of the arrest, orders were received from the commander of the Huertista forces at Tampico for the release of the paymaster and his men. The release was followed by apologies from the commander and also by an expression of regret by General Huerta himself. General Huerta urged that martial law obtained at the time at Tampico, that orders had been issued that no one should be allowed to land at the Iturbide bridge, and that our sailors had no right to land there. Our naval commanders at the port had not been notified of any such prohibition, and, even if they had been, the only justifiable course open to the local authorities would have been to request the paymaster and his crew to withdraw and to lodge a protest with the commanding officer of the fleet. Admiral [Henry T.] Mayo regarded the arrest as so serious an affront that he was not satisfied with the apologies offered, but demanded that the flag of the United States be saluted with special ceremony by the military commander of the port.[1]

The incident can not be regarded as a trivial one, especially as two of the men arrested were taken from the boat itself—that is to say, from the territory of the United States; but had it stood by itself, it might have been attributed to the ignorance or arrogance of a single officer.

Unfortunately, it was not an isolated case. A series of incidents have recently occurred which can not but create the impression that the representatives of General Huerta were willing to go out of their way to show disregard for the dignity and rights of this Government, and felt perfectly safe in doing what they pleased, making free to show in many ways their irritation and contempt.

A few days after the incident at Tampico an orderly from the U.S.S. *Minnesota* was arrested at Vera Cruz while ashore in uniform to obtain the ship's mail, and was for a time thrown into jail. An official dispatch from this Government to its embassy at Mexico City was withheld by the authorities of the telegraphic service until peremptorily demanded by our Chargé d'Affaires in person.

So far as I can learn, such wrongs and annoyances have been suffered to occur only against representatives of the United States. I have heard of no complaints from other governments of similar treatment. Subsequent explanations and formal apologies did not and could not alter the popular impression, which it is possible it had been the object of the Huertista authorities to create, that the Government of the United States was being singled out, and might be singled out with impunity, for slights and affronts in retaliation for its refusal to recognize the pretensions of General Huerta to be regarded as the Constitutional Provisional President of the Republic of Mexico.

The manifest danger of such a situation was that such offenses might grow from bad to worse until something happened of so gross and intolerable a sort as to lead directly and inevitably to armed conflict. It was necessary that the apologies of General Huerta and his representatives should go much further, that they should be such as to attract the attention of the

---

[1] At the time of the incident, Admiral Mayo was commanding the U.S. naval squadron in the Caribbean.

whole population to their significance, and such as to impress upon General Huerta himself the necessity of seeing to it that no further occasion for explanations and professed regrets should arise. I, therefore, felt it my duty to sustain Admiral Mayo in the whole of his demand and to insist that the flag of the United States should be saluted in such a way as to indicate a new spirit and attitude on the part of the Huertistas.

Such a salute General Huerta has refused, and I have come to ask your approval and support in the course I now propose to pursue.

This Government can, I earnestly hope, in no circumstances be forced into war with the people of Mexico. Mexico is torn by civil strife. If we are to accept the tests of its own Constitution, it has no government. General Huerta has set his power up in the City of Mexico, such as it is, without right and by methods for which there can be no justification. Only part of the country is under his control.

If armed conflict should unhappily come as a result of his attitude of personal resentment toward this Government, we should be fighting only General Huerta and those who adhere to him and give him their support, and our object would be only to restore to the people of the distracted republic the opportunity to set up again their own laws and their own government.

But I earnestly hope that war is not now in question. I believe that I speak for the American people when I say that we do not desire to control in any degree the affairs of our sister republic. Our feeling for the people of Mexico is one of deep and genuine friendship, and everything that we have so far done or refrained from doing has proceeded from our desire to help them, not to hinder or embarrass them. We would not wish even to exercise the good offices of friendship without their welcome and consent.

The people of Mexico are entitled to settle their own domestic affairs in their own way, and we sincerely desire to respect their right. The present situation need have none of the grave complications of interference if we deal with it promptly, firmly, and wisely.

No doubt I could do what is necessary in the circumstances to enforce respect for our Government without recourse to the Congress, and yet not exceed my constitutional power as President; but I do not wish to act in a matter possibly of so grave consequence except in close conference and co-operation with both the Senate and House. I therefore come to ask your approval that I should use the armed forces of the United States in such ways and to such an extent as may be necessary to obtain from General Huerta and his adherents the fullest recognition of the rights and dignity of the United States, even amid the distressing conditions now unhappily obtaining in Mexico.

There can in what we do be no thought of aggression or selfish aggrandizement. We seek to maintain the dignity and authority of the United States only because we wish always to keep our great influence unimpaired for the uses of liberty, both in the United States and wherever else it may be employed for the benefit of mankind.[2]

SOURCE: U.S. State Department, *Foreign Relations of the United States, 1914* (Washington, DC: Government Printing Office, 1922), 474–76.

DOCUMENT 37

PRESIDENT WILSON WARNS THE AMERICAN PUBLIC OF TROUBLES IN MEXICO. JUNE 2, 1915.

For more than two years revolutionary conditions have existed in Mexico. The purpose of the revolution was to rid Mexico of men who ignored the constitution of the Republic and used their power in contempt of the rights of its people; and with these purposes the people of the United States instinctively and generously sympathized. But the leaders of the revolution, in the very hour of their success, have disagreed and turned their arms against one another. All professing the same objects, they are nevertheless unable or unwilling to cooperate. A central authority at Mexico City is no sooner set up than it is undermined and its authority denied by those who were expected to support it. Mexico is apparently no nearer a solution of her tragical troubles than she was when the revolution was first kindled. And she has been swept by civil war as if by fire. Her crops are destroyed, her fields lie unseeded, her work cattle are confiscated for the use of the armed factions, her people flee to the mountains to escape being drawn into unavailing bloodshed, and no man seems to see or lead the way to peace and settled order. There is no proper protection either for her own citizens or for the citizens of other nations resident and at work within her territory. Mexico is starving and without a government.

[2] A congressional joint resolution on April 22 gave President Wilson the approval to use U.S. armed forces, if necessary, to require that General Huerta make unequivocal amends to "the dignity and authority of the United States."

In these circumstances the people and Government of the United States can not stand indifferently by and do nothing to serve their neighbor. They want nothing for themselves in Mexico. Least of all do they desire to settle her affairs for her, or claim any right to do so. But neither do they wish to see utter ruin come upon her, and they deem it their duty as friends and neighbors to lend any aid they properly can to any instrumentality which promises to be effective in bringing about a settlement which will embody the real objects of the revolution—constitutional government and the rights of the people. Patriotic Mexicans are sick at heart and cry out for peace and for every self-sacrifice that may be necessary to procure it. Their people cry out for food and will presently hate as much as they fear every man, in their country or out of it, who stands between them and their daily bread.

It is time, therefore, that the Government of the United States should frankly state the policy which in these extraordinary circumstances it becomes its duty to adopt. It must presently do what it has not hitherto done or felt at liberty to do: lend its active moral support to some man or group of men, if such may be found, who can rally the suffering people of Mexico to their support in an effort to ignore, if they cannot unite, the warring factions of the country, return to the constitution of the Republic so long in abeyance, and set up a government at Mexico City which the great powers of the world can recognize and deal with, a government with whom the program of the revolution will be a business and not merely a platform. I, therefore, publicly and very solemnly, call upon the leaders of faction in Mexico to act, to act together, and to act promptly for the relief and redemption of their prostrate country. I feel it to be my duty to tell them that, if they cannot accommodate their differences and unite for this great purpose within a very short time, this Government will be constrained to decide what means should be employed by the United States in order to help Mexico save herself and serve her people.

SOURCE: *Foreign Relations of the United States, 1915,* 694–95.

DOCUMENT 38

PRESIDENT WILSON'S STATE OF THE UNION MESSAGE ON RELATIONS WITH MEXICO. DECEMBER 7, 1915.

...There was a time in the early days of our own great nation and of the republics lighting their way to independence in Central and South

America when the government of the United States looked upon itself as in some sort the guardian of the republics to the south of her as against any encroachments or efforts at political control from the other side of the water; felt it its duty to play the part even without invitation from them; and I think that we can claim that the task was undertaken with a true and disinterested enthusiasm for the freedom of the Americas and the unmolested self-government of her independent peoples. But it was always difficult to maintain such a role without offence to the pride of the peoples whose freedom of action we sought to protect, and without provoking serious misconceptions of our motives, and every thoughtful man of affairs must welcome the altered circumstances of the new day in whose light we now stand, when there is no claim of guardianship or thought of wards but, instead, a full and honorable association as of partners between ourselves and our neighbours, in the interest of all America, north and south. Our concern for the independence and prosperity of the states of Central and South America is not altered. We retain unabated the spirit that has inspired us throughout the whole life of our government and which was so frankly put into words by President Monroe. We still mean always to make a common cause of national independence and of political liberty in America. But that purpose is now better understood so far as it concerns ourselves. It is known not to be a selfish purpose. It is known to have in it no thought of taking advantage of any government in this hemisphere or playing its political fortunes for our own benefit. All the governments of America stand, so far as we are concerned, upon a footing of genuine equality and unquestioned independence.

We have been put to the test in the case of Mexico, and we have stood the test. Whether we have benefited Mexico by the course we have pursued remains to be seen. Her fortunes are in her own hands. But we have at least proved that we will not take advantage of her in her distress and undertake to impose upon her an order and government of our own choosing. Liberty is often a fierce and intractable thing, to which no bounds can be set, and to which no bounds of a few men's choosing ought ever to be set. Every American who has drunk at the true fountains of principle and tradition must subscribe without reservation to the high doctrine of the Virginia Bill of Rights, which in the great days in which our government was set up was everywhere amongst us accepted as the creed of freemen. That doctrine is, "That government is, or ought to be, instituted for the common benefit, protection, and security of the people, nation, or community"; that "of all the various modes and forms of government, that is the best which is capable of producing the greatest degree of happiness and safety, and is most effectually secured against the danger of maladministration; and that, when any government shall be found inadequate or contrary to these purposes, a majority of the community hath an indubitable, inalienable, and indefeasible right to reform, alter, or abolish it, in such manner as shall be judged most conducive to the public weal." We have unhesitatingly applied that heroic principle to the case of Mexico, and now hopefully await the rebirth of the troubled Republic, which had so much of which to purge itself and so little sympathy from any outside quarter in the radical but necessary process. We will aid and befriend Mexico, but we will not coerce her; and our course with regard to her ought to be sufficient proof to all America that we seek no political suzerainty or selfish control.

The moral is, that the states of America are not hostile rivals but cooperating friends, and that their growing sense of community of interest, alike in matters political and in matters economic, is likely to give them a new significance as factors in international affairs and in the political history of the world. It presents them as in a very deep and true sense a unit in world affairs, spiritual partners, standing together because thinking together, quick with common sympathies and common ideals. Separated they are subject to all the cross currents of the confused politics of a world of hostile rivalries; united in spirit and purpose they cannot be disappointed of their peaceful destiny.

This is Pan-Americanism. It has none of the spirit of empire in it. It is the embodiment, the effectual embodiment, of the spirit of law and independence and liberty and mutual service.

SOURCE: U.S. State Department, *Foreign Relations of the United States, 1915* (Washington, DC: Government Printing Office, 1924), ix–xi.

DOCUMENT 39
WHITE HOUSE PRESS RELEASE FOLLOWING PANCHO VILLA'S RAID ON COLUMBUS, NEW MEXICO. MARCH 10, 1916.

An adequate force will be sent at once in pursuit of Villa with the single object of capturing him and putting a stop to his forays. This can and will be done in entirely friendly aid of the constituted authorities in Mexico and with scrupulous respect for the sovereignty of that Republic.

SOURCE: U.S. State Department, *Foreign Relations of the United States, 1916* (Washington, DC: Government Printing Office, 1925), 486.

DOCUMENT 40

PRESIDENT WILSON NOTIFIES HIS SECRETARIES OF STATE AND WAR OF HIS PUNITIVE EXPEDITION RESPONSE TO VILLA'S RAID. MARCH 13, 1916.

My Dear Mr. Secretary [of State, Robert Lansing]:

Here is the statement I suggested during our conversation this afternoon. I would be very much obliged if you would issue it at your ea[r]ly convenience. . . .

Will you not be kind enough to communicate this immediately to the Secretary of War [Newton D. Baker].

ENCLOSURE

In order to remove any apprehensions that may exist either in the United States or in Mexico, the President has authorized me to give in his name the public assurance that the military operations now in contemplation by this Government will be scrupulously confined to the object already announced, and that in no circumstances will they be suffered to infringe in any degree upon the sovereignty of Mexico or develop into intervention of any kind in the internal affairs of our sister Republic. On the contrary, what is now being done is deliberately intended to preclude the possibility of intervention.

SOURCE: *Foreign Relations of the United States, 1916*, 489; and Arthur S. Link, ed., *The Papers of Woodrow Wilson*, 58 vols. (Princeton, NJ: Princeton University Press, 1981), 36:298.

DOCUMENT 41

PRESIDENT WILSON'S INSTRUCTIONS ON PRESS COVERAGE OF THE MILITARY EXPEDITION INTO MEXICO. MARCH 14, 1916.

My Dear Mr. [Acting Secretary of State Frank L.] Polk:

Here is a letter from a newspaper man whom I think you know that contains some interesting suggestions. I would be very much obliged if you would prepare such a request as is suggested in the paragraph marked "3" so that we may discuss it together, and, if we finally think it wise, may send for the representatives of the three principal press associations and ask their cooperation.

Cordially and sincerely yours, *Woodrow Wilson*

ENCLOSURE

Personal March 13, 1916

Dear Mr. President:

In the present delicate situation the press can be a helpful as well as a dangerous factor, and I want to draw your attention to some steps that might be taken by you to keep the newspapers from causing trouble.

1. The head of every bureau and news service in Washington, the *head* of each Washington newspaper, and correspondents especially of newspapers published in the border states, should be summoned to the White House and impressed with the fact that the news dispatches they write must be tempered; that they must consider the sensitiveness of the Mexican people and at this time refrain from any unfavorable mention of [President Venustiano] Carranza or his government, the spread of stories about our relations with the Carranza government that might indicate friction or a likelihood of it; that above all stories hinting at a general invasion or talk of preparations that would give the impression of a large military movement should be avoided.

2. This should be supplemented by a statement from you calling on the press of the United States and especially the newspapers published in border towns and states to refrain at this time from publishing any stories that might inflame public opinion, anatagonize [antagonize] the Carranza government or Mexicans generally, or which might give to the present small expedition the character of a general invasion or intervention.

3. Each of the news services—the Associated Press, the United Press, the International News Service, and the Central News—should be asked to send privately to all their clients, both day and night, a request that stories of troop movements or preparations that might be interpreted as meaning war be withheld, and that the requests made in your public statement be scrupulously observed.

4. Our military commanders at the border points should be instructed to give interviews to the local papers where they are stationed

pointing out that there is no intention of invading Mexico but to pursue Villa in accordance with the precedents; that, of course, as soon as the Carranza troops are in control and Villa is captured our forces will be withdrawn and that just now the American government is viewing favorably the request of Gen. Carranza for the reciprocal privilege asked for in his communication. (I am satisfied that this privilege was asked for not to be exercised for it need not be if we have sufficient troops alone [along] our boundary but to calm Mexican public opinion).

Much importance is always attached in border towns to interviews given by military commanders. It calms our own people as well.

All these steps may seem to you to be making a mountain out of a molehill but each day that the situation continues as it is increases the danger of a general uprising against our troops the end of which would be a purposeless war. The newspapers have been saying too much about "US refuses to cooperate with Carranza troops" and have been doing a great deal of damage giving the impression that we do not want Carranza's help etc. I particularly fear the effect of all this on that garrison at Juarez and I would even advise that special request be made of the two El Paso newspapers to do everything possible to avoid friction.

Very sincerely, *David Lawrence*

SOURCE: Link, *Papers of Woodrow Wilson*, 36:307–9.

DOCUMENT 42
PRESIDENT WILSON'S STATEMENT OF INTENT FOR THE PUNITIVE EXPEDITION INTO MEXICO AND WARNING TO THE AMERICAN PRESS. MARCH 25, 1916.

As has already been announced, the expedition into Mexico was ordered under an agreement with the de facto Government of Mexico for the single purpose of taking the bandit Villa, whose forces had actually invaded the territory of the United States, and is in no sense intended as an invasion of the republic or as an infringement of its sovereignty.

I have, therefore, asked the several news services to be good enough to assist the Administration in keeping this view of the expedition constantly before both the people of this country and the distressed and sensitive people of Mexico, who are very susceptible, indeed, to impressions received from the American press, not only, but also very ready to believe that those impressions proceed from the views and objects of our Government itself. Such conclusions, it must be said, are not unnatural, because the main, if not the only, source of information for the people on both sides of the border is the public press of the United States.

In order to avoid the creation of erroneous and dangerous impressions in this way I have called upon the several news agencies to use the utmost care not to give news stories regarding this expedition the color of war, to withhold stories of troop movements and military preparations which might be given that interpretation, and to refrain from publishing unverified rumors of unrest in Mexico.

I feel that it is most desirable to impress upon both our own people and the people of Mexico the fact that the expedition is simply a necessary punitive measure, aimed solely at the elimination of the marauders, who raided Columbus and who infest an unprotected district near the border, which they use as a base in making attacks upon the lives and property of our citizens within our own territory. It is the purpose of our commanders to co-operate in every possible way with the forces of General Carranza in removing this cause of irritation to both Governments, and retire from Mexican territory so soon as that object is accomplished.

It is my duty to warn the people of the United States that there are persons all along the border who are actively engaged in originating and giving as wide currency as they can to rumors of the most sensational and disturbing sort, which are wholly unjustified by the facts. The object of this traffic in falsehood is obvious. It is to create intolerable friction between the Government of the United States and the de facto Government of Mexico for the purpose of bringing about intervention in the interest of certain American owners of Mexican properties. This object can not be attained so long as sane and honorable men are in control of this Government, but very serious conditions may be created, unnecessary bloodshed may result, and the relations between the two republics may be very much embarrassed.

The people of the United States should know the sinister and unscrupulous influences that are afoot, and should be on their guard against accepting any story coming from the border; and those who disseminate the news should make it a matter of patriotism and of conscience to test the source and authenticity of every report they receive from that quarter.

SOURCE: Link, *Papers of Woodrow Wilson*, 36:364–66.

DOCUMENT 43

PRESIDENT WILSON'S PRESS CONFERENCE REMARKS CONCERNING U.S. INTERVENTION IN HAITI AND THE DOMINICAN REPUBLIC. JULY 23, 1914.

Mr. President, can you tell us something about the government's attitude in the Haitian situation? I refer particularly to the fact that announcement was made by the War and Navy Departments that several marines were going to be sent to Guantánamo, to be held in readiness there for eventualities in Haiti and Santo Domingo, although we understood that Haiti was meant particularly. That indicates that the administration certainly has some policy in view that might involve the use of force.

President Wilson: No. It indicates only that the administration has some anxiety with regard to the case. It is one of those situations that is just bristling with interrogation points. I don't know what is going to happen from day to day. We didn't feel at liberty to be so far away that if it should appear with regard to saving lives, for example, or interests that ought to be protected, then we could not act, but it doesn't in any way seem plain.

Could you say, Mr. President, whether any negotiations are afoot now for taking over the customs revenues of Haiti under the—

President Wilson: No, sir. There are no negotiations.

Mr. President, has this government sent anything to the government of Haiti and Santo Domingo about the necessity of restoring order?

President Wilson: Yes, sir. We have been very eloquent on that.

Do the representations approach an ultimatum?

President Wilson: We can't get the audience to sit still long enough to hear us, like some other audiences that I have addressed.

Could you tell us, when you catch them, what you are going to say to them?

President Wilson: No, that's too conjectural.

SOURCE: Link, *Papers of Woodrow Wilson*, 30:296–97.

DOCUMENT 44

PRESIDENT WILSON'S MESSAGE TO CONGRESS REQUESTING DECLARATION OF WAR AGAINST GERMANY. APRIL 2, 1917.

Gentlemen of the Congress:

I have called the Congress into extraordinary session because there are serious, very serious, choices of policy to be made, and made immediately which it was neither right nor constitutionally permissible that I should assume the responsibility of making.

On the third of February last, I officially laid before you the extraordinary announcement of the Imperial German Government that on and after the first day of February it was its purpose to put aside all restraints of law or of humanity and use its submarines to sink every vessel that sought to approach either the ports of Great Britain and Ireland or the western coast of Europe or any of the ports controlled by the enemies of Germany within the Mediterranean. That had seemed to be the object of the German submarine warfare earlier in the war; but since April of last year the Imperial Government had somewhat restrained the commanders of its undersea craft, in conformity with its promise then given to us that passenger boats should not be sunk, and that due warning would be given to all other vessels which its submarines might seek to destroy, when no resistance was offered or escape attempted, and care taken that their crews were given at least a fair chance to save their lives in their open boats. The precautions taken were meager and haphazard enough, as was proved in distressing instance after instance in the progress of the cruel and unmanly business, but a certain degree of restraint was observed.

The new policy has swept every restriction aside. Vessels of every kind, whatever their flag, their character, their cargo, their destination, their errand, have been ruthlessly sent to the bottom without warning and without thought of help or mercy for those on board—the vessels of friendly neutrals along with those of belligerents. Even hospital ships and ships carrying relief to the sorely bereaved and stricken people of Belgium, though the latter were provided with safe conduct through the proscribed areas by the German Government itself, and were distinguished by unmistakable marks of identity, have been sunk with the same reckless lack of compassion or of principle.

I was for a little while unable to believe that such things would in fact be done by any government that had hitherto subscribed to the humane practices of civilized nations. International law had its origin in the attempt to set up some law which would be respected and observed upon the seas, where no nation had right of dominion and where lay the free highways of the world. By painful stage after stage has that law been built up, with meager enough results, indeed, after all was accomplished that could be accomplished, but always with a clear view, at least, of what the heart and conscience of mankind demanded.

This minimum of right the German Government has swept aside under the plea of retaliation and necessity, and because it had no weapons which it could use at sea except these which it is impossible to employ as it is employing them without throwing to the winds all scruples of humanity or of respect for the understandings that were supposed to underlie the intercourse of the world.

I am not now thinking of the loss of property involved, immense and serious as that is, but only of the wanton and wholesale destruction of the lives of non-combatants, men, women, and children, engaged in pursuits which have always, even in the darkest period of modern history, been deemed innocent and legitimate. Property can be paid for; the lives of peaceful and innocent people can not be.

The present German submarine warfare against commerce is a warfare against mankind. It is a war against all nations. American ships have been sunk, American lives taken in ways which it has stirred us very deeply to learn of, but the ships and people of other neutral and friendly nations have been sunk and overwhelmed in the waters in the same way. There has been no discrimination. The challenge is to all mankind. Each nation must decide for itself how it will meet it. The choice we make for ourselves must be made with a moderation of counsel and a temperateness of judgment befitting our character and our motives as a nation.

We must put excited feeling away. Our motive will not be revenge or the victorious assertion of the physical might of the nation, but only the vindication of right, of human right, of which we are only a single champion.

When I addressed the Congress on the 26th of February last, I thought that it would suffice to assert our neutral right with arms; our right to use the sea against unlawful interference; our right to keep our people safe against unlawful violence. But armed neutrality, it now appears, is impracticable. Because submarines are in effect outlaws when used as the German submarines have been used against merchant shipping, it is impossible to defend ships against their attacks as the law of nations has assumed that merchantmen would defend themselves against privateers or cruisers, visible craft giving chase upon the open sea. It is common prudence in such circumstances, grim necessity indeed, to endeavor to destroy them before they have shown their own intention. They must be dealt with upon sight, if dealt with at all.

The German Government denies the right of neutrals to use arms at all within the areas of the sea which it has proscribed, even in the defense of rights which no modern publicist has ever before questioned their right to defend. The intimation is conveyed that the armed guards which we have placed on our merchant ships will be treated as beyond the pale of law and subject to be dealt with as pirates would be. Armed neutrality is ineffectual enough at best; in such circumstances and in the face of such pretensions, it is worse than ineffectual; it is likely only to produce what it was meant to prevent; it is practically certain to draw us into the war without either the rights or the effectiveness of belligerents.

There is one choice we cannot make, we are incapable of making—we will not choose the path of submission and suffer the most sacred rights of our nation and our people to be ignored or violated. The wrongs against which we now array ourselves are no common wrongs; they cut to the very roots of human life.

With a profound sense of the solemn and even tragical character of the step I am taking and of the grave responsibilities which it involves, but in unhesitating obedience to what I deem my constitutional duty, I advise that the Congress declare the recent course of the Imperial German Government to be, in fact, nothing less than war against the Government and people of the United States; that it formally accept the status of belligerent which has thus been thrust upon it; and that it take immediate steps not only to put the country in a more thorough state of defense, but also to exert all its power and employ all its resources to bring the Government of the German Empire to terms and end the war.

What this will involve is clear. It will involve the utmost practicable cooperation in counsel and action with the governments now at war with Germany; and, as incident to that, the extension to those governments of the most liberal financial credits, in order that our resources may, so far as possible, be added to theirs. It will involve the organization and mobilization of all the material resources of the country to supply the materials of war and serve the incidental needs of the nation in the most abundant and yet the most economical and efficient way possible. It will involve the immediate full equipment of the navy in all respects, but particularly in supplying it with the best means of dealing with the enemy's submarines. It will involve the immediate addition to the armed forces of the United States already provided for by law in case of war at least 500,000 men, who should, in my opinion, be chosen upon the principle of universal liability to service, and also the authorization of subsequent additional increments of equal force so soon as they may be needed and can be handled in training.

It will involve also, of course, the granting of adequate credits to the Government, sustained, I hope, so far as they can equitably be sustained, by the present generation, by well-conceived taxation. I say sustained so far as may be equitable by taxation because it seems to me that it would be most unwise to base the credits which will now be necessary entirely on money borrowed. It is our duty, I most respectfully urge, to protect our people so far as we may against the very serious hardships and evils which would be likely to arise out of the inflation which would be produced by vast loans.

In carrying out the measures by which these things are to be accomplished, we should keep constantly in mind the wisdom of interfering as little as possible in our own preparation and in the equipment of military forces with the duty—for it will be a very practical duty—of supplying the nations already at war with Germany with the materials which they can obtain only from us or by our assistance. They are in the field, and we should help them in every way to be effective there.

I shall take the liberty of suggesting, through the several executive departments of the Government, for the consideration of your committees, measures for the accomplishment of the several objects I have mentioned. I hope that it will be your pleasure to deal with them as having been framed after very careful thought by the branch of the Government upon which the responsibility of conducting the war and safeguarding the nation will most directly fall.

While we do these things, these deeply momentous things, let us be very clear, and make very clear to all the world what our motives and our objects are. My own thought has not been driven from its habitual and normal course by the unhappy events of the last two months, and I do not believe that the thought of the nation has been altered or clouded by them.

I have exactly the same things in mind now that I had in mind when I addressed the Senate on the 22d of January last; the same that I had in mind when I addressed the Congress on the 3d of February and on the 26th of February. Our object now, as then, is to vindicate the principles of peace and justice in the life of the world as against selfish and autocratic power and to set up among the really free and self-governed peoples of the world such a concert of purpose and of action as will henceforth insure the observance of those principles.

Neutrality is no longer feasible or desirable where the peace of the world is involved and the freedom of its peoples, and the menace to that peace and freedom lies in the existence of autocratic governments backed by organized force which is controlled wholly by their will, not by the will of their people. We have seen the last of neutrality in such circumstances.

We are at the beginning of an age where it will be insisted that the same standards of conduct and of responsibility for wrong done shall be observed among nations and their governments that are observed among the individual citizens of civilized states.

We have no quarrel with the German people. We have no feeling toward them but one of sympathy and friendship. It was not upon their impulse that their Government acted in entering this war. It was not with their previous knowledge or approval.

It was a war determined upon as wars used to be determined upon in the old, unhappy days when peoples were nowhere consulted by their rulers and wars were provoked and waged in the interest of dynasties or of little groups of ambitious men who were accustomed to use their fellow-men as pawns and tools.

Self-governed nations do not fill their neighbor states with spies or set the course of intrigue to bring about some critical posture of affairs which will give them an opportunity to strike and make conquest. Such designs can be successfully worked out only under cover and where no one has the right to ask questions.

Cunningly contrived plans of deception or aggression, carried, it may be, from generation to generation, can be worked out and kept from the light only within the privacy of courts or behind the carefully guarded confidences of a narrow and privileged class. They are happily impossible where public opinion commands and insists upon full information concerning all the nation's affairs.

A steadfast concert for peace can never be maintained except by a partnership of democratic nations. No autocratic government could be trusted to keep faith within it or observe its covenants. It must be a league of honor, a partnership of opinion. Intrigue would eat its vitals away; the plottings of inner circles who could plan what they would and render account to no one would be a corruption seated at its very heart. Only free peoples can hold their purpose and their honor steady to a common end and prefer the interests of mankind to any narrow interest of their own.

Does not every American feel that assurance has been added to our hope for the future peace of the world by the wonderful and heartening things that have been happening within the last few weeks in Russia?[1]

---

[1]President Wilson is referring to the March revolution of 1917 that replaced Czar Nicholas II with a social-democratic government.

Russia was known by those who knew her best to have been always in fact democratic at heart, in all the vital habits of her thought, in all the intimate relationships of her people that spoke their natural instinct, their habitual attitude toward life.

The autocracy that crowned the summit of her political structure, long as it had stood and terrible as was the reality of its power, was not in fact Russian in origin, character, or purpose; and now it has been shaken off and the great generous Russian people have been added in all their native majesty and might to the forces that are fighting for freedom in the world, for justice and for peace. Here is a fit partner for a league of honor.

One of the things that has served to convince us that the Prussian autocracy was not and could never be our friend is that from the very outset of the present war it has filled our unsuspecting communities and even our offices of government with spies and set criminal intrigues everywhere afoot against our national unity of council, our peace within and without, our industries and our commerce.

Indeed, it is now evident that its spies were here even before the war began; and it unhappily is not a matter of conjecture, but a fact proved in our courts of justice, that the intrigues which have more than once come perilously near to disturbing the peace and dislocating the industries of the country have been carried on at the instigation, with the support, and even under the personal direction of official agents of the Imperial Government accredited to the Government of the United States.

Even in checking these things and trying to extirpate them, we have sought to put the most generous interpretation possible upon them because we knew that their source lay, not in any hostile feeling or purpose of the German people toward us (who were, no doubt, as ignorant of them as we ourselves were), but only in the selfish designs of a government that did what it pleased and told its people nothing. But they have played their part in serving to convince us at last that that government entertains no real friendship for us and means to act against our peace and security at its convenience. That it means to stir up enemies against us at our very doors, the intercepted note to the German Minister at Mexico City is eloquent evidence.[2]

---

[2]In early 1917, German Foreign Minister Arthur Zimmermann secretly proposed an alliance with Mexico if the Mexican government would declare war on the United States. In return, Germany was prepared to support Mexican claims to Texas, New Mexico, and Arizona. Germany hoped that an American war against Mexico would keep the United States out of the war in Europe. The disclosure of the British-intercepted Zimmermann Telegram, detailing the proposed alliance, inflamed American public opinion against Germany and was one of the proximate causes of America's entry into the World War.

We are accepting this challenge of hostile purpose because we know that in such a government, following such methods, we can never have a friend; and that in the presence of its organized power always lying in wait to accomplish we know not what purpose, there can be no assured security for the democratic governments of the world.

We are now about to accept a gage of battle with this natural foe to liberty and shall, if necessary, spend the whole force of the nation to check and nullify its pretensions and end its power. We are glad, now that we see the facts with no veil of false pretense about them, to fight thus for the ultimate peace of the world and for the liberation of its peoples, the German peoples included; for the rights of nations great and small and the privilege of men everywhere to choose their way of life and of obedience. The world must be made safe for democracy. Its peace must be planted upon the tested foundations of political liberty.

We have no selfish ends to serve. We desire no conquest, no dominion. We seek no indemnities for ourselves, no material compensation for the sacrifices we shall freely make. We are but one of the champions of the rights of mankind. We shall be satisfied when those rights have been made as secure as the faith and the freedom of the nations can make them.

Just because we fight without rancor and without selfish object, seeking nothing for ourselves but what we shall wish to share with all free peoples, we shall, I feel confident, conduct our operations as belligerents without passion and ourselves observe with proud punctilio the principles of right and of fair play we profess to be fighting for.

I have said nothing of the Governments allied with the Imperial Government of Germany because they have not made war upon us or challenged us to defend our right and our honor. The Austro-Hungarian Government has, indeed, avowed its unqualified endorsement and acceptance of the reckless and lawless submarine warfare adopted now without disguise by the Imperial German Government, and it has therefore not been possible for this Government to receive Count [Adam] Tarnowski, the Ambassador recently accredited to this Government by the Imperial and Royal Government of Austria-Hungary; but that Government has not actually engaged in warfare against citizens of the United States on the seas, and I take the liberty, for the present at least, of postponing a discussion of our relations with the authorities at Vienna. We enter this war only where we are clearly forced into it because there are no other means of defending our rights.

It will be all the easier for us to conduct ourselves as belligerents in a high spirit of right and fairness because we act without animus, not in enmity toward a people nor with the desire to bring any injury or disadvantage upon them, but only in armed opposition to an irresponsible Government which has thrown aside all considerations of humanity and of right and is running amuck.

We are, let me say again, the sincere friends of the German people, and shall desire nothing so much as the early re-establishment of intimate relations of mutual advantage between us—however hard it may be for them, for the time being, to believe that this is spoken from our hearts. We have borne with their present Government through all these bitter months because of that friendship—exercising a patience and forbearance which would otherwise have been impossible. We shall, happily, still have an opportunity to prove that friendship in our daily attitude and actions toward the millions of men and women of German birth and native sympathy who live among us and share our life, and we shall be proud to prove it toward all who are in fact loyal to their neighbors and to the Government in the hour of test. They are, most of them, as true and loyal Americans as if they had never known any other fealty or allegiance. They will be prompt to stand with us in rebuking and restraining the few who may be of a different mind and purpose.

If there should be disloyalty, it will be dealt with with a firm hand of stern repression; but if it lifts its head at all, it will lift it only here and there and without countenance, except from a lawless and malignant few.

It is a distressing and oppressive duty, gentlemen of the Congress, which I have performed in thus addressing you. There are, it may be, many months of fiery trial and sacrifice ahead of us. It is a fearful thing to lead this great peaceful people into war, into the most terrible and disastrous of all wars, civilization itself seeming to be in the balance. But the right is more precious than peace, and we shall fight for the things which we have always carried nearest our hearts—for democracy, for the right of those who submit to authority to have a voice in their own governments, for the rights and liberties of small nations, for a universal domination of right by such a concert of free peoples as shall bring peace and safety to all nations and make the world itself at last free. To such a task we can dedicate our lives and our fortunes, everything that we are and everything that we have, with the price of those who know that the day has come when America is privileged to spend her blood and her might for the principles that gave her birth and happiness and the peace which she has treasured. God helping her, she can do no other.

SOURCE: U.S. State Department, *Foreign Relations of the United States, 1917*, 3 vols. (Washington, DC: Government Printing Office, 1924), 2:195–203.

DOCUMENT 45

PRESIDENT WILSON'S AIDE-MÉMOIRE OF U.S. INTERVENTION IN RUSSIA AS COMMUNICATED TO BRITAIN, FRANCE, ITALY, AND JAPAN. JULY 17, 1918.

The whole heart of the people of the United States is in the winning of this war. The controlling purpose of the Government of the United States is to do everything that is necessary and effective to win it. It wishes to cooperate in every practicable way with the allied governments, and to cooperate ungrudgingly; for it has no ends of its own to serve and believes that the war can be won only by common counsel and intimate concert of action. It has sought to study every proposed policy or action in which its cooperation has been asked in this spirit, and states the following conclusions in the confidence that, if it finds itself obliged to decline participation in any undertaking or course of action, it will be understood that it does so only because it deems itself precluded from participating by imperative considerations either of policy or of fact.

In full agreement with the allied governments and upon the unanimous advice of the Supreme War Council, the Government of the United States adopted, upon its entrance into the war, a plan for taking part in the fighting on the western front into which all its resources of men and material were to be put, and put as rapidly as possible, and it has carried out that plan with energy and success, pressing its execution more and more rapidly forward and literally putting into it the entire energy and executive force of the nation. This was its response, its very willing and hearty response, to what was the unhesitating judgment alike of its own military advisers and of the advisers of the allied governments. It is now considering, at the suggestion of the Supreme War Council, the possibility of making very considerable additions even to this immense programme which, if they should prove feasible at all, will tax the industrial processes of the United States and the shipping facilities of the whole group of associated nations to the utmost. It has thus concentrated all its plans and all its resources upon this single absolutely necessary object.

In such circumstances it feels it to be its duty to say that it cannot, so long as the military situation on the western front remains critical, consent to break or slacken the force of its present effort by diverting any part of its military force to other points or objectives. The United States is at a great distance from the field of action on the western front; it is at a much greater distance from any other field of action. The instrumentalities by which it is to handle its armies and its stores have at great cost and with great difficulty been created in France. They do not exist elsewhere. It is practicable for her to do a great deal in France; it is not practicable for her to do anything of importance or on a large scale upon any other field. The American Government, therefore, very respectfully requests its Associates to accept its deliberate judgment that it should not dissipate its force by attempting important operations elsewhere.

It regards the Italian front as closely coordinated with the western front, however, and is willing to divert a portion of its military forces from France to Italy if it is the judgment and wish of the Supreme Command that it should do so. It wishes to defer to the decision of the Commander-in-chief in this matter, as it would wish to defer in all others, particularly because it considers these two fronts so closely related as to be practically but separate parts of a single line and because it would be necessary that any American troops sent to Italy should be subtracted from the number used in France and be actually transported across French territory from the ports now used by the armies of the United States.

It is the clear and fixed judgment of the Government of the United States, arrived at after repeated and very searching reconsiderations of the whole situation in Russia, that military intervention there would add to the present sad confusion in Russia rather than cure it, injure her rather than help her, and that it would be of no advantage in the prosecution of our main design, to win the war against Germany. It cannot, therefore, take part in such intervention or sanction it in principle. Military intervention would, in its judgment, even supposing it to be efficacious in its immediate avowed object of delivering an attack upon Germany from the east, be merely a method of making use of Russia, not a method of serving her. Her people could not profit by it, if they profited by it at all, in time to save them from their present distresses, and their substance would be used to maintain foreign armies, not to reconstitute their own. Military action is admissible in Russia, as the Government of the United States sees the circumstances, only to help the Czecho-Slovaks consolidate their forces and get into successful cooperation with their Slavic kinsmen and to steady any efforts at self-government or self-defence in which the Russians themselves may be willing to accept assistance. Whether from Vladivostok or from Murmansk and Archangel, the only legitimate object for which American or allied troops can be employed, it submits, is to guard military stores which may subsequently be needed by Russian forces and to render such aid as may be acceptable to the Russians in the organization of their own self-defence. For helping the Czecho-Slovaks there is immediate necessity and sufficient justification. Recent developments have made it evident that that is in the interest of what the Russian people themselves desire, and the Government of the United States is glad to contribute the small force at its disposal for that purpose. It yields, also, to the judgment of the Supreme Command in the matter of establishing a small force at Murmansk, to guard the military stores at Kola and to make it safe for Russian forces to come together in organized bodies in the north. But it owes it to frank counsel to say that it can go no further than these modest and experimental plans. It is not in a position, and has no expectation of being in a position, to take part in organized intervention in adequate force from either Vladivostok or Murmansk and Archangel. It feels that it ought to add, also, that it will feel at liberty to use the few troops it can spare only for the purposes here stated and shall feel obliged to withdraw those forces, in order to add them to the forces at the western front, if the plans in whose execution it is now intended that they should cooperate should develop into others inconsistent with the policy to which the Government of the United States feels constrained to restrict itself.

At the same time the Government of the United States wishes to say with the utmost cordiality and good will that none of the conclusions here stated is meant to wear the least color of criticism of what the other governments associated against Germany may think it wise to undertake. It wishes in no way to embarrass their choices of policy. All that is intended here is a perfectly frank and definite statement of the policy which the United States feels obliged to adopt for herself and in the use of her own military forces. The Government of the United States does not wish it to be understood that in so restricting its own activities it is seeking, even by implication, to set limits to the action or to define the policies of its Associates.

It hopes to carry out the plans for safeguarding the rear of the Czecho-Slovaks operating from Vladivostok in a way that will place it and keep it in close cooperation with a small military force like its own from Japan, and if necessary from the other allies, and that will assure it of the cordial accord of all the allied powers; and it proposes to ask all associated in this course of action to unite in assuring the people of Russia in the most public and solemn manner that none of the governments uniting in action either in Siberia or in northern Russia contemplates any interference of any kind with the political sovereignty of Russia, any intervention in her internal affairs, or any impairment of her territorial integrity either now or hereafter, but that each of the associated powers has the single object of affording such aid as shall be acceptable, and only such aid as shall be acceptable, to the Russian people in their endeavor to regain control of their own affairs, their own territory, and their own destiny.

It is the hope and purpose of the Government of the United States to take advantage of the earliest opportunity to send to Siberia a commission of merchants, agricultural experts, labour advisers, Red Cross representatives, and agents of the Young Men's Christian Association accustomed to organizing the best methods of spreading useful information and rendering educational help of a modest sort, in order in some systematic manner to relieve the immediate economic necessities of the people there in every way for which opportunity may open. The execution of this plan will follow and will not be permitted to embarrass the military assistance rendered in the rear of the westward-moving forces of the Czecho-Slovaks.

SOURCE: U.S. State Department, *Foreign Relations of the United States, 1918: Russia*, 3 vols. (Washington, DC: Government Printing Office, 1932), 2:286–90.

DOCUMENT 46
PRESIDENT WILSON'S PRESS STATEMENT CONCERNING AMERICAN-JAPANESE INTERVENTION IN RUSSIA.
AUGUST 5, 1918.

In the judgment of the Government of the United States,—a judgment arrived at after repeated and very searching considerations of the whole situation,—military intervention in Russia would be more likely to add to the present sad confusion there than to cure it, and would injure Russia rather than help her out of her distresses. Such military intervention as has been most frequently proposed, even supposing it to be efficacious in its immediate object of delivering an attack upon Germany from the east, would, in its judgment, be more likely to turn out to be merely a method of making use of Russia than to be a method of serving her. Her people, if they profited by it at all, could not profit by it in time to deliver them from their present desperate difficulties, and their substance would meantime be used to maintain foreign armies, not to reconstitute their own or to feed their own men, women, and children. We are bending all our energies now to the purpose, the resolute and confident purpose, of winning on the western front, and it would in the judgment of the Government of the United States be most unwise to divide or dissipate our forces.

As the Government of the United States sees the present circumstances, therefore, military action is admissible in Russia now only to render such protection and help as is possible to the Czecho-Slovaks against the armed Austrian and German prisoners who are attacking them and to steady any efforts at self-government or self-defense in which the Russians themselves may be willing to accept assistance. Whether from Vladivostok or from Murmansk and Archangel, the only present object for which American troops will be employed will be to guard military stores which may subsequently be needed by Russian forces and to render such aid as may be acceptable to the Russians in the organization of their own self-defence.

With such objects in view the Government of the United States is now cooperating with the governments of France and Great Britain in the neighborhood of Murmansk and Archangel. The United States and Japan are the only powers which are just now in a position to act in Siberia in sufficient force to accomplish even such modest objects as those that have been outlined. The Government of the United States has, therefore, proposed to the Government of Japan that each of the two governments send a force of a few thousand men to Vladivostok, with the purpose of cooperating as a single force in the occupation of Vladivostok and in safeguarding, so far as it may, [the] country to the rear of the westward-moving Czecho-Slovaks; and the Japanese Government has consented.

In taking this action the Government of the United States wishes to announce to the people of Russia in the most public and solemn manner that it contemplates no interference with the political sovereignty of Russia, no intervention in her internal affairs,—not even in the local affairs of the limited areas which her military force may be obliged to occupy,— and no impairment of her territorial integrity either now or hereafter; but that what we are about to do has as its single and only object the rendering of such aid as shall be acceptable to the Russian people themselves in their endeavors to regain control of their own affairs, their own territory, and their own destiny. The Japanese Government, it is understood, will issue a similar assurance.

These plans and purposes of the Government of the United States have been communicated to the governments of Great Britain, France, and Italy, and those governments have advised the Department of State that they assent to them in principle. No conclusion that the Government of the United States has arrived at in this important matter is intended, however, as an effort to restrict the actions or interfere with the independent judgment of the governments with which we are now associated in the war.

It is also the hope and purpose of the Government of the United States to take advantage of the earliest opportunity to send to Siberia a commission of merchants, agricultural experts, labour advisers, Red Cross representatives, and agents of the Young Men's Christian Association accustomed to organ-izing the best methods of spreading useful information and rendering edu-cational help of a modest kind, in order in some systematic way to relieve the immediate economic necessities of the people there in every way for which an opportunity may open. The execution of this plan will follow and will not be permitted to embarrass the military assistance rendered to the Czecho-Slovaks.

It is the hope and expectation of the Government of the United States that the governments with which it is associated will, wherever necessary or possible, lend their active aid in the execution of these military and eco-nomic plans.

SOURCE: *Foreign Relations of the United States, 1918: Russia*, 2:286–90.

DOCUMENT 47

PRESIDENT WILSON'S RESPONSE—LETTER TO THE
U.S. SENATE CONCERNING AMERICAN-JAPANESE
INTERVENTION IN RUSSIA. JULY 22, 1919.

For the information of the Senate, and in response to the resolution adopted June 23 [27], 1919, requesting the President to inform the Senate, if not incompatible with the public interest, of the reasons for sending United States soldiers to Siberia, the duties that are to be performed by these soldiers, how long they are to remain, and generally to advise the Senate of the policy of the United States Government in respect to Siberia and the maintenance of United States soldiers there, I have the honor to say that the decision to send American troops to Siberia was announced to the press on August 5, 1918, in a statement from the Acting Secretary of State [Frank L. Polk]. . . .

This measure was taken in conjunction with Japan and in concert of purpose with the other allied powers, first of all to save the Czecho-Slovak armies, which were threatened with destruction by hostile armies appar-ently organized by and often largely composed of enemy prisoners of war. The second purpose in view was to steady any efforts of the Russians at self-defense, or the establishment of law and order in which they might be willing to accept assistance.

Two regiments of infantry, with auxiliary troops—about 8,000 effectives —comprising a total of approximately 10,000 men, were sent under the command of Major General William S. Graves. The troops began to arrive at Vladivostok in September, 1918. Considerably larger forces were dispatched by Japan at about the same time, and much smaller forces by others of the allied powers. The net result was the successful reunion of the separated Czecho-Slovak armies and the substantial elimination in eastern Siberia of the active efforts of enemy prisoners of war. A period of relative quiet then ensued.

In February, 1919, at a conclusion of negotiations begun early in the summer of 1918, the United States accepted a plan proposed by Japan for the supervision of the Siberian railways by an international committee, under which committee Mr. John F. Stevens would assume the operation of the Russian Railway Service Corps. In this connection it is to be recalled that Mr. John F. Stevens, in response to a request of the provisional government of Russia, went to Russia in the spring of 1917. A few months later he was made official adviser to the minister of ways of communication at Petrograd under the provisional government. At the request of the provisional government, and with the support of Mr. John F. Stevens, there was organized the so-called Russian Railway Service Corps, composed of American engineers. As originally organized, the personnel of this corps constituted 14 skeleton division units as known in this country, the idea being that the skeleton units would serve as practical advisers and assistants on 14 different sections of the Siberian Railway and assist the Russians by their knowledge of long-haul problems as known in this country, and which are the rule and not the exception in Siberia.

Owing to the Bolshevik uprising and the general chaotic conditions, neither Mr. Stevens nor the Russian Railway Service Corps was able to begin work in Siberia until March, 1918. They have been able to operate effectively only since the railway plan was adopted in February, 1919.

The most recent report from Mr. Stevens shows that on parts of the Chinese-Eastern and Trans-Baikal Railway he is now running six trains a day each way, while only a little while ago they were only able to run that many trains a week.

In accepting the railway plan it was provided that some protection should be given by the allied forces. Mr. Stevens stated frankly that he would not undertake the arduous task before him unless he could rely upon support from American troops in an emergency. Accordingly, as provided in the railway plan and with the approval of the interallied committee, the military commanders in Siberia have established troops where it is necessary to maintain order at different parts of the line. The American forces under Gen. Graves are understood to be protecting parts of the line near Vladivostok, and also on the section around Verchne Udinsk. There is also understood to be a small body of American troops at Harbin. The exact location from time to time of American troops is, however, subject to change by the direction of Gen. Graves.

The instructions to Gen. Graves direct him not to interfere in Russian affairs, but to support Mr. Stevens wherever necessary. The Siberian Railway is not only the main artery for transportation in Siberia, but is the only open access to European Russia today. The population of Siberia, whose resources have been almost exhausted by the long years of war and the chaotic conditions which have existed there, can be protected from a further period of chaos and anarchy only by the restoration and maintenance of traffic on the Siberian Railway.

Partisan bands under leaders having no settled connection with any organized government, and bands under leaders whose allegiance to any settled authority is apparently temporary and transitory, are constantly menacing the operation of the railway and the safety of its permanent structures.

The situation of the people of Siberia meantime is that they have no shoes or warm clothing; they are pleading for agricultural machinery and for many of the simpler articles of commerce upon which their own domestic economy depends and which are necessary to fruitful and productive industry among them. Having contributed their quota to the Russian armies which fought the Central Empires for three and one-half years, they now look to the allies and the United States for economic assistance.

The population of western Siberia and the forces of Admiral [Aleksandr Vasilyevich] Kolchak are entirely dependent upon these railways.

The Russian authorities in this country have succeeded in shipping large quantities of Russian supplies to Siberia, and the Secretary of War is now contracting with the great cooperative societies which operate throughout European and Asiatic Russia to ship further supplies to meet the needs of the civilian population. The Kolchak Government is also endeavoring to arrange for the purchase of medical and other Red Cross supplies from the War Department, and the American Red Cross is itself attempting the forms of relief for which it is organized. All elements of the population in Siberia look to the United States for assistance. This assistance can not be given to the population of Siberia, and ultimately to Russia, if the purpose entertained for two years to restore railway traffic is abandoned. The presence of American troops is a vital element in this effort. The services of Mr. Stevens depend upon it, and, a point of serious moment, the plan proposed by Japan expressly provides that Mr. Stevens and all foreign railway experts shall be withdrawn when the troops are withdrawn.

From these observations it will be seen that the purpose of the continuance of American troops in Siberia is that we, with the concurrence of the great allied powers, may keep open a necessary artery of trade and extend to the vast population of Siberia the economic aid essential to it in peace time, but indispensable under the conditions which have followed the prolonged and exhausting participation by Russia in the war against the Central Powers. This participation was obviously of incalculable value to the allied cause, and in a very particular way commends the exhausted people who suffered from it to such assistance as we can render to bring about their industrial and economic rehabilitation.

SOURCE: U.S. State Department, *Foreign Relations of the United States, 1919: Russia* (Washington, DC: Government Printing Office, 1937), 391–94.

12

CALVIN COOLIDGE

DOCUMENT 48

PRESIDENT CALVIN COOLIDGE DELIVERS SPECIAL MESSAGE TO CONGRESS CONCERNING U.S. INTERVENTION IN NICARAGUA. JANUARY 10, 1927.

To the Congress of the United States:

While conditions in Nicaragua and the action of this Government pertaining thereto have in general been made public, I think the time has arrived for me officially to inform the Congress more in detail of the events leading up to the present disturbances and conditions which seriously threaten American lives and property, endanger the stability of all Central America, and put in jeopardy the rights granted by Nicaragua to the United States for the construction of a canal. It is well known that in 1912 the United States intervened in Nicaragua with a large force and put down a revolution, and that from that time to 1925 a legation guard of American marines was, with the consent of the Nicaraguan Government, kept in Managua to protect American lives and property. In 1923 representatives of the five Central American countries, namely, Costa Rica, Guatemala, Honduras, Nicaragua, and Salvador, at the invitation of the United States, met in Washington and entered into a series of treaties. These treaties dealt with limitation of armament, a Central American tribunal for arbitration, and the general subject of peace and amity. The treaty last referred to specifically provides in Article II that the Governments of the contracting parties will not recognize any other government which may come into power in any of the five Republics through a coup d'état or revolution and disqualifies the leaders of such coup d'état or revolution from assuming the presidency or vice presidency. Article II is as follows:

> Desiring to make secure in the Republics of Central America the benefits which are derived from the maintenance of free institutions and to contribute at the same time toward strengthening their stability, and the prestige

with which they should be surrounded, they declare that every act, disposition or measure which alters the constitutional organization in any of them is to be deemed a menace to the peace of said Republics, whether it proceed from any public power or from the private citizens.

Consequently, the Governments of the Contracting Parties will not recognize any other Government which may come into power in any of the five Republics through a coup d'etat or a revolution against a recognized Government so long as the freely elected representatives of the people thereof have not constitutionally reorganized the country. And even in such a case they obligate themselves not to acknowledge the recognition if any of the persons elected as President, Vice-President or Chief of State designate should fall under any of the following heads:

1) If he should be the leader or one of the leaders of a coup d'etat or revolution, or through blood relationship or marriage, be an ascendent or descendent or brother of such leader or leaders.

2) If he should have been a Secretary of State or should have held some high military command during the accomplishment of the coup d'etat, the revolution, or while the election was being carried on, or if he should have held this office, or command within the six months preceding the coup d'etat, revolution, or the election.

Furthermore, in no case shall recognition be accorded to a government which arises from election to power of a citizen expressly and unquestionably disqualified by the Constitution of his country as eligible to election as President, Vice-President or Chief of State designate.

The United States was not a party to this treaty, but it was made in Washington under the auspices of the Secretary of State [Charles Evans Hughes], and this Government has felt a moral obligation to apply its principles in order to encourage the Central American States in their efforts to prevent revolution and disorder. The treaty, it may be noted in passing, was signed on behalf of Nicaragua by Emiliano Chamorro himself, who afterwards assumed the presidency in violation thereof and thereby contributed to the creation of the present difficulty.

In October, 1924, an election was held in Nicaragua for President, Vice President, and members of the Congress. This resulted in the election of a coalition ticket embracing Conservatives and Liberals. Carlos Solorzano, a Conservative Republican, was elected President and Juan B. Sacasa, a Liberal, was elected Vice President. This Government was recognized by the other Central American countries and by the United States. It had been the intention of the United States to withdraw the marines immediately after this election, and notice was given of the intention to withdraw them in January, 1925. At the request of the President of Nicaragua this time was extended to September 1, 1925. Pursuant to this determination and notice, the marines were withdrawn in August, 1925, and it appeared at that time as though tranquility in Nicaragua was assured. Within two months, however, further disturbances broke out between the supporters of General Chamorro and the supporters of the President, culminating in the seizure of the Loma, a fortress dominating the city of Managua. Once in possession of the Loma, General Chamorro dictated an agreement which President Solorzano signed the next day. According to the terms of this agreement the President agreed to substitute supporters of General Chamorro for certain members of his cabinet, to pay General Chamorro $10,000 for the expenses of the uprising, and to grant amnesty to all those who participated in it. Vice President Sacasa thereupon left the country. In the meantime General Chamorro, who, while he had not actually taken over the office of President, was able to dictate his will to the actual Executive, brought about the expulsion from the Congress of 18 members, on the ground that their election had been fraudulent, and caused to be put in their places candidates who had been defeated at the election of 1924. Having thus gained the control of Congress, he caused himself to be appointed by the Congress as designate on January 16, 1926. On January 16, 1926, Solorzano resigned as President and immediately General Chamorro took office. The four Central American countries and the United States refused to recognize him as President. On January 22 the Secretary of State addressed to the Nicaraguan representative in Washington the following letter:

Dear Doctor Castrillo:

In your communication of the 19th instant addressed to the Secretary of State you advise that President Solorzano having resigned his office General Emiliano Chamorro took charge of the executive power on January 17.

The hope expressed in your letter that the relations which have been close and cordial for so many years between Nicaragua and the United States will continue and grow stronger has been noted with pleasure. The Government and people of the United States have feelings of sincerest friendship for Nicaragua and the people of Nicaragua and the Government of the United States will of course continue to maintain the most friendly relations with the people of Nicaragua. This Government has felt privileged to be able to be of assistance in the past at their request not only to Nicaragua but to all countries of Central

America more especially during the Conference on Central American Affairs which resulted in the signing of a General Treaty of Peace and Amity on February 7, 1923, between the five Republics of Central America. The object of the Central American countries with which the United States was heartily in accord, was to promote constitutional government and orderly procedure in Central America and those Governments agreed upon a joint course of action with regard to the nonrecognition of governments coming into office through coup d'etat or revolution. The United States has adopted the principles of that Treaty as its policy in the future recognition of Central American Governments as it feels that by so doing it can best show its friendly disposition towards and its desire to be helpful to the Republics of Central America.

It is therefore with regret that I have to inform you that the Government of the United States has not recognized and will not recognize as the Government of Nicaragua the regime now headed by General Chamorro, as the latter was duly advised on several occasions by the American Minister after General Chamorro had taken charge of the citadel at Managua on October 25th last. This action is, I am happy to learn, in accord with that taken by all the Governments that signed with Nicaragua the Treaty of 1923.

Notwithstanding the refusal of this Government and of the other Central American Governments to recognize him, General Chamorro continued to exercise the functions of President until October 30, 1926. In the meantime, a revolution broke out in May on the east coast in the neighborhood of Bluefields and was speedily suppressed by the troops of General Chamorro. However, it again broke out with considerably more violence. The second attempt was attended with some success and practically all of the east coast of Nicaragua fell into the hands of the revolutionists. Throughout these events Sacasa was at no time in the country, having remained in Mexico and Guatemala during this period.

Repeated requests were made of the United States for protection, especially on the east coast, and, on August 24, 1926, the Secretary of State addressed to the Secretary of the Navy the following communication:

I have the honor to suggest that war vessels of the Special Service Squadron proceed as soon as possible to the Nicaraguan ports of Corinto and Bluefields for the protection of American and foreign lives and property in case that threatened emergencies materialize. The American Chargé d'Affaires at Managua has informed the Department that he considers the presence of war vessels at these ports desirable, and the American Consul at Bluefields has reported that a warship is urgently needed to protect life and property at that port. An attack on The Bluff and Bluefields is expected momentarily.

Accordingly, the Navy Department ordered Admiral [Julian K.] Latimer, in command of the Special Service Squadron, to proceed to Bluefields. Upon arriving there he found it necessary for the adequate protection of American lives and property to declare Bluefields a neutral zone. This was done with the consent of both factions, afterwards, on October 26, 1926, reduced to a written agreement, which is still in force. In October [September], 1926, the good offices of the United States were sought by both parties for the purpose of effecting a settlement of the conflict. Admiral Latimer, commanding the Special Service Squadron, brought about an armistice to permit a conference being held between the delegates of the two factions. The armistice was originally for 15 days and was later extended for 15 days more. At the request of both parties, marines were landed at Corinto to establish a neutral zone in which the conference could be held. Doctor Sacasa was invited to attend this conference but refrained from doing so and remained in Guatemala City. The United States Government did not participate in the conference except to provide a neutral chairman; it simply offered its good offices to make the conference possible and arranged a neutral zone at Corinto at the request of both parties during the time the conference was held. I understand that at this conference General Chamorro offered to resign and permit the Congress to elect a new designate to assume the presidency. The conference led to no result, since just at the time when it seemed as though some compromise agreement would be reached the representatives of Doctor Sacasa suddenly broke off negotiations.

According to our reports, the Sacasa delegates on this occasion stated freely that to accept any government other than one presided over by Doctor Sacasa himself would be a breach of faith with their Mexican allies. Hostilities were resumed on October 30, 1926. On the same date General Chamorro formally turned over the executive power to Sebastian Uriza, who had been appointed designate by the Congress controlled by General Chamorro. The United States Government refused to recognize Señor Uriza, on the ground that his assumption of the Presidency had no constitutional basis. Uriza thereupon convoked Congress in extraordinary session, and the entire 18 members who had been expelled during the Chamorro regime were notified to resume their seats. The Congress which met in extraordinary session on November 10 had, therefore, substantially the same membership as when first convened following the election of 1924. This Congress, whose acts may be considered as constitutional, designated Señor Adolfo Díaz as first designate. At this session of Congress 53 members were present out of a total membership of 67, of whom 44 voted for Díaz and 2 for Solorzano. The balance abstained from voting. On November 11 Señor Uriza turned over the executive power to Díaz, who was inaugurated on the 14th.

The Nicaraguan constitution provides in Article 106 that in the absence of the President and Vice President the Congress shall designate one of its members to complete the unexpired term of President. As President Solorzano had resigned and was then residing in California, and as the Vice President, Doctor Sacasa, was in Guatemala, having been out of the country since November, 1925, the action of Congress in designating Señor Díaz was perfectly legal and in accordance with the constitution. Therefore the United States Government on November 17 extended recognition to Señor Díaz.

Following his assumption of office, President Díaz, in the following note, dated November 15, 1926, requested the assistance of the United States Government to protect American and foreign lives and property:

Upon assuming the presidency I found the Republic in a very difficult situation because of the attitude, assumed without motive, by the Government of Mexico in open hostility to Nicaragua. It must be clear to you that, given the forces which that Government disposes of its elements of attack are irresistible for this feeble and small Nation. This condition places in imminent risk the sovereignty and independence of Nicaragua, and consequently, the continental equilibrium on which the Pan-Americanism is founded which the United States has fostered with such lofty spirit.

Naturally the emergency resulting from these conditions places in peril the interests of American citizens and other foreigners residing in our territory and renders it impossible for a Government so rudely attacked, to protect them as is its duty and as it desires.

For these reasons and appreciating the friendly disposition of the United States toward weak Republics and the intentions which your Government has always manifested for the protection of the sovereignty and independence of all the countries of America by morally supporting legitimate Governments in order to enable them [to] afford a tranquil field of labor for foreigners which is needed for the stimulation of the growth of the prosperity of these countries, I address myself to you in order that, with the same good will with which you have aided in Nicaraguan reconciliation, you may solicit for my government and in my name the support of the Department of State in order to reach a solution in the present crisis and avoid further hostilities and invasions on the part of the Government of Mexico.

I desire to manifest to you at the same time that whatever may be the means chosen by the Department of State, they will meet with the approval of my absolute confidence in the high spirit of justice of the Government of the United States.

Immediately following the inauguration of President Díaz and frequently since that date he has appealed to the United States for support, has informed this Government of the aid which Mexico is giving to the revolutionists, and has stated that he is unable solely because of the aid given by Mexico to the revolutionists to protect the lives and property of American citizens and other foreigners. When negotiations leading up to the Corinto conference began, I immediately placed an embargo on the shipment of arms and ammunition to Nicaragua. The Department of State notified the other Central American States, to wit, Costa Rica, Honduras, Salvador, and Guatemala, and they assured the department that they would cooperate in this measure. So far as known, they have done so. The State Department also notified the Mexican Government of this embargo and informally suggested to that Government like action. The Mexican Government did not adopt the suggestion to put on an embargo, but informed the American ambassador at Mexico City that in the absence of manufacturing plants in Mexico for the making of arms and ammunition the matter had little practical importance.

As a matter of fact, I have the most conclusive evidence that arms and munitions in large quantities have been on several occasions since August, 1926, shipped to the revolutionists in Nicaragua. Boats carrying these munitions have been fitted out in Mexican ports, and some of the munitions bear evidence of having belonged to the Mexican Government. It also appears that the ships were fitted out with the full knowledge of and, in some cases, with the encouragement of Mexican officials and were in one instance, at least, commanded by a Mexican naval reserve officer. At the end of November, after spending some time in Mexico City, Doctor Sacasa went back to Nicaragua, landing at Puerto Cabezas, near Bragmans Bluff. He immediately placed himself at the head of the insurrection and declared himself President of Nicaragua. He has never been recognized by any of the Central American Republics nor by any other Government, with the exception of Mexico, which recognized him immediately. As arms and munitions in large quantities were reaching the revolutionists, I deemed it unfair to prevent the recognized Government from purchasing arms abroad, and, accordingly, the Secretary of State has notified the Díaz Government that licenses would be issued for the export of arms and munitions purchased in this country. It would be thoroughly inconsistent for this country not to support the Government recognized by it while the revolutionists were receiving arms and munitions from abroad.

During the last two months the Government of the United States has received repeated requests from various American citizens, both directly and through our consuls and legation, for the protection of their lives and property. The Government of the United States has also received requests from the British Chargé at Managua, and from the Italian ambassador at Washington for the protection of their respective nationals. Pursuant to such requests, Admiral Latimer, in charge of the Special Service Squadron, has not only maintained the neutral zone at Bluefields under the agreement of both parties but has landed forces at Puerto Cabezas and Rio Grande, and established neutral zones at these points where considerable numbers of Americans live and are engaged in carrying on various industries. He has also been authorized to establish such other neutral zones as are necessary for the purposes above mentioned.

For many years numerous Americans have been living in Nicaragua developing its industries and carrying on business. At the present time there are large investments in lumbering, mining, coffee growing, banana culture, shipping, and also in general mercantile and other collateral business. All these people and these industries have been encouraged by the Nicaraguan Government. That Government has at all times owed them protection, but the United States has occasionally been obliged to send naval forces for their proper protection. In the present crisis such forces are requested by the Nicaraguan Government, which protests to the United States its inability to protect these interests and states that any measures which the United States deems appropriate for their protection will be satisfactory to the Nicaraguan Government.

In addition to these industries now in existence, the Government of Nicaragua, by a treaty entered into on the 5th day of August, 1914, granted in perpetuity to the United States the exclusive proprietary rights necessary and convenient for the construction, operation, and maintenance of an oceanic canal. Articles I and II of said treaty are as follows:

Article I. The Government of Nicaragua grants in perpetuity to the Government of the United States, forever free from all taxation or other public charge, the exclusive proprietary rights necessary and convenient for the construction, operation and maintenance of an interoceanic canal by way of the San Juan River and the great Lake of Nicaragua or by way of any route over Nicaraguan territory, the details of the terms upon which such canal shall be constructed, operated and maintained to be agreed to by the two governments whenever the Government of the United States shall notify the Government of Nicaragua of its desire or intention to construct such canal.

Article II. To enable the Government of the United States to protect the Panama Canal and the proprietary rights granted to the Government of the United States by the foregoing article, and also to enable the Government of the United States to take any measure necessary to the ends contemplated herein, the Government of Nicaragua hereby leases for a term of ninety-nine years to the Government of the United States the islands in the Caribbean Sea known as Great Corn Island and Little Corn Island; and the Government of Nicaragua further grants to the Government of the United States for a like period of ninety-nine years the right to establish, operate and maintain a naval base at such place on the territory of Nicaragua bordering upon the Gulf of Fonseca as the Government of the United States may select. The Government of the United States shall have the option of renewing for a further term of ninety-nine years the above leases and grants upon the expiration of their respective terms, it being expressly agreed that the territory hereby leased and the naval base which may be maintained under the grant aforesaid shall be subject exclusively to the laws and sovereign authority of the United States during the terms of such lease and grant and of any renewal or renewals thereof.

The consideration paid by the United States to Nicaragua was the sum of $3,000,000. At the time of the payment of this money a financial plan was drawn up between the Nicaraguan Government and its creditors which provided for the consolidation of Nicaragua's obligations. At that time the bondholders holding the Nicaraguan external debt consented to a reduction in interest from 6 to 5 per cent, providing the service of this loan was handled through the American collector of customs, and at the same time a series of internal guaranteed customs bonds amounting to $3,744,000 was issued by the Nicaraguan Government to pay off the claims which had arisen against it because of revolutionary disturbances from 1909 to 1912. The other outstanding external bonds, amounting on February 1, 1926, to about £772,000, are held in Great Britain. Of the guaranteed customs bonds, $2,867,000 were on February 1, 1926, still in circulation, and of these about $1,000,000 were held by Nicaraguans, $1,000,000 by American citizens, and the balance by nationals of other countries. The bonds held in the United States are held by the public in general circulation and, so far as the department knows, no American bankers are directly interested in the Nicaraguan indebtedness. This financial plan was adopted by an act of the Congress of Nicaragua on August 31, 1917. The National Bank of Nicaragua was made the depository of all Government revenues. The internal revenues were, as heretofore, to be collected by the Government. Collection of the internal revenue, however, was to be taken over by the collector general of customs, an American citizen appointed by the Nicaraguan Government and approved by the Secretary of State of the United States, if the products should average less than $60,000 a month for three consecutive months. This has never yet been necessary. The proceeds of the customs revenues were to be applied, first, to the payment of such sums as might be agreed upon in the contemplated contracts for the service of the foreign loan, the internal loan, and claims against the Nicaraguan Government. From the balance of the revenue $80,000 a month was to be used for the ordinary budget expenses and an additional $15,000 for extraordinary expenses.

Under this financial plan the finances of Nicaragua have been rehabilitated in a very satisfactory manner. Of the $3,744,000 of internal customs bonds issued in 1917 about $900,000 have been paid. Of the external debt, bonds issued in 1909 amounting to £1,250,000, there now remain only about £770,000. The total public debt of Nicaragua has been reduced from about $22,000,000 in 1917 to $6,625,203 at the beginning of 1926. Furthermore, the country in time of peace has ample revenues for its ordinary budget expenses and a surplus which has been used in extensive public improvements. The Nicaraguan National Bank and the National Railroad, controlling interests in which were formerly owned by American bankers, were repurchased by the Nicaraguan Government in 1920 and 1924, and are now wholly owned by that Government.

There is no question that if the revolution continues American investments and business interests in Nicaragua will be very seriously affected, if not destroyed. The currency, which is now at par, will be inflated. American as well as foreign bondholders will undoubtedly look to the United States for the protection of their interests.

It is true that the United States did not establish the financial plan by any treaty, but it nevertheless did aid through diplomatic channels and advise in the negotiation and establishment of this plan for the financial rehabilitation of Nicaragua.

Manifestly the relation of this Government to the Nicaraguan situation, and its policy in the existing emergency, are determined by the facts which I have described. The proprietary rights of the United States in the Nicaraguan canal route, with the necessary implications growing out of it affecting the Panama Canal, together with the obligations flowing from the investments of all classes of our citizens in Nicaragua, place us in a position of peculiar responsibility. I am sure it is not the desire of the United States to intervene in the internal affairs of Nicaragua or of any other Central American Republic. Nevertheless it must be said that we have a very definite and special interest in the maintenance of order and good government in Nicaragua at the present time, and that the stability, prosperity, and independence of all Central American countries can never be a matter of indifference to us. The United States can not, therefore, fail to view with deep concern any serious threat to stability and constitutional government in Nicaragua tending toward anarchy and jeopardizing American interests, especially if such state of affairs is contributed to or brought about by outside influences or by any foreign power. It has always been and remains the policy of the United States in such circumstances to take the steps that may be necessary for the preservation and protection of the lives, the property, and the interests of its citizens and of this Government itself. In this respect I propose to follow the path of my predecessors.

Consequently, I have deemed it my duty to use the powers committed to me to insure the adequate protection of all American interests in Nicaragua, whether they be endangered by internal strife or by outside interference in the affairs of that Republic.

SOURCE: U.S. State Department, *Foreign Relations of the United States, 1927*, 3 vols. (Washington, DC: Government Printing Office, 1942), 3:288–98.

DOCUMENT 49

PRESIDENT COOLIDGE'S STATE OF THE UNION ADDRESS CONCERNING U.S. INTERVENTION IN NICARAGUA. DECEMBER 4, 1928.

. . . When a destructive and bloody revolution lately broke out in Nicaragua, at the earnest and repeated entreaties of its Government I dispatched our Marine forces there to protect the lives and interests of our citizens. To compose the contending parties, I sent there Col. Henry L. Stimson, former Secretary of War and now Governor General of the Philippine Islands, who secured an agreement that warfare should cease, a national election should be held and peace should be restored. Both parties conscientiously carried out this agreement, with the exception of a few bandits who later mostly surrendered or left the country. President Díaz appointed Brig. Gen. Frank R. McCoy, United States Army, president of the election board, which included also one member of each political party.

A free and fair election has been held and has worked out so successfully that both parties have joined in requesting like cooperation from this country at the election four years hence, to which I have refrained from making any commitments, although our country must be gratified at such an exhibition of success and appreciation. Nicaragua is regaining its prosperity and has taken a long step in the direction of peaceful self-government.

SOURCE: U.S. State Department, *Foreign Relations of the United States, 1928*, 3 vols. (Washington, DC: Government Printing Office, 1942), 1:ix.

DOCUMENT 50
PRESIDENT COOLIDGE'S STATEMENT CONCERNING U.S. INTERVENTION IN CHINA. APRIL 25, 1927.

... Our main difficulty here (in China) is the protection of the life and property of our citizens. Our citizens are being concentrated in ports where we can protect them and remove them. It is solely for this purpose that our warships and marines are in that territory.

While this process was going on the unfortunate incident arose at Nanking. One of our citizens was murdered, another was wounded, our consulate was violated, and when the house in which our people had taken refuge was surrounded and they were actually under fire it became necessary for one of our ships, and one of the British ships in the harbor, to lay down a barrage, to drive away the soldiers and the mob who were making the attack and to enable our citizens to reach a place of safety on our ships in the river. We presented with the other powers who had suffered like attacks identic notes of protest, to which a reply has been made, which although conciliatory in tone and to a certain degree responsive, leaves the final disposition of the issue a matter for further consideration by our Government. . . .

The friendship of America for China has become proverbial. We feel for her the deepest sympathy in these times of her distress. We have no disposition to do otherwise than to assist and encourage every legitimate aspiration for freedom, for unity, for the cultivation of a national spirit, and the realization of a republican form of government. In the turmoil and strife of the present time we realize fully that forces may be let loose temporarily beyond their power to control, which may do injury to American nationals. It is to guard against that eventuality that our forces are in Chinese waters and to do what China itself would do if peace prevailed. We do not wish to pursue any course of aggression against the Chinese people. We are there to prevent aggression against our people by any of their disorderly elements. Ultimately the turmoil will quiet down and some form of authority will emerge, which will no doubt be prepared to make adequate settlement for any wrongs we have suffered. We shall of course maintain the dignity of our Government and insist upon proper respect being extended to our authority. But our actions will at all times be those of a friend solicitous for the well-being of the Chinese people.

SOURCE: *Foreign Relations of the United States, 1927*, 2:118–19.

13

FRANKLIN D. ROOSEVELT

DOCUMENT 51
PRESIDENT FRANKLIN ROOSEVELT'S WAR MESSAGE
TO CONGRESS. DECEMBER 8, 1941.

Yesterday, December 7, 1941—a date which will live in infamy—the United States of America was suddenly and deliberately attacked by naval and air forces of the Empire of Japan.

The United States was at peace with that nation and, at the solicitation of Japan, was still in conversation with its Government and its Emperor [Hirohito] looking toward the maintenance of peace in the Pacific. Indeed, one hour after Japanese air squadrons had commenced bombing in the American Island of Oahu, the Japanese Ambassador to the United States and his colleague [Admiral Kichisaburo Nomura and Saburo Kurusu] delivered to our Secretary of State [Cordell Hull] a formal reply to a recent American message. And while this reply stated that it seemed useless to continue the existing diplomatic negotiations, it contained no threat or hint of war or of armed attack.

It will be recorded that the distance of Hawaii from Japan makes it obvious that the attack was deliberately planned many days or even weeks ago. During the intervening time the Japanese Government has deliberately sought to deceive the United States by false statements and expressions of hope for continued peace.

The attack yesterday on the Hawaiian Islands has caused severe damage to American naval and military forces. I regret to tell you that very many American lives have been lost. In addition American ships have been reported torpedoed on the high seas between San Francisco and Honolulu.

Yesterday the Japanese Government also launched an attack against Malaya.

Last night Japanese forces attacked Hong Kong.

Last night Japanese forces attacked Guam.

Last night Japanese forces attacked the Philippine Islands.

Last night the Japanese attacked Wake Island.

And this morning the Japanese attacked Midway Island.

Japan has, therefore, undertaken a surprise offensive extending through-out the Pacific area. The facts of yesterday and today speak for themselves. The people of the United States have already formed their opinions and well understand the implications to the very life and safety of our nation.

As Commander-in-Chief of the Army and Navy I have directed that all measures be taken for our defense.

But always will our whole nation remember the character of the on-slaught against us.

No matter how long it may take us to overcome this premeditated inva-sion, the American people in their righteous might will win through to absolute victory.

I believe that I interpret the will of the Congress and of the people when I assert that we will not only defend ourselves to the uttermost but will make it very certain that this form of treachery shall never again endanger us.

Hostilities exist. There is no blinking at the fact that our people, our ter-ritory and our interests are in grave danger.

With confidence in our armed forces—with the unbounding determi-nation of our people—we will gain the inevitable triumph—so help us God.

I ask that the Congress declare that since the unprovoked and dastardly attack by Japan on Sunday, December seventh, 1941, a state of war has existed between the United States and the Japanese Empire.

SOURCE: U.S. State Department, *Foreign Relations of the United States, Japan, 1931–1941,* 2 vols. (Washington, DC: Government Printing Office, 1942), 2:793.

DOCUMENT 52

PRESIDENT ROOSEVELT'S STATE OF THE UNION MESSAGE CALLING AMERICA TO FIGHT AGAINST GERMANY, ITALY, AND JAPAN. JANUARY 6, 1942.

Mr. President, Mr. Speaker, Members of the Seventy-seventh Congress:

In fulfilling my duty to report upon the state of the Union, I am proud to say to you that the spirit of the American people was never higher than it is today—the Union was never more closely knit together—this coun-try was never more deeply determined to face the solemn tasks before it.

The response of the American people has been instantaneous. It will be sustained until our security is assured.

Exactly one year ago today I said to this Congress: "When the dictators are ready to make war upon us, they will not wait for an act of war on our part. They—not we—will choose the time and the place and the method of their attack."

We now know their choice of the time. A peaceful Sunday morning—December 7, 1941.

We know their choice of the place. An American outpost in the Pacific.

We know their choice of the method. The method of Hitler himself.

Japan's scheme of conquest goes back half a century. It was not merely a policy of seeking living room; it was a plan which included the subjugation of all the peoples in the Far East and in the islands of the Pacific, and the domination of that ocean by Japanese military and naval control of the western coasts of North, Central, and South America.

The development of this ambitious conspiracy was marked by the war against China in 1894; the subsequent occupation of Korea; the war against Russia in 1904; the illegal fortification of the mandated Pacific Islands following 1920; the seizure of Manchuria in 1931; and the invasion of China in 1937.

A similar policy of criminal conquest was adopted by Italy [under Benito Mussolini]. The fascists first revealed their imperial designs in Libya and Tripoli. In 1935 they seized Abyssinia [Ethiopia]. Their goal was the domination of all North Africa, Egypt, parts of France, and the entire Mediterranean world.

But the dreams of empire of the Japanese and fascist leaders were modest in comparison with the gargantuan aspirations of [Adolf] Hitler and his Nazis. Even before they came to power in 1933, their plans for conquest had been drawn. Those plans provided for ultimate domination, not of any one section of the world, but of the whole Earth and all the oceans on it.

With Hitler's formation of the Berlin-Rome-Tokyo alliance,[1] all these plans of conquest became a single plan. Under this, in addition to her own schemes of conquest, Japan's role was to cut off our supply of weapons of war to Britain, Russia, and China—weapons which increasingly were

---

[1] This was the Tripartite Pact signed on September 27, 1940, in which the Japanese agreed to German and Italian supremacy in Europe, while Germany and Italy recognized Japan's dominance in Asia. The three signatories also agreed to come to the defense of one another if any of them was attacked by a country not then engaged in either the European or Sino-Japanese War. This defensive alliance was clearly aimed at the United States because a separate codicil exempted the Soviet Union.

speeding the day of Hitler's doom. The act of Japan at Pearl Harbor was intended to stun us—to terrify us to such an extent that we would divert our industrial and military strength to the Pacific area, or even to our own continental defense.

The plan failed in its purpose. We have not been stunned. We have not been terrified or confused. The reassembling of the 77th Congress is proof of that; for the mood of quiet, grim resolution which here prevails, bodes ill for those who conspired and collaborated to murder world peace.

That mood is stronger than any mere desire for revenge. It expresses the will of the American people to make very certain that the world will never so suffer again.

Admittedly, we have been faced with hard choices. It was bitter, for example, not to be able to relieve the heroic and historic defenders of Wake Island. It was bitter for us not to be able to land a million men and a thousand ships in the Philippine Islands.

But this adds only to our determination to see to it that the Stars and Stripes will fly again over Wake and Guam[2]; and that the brave people of the Philippines will be rid of Japanese imperialism; and will live in freedom, security, and independence.

Powerful and offensive actions must and will be taken in proper time. The consolidation of the United Nations' total war effort against our common enemies is being achieved.

That is the purpose of conferences which have been held during the past two weeks in Washington, in Moscow, and in Chungking. That is the primary objective of the declaration of solidarity signed in Washington on January 1, 1942, by 26 nations united against the Axis powers.

Difficult choices may have to be made in the months to come. We will not shrink from such decisions. We and those united with us will make those decisions with courage and determination.

Plans have been laid here and in the other capitals for coordinated and cooperative action by all the united nations—military action and economic action. Already we have established unified command of land, sea, and air forces in the southwestern Pacific theater of war. There will be a continuation of conferences and consultations among military staffs, so that the plans and operations of each will fit into a general strategy designed to crush the enemy. We shall not fight isolated wars—each nation going its own way. These 26 nations are united—not in spirit and determination alone, but in the broad conduct of the war in all its phases.

---

[2]Guam fell to the Japanese on December 11 and Wake Island on December 23.

For the first time since the Japanese and the fascists and the Nazis started along their bloodstained course of conquest they now face the fact that superior forces are assembling against them. Gone forever are the days when the aggressors could attack and destroy their victims one by one without unity of resistance. We of the united nations will so dispose our forces that we can strike at the common enemy wherever the greatest damage can be done.

The militarists in Berlin and Tokyo started this war. But the massed, angered forces of common humanity will finish it.

Destruction of the material and spiritual centers of civilization—this has been and still is the purpose of Hitler and his Italian and Japanese chessmen. They would wreck the power of the British Commonwealth and Russia and China and the Netherlands—and then combine all their forces to achieve their ultimate goal, the conquest of the United States.

They know that victory for us means victory for freedom.

They know that victory for us means victory for the institution of democracy—the ideal of the family, the simple principles of common decency and humanity.

They know that victory for us means victory for religion.

And they could not tolerate that. The world is too small to provide adequate "living room" for both Hitler and God. In proof of that, the Nazis have now announced their plan for enforcing their new German, pagan religion throughout the world—the plan by which the Holy Bible and the Cross of Mercy would be displaced by *Mein Kampf* and the swastika and the naked sword.

Our own objectives are clear; the objective of smashing the militarism imposed by war lords upon their enslaved peoples—the objective of liberating the subjugated nations—the objective of establishing and securing freedom of speech, freedom of religion, freedom from want, and freedom from fear everywhere in the world.[3]

We shall not stop short of these objectives—nor shall we be satisfied merely to gain them and then call it a day. I know that I speak for the American people—and I have good reason to believe I speak also for all the other peoples who fight with us—when I say that this time we are determined not only to win the war, but also to maintain the security of the peace which will follow.

---

[3]President Roosevelt had earlier spoken of the Four Freedoms in his Lend-Lease Message to Congress on January 6, 1941.

But modern methods of warfare make it a task, not only of shooting and fighting, but an even more urgent one of working and producing.

Victory requires the actual weapons of war and the means of transporting them to a dozen points of combat.

It will not be sufficient for us and the other united nations to produce a slightly superior supply of munitions to that of Germany, Japan, Italy, and the stolen industries in the countries which they have overrun.

The superiority of the united nations in munitions and ships must be overwhelming—so overwhelming that the Axis nations can never hope to catch up with it. In order to attain this overwhelming superiority the United States must build planes and tanks and guns and ships to the utmost limit of our national capacity. We have the ability and capacity to produce arms not only for our own forces, but also for the armies, navies, and air forces fighting on our side.[4]

And our overwhelming superiority of armament must be adequate to put weapons of war at the proper time into the hands of those men in the conquered nations, who stand ready to seize the first opportunity to revolt against their German and Japanese oppressors, and against the traitors in their own ranks, known by the already infamous name of "Quislings."[5] As we get guns to the patriots in those lands, they, too, will fire shots heard round the world.

This production of ours in the United States must be raised far above its present levels, even though it will mean the dislocation of the lives and occupations of millions of our own people. We must raise our sights all along the production line. Let no man say it cannot be done. It must be done—and we have undertaken to do it.

I have just sent a letter of directive to the appropriate departments and agencies of our government, ordering that immediate steps be taken:

1. To increase our production rate of airplanes so rapidly that in this year, 1942, we shall produce 60,000 planes, 10,000 more than the

---

[4] In his first Fireside Chat since elected to his unprecedented third term as president, Franklin Roosevelt warned the nation on December 29, 1940, that American security required providing war matériel to the British. This "arsenal of democracy" address to the nation came after months of Fascist victories in Europe.

---

[5] **Vidkun Quisling**, 1887–1945; the Norwegian Fascist whom the Germans placed in control of Norway after the Wehrmacht seized the country. His name became synonymous with "traitor." Quisling was executed after the Nazi surrender in 1945.

goal set a year and a half ago. This includes 45,000 combat planes—bombers, dive-bombers, pursuit planes. The rate of increase will be continued, so that next year, 1943, we shall produce 125,000 airplanes, including 100,000 combat planes.

2. To increase our production rate of tanks so rapidly that in this year, 1942, we shall produce 45,000 tanks; and to continue that increase so that next year, 1943, we shall produce 75,000 tanks.

3. To increase our production rate of anti-aircraft guns so rapidly that in this year, 1942, we shall produce 20,000 of them; and to continue that increase so that next year, 1943, we shall produce 35,000 anti-aircraft guns.

4. To increase our production rate of merchant ships so rapidly that in this year, 1942, we shall build 8,000,000 deadweight tons as compared with a 1941 production of 1,100,000. We shall continue that increase so that next year, 1943, we shall build 10,000,000 tons.

These figures and similar figures for a multitude of other implements of war will give the Japanese and Nazis a little idea of just what they accomplished in the attack on Pearl Harbor.

Our task is hard—our task is unprecedented—and the time is short. We must strain every existing armament-producing facility to the utmost. We must convert every available plant and tool to war production. That goes all the way from the greatest plants to the smallest—from the huge automobile industry to the village machine shop.

Production for war is based on men and women—the human hands and brains which collectively we call Labor. Our workers stand ready to work long hours; to turn out more in a day's work; to keep the wheels turning and the fires burning twenty-four hours a day, and seven days a week. They realize well that on the speed and efficiency of their work depend the lives of their sons and their brothers on the fighting fronts.

Production for war is based on metals and raw materials—steel, copper, rubber, aluminum, zinc, tin. Greater and greater quantities of them will have to be diverted to war purposes. Civilian use of them will have to be cut further and still further—and, in many cases, completely eliminated.

War costs money. So far, we have hardly even begun to pay for it. We have devoted only fifteen percent of our national income to national defense. As will appear in my budget message tomorrow, our war program for the coming fiscal year will cost $56,000,000,000, or, in other words, more than one-half of the estimated annual national income. This means taxes and bonds and bonds and taxes. It means cutting luxuries and other nonessentials. In a word, it means an "all-out" war by individual effort and family effort in a united country.

Only this all-out scale of production will hasten the ultimate all-out victory. Speed will count. Lost ground can always be regained—lost time never. Speed will save lives; speed will save this nation which is in peril; speed will save our freedom and civilization—and slowness has never been an American characteristic.

As the United States goes into its full stride, we must always be on guard against misconceptions which will arise naturally or which will be planted among us by our enemies.

We must guard against complacency. We must not underrate the enemy. He is powerful and cunning—and cruel and ruthless. He will stop at nothing which gives him a chance to kill and to destroy. He has trained his people to believe that their highest perfection is achieved by waging war. For many years he has prepared for this very conflict—planning, plotting, training, arming, fighting. We have already tasted defeat. We may suffer further setbacks. We must face the fact of a hard war, a long war, a bloody war, a costly war.

We must, on the other hand, guard against defeatism. That has been one of the chief weapons of Hitler's propaganda machine used time and again with deadly results. It will not be used successfully on the American people.

We must guard against divisions among ourselves and among all the other united nations. We must be particularly vigilant against racial discrimination in any of its ugly forms. Hitler will try again to breed mistrust and suspicion between one individual and another, one group and another, one race and another, one government and another. He will try to use the same technique of falsehood and rumor-mongering with which he divided France from Britain. He is trying to do this with us even now. But he will find a unity of will and purpose against him, which will persevere until the destruction of all his black designs upon the freedom and safety of the people of the world.

We cannot wage this war in a defensive spirit. As our power and our resources are fully mobilized, we shall carry the attack against the enemy— we shall hit him and hit him again wherever and whenever we can reach him.

We must keep him far from our shores, for we intend to bring this battle to him on his own home grounds.

American armed forces must be used at any place in all the world where it seems advisable to engage the forces of the enemy. In some cases these operations will be defensive, in order to protect key positions. In other cases, these operations will be offensive, in order to be at the common enemy, with a view to his complete encirclement and eventual total defeat.

American armed forces will operate at many points in the Far East.

American armed forces will be on all the oceans—helping to guard the essential communications which are vital to the united nations.

American land and air and sea forces will take stations in the British Isles—which constitute an essential fortress in this world struggle.

American armed forces will help to protect this hemisphere—and also bases outside this hemisphere, which could be used for an attack on the Americas.

If any of our enemies, from Europe or from Asia, attempt long-range raids by "suicide" squadrons of bombing planes, they will do so only in the hope of terrorizing our people and disrupting our morale. Our people are not afraid of that. We know that we may have to pay a heavy price for freedom. We will pay this price with a will. Whatever the price, it is a thousand times worth it. No matter what our enemies in their desperation may attempt to do to us—we will say, as the people of London have said, "We can take it." And what's more, we can give it back—and we will give it back—with compound interest.

When our enemies challenged our country to stand up and fight, they challenged each and every one of us. And each and every one of us has accepted the challenge—for himself and for the nation.

There were only some 400 United States marines who in the heroic and historic defense of Wake Island inflicted such great losses on the enemy. Some of those men were killed in action: and others are now prisoners of war. When the survivors of that great fight are liberated and restored to their homes, they will learn that a hundred and thirty million of their fellow citizens have been inspired to render their own full share of service and sacrifice.

Our men on the fighting fronts have already proved that Americans today are just as rugged and just as tough as any of the heroes whose exploits we celebrate on the Fourth of July.

Many people ask, "When will this war end?" There is only one answer to that. It will end just as soon as we make it end, by our combined efforts, our combined strength, our combined determination to fight through and work through until the end—the end of militarism in Germany and Italy and Japan. Most certainly we shall not settle for less.

That is the spirit in which discussions have been conducted during the visit of the British Prime Minister to Washington.[6] Mr. Churchill and I understand each other, our motives, and our purposes. Together, during the past two weeks, we have faced squarely the major military and economic problems of this greatest world war.

All in our nation have been cheered by Mr. Churchill's visit. We have been deeply stirred by his great message to us. We wish him a safe return to his home. He is welcome in our midst, now and in days to come.

We are fighting on the same side with the British people, who fought alone for long, terrible months, and withstood the enemy with fortitude and tenacity and skill.[7]

We are fighting on the same side with the Russian people who have seen the Nazi hordes swarm up to the very gates of Moscow, and who with almost superhuman will and courage have forced the invaders back into retreat.

We are fighting on the same side as the brave people of China who for four and a half long years have withstood bombs and starvation and have whipped the invaders time and again in spite of superior Japanese equipment and arms.

We are fighting on the same side as the indomitable Dutch.

We are fighting on the same side as all the other governments in exile, whom Hitler and all his armies and all his Gestapo have not been able to conquer.

But we of the united nations are not making all this sacrifice of human effort and human lives to return to the kind of world we had after the last World War.

---

[6] Ten days after Adolf Hitler declared war on the United States (December 11, 1941), Prime Minister Winston Churchill flew to Washington for Christmas talks directly with President Roosevelt. The Arcadia Conference (December 22–January 14, 1942) reaffirmed their resolve to defeat Nazi Germany first, then crush Japan. After the military Chiefs of Staff from both countries met to establish a method of unified command, Roosevelt declared an accelerated increase of Lend-Lease supplies to Britain.

---

[7] In January 1941 the situation appeared grim for Britain. For over six months the Germans had been attempting to gain air superiority over England through massive bombing raids on London, "the Blitz." This air phase of the Battle of Britain was preparatory to a German amphibious and airborne landing. In November, Prime Minister Churchill and President Roosevelt concluded a deal that involved giving fifty American destroyers to the British for U.S. access to a string of British bases in the Atlantic. The agreement was significant because the president's executive agreement bypassed Congress and constituted a virtual act of war by nullifying any U.S. pretense of neutrality.

We are fighting today for security, for progress and for peace, not only for ourselves, but for all men, not only for one generation but for all generations. We are fighting to cleanse the world of ancient evils, ancient ills.

Our enemies are guided by brutal cynicism, by unholy contempt for the human race. We are inspired by a faith which goes back through all the years to the first chapter of the Book of Genesis: "God created man in His own image."

We on our side are striving to be true to that divine heritage. We are fighting as our fathers have fought, to uphold the doctrine that all men are equal in the sight of God. Those on the other side are striving to destroy this deep belief and to create a world in their own image—a world of tyranny and cruelty and serfdom.

That is the conflict that day and night now pervades our lives. No compromise can end that conflict. There never has been—there never can be—successful compromise between good and evil. Only total victory can reward the champions of tolerance and decency and freedom and faith.

SOURCE: U.S. State Department, *Bulletin* 6, no. 133 (January 10, 1942): 39–43.

14

HARRY S. TRUMAN

DOCUMENT 53

PRESIDENT HARRY TRUMAN'S STATEMENT APPOINTING GENERAL DOUGLAS MacARTHUR COMMANDER OF UN FORCES IN KOREA. JULY 8, 1950.

The Security Council of the United Nations in its resolution of July 7, 1950, has recommended that all members providing military forces and other assistance pursuant to the Security Council resolutions of June 25 and 27 make such forces and other assistance available to a unified command under the United States.

The Security Council resolution also requests that the United States designate the commander of such forces, and authorize the unified command at its discretion to use the United Nations flag in the course of operations against the North Korean forces concurrently with the flags of the various nations participating.

I am responding to the recommendation of the Security Council and have designated General Douglas A. MacArthur as the Commanding General of the military forces which the members of the United Nations place under the unified command of the United States pursuant to the United Nations' assistance to the Republic of Korea in repelling the unprovoked armed attack against it.*

I am directing General MacArthur, pursuant to the Security Council resolution, to use the United Nations flag in the course of operations against the North Korean forces concurrently with the flags of the various nations participating.

SOURCE: *Public Papers of the Presidents: Harry S. Truman, 1950* (Washington, DC: Government Printing Office, 1965), 491–92.

*****Douglas MacArthur**, 1880–1964; a career officer who emerged during World War II as one of the ablest commanders in the Far East. After accepting the Japanese surrender in September 1945 aboard the USS *Missouri*, MacArthur remained in occupied Japan as Supreme Allied Military Governor. His father, Arthur MacArthur, was military governor of the Philippines during the McKinley administration.

DOCUMENT 54

PRESIDENT TRUMAN'S SPECIAL MESSAGE TO CONGRESS REPORTING THE SITUATION IN KOREA. JULY 19, 1950.

To the Congress of the United States:

I am reporting to the Congress on the situation which has been created in Korea, and on the actions which this Nation has taken, as a member of the United Nations, to meet this situation. I am also laying before the Congress my views concerning the significance of these events for this Nation and the world, and certain recommendations for legislative action which I believe should be taken at this time.

At four o'clock in the morning, Sunday June 25th, Korean time, armed forces from north of the thirty-eighth parallel invaded the Republic of Korea.

The Republic of Korea was established as an independent nation in August, 1948, after a free election held under the auspices of the United Nations. This election, which was originally intended to cover all of Korea, was held only in the part of the Korean peninsula south of the thirty-eighth parallel, because the Soviet Government, which occupied the peninsula north of that parallel, refused to allow the election to be held in the area under its control.

The United States, and a majority of the other members of the United Nations, have recognized the Republic of Korea. The admission of Korea to the United Nations has been blocked by the Soviet veto.[1]

In December, 1948, the Soviet Government stated that it had withdrawn its occupation troops from northern Korea, and that a local regime had been established there. The authorities in northern Korea continued to refuse to permit United Nations observers to pass the thirty-eighth parallel to supervise or observe a free election, or to verify the withdrawal of Soviet troops.

Nevertheless, the United Nations continued its efforts to obtain a freely-elected government for all of Korea, and at the time of the attack, a United Nations Commission, made up of representatives of seven nations—Australia, China, El Salvador, France, India, the Philippines and Turkey—was in the Republic of Korea.

---

[1] The UN Charter was signed in 1945. As one of the five standing members of the United Nations Security Council, the Soviet Union had veto power over any issue before the United Nations.

Just one day before the attack of June 25th, field observers attached to the United Nations Commission on Korea had completed a routine tour, lasting two weeks, of the military positions of the Republic of Korea south of the thirty-eighth parallel.

The report of these international observers stated that the Army of the Republic of Korea was organized entirely for defense. The observers found the parallel guarded on the south side by small bodies of troops in scattered outposts, with roving patrols. They found no concentration of troops and no preparation to attack. The observers concluded that the absence of armor, air support, heavy artillery, and military supplies precluded any offensive action by the forces of the Republic of Korea.

On June 25th, within a few hours after the invasion was launched from the north, the Commission reported to the United Nations that the attack had come without warning and without provocation.

The reports from the Commission make it unmistakably clear that the attack was naked, deliberate, unprovoked aggression, without a shadow of justification.

This outright breach of the peace, in violation of the United Nations Charter, created a real and present danger to the security of every nation. This attack was, in addition, a demonstration of contempt for the United Nations, since it was an attempt to settle, by military aggression, a question which the United Nations had been working to settle by peaceful means.

The attack on the Republic of Korea, therefore, was a clear challenge to the basic principles of the United Nations Charter and to the specific actions taken by the United Nations in Korea. If this challenge had not been met squarely, the effectiveness of the United Nations would have been all but ended, and the hope of mankind that the United Nations would develop into an institution of world order would have been shattered.

Prompt action was imperative. The Security Council of the United Nations met, at the request of the United States, in New York at two o'clock in the afternoon, Sunday, June 25th, eastern daylight time. Since there is a 14-hour difference in time between Korea and New York, this meant that the Council convened just 24 hours after the attack began.

At this meeting, the Security Council passed a resolution which called for the immediate cessation of hostilities and for the withdrawal of the invading troops to the thirty-eighth parallel, and which requested the members of the United Nations to refrain from giving aid to the northern aggressors and to assist in the execution of this resolution. The representative of the Soviet Union to the Security Council stayed away from the meetings, and the Soviet Government has refused to support the Council's resolution.

The attack launched on June 25th moved ahead rapidly. The tactical surprise gained by the aggressors, and their superiority in planes, tanks, and artillery, forced the lightly-armed defenders to retreat. The speed, the scale, and the coordination of the attack left no doubt that it had been plotted long in advance.

When the attack came, our Ambassador to Korea, John J. Muccio, began the immediate evacuation of American women and children from the danger zone. To protect this evacuation, air cover and sea cover were provided by the Commander in Chief of United States Forces in the Far East, General of the Army Douglas MacArthur. In response to urgent appeals from the Government of Korea, General MacArthur was immediately authorized to send supplies of ammunition to the Korean defenders. These supplies were sent by air transport, with fighter protection. The United States Seventh Fleet was ordered north from the Philippines, so that it might be available in the area in case of need.

Throughout Monday, June 26th, the invaders continued their attack with no heed to the resolution of the Security Council of the United Nations. Accordingly, in order to support the resolution, and on the unanimous advice of our civil and military authorities, I ordered United States air and sea forces to give the Korean Government troops cover and support.

On Tuesday, June 27th, when the United Nations Commission in Korea had reported that the northern troops had neither ceased hostilities nor withdrawn to the thirty-eighth parallel, the United Nations Security Council met again and passed a second resolution recommending that members of the United Nations furnish to the Republic of Korea such aid as might be necessary to repel the attack and to restore international peace and security in the area. The representative of the Soviet Union to the Security Council stayed away from this meeting also,[2] and the Soviet Government has refused to support the Council's resolution.

The vigorous and unhesitating actions of the United Nations and the United States in the face of this aggression met with an immediate and overwhelming response throughout the free world. The first blow of aggression had brought dismay and anxiety to the hearts of men the world

---

[2]The Soviet Union had no official UN representative serving during the initial days of the conflict because of a self-imposed boycott.

over. The fateful events of the 1930s, when aggression unopposed bred more aggression and eventually war, were fresh in our memory.

But the free nations had learned the lesson of history. Their determined and united actions uplifted the spirit of free men everywhere. As a result, where there had been dismay there is hope; where there had been anxiety there is firm determination.

Fifty-two of the fifty-nine member nations have supported the United Nations action to restore peace in Korea.

A number of member nations have offered military support or other types of assistance for the United Nations action to repel the aggressors in Korea. In a third resolution, passed on July 7th, the Security Council requested the United States to designate a commander for all the forces of the members of the United Nations in the Korean operation, and authorized these forces to fly the United Nations flag. In response to this resolution, General MacArthur has been designated as commander of these forces. These are important steps forward in the development of a United Nations system of collective security. Already, aircraft of two nations—Australia and Great Britain—and naval vessels of five nations—Australia, Canada, Great Britain, the Netherlands and New Zealand—have been made available for operations in the Korean area, along with forces of Korea and the United States, under General MacArthur's command. The other offers of assistance that have been and will continue to be made will be coordinated by the United Nations and by the unified command, in order to support the effort in Korea to maximum advantage.

All the members of the United Nations who have indorsed the action of the Security Council realize the significance of the step that has been taken. This united and resolute action to put down lawless aggression is a milestone toward the establishment of a rule of law among nations.

Only a few countries have failed to support the common action to restore the peace. The most important of these is the Soviet Union.

Since the Soviet representative had refused to participate in the meetings of the Security Council which took action regarding Korea, the United States brought the matter directly to the attention of the Soviet Government in Moscow. On June 27th, we requested the Soviet Government, in view of its known close relations with the north Korean regime, to use its influence to have the invaders withdraw at once.

The Soviet Government, in its reply on June 29th and in subsequent statements, has taken the position that the attack launched by the north Korean forces was provoked by the Republic of Korea, and that the actions of the United Nations Security Council were illegal.

These Soviet claims are flatly disproved by the facts.

The attitude of the Soviet Government toward the aggression against the Republic of Korea, is in direct contradiction to its often expressed intention to work with other nations to achieve peace in the world.

For our part, we shall continue to support the United Nations action to restore peace in the Korean area.

As the situation has developed, I have authorized a number of measures to be taken. Within the first week of the fighting, General MacArthur reported, after a visit to the front, that the forces from north Korea were continuing to drive south, and further support to the Republic of Korea was needed. Accordingly, General MacArthur was authorized to use United States Army troops in Korea, and to use United States aircraft of the Air Force and the Navy to conduct missions against specific military targets in Korea north of the thirty-eighth parallel, where necessary to carry out the United Nations resolution. General MacArthur was also directed to blockade the Korean coast.

The attacking forces from the north have continued to move forward, although their advance has been slowed down. The troops of the Republic of Korea, though initially overwhelmed by the tanks and artillery of the surprise attack by the invaders, have been reorganized and are fighting bravely.

United States forces, as they have arrived in the area, have fought with great valor. The Army troops have been conducting a very difficult delaying operation with skill and determination, outnumbered many times over by attacking troops, spearheaded by tanks. Despite the bad weather of the rainy season, our troops have been valiantly supported by the air and naval forces of both the United States and other members of the United Nations.

In this connection, I think it is important that the nature of our military action in Korea be understood. It should be made perfectly clear that the action was undertaken as a matter of basic moral principle. The United States was going to the aid of a nation established and supported by the United Nations and unjustifiably attacked by an aggressor force. Consequently, we were not deterred by the relative immediate superiority of the attacking forces, by the fact that our base of supplies was 5,000 miles away, or by the further fact that we would have to supply our forces through port facilities that are far from satisfactory.

We are moving as rapidly as possible to bring to bear on the fighting front larger forces and heavier equipment, and to increase our naval and air superiority. But it will take time, men, and material to slow down the forces of aggression, bring those forces to a halt, and throw them back.

Nevertheless, our assistance to the Republic of Korea has prevented the invaders from crushing that nation in a few days—as they had evidently expected to do. We are determined to support the United Nations in its effort to restore peace and security to Korea, and its effort to assure the people of Korea an opportunity to choose their own form of government free from coercion, as expressed in the General Assembly resolutions of November 14, 1947, and December 12, 1948.

In addition to the direct military effort we and other members of the United Nations are making in Korea, the outbreak of aggression there requires us to consider its implications for peace throughout the world. The attack upon the Republic of Korea makes it plain beyond all doubt that the international communist movement is prepared to use armed invasion to conquer independent nations. We must therefore recognize the possibility that armed aggression may take place in other areas.

In view of this, I have already directed that United States forces in support of the Philippines be strengthened, and that military assistance be speeded up to the Philippine Government and to the Associated States of Indo-China and to the forces of France in Indo-China. I have also ordered the United States Seventh Fleet to prevent any attack upon Formosa, and I have requested the Chinese Government on Formosa to cease all air and sea operations against the mainland. These steps were at once reported to the United Nations Security Council.

Our action in regard to Formosa was a matter of elementary security. The peace and stability of the Pacific area had been violently disturbed by the attack on Korea.

Attacks elsewhere in the Pacific area would have enlarged the Korean crisis, thereby rendering much more difficult the carrying out of our obligations to the United Nations in Korea.

In order that there may be no doubt in any quarter about our intentions regarding Formosa, I wish to state that the United States has no territorial ambitions whatever concerning that island, nor do we seek for ourselves any special position or privilege on Formosa. The present military neutralization of Formosa is without prejudice to political questions affecting that island. Our desire is that Formosa not become embroiled in hostilities disturbing to the peace of the Pacific and that all questions affecting Formosa be settled by peaceful means as envisaged in the Charter of the United Nations. With peace re-established, even the most complex political questions are susceptible of solution. In the presence of brutal and unprovoked aggression, however, some of these questions may have to be held in abeyance in the interest of the essential security of all.

The outbreak of aggression in the Far East does not, of course, lessen, but instead increases, the importance of the common strength of the free nations in other parts of the world. The attack on the Republic of Korea gives added urgency to the efforts of the free nations to increase and to unify their common strength, in order to deter a potential aggressor.

To be able to accomplish this objective, the free nations must maintain a sufficient defensive military strength in being, and, even more important, a solid basis of economic strength, capable of rapid mobilization in the event of emergency. . . .

We have been increasing our common defensive strength under the treaty of Rio de Janeiro,[3] which are collective security arrangements within the framework of the United Nations Charter. We have also taken action to bolster the military defenses of individual free nations, such as Greece, Turkey, and Iran.

The defenses of the North Atlantic Treaty area were considered a matter of great urgency by the North Atlantic Council in London this spring. Recent events make it even more urgent than it was at that time to build and maintain these defenses.[4]

Under all the circumstances, it is apparent that the United States is required to increase its military strength and preparedness not only to deal with the aggression in Korea but also to increase our common defense, with other free nations, against further aggression.

The increased strength which is needed falls into three categories.

In the first place, to meet the situation in Korea, we shall need to send additional men, equipment and supplies to General MacArthur's command as rapidly as possible.

In the second place, the world situation requires that we increase substantially the size and materiel support of our armed forces, over and above the increases which are needed in Korea.

In the third place, we must assist the free nations associated with us in common defense to augment their military strength.

Of the three categories I have just enumerated, the first two involve increases in our own military manpower, and in the material support that our men must have.

---

[3] U.S.-Latin American alliance signed in 1947 to protect inter-American security by providing U.S. military assistance to countries in the region.

---

[4] Signed in 1949 the North Atlantic Treaty Organization (NATO) was a defensive alliance between the United States, Canada, and major European countries against further Soviet expansionism into Western Europe.

To meet the increased requirements for military manpower, I have authorized the Secretary of Defense [Louis Johnson] to exceed the budgeted strength of military personnel for the Army, Navy, and Air Force, and to use the Selective Service system to such extent as may be required in order to obtain the increased strength which we must have. I have also authorized the Secretary of Defense to meet the need for military manpower by calling into active Federal service as many National Guard units and as many units and individuals of the Reserve forces of the Army, Navy, and Air Forces as may be required.

I have directed the Secretary of Defense and the Joint Chiefs of Staff to keep our military manpower needs under constant study, in order that further increases may be made as required. There are now statutory limits on the sizes of the armed forces, and since we may need to exceed these limits, I recommend that they be removed.

To increase the level of our military strength will also require additional supplies and equipment. Procurement of many items has already been accelerated, in some cases for use in Korea, in others to replace reserve stocks which are now being sent to Korea, and in still others to add to our general level of preparedness. Further increases in procurement, resulting in a higher rate of production of military equipment and supplies, will be necessary.

The increases in the size of the armed forces, and the additional supplies and equipment which will be needed, will require additional appropriations. Within the next few days, I will transmit to the Congress specific requests for appropriations in the amount of approximately ten billion dollars.

These requests for appropriations will be addressed to the needs of our own military forces. Earlier, I referred to the fact that we must also assist other free nations in the strengthening of our common defenses. The action we must take to accomplish this is just as important as the measures required to strengthen our own forces.

The authorization bill for the Mutual Defense Assistance [military aid] Program for 1951 now before the House of Representatives, is an important immediate step toward the strengthening of our collective security. It should be enacted without delay.

But it is now clear that the free nations of the world must step up their common security program. The other nations associated with us in the Mutual Defense Assistance Program, like ourselves, will need to divert additional economic resources to defense purposes. In order to enable the nations associated with us to make their maximum contribution to our common defense, further assistance on our part will be required. Additional assistance may also be needed to increase the strength of certain other free nations whose security is vital to our own.

In the case of the North Atlantic area these requirements will reflect the consultations now going on with the other nations associated with us in the North Atlantic Treaty. As soon as it is possible to determine what each nation will need to do, I shall lay before the Congress a request for such funds as are shown to be necessary to the attainment and maintenance of our common strength at an adequate level.

The steps which we must take to support the United Nations action in Korea, and to increase our own strength and the common defense of the free world, will necessarily have repercussions upon our domestic economy.

Many of our young men are in battle now, or soon will be. Others must be trained. The equipment and supplies they need, and those required for adequate emergency reserves, must be produced. They must be available promptly, at reasonable cost, and without disrupting the efficient functioning of the economy.

We must continue to recognize that our strength is not to be measured in military terms alone. Our power to join in a common defense of peace rests fundamentally on the productive capacity and energies of our people. In all that we do, therefore, we must make sure that the economic strength which is at the base of our security is not impaired, but continues to grow.

Our economy has tremendous productive power. Our total output of goods and services is now running at an annual rate of nearly 270 billion dollars—over 100 billion dollars higher than in 1939. The rate is now about 13 billion dollars higher than a year ago, and about 8 billion dollars higher than the previous record rate reached in 1948. All the foregoing figures have been adjusted for price changes, and are therefore a measure of actual output. The index of industrial production, now at 197, is 12 percent higher than the average for last year, and 81 percent higher than in 1939.

We now have 61½ million people in civilian employment. There are 16 million more people in productive jobs than there were in 1939. We are now producing 11 million more tons of steel a year than in the peak war year 1944. Electric power output has risen from 128 billion kilowatt hours in 1939, to 228 billion hours in 1944, to 317 billion hours now. Food production is about a third higher than it ever was before the war, and is practically as high as it was during the war years, when we were sending far more food abroad than we are now.

The potential productive power of our economy is even greater. We can achieve some immediate increase in production by employing men and facilities not now fully utilized. And we can continue to increase our total annual output each year, by putting to use the increasing skills of our growing population and the higher productive capacity which results from plant expansion, new inventions, and more efficient methods of production.

With this enormous economic strength, the new and necessary programs I am now recommending can be undertaken with confidence in the ability of our economy to bear the strains involved. Nevertheless, the magnitude of the demands for military purposes that are now foreseeable, in an economy which is already operating at a very high level, will require substantial redirection of economic resources.

Under the program for increasing military strength which I have outlined above, military and related procurement will need to be expanded at a more rapid rate than total production can be expanded. Some materials were in short supply even before the Korean situation developed. The steel industry, for example, was operating at capacity levels, and even so was not able to satisfy all market demands. Some other construction materials, and certain other products, were also under pressure and their prices were rising—even before the outbreak in Korea.

The substantial speed-up of military procurement will intensify these shortages. Action must be taken to insure that these shortages do not interfere with or delay the materials and the supplies needed for the national defense.

Further, the dollars spent now for military purposes will have a magnified effect upon the economy as a whole, since they will be added to the high level of current civilian demand. These increased pressures, if neglected, could drive us into a general inflationary situation. The best evidence of this is the recent price advances in many raw materials and in the cost of living, even upon the mere expectancy of increased military outlays.

In these circumstances, we must take action to insure that the increased national defense needs will be met, and that in the process we do not bring on an inflation, with its resulting hardship for every family.

At the same time, we must recognize that it will be necessary for a number of years to support continuing defense expenditures, including assistance to other nations at a higher level than we had previously planned. Therefore, the economic measures we take now must be planned and used in such a manner as to develop and maintain our economic strength for the long run as well as the short run.

I am recommending certain legislative measures to help achieve these objectives. I believe that each of them should be promptly enacted. We must be sure to take the steps that are necessary now, or we shall surely be required to take much more drastic steps later on.

First, we should adopt such direct measures as are now necessary to assure prompt and adequate supplies of goods for military and essential civilian use. I therefore recommend that the Congress now enact legislation authorizing the Government to establish priorities and allocate materials as necessary to promote the national security; to limit the use of materials for nonessential purposes; to prevent inventory hoarding; and to requisition supplies and materials needed for the national defense, particularly excessive and unnecessary inventories.

Second, we must promptly adopt some general measures to compensate for the growth of demand caused by the expansion of military programs in a period of high civilian incomes. I am directing all executive agencies to conduct a detailed review of Government programs, for the purpose of modifying them wherever practicable to lessen the demand upon services, commodities, raw materials, manpower, and facilities which are in competition with those needed for national defense. The Government, as well as the public, must exercise great restraint in the use of those goods and services which are needed for our increased defense efforts.

Nevertheless, the increased appropriations for the Department of Defense, plus the defense-related appropriations which I have recently submitted for power development and atomic energy, and others which will be necessary for such purposes as stockpiling, will mean sharply increased Federal expenditures. For this reason, we should increase Federal revenues more sharply than I have previously recommended, in order to reduce the inflationary effect of the Government deficit.

There are two fundamental principles which must guide us in framing measures to obtain these additional revenues:

(A) We must make every effort to finance the greatest possible amount of needed expenditures by taxation. The increase of taxes is our basic weapon in offsetting the inflationary pressures exerted by enlarged government expenditures. Heavier taxes will make general controls less necessary.

(B) We must provide for a balanced system of taxation which makes a fair distribution of the tax burden among the different groups of individuals and business concerns in the Nation. A balanced tax program should also have as a major aim the elimination of profiteering.

At an appropriate time, as soon as the necessary studies are completed, I shall present to the Congress a program based on these principles to assure the financing of our needs in a manner which will be fair to all our citizens, which will help prevent inflation, and which will maintain the fiscal position of the Nation in the soundest possible condition.

As a further important safeguard against inflation, we shall need to restrain credit expansion. I recommend that the Congress now authorize the control of consumer credit and credit used for commodity speculation. In the housing field, where Government credit is an important factor, I have directed that certain available credit restraints be applied, and I recommend that further controls be authorized, particularly to restrain expansion of privately-financed real estate credit. These actions will not only reduce the upward pressure on prices, but will also reduce the demand for certain critical materials which are required for the production of military equipment.

Third, we must take steps to accelerate and increase the production of essential materials, products, and services. I recommend, therefore, that the Congress authorize, for national defense purposes, production loan guarantees and loans to increase production. I also recommend that the Congress authorize the making of long-term contracts and other means to encourage the production of certain materials in short supply.

In the forthcoming Mid-year Economic Report, I shall discuss in greater detail the current economic situation, and the economic measures which I have recommended. If these measures are made available promptly, and firmly administered, I believe we will be able to meet military needs without serious disruption of the economy.

If we are to be successful, there must be sensible and restrained action by businessmen, labor, farmers and consumers. The people of this country know the seriousness of inflation, and will, I am sure, do everything they can to see that it does not come upon us. However, if a sharp rise in prices should make it necessary, I shall not hesitate to recommend the more drastic measures of price control and rationing.

The hard facts of the present situation require relentless determination and firm action. The course of the fighting thus far in Korea shows that we can expect no easy solution to the conflict there. We are confronted in Korea with well-supplied, well-led forces which have been long trained for aggressive action. We and the other members of the United Nations who have joined in the effort to restore peace in Korea must expect a hard and costly military operation.

We must also prepare ourselves better to fulfill our responsibilities toward the preservation of international peace and security against possible further aggression. In this effort, we will not flinch in the face of danger or difficulty.

The free world has made it clear, through the United Nations, that lawless aggression will be met with force. This is the significance of Korea— and it is a significance whose importance cannot be over-estimated. I shall not attempt to predict the course of events. But I am sure that those who have it in their power to unleash or withhold acts of armed aggression must realize that new recourse to aggression in the world today might well strain to the breaking point the fabric of world peace.

The United States can be proud of the part it has played in the United Nations action in this crisis. We can be proud of the unhesitating support of the American people for the resolute actions taken to halt the aggression in Korea and to support the cause of world peace.

The Congress of the United States, by its strong, bipartisan support of the steps we are taking and by repeated actions in support of international cooperation, has contributed most vitally to the cause of peace. The expressions of support which have been forthcoming from the leaders of both political parties for the actions of our Government and of the United Nations in dealing with the present crisis, have buttressed the firm morale of the entire free world in the face of this challenge.

The American people, together with other free peoples, seek a new era in world affairs. We seek a world where all men may live in peace and freedom, with steadily improving living conditions, under governments of their own free choice.

For ourselves, we seek no territory or domination over others. We are determined to maintain our democratic institutions so that Americans now and in the future can enjoy personal liberty, economic opportunity, and political equality. We are concerned with advancing our prosperity and our well-being as a Nation, but we know that our future is inseparably joined with the future of other free peoples.

We will follow the course we have chosen with courage and with faith, because we carry in our hearts the flame of freedom. We are fighting for liberty and for peace—and with God's blessing we shall succeed.

SOURCE: *Public Papers: Truman, 1950,* 527–37.

DOCUMENT 55
PRESIDENT TRUMAN'S TELEVISED ADDRESS TO THE NATION ON THE DEPLOYMENT OF U.S. FORCES TO KOREA. JULY 19, 1950.

My Fellow Citizens:

At noon today I sent a message to the Congress about the situation in Korea. I want to talk to you tonight about that situation, and about what it means to the security of the United States and to our hopes for peace in the world.

Korea is a small country, thousands of miles away, but what is happening there is important to every American.

On Sunday, June 25th, Communist forces attacked the Republic of Korea.

This attack has made it clear, beyond all doubt, that the international Communist movement is willing to use armed invasion to conquer independent nations. An act of aggression such as this creates a very real danger to the security of all free nations.

The attack upon Korea was an outright breach of the peace and a violation of the Charter of the United Nations. By their actions in Korea, Communist leaders have demonstrated their contempt for the basic moral principles on which the United Nations is founded. This is a direct challenge to the efforts of the free nations to build the kind of world in which men can live in freedom and peace.

This challenge has been presented squarely. We must meet it squarely.

It is important for all of us to understand the essential facts as to how the situation in Korea came about.

Before and during World War II, Korea was subject to Japanese rule. When the fighting stopped, it was agreed that troops of the Soviet Union would accept the surrender of the Japanese soldiers in the northern part of Korea, and that American forces would accept the surrender of the Japanese in the southern part. For this purpose, the 38th parallel was used as the dividing line.* Later, the United Nations sought to establish Korea as a free and independent nation. A commission was sent out to supervise a free election in the whole of Korea. However, this election was held only in the southern part of the country, because the Soviet Union refused to permit an election for this purpose to be held in the northern part. Indeed, the Soviet authorities even refused to permit the United Nations Commission to visit northern Korea.

Nevertheless, the United Nations decided to go ahead where it could. In August 1948 the Republic of Korea was established as a free and independent nation in that part of Korea south of the 38th parallel.

In December 1948, the Soviet Union stated that it had withdrawn its troops from northern Korea and that a local government had been established

---

*In August 1945, Soviet and U.S. policymakers decided on the 38th parallel as the line to separate their forces in order to disarm the defeated forces of Japan and to rebuild an occupied Korea.

there. However, the Communist authorities never have permitted the United Nations observers to visit northern Korea to see what was going on behind that part of the Iron Curtain.

It was from that area, where the Communist authorities have been unwilling to let the outside world see what was going on, that the attack was launched against the Republic of Korea on June 25th. That attack came without provocation and without warning. It was an act of raw aggression, without a shadow of justification.

I repeat that it was an act of raw aggression. It had no justification whatever.

The Communist invasion was launched in great force, with planes, tanks, and artillery. The size of the attack, and the speed with which it was followed up, make it perfectly plain that it had been plotted long in advance.

As soon as word of the attack was received, Secretary of State [Dean] Acheson called me at Independence, Missouri, and informed me that, with my approval, he would ask for an immediate meeting of the United Nations Security Council. The Security Council met just 24 hours after the Communist invasion began.

One of the main reasons the Security Council was set up was to act in such cases as this—to stop outbreaks of aggression in a hurry before they develop into general conflicts. In this case the Council passed a resolution which called for the invaders of Korea to stop fighting, and to withdraw. The Council called on all members of the United Nations to help carry out this resolution. The Communist invaders ignored the action of the Security Council and kept right on with their attack.

The Security Council then met again. It recommended that members of the United Nations help the Republic of Korea repel the attack and help restore peace and security in that area.

Fifty-two of the 59 countries which are members of the United Nations have given their support to the action taken by the Security Council to restore peace in Korea.

These actions by the United Nations and its members are of great importance. The free nations have now made it clear that lawless aggression will be met with force. The free nations have learned the fateful lesson of the 1930s. That lesson is that aggression must be met firmly. Appeasement leads only to further aggression and ultimately to war.

The principal effort to help the Koreans preserve their independence, and to help the United Nations restore peace, has been made by the United States. We have sent land, sea, and air forces to assist in these operations. We have done this because we know that what is at stake here is nothing less than our own national security and the peace of the world.

So far, two other nations—Australia and Great Britain—have sent planes to Korea; and six other nations—Australia, Canada, France, Great Britain, the Netherlands, and New Zealand—have made naval forces available.

Under the flag of the United Nations a unified command has been established for all forces of the members of the United Nations fighting in Korea. Gen. Douglas MacArthur is the commander of this combined force.

The prompt action of the United Nations to put down lawless aggression, and the prompt response to this action by free peoples all over the world, will stand as a landmark in mankind's long search for a rule of law among nations.

Only a few countries have failed to endorse the efforts of the United Nations to stop the fighting in Korea. The most important of these is the Soviet Union. The Soviet Union has boycotted the meetings of the United Nations Security Council. It has refused to support the actions of the United Nations with respect to Korea.

The United States requested the Soviet Government, 2 days after the fighting started, to use its influence with the North Koreans to have them withdraw. The Soviet Government refused.

The Soviet Government has said many times that it wants peace in the world, but its attitude toward this act of aggression against the Republic of Korea is in direct contradiction of its statements.

For our part, we shall continue to support the United Nations action to restore peace in the world.

We know that it will take a hard, tough fight to halt the invasion, and to drive the Communists back. The invaders have been provided with enough equipment and supplies for a long campaign. They overwhelmed the lightly armed defense forces of the Korean Republic in the first few days and drove southward.

Now, however, the Korean defenders have reorganized and are making a brave fight for their liberty, and an increasing number of American troops have joined them. Our forces have fought a skillful, rearguard delaying action, pending the arrival of reinforcements. Some of these reinforcements are now arriving; others are on the way from the United States.

I should like to read you a part of a report I have received from General [J. Lawton] Collins, Chief of Staff of the United States Army. General Collins and General [Hoyt S.] Vandenberg, Chief of Staff of the Air Force, have just returned from an inspection trip to Korea and Japan.

This is what General Collins had to say:

"The United States Armed Forces in Korea are giving a splendid account of themselves.

"Our Far Eastern forces were organized and equipped primarily to perform peaceful occupation duties in Japan. However, under General MacArthur's magnificent leadership, they have quickly adapted themselves to meet the deliberately planned attack of the North Korean Communist forces, which are well-equipped, well-led, and battle-trained, and which have at times outnumbered our troops by as much as 20 to 1.

"Our Army troops, ably supported by tactical aircraft of the United States Air Force and Navy and our Australian friends, flying under the most adverse conditions of weather, have already distinguished themselves in the most difficult of military operations—a delaying action. The fact that they are preventing the Communists from overrunning Korea—which this calculated attack had been designed to accomplish—is a splendid tribute to the ability of our Armed Forces to convert quickly from the peaceful duties of occupation to the grim duties of war.

"The task that confronts us is not an easy one, but I am confident of the outcome."

I shall also read to you part of a report that I received from General MacArthur within the last few hours.

General MacArthur says:

"It is, of course, impossible to predict with any degree of accuracy the future incidents of a military campaign. Over a broad front involving continuous local struggles, there are bound to be ups and downs, losses as well as successes. . . . But the issue of battle is now fully joined and will proceed along lines of action in which we will not be without choice. Our hold upon the southern part of Korea represents a secure base. Our casualties, despite overwhelming odds, have been relatively light. Our strength will continually increase while that of the enemy will relatively decrease. His supply line is insecure. He has had his great chance and failed to exploit it. We are now in Korea in force, and with God's help we are there to stay until the constitutional authority of the Republic of Korea is fully restored."

These and other reports I have received show that our Armed Forces are acting with close teamwork and efficiency to meet the problems facing us in Korea.

These reports are reassuring, but they also show that the job ahead of us in Korea is long and difficult.

Furthermore, the fact that Communist forces have invaded Korea is a warning that there may be similar acts of aggression in other parts of the world. The free nations must be on their guard, more than ever before, against this kind of sneak attack.

It is obvious that we must increase our military strength and preparedness immediately. There are three things we need to do.

First, we need to send more men, equipment, and supplies to General MacArthur.

Second, in view of the world situation, we need to build up our own Army, Navy, and Air Force over and above what is needed in Korea.

Third, we need to speed up our work with other countries in strengthening our common defenses.

To help meet these needs, I have already authorized increases in the size of our Armed Forces. These increases will come in part from volunteers, in part from Selective Service, and in part from the National Guard and the Reserves.

I have also ordered that military supplies and equipment be obtained at a faster rate.

The necessary increases in the size of our Armed Forces, and the additional equipment they must have, will cost about $10 billion, and I am asking the Congress to appropriate the amount required.

These funds will be used to train men and equip them with tanks, planes, guns, and ships, in order to build the strength we need to help assure peace in the world.

When we have worked out with other free countries an increased program for our common defense, I shall recommend to the Congress that additional funds be provided for this purpose. This is of great importance. The free nations face a worldwide threat. It must be met with a worldwide defense. The United States and other free nations can multiply their strength by joining with one another in a common effort to provide this defense. This is our best hope for peace.

The things we need to do to build up our military defense will require considerable adjustment in our domestic economy. We have a tremendously rich and productive economy, and it is expanding every year.

Our job now is to divert to defense purposes more of that tremendous productive capacity—more steel, more aluminum, more of a good many things.

Some of the additional production for military purposes can come from making fuller use of plants which are not operating at capacity. But many of our industries are already going full tilt, and until we can add new capacity, some of the resources we need for the national defense will have to be taken from civilian uses.

This requires us to take certain steps to make sure that we obtain the things we need for national defense, and at the same time guard against inflationary price rises.

The steps that are needed now must be taken promptly.

In the message which I sent to the Congress today, I described the economic measures which are required at this time.

First, we need laws which will insure prompt and adequate supplies for military and essential civilian use. I have therefore recommended that the Congress give the Government power to guide the flow of materials into essential uses, to restrict their use for nonessential purposes, and to prevent the accumulation of unnecessary inventories.

Second, we must adopt measures to prevent inflation and to keep our Government in a sound financial condition. One of the major causes of inflation is the excessive use of credit. I have recommended that the Congress authorize the Government to set limits on installment buying and to curb speculation in agricultural commodities. In the housing field, where Government credit is an important factor, I have already directed that credit restraints be applied, and I have recommended that the Congress authorize further controls.

As an additional safeguard against inflation, and to help finance our defense needs, it will be necessary to make substantial increases in taxes. This is a contribution to our national security that every one of us should stand ready to make. As soon as a balanced and fair tax program can be worked out, I shall lay it before the Congress. This tax program will have as a major aim the elimination of profiteering.

Third, we should increase the production of goods needed for national defense. We must plan to enlarge our defense production, not just for the immediate future, but for the next several years. This will be primarily a task for our businessmen and workers. However, to help obtain the necessary increases, the Government should be authorized to provide certain types of financial assistance to private industry to increase defense production.

Our military needs are large, and to meet them will require hard work and steady effort. I know that we can produce what we need if each of us does his part—each man, each woman, each soldier, each civilian. This is a time for all of us to pitch in and work together.

I have been sorry to hear that some people have fallen victim to rumors in the last week or two, and have been buying up various things they have heard would be scarce. That is foolish—I say that is foolish, and it is selfish, very selfish, because hoarding results in entirely unnecessary local shortages.

Hoarding food is especially foolish. There is plenty of food in this country. I have read that there have been runs on sugar in some cities. That is perfectly ridiculous. We now have more sugar available than ever before. There are ample supplies of our other basic foods also.

Now, I sincerely hope that every American housewife will keep this in mind when she does her daily shopping.

If I had thought that we were actually threatened by shortages of essential consumer goods, I should have recommended that price control and rationing be immediately instituted. But there is no such threat. We have to fear only those shortages which we ourselves artificially create.

Every businessman who is trying to profiteer in time of national danger —and every person who is selfishly trying to get more than his neighbor —is doing just exactly the thing that any enemy of this country would want him to do.

If prices should rise unduly because of excessive buying or speculation, I know our people will want the Government to take action, and I will not hesitate to recommend rationing and price control.

We have the resources to meet our needs. Far more important, the American people are unified in their belief in democratic freedom. We are united in detesting Communist slavery.

We know that the cost of freedom is high. But we are determined to preserve our freedom—no matter what the cost.

I know that our people are willing to do their part to support our soldiers and sailors and airmen who are fighting in Korea. I know that our fighting men can count on each and every one of you.

Our country stands before the world as an example of how free men, under God, can build a community of neighbors, working together for the good of all.

That is the goal we seek not only for ourselves, but for all people. We believe that freedom and peace are essential if men are to live as our Creator intended us to live. It is this faith that has guided us in the past, and it is this faith that will fortify us in the stern days ahead.

SOURCE: *Public Papers: Truman, 1950*, 537–42.

15

DWIGHT D. EISENHOWER

DOCUMENT 56

PRESIDENT DWIGHT EISENHOWER'S MESSAGE TO CONGRESS ON THE DEFENSE OF FORMOSA. JANUARY 24, 1955.

The most important objective of our Nation's foreign policy is to safe-guard the security of the United States by establishing and preserving a just and honorable peace. In the Western Pacific a situation is developing in the Formosa Straits that seriously imperils the peace and our security.

Since the end of Japanese hostilities in 1945, Formosa [Taiwan] and the Pescadores [small islands in the South China Sea] have been in the friendly hands of our loyal ally, the Republic of China. We have recognized that it was important that these islands should remain in friendly hands. In unfriendly hands, Formosa and the Pescadores would seriously dislocate the existing, even if unstable, balance of moral, economic, and military forces upon which the peace of the Pacific depends. It would create a breach in the island chain of the Western Pacific that constitutes, for the United States and other free nations, the geographical backbone of their security structure in that ocean. In addition, this breach would interrupt north-south communications between other important elements of that barrier, and damage the economic life of countries friendly to us.

The United States and the friendly Government of the Republic of China [Nationalist government of Chiang Kai-shek], and indeed all the free nations, have a common interest that Formosa and the Pescadores should not fall into the control of aggressive Communist forces.

Influenced by such considerations, our Government was prompt, when the Communists committed armed aggression in Korea in June 1950, to direct our Seventh Fleet to defend Formosa from possible invasion from the Communist mainland.

These considerations are still valid. The Seventh Fleet continues under Presidential directive to carry out that defensive mission. We also provide military and economic support to the Chinese Nationalist Government and we cooperate in every proper and feasible way with that Government in order to promote its security and stability. All of these military and related activities will be continued.

In addition, there was signed last December a Mutual Defense Treaty between this Government and the Republic of China,[1] covering Formosa and the neighboring Pescadores. It is a treaty of purely defensive character. That treaty is now before the Senate of the United States.

Meanwhile, Communist China has pursued a series of provocative political and military actions, establishing a pattern of aggressive purpose. That purpose, they proclaim, is the conquest of Formosa.

In September 1954 the Chinese Communists opened up heavy artillery fire upon Quemoy Island,[2] one of the natural approaches to Formosa, which had for several years been under the uncontested control of the Republic of China. Then came air attacks of mounting intensity against other Free China islands, notably those in the vicinity of the Tachen group to the north of Formosa. One small island (Ichiang) was seized last week by air and amphibious operations after a gallant few fought bravely for days against overwhelming odds. There have been recent heavy air attacks and artillery fire against the main Tachen Islands themselves.

The Chinese Communists themselves assert that these attacks are a prelude to the conquest of Formosa. For example, after the fall of Ichiang, the Peiping radio said that it showed a "determined will to fight for the liberation of Taiwan. Our people will use all their strength to fulfill that task."

Clearly, this existing and developing situation poses a serious danger to the security of our country and of the entire Pacific area and indeed to the peace of the world. We believe that the situation is one for appropriate action of the United Nations under its charter, for the purpose of ending the present hostilities in that area. We would welcome assumption of such jurisdiction by that body.

Meanwhile, the situation has become sufficiently critical to impel me, without awaiting action by the United Nations, to ask the Congress to participate now, by specific resolution, in measures designed to improve the prospects for peace. These measures would contemplate the use of the

---

[1] U.S. alliance to protect the Nationalist Chinese government on Taiwan.

---

[2] In the South China Sea within the territorial waters of the People's Republic of China.

Armed Forces of the United States if necessary to assure the security of Formosa and the Pescadores. . . .

Authority for some of the actions which might be required would be inherent in the authority of the Commander in Chief. Until Congress can act I would not hesitate, so far as my constitutional powers extend, to take whatever emergency action might be forced upon us in order to protect the rights and security of the United States.

SOURCE: *Public Papers of the President: Dwight D. Eisenhower, 1955* (Washington, DC: Government Printing Office, 1959), 207–11.

DOCUMENT 57

PRESIDENT EISENHOWER'S RADIO-TELEVISION ADDRESS TO THE NATION CONCERNING THE LANDING OF MARINES IN LEBANON. JULY 15, 1958.

Yesterday was a day of grave developments in the Middle East. In Iraq a highly organized military blow struck down the duly constituted government and attempted to put in its place a committee of army officers. The attack was conducted with great brutality. Many of the leading personalities were beaten to death or hanged and their bodies dragged through the streets.

At about the same time there was discovered a highly organized plot to overthrow the lawful government of Jordan.

Warned and alarmed by these developments, President [Camille] Chamoun of Lebanon sent me an urgent plea that the United States station some military units in Lebanon to evidence our concern for the independence of Lebanon, that little country, which itself has for about two months been subjected to civil strife. This has been actively fomented by Soviet and Cairo broadcasts* and abetted and aided by substantial amounts of arms, money and personnel infiltrated into Lebanon across the Syrian border.

President Chamoun stated that without an immediate show of United States support, the government of Lebanon would be unable to survive against the forces which had been set loose in the area.

The plea of President Chamoun was supported by the unanimous action of the Lebanese cabinet.

*Radio and televised broadcasts from Cairo were state-sponsored, Pan-Arab, and anti-West propaganda from Nasserite Egypt.

After giving this plea earnest thought and after taking advice from leaders of both the executive and congressional branches of the government, I decided to comply with the plea of the government of Lebanon. A few hours ago a battalion of United States marines landed and took up stations in and about the city of Beirut.

The mission of these forces is to protect American lives—there are about 2,500 Americans in Lebanon—and by their presence to assist the government of Lebanon to preserve its territorial integrity and political independence.

The United States does not, of course, intend to replace the United Nations which has a primary responsibility to maintain international peace and security. We reacted as we did within a matter of hours because the situation was such that only prompt action would suffice. We have, however, with equal promptness moved in the United Nations. This morning there was held at our request an emergency meeting of the United Nations Security Council. At this meeting we reported the action which we had taken. We stated the reasons therefor. We expressed the hope that the United Nations would itself take measures which would be adequate to preserve the independence of Lebanon and permit of the early withdrawal of the United States forces.

I should like now to take a few minutes to explain the situation in Lebanon.

Lebanon is a small country, a little less than the size of Connecticut, with a population of about one and one half million. It has always had close and friendly relations with the United States. Many of you no doubt have heard of the American University at Beirut which has a distinguished record. Lebanon has been a prosperous, peaceful country, thriving on trade largely with the West. A little over a year ago there were general elections, held in an atmosphere of total calm, which resulted in the establishment, by an overwhelming popular vote, of the present Parliament for a period of four years. The term of the president, however, is of a different duration and would normally expire next September. The president, Mr. Chamoun, has made clear that he does not seek reelection.

When the attacks on the government of Lebanon began to occur, it took the matter to the United Nations Security Council, pointing out that Lebanon was the victim of indirect aggression from without. As a result, the Security Council sent observers to Lebanon in the hope of thereby insuring that hostile intervention would cease. Secretary General [Dag] Hammarskjöld undertook a mission to the area to reinforce the work of the observers.

We believe that his efforts and those of the United Nations observers were helpful. They could not eliminate arms or ammunition or remove persons already sent into Lebanon. But we believe they did reduce such aid from across the border. It seemed, last week, that the situation was moving toward a peaceful solution which would preserve the integrity of Lebanon, and end indirect aggression from without.

Those hopes were, however, dashed by the events of yesterday in Iraq and Jordan. These events demonstrate a scope of aggressive purpose which tiny Lebanon could not combat without further evidence of support. That is why Lebanon's request for troops from the United States was made. That is why we have responded to that request.

Some will ask, does the stationing of some United States troops in Lebanon involve any interference in the internal affairs of Lebanon? The clear answer is "no."

First of all we have acted at the urgent plea of the government of Lebanon, a government which has been freely elected by the people only a little over a year ago. It is entitled, as are we, to join in measures of collective security for self-defense. Such action, the United Nations Charter recognizes, is an "inherent right."

In the second place what we now see in the Middle East is the same pattern of conquest with which we became familiar during the period of 1945 to 1950. This involves taking over a nation by means of indirect aggression; that is, under the cover of a fomented civil strife the purpose is to put into domestic control those whose real loyalty is to the aggressor.

It was by such means that the communists attempted to take over Greece in 1947. That effort was thwarted by the Truman Doctrine.

It was by such means that the communists took over Czechoslovakia in 1948.

It was by such means that the communists took over the mainland of China in 1949.

It was by such means that the communists attempted to take over Korea and Indochina, beginning in 1950.

You will remember at the time of the Korean war that the Soviet government claimed that this was merely a civil war, because the only attack was by North Koreans upon South Koreans. But all the world knew that the North Koreans were armed, equipped and directed from without for the purpose of aggression.

This means of conquest was denounced by the United Nations General Assembly when it adopted in November 1950 its resolution entitled, "Peace through Deeds." It thereby called upon every nation to refrain from "fomenting civil strife in the interest of a foreign power" and denounced such action as "the gravest of all crimes against peace and security throughout the world."

We had hoped that these threats to the peace and to the independence and integrity of small nations had come to an end. Unhappily, now they reappear. Lebanon was selected to become a victim. . . .

I believe that the presence of the United States forces now being sent to Lebanon will have a stabilizing effect which will preserve the independence and integrity of Lebanon. It will also afford an increased measure of security to the thousands of Americans who reside in Lebanon.

We know that stability and well-being cannot be achieved purely by military measures. The economy of Lebanon has been gravely strained by civil strife. Foreign trade and tourist traffic have almost come to a standstill. The United States stands ready, under its Mutual Security Program, to cooperate with the government of Lebanon to find ways to restore its shattered economy. Thus we shall help to bring back to Lebanon a peace which is not merely the absence of fighting but the well-being of the people.

I am well aware of the fact that landing of United States troops in Lebanon could have some serious consequences. That is why this step was taken only after the most serious consideration and broad consultation. I have, however, come to the sober and clear conclusion that the action taken was essential to the welfare of the United States. It was required to support the principles of justice and international law upon which peace and a stable international order depend.

That, and that alone, is the purpose of the United States. We are not actuated by any hope of material gain or by any emotional hostility against any person or any government. Our dedication is to the principles of the United Nations Charter and to the preservation of the independence of every state. That is the basic pledge of the United Nations Charter.

Yet indirect aggression and violence are being promoted in the Near East in clear violation of the provisions of the United Nations Charter.

There can be no peace in the world unless there is fuller dedication to the basic principles of the United Nations Charter. If ever the United States fails to support these principles the result would be to open the flood gates to direct and indirect aggression throughout the world.

In the 1930s the members of the League of Nations became indifferent to direct and indirect aggression in Europe, Asia and Africa. The result was to strengthen and stimulate aggressive forces that made World War II inevitable.

The United States is determined that that history shall not now be repeated. We are hopeful that the action which we are taking will both preserve the independence of Lebanon and check international violations which, if they succeeded, would endanger world peace.

We hope that this result will quickly be attained and that our forces can be promptly withdrawn. We must, however, be prepared to meet the situation, whatever be the consequences. We can do so, confident that we strive for a world in which nations, be they great or be they small, can preserve their independence. We are striving for an ideal which is close to the heart of every American and for which in the past many Americans have laid down their lives.

To serve these ideals is also to serve the cause of peace, security and well-being, not only for us, but for all men everywhere.

SOURCE: U.S. State Department, *Bulletin* 39, no. 997 (August 4, 1958): 183–86.

16

JOHN F. KENNEDY

DOCUMENT 58

PRESIDENT JOHN KENNEDY'S RADIO-TELEVISION ADDRESS TO THE NATION ON SOVIET NUCLEAR MISSILES IN CUBA. OCTOBER 22, 1962.

This government, as promised, has maintained the closest surveillance of the Soviet military buildup on the island of Cuba. Within the past week, unmistakable evidence has established the fact that a series of offensive missile sites is now in preparation on that imprisoned island. The purpose of these bases can be none other than to provide a nuclear strike capability against the Western Hemisphere.

Upon receiving the first preliminary hard information of this nature last Tuesday morning at 9 A.M., I directed that our surveillance be stepped up. And having now confirmed and completed our evaluation of the evidence and our decision on a course of action, this government feels obliged to report this new crisis to you in fullest detail.

The characteristics of these new missile sites indicate two distinct types of installations. Several of them include medium range ballistic missiles, capable of carrying a nuclear warhead for a distance of more than 1,000 nautical miles. Each of these missiles, in short, is capable of striking Washington, D.C., the Panama Canal, Cape Canaveral, Mexico City, or any other city in the southeastern part of the United States, in Central America, or in the Caribbean area.

Additional sites not yet completed appear to be designed for intermediate range ballistic missiles—capable of traveling more than twice as far—and thus capable of striking most of the major cities in the Western Hemisphere, ranging as far north as Hudson Bay, Canada, and as far south as Lima, Peru. In addition, jet bombers, capable of carrying nuclear weapons, are now being uncrated and assembled in Cuba, while the necessary air bases are being prepared.

This urgent transformation of Cuba into an important strategic base—by the presence of these large, long-range, and clearly offensive weapons of sudden mass destruction—constitutes an explicit threat to the peace and security of all the Americas, in flagrant and deliberate defiance of the Rio Pact of 1947,[1] the traditions of this nation and hemisphere, the joint resolution of the 87th Congress, the Charter of the United Nations, and my own public warnings to the Soviets on September 4 and 13.[2] This action also contradicts the repeated assurances of Soviet spokesmen, both publicly and privately delivered, that the arms buildup in Cuba would retain its original defensive character, and that the Soviet Union had no need or desire to station strategic missiles on the territory of any other nation.

The size of this undertaking makes clear that it has been planned for some months. Yet only last month, after I had made clear the distinction between any introduction of ground-to-ground missiles and the existence of defensive antiaircraft missiles, the Soviet government publicly stated on September 11 that, and I quote, "the armaments and military equipment sent to Cuba are designed exclusively for defensive purposes," that, and I quote the Soviet government, "there is no need for the Soviet government to shift its weapons . . . for a retaliatory blow to any other country, for instance Cuba," and that, and I quote their government, "the Soviet Union has so powerful rockets to carry these nuclear warheads that there is no need to search for sites for them beyond the boundaries of the Soviet Union." That statement was false.

Only last Thursday, as evidence of this rapid offensive buildup was already in my hand, Soviet Foreign Minister [Andrei] Gromyko told me in my office that he was instructed to make it clear once again, as he said his government had already done, that Soviet assistance to Cuba, and I quote, "pursued solely the purpose of contributing to the defense capabilities of Cuba," that, and I quote him, "training by Soviet specialists of Cuban nationals in handling defensive armaments was by no means offensive, and if it were otherwise," Mr. Gromyko went on, "the Soviet government would never become involved in rendering such assistance." That statement also was false.

Neither the United States of America nor the world community of nations can tolerate deliberate deception and offensive threats on the part of any nation, large or small. We no longer live in a world where only the

---

[1] The pact was a U.S.-initiated, inter-American alliance for military assistance.

---

[2] The joint resolution and President Kennedy's warnings were against a Soviet military presence on the island of Cuba.

actual firing of weapons represents a sufficient challenge to a nation's security to constitute maximum peril. Nuclear weapons are so destructive and ballistic missiles are so swift, that any substantially increased possibility of their use or any sudden change in their deployment may well be regarded as a definite threat to peace.

For many years, both the Soviet Union and the United States, recognizing this fact, have deployed strategic nuclear weapons with great care, never upsetting the precarious status quo which insured that these weapons would not be used in the absence of some vital challenge. Our own strategic missiles have never been transferred to the territory of any other nation under a cloak of secrecy and deception; and our history—unlike that of the Soviets since the end of World War II—demonstrates that we have no desire to dominate or conquer any other nation or impose our system upon its people. Nevertheless, American citizens have become adjusted to living daily on the bull's-eye of Soviet missiles located inside the U.S.S.R. or in submarines.[3] In that sense, missiles in Cuba add to an already clear and present danger—although it should be noted the nations of Latin America have never previously been subjected to a potential nuclear threat.

But this secret, swift, and extraordinary buildup of communist missiles—in an area well known to have a special and historical relationship to the United States and the nations of the Western Hemisphere, in violation of Soviet assurances, and in defiance of American and hemispheric policy—this sudden, clandestine decision to station strategic weapons for the first time outside of Soviet soil—is a deliberately provocative and unjustified change in the status quo which cannot be accepted by this country, if our courage and our commitments are ever to be trusted again by either friend or foe.

The 1930s taught us a clear lesson; aggressive conduct, if allowed to go unchecked and unchallenged, ultimately leads to war. This nation is opposed to war. We are also true to our word. Our unswerving objective, therefore, must be to prevent the use of these missiles against this or any other country, and to secure their withdrawal or elimination from the Western Hemisphere.

Our policy has been one of patience and restraint, as befits a peaceful and powerful nation, which leads a worldwide alliance. We have been determined not to be diverted from our central concerns by mere irritants and fanatics. But now further action is required—and it is under way; and these actions may only be the beginning. We will not prematurely or

---

[3] The Soviets arguably made the case that they had a more immediate "adjustment" following the stationing of U.S. Jupiter missiles to Turkey in the late 1950s.

unnecessarily risk the costs of worldwide nuclear war in which even the fruits of victory would be ashes in our mouth—but neither will we shrink from that risk at any time it must be faced.

Acting, therefore, in the defense of our own security and of the entire Western Hemisphere, and under the authority entrusted to me by the Constitution as endorsed by the resolution of the Congress, I have directed that the following initial steps be taken immediately:

First: To halt this offensive buildup, a strict quarantine on all offensive military equipment under shipment to Cuba is being initiated. All ships of any kind bound for Cuba from whatever nation or port will, if found to contain cargoes of offensive weapons, be turned back. This quarantine will be extended, if needed, to other types of cargo and carriers. We are not at this time, however, denying the necessities of life as the Soviets attempted to do in their Berlin blockade of 1948.[4]

Second: I have directed the continued and increased close surveillance of Cuba and its military buildup. The foreign ministers of the OAS in their communique of October 6, rejected secrecy on such matters in this hemisphere.[5] Should these offensive military preparations continue, thus increasing the threat to the hemisphere, further action will be justified. I have directed the armed forces to prepare for any eventualities; and I trust that in the interest of both the Cuban people and the Soviet technicians at the sites, the hazards to all concerned of continuing this threat will be recognized.

Third: It shall be the policy of this nation to regard any nuclear missile launched from Cuba against any nation in the Western Hemisphere as an attack by the Soviet Union on the United States, requiring a full retaliatory response upon the Soviet Union.

Fourth: As a necessary military precaution, I have reinforced our base at Guantánamo, evacuated today the dependents of our personnel there, and ordered additional military units to be on a standby alert basis.[6]

Fifth: We are calling tonight for an immediate meeting of the Organ of Consultation under the Organization of American States, to consider this

---

[4] The Soviet road and rail blockade on the divided city of Berlin was largely broken by the almost year-long airlift of supplies by the British and Americans.

[5] The Organization of American States (OAS) was designed for the collective security of the Western Hemisphere.

[6] As part of the Platt Amendment to the Cuban constitution of 1903, the United States acquired legal jurisdiction for a U.S. Navy/Marine base at Guantánamo Bay, Cuba.

threat to hemispheric security and to invoke Articles 6 and 8 of the Rio Treaty in support of all necessary action. The United Nations Charter allows for regional security arrangements—and the nations of this hemisphere decided long ago against the military presence of outside powers. Our other allies around the world have also been alerted.

Sixth: Under the Charter of the United Nations, we are asking tonight that an emergency meeting of the Security Council be convoked without delay to take action against this latest Soviet threat to world peace. Our resolution will call for the prompt dismantling and withdrawal of all offensive weapons in Cuba, under the supervision of U.N. observers, before the quarantine can be lifted.

Seventh and finally: I call upon Chairman [Nikita] Khrushchev to halt and eliminate this clandestine, reckless, and provocative threat to world peace and to stable relations between our two nations. I call upon him further to abandon this course of world domination, and to join in an historic effort to end the perilous arms race and to transform the history of man. He has an opportunity now to move the world back from the abyss of destruction—by returning to his government's own words that it had no need to station missiles outside its own territory, and withdrawing these weapons from Cuba—by refraining from any action which will widen or deepen the present crisis and then by participating in a search for peaceful and permanent solutions.

This nation is prepared to present its case against the Soviet threat to peace, and our own proposals for a peaceful world, at any time and in any forum—in the OAS, in the United Nations, or in any other meeting that could be useful—without limiting our freedom of action. We have in the past made strenuous efforts to limit the spread of nuclear weapons. We have proposed the elimination of all arms and military bases in a fair and effective disarmament treaty. We are prepared to discuss new proposals for the removal of tensions on both sides—including the possibilities of a genuinely independent Cuba, free to determine its own destiny. We have no wish to war with the Soviet Union—for we are a peaceful people who desire to live in peace with all other peoples.

But it is difficult to settle or even discuss these problems in an atmosphere of intimidation. That is why this latest Soviet threat—or any other threat which is made either independently or in response to our actions this week—must and will be met with determination. Any hostile move anywhere in the world against the safety and freedom of peoples to whom we are committed—including in particular the brave people of West Berlin—will be met by whatever action is needed.

Finally, I want to say a few words to the captive people of Cuba, to whom this speech is being directly carried by special radio facilities.[7] I speak to you as a friend, as one who knows of your deep attachment to your fatherland, as one who shares your aspirations for liberty and justice for all. And I have watched and the American people have watched with deep sorrow how your nationalist revolution was betrayed—and how your fatherland fell under foreign domination. Now your leaders are no longer Cuban leaders inspired by Cuban ideals. They are puppets and agents of an international conspiracy which has turned Cuba against your friends and neighbors in the Americas—and turned it into the first Latin American country to become a target for nuclear war—the first Latin American country to have these weapons on its soil.

These new weapons are not in your interest. They contribute nothing to your peace and well-being. They can only undermine it. But this country has no wish to cause you to suffer or to impose any system upon you. We know that your lives and land are being used as pawns by those who deny your freedom.

Many times in the past, the Cuban people have risen to throw out tyrants who destroyed their liberty. And I have no doubt that most Cubans today look forward to the time when they will be truly free—free from foreign domination, free to choose their own leaders, free to select their own system, free to own their own land, free to speak and write and worship without fear or degradation. And then shall Cuba be welcomed back to the society of free nations and to the associations of this hemisphere.

My fellow citizens: let no one doubt that this is a difficult and dangerous effort on which we have set out. No one can foresee precisely what course it will take or what costs or casualties will be incurred. Many months of sacrifice and self-discipline lie ahead—months in which both our patience and our will will be tested—months in which many threats and denunciations will keep us aware of our dangers. But the greatest danger of all would be to do nothing.

The path we have chosen for the present is full of hazards, as all paths are—but it is the one most consistent with our character and courage as a nation and our commitments around the world. The cost of freedom is always high—but Americans have always paid it. And one path we shall never choose, and that is the path of surrender or submission.

---

[7] The U.S. government-sponsored Radio Martí.

Our goal is not the victory of might, but the vindication of right—not peace at the expense of freedom, but both peace and freedom, here in this hemisphere, and, we hope, around the world. God willing, that goal will be achieved.

Thank you and good night.

SOURCE: *Public Papers of the Presidents: John F. Kennedy, 1962* (Washington, DC: Government Printing Office, 1963), 806–9.

17

LYNDON B. JOHNSON

DOCUMENT 59
PRESIDENT LYNDON JOHNSON'S ADDRESS TO THE NATION
ON THE GULF OF TONKIN INCIDENT AND U.S. RAID
AGAINST NORTH VIETNAM. AUGUST 4, 1964.

My Fellow Americans:

As President and Commander in Chief, it is my duty to the American people to report that renewed hostile actions against United States ships on the high seas in the Gulf of Tonkin have today required me to order the military forces of the United States to take action in reply.

The initial attack on the destroyer *Maddox*, on August 2, was repeated today by a number of hostile vessels attacking two U.S. destroyers with torpedoes. The destroyers and supporting aircraft acted at once on the orders I gave after the initial act of aggression. We believe at least two of the attacking boats were sunk. There were no U.S. losses.

The performance of commanders and crews in this engagement is in the highest tradition of the United States Navy. But repeated acts of violence against the Armed Forces of the United States must be met not only with alert defense, but with positive reply. That reply is being given as I speak to you tonight. Air action is now in execution against gunboats and certain supporting facilities in North Viet-Nam which have been used in these hostile operations.

In the larger sense this new act of aggression, aimed directly at our own forces, again brings home to all of us in the United States the importance of the struggle for peace and security in southeast Asia. Aggression by terror against the peaceful villagers of South Viet-Nam has now been joined by open aggression on the high seas against the United States of America.

The determination of all Americans to carry out our full commitment to the people and the government of South Viet-Nam will be redoubled by this outrage. Yet our response, for the present, will be limited and fitting.

We Americans know, although others appear to forget, the risks of spreading conflict. We still seek no wider war.

I have instructed the Secretary of State to make this position totally clear to friends and to adversaries and, indeed, to all. I have instructed [UN] Ambassador [Adlai] Stevenson to raise this matter immediately and urgently before the Security Council of the United Nations. Finally, I have today met with the leaders of both parties in the Congress of the United States and I have informed them that I shall immediately request the Congress to pass a resolution making it clear that our Government is united in its determination to take all necessary measures in support of freedom and in defense of peace in southeast Asia.

I have been given encouraging assurance by these leaders of both parties that such a resolution will be promptly introduced, freely and expeditiously debated, and passed with overwhelming support. And just a few minutes ago I was able to reach [Republican presidential candidate] Senator [Barry] Goldwater and I am glad to say that he has expressed his support of the statement that I am making to you tonight.

It is a solemn responsibility to have to order even limited military action by forces whose overall strength is as vast and as awesome as those of the United States of America, but it is my considered conviction, shared throughout your Government, that firmness in the right is indispensable today for peace; that firmness will always be measured. Its mission is peace.

SOURCE: U.S. State Department, *Bulletin* 51, no. 1313 (August 24, 1964): 259.

DOCUMENT 60

PRESIDENT JOHNSON'S MESSAGE TO CONGRESS ON THE GULF OF TONKIN INCIDENT AND U.S. RAID AGAINST NORTH VIETNAM. AUGUST 5, 1964.

To the Congress of the United States:

Last night I announced to the American people that the North Vietnamese regime had conducted further deliberate attacks against U.S. naval vessels operating in international waters, and that I had therefore directed air action against gunboats and supporting facilities used in these hostile operations. This air action has now been carried out with substantial damage to the boats and facilities. Two U.S. aircraft were lost in the action.

After consultation with the leaders of both parties in the Congress, I further announced a decision to ask the Congress for a resolution expressing the unity and determination of the United States in supporting freedom and in protecting peace in southeast Asia.

These latest actions of the North Vietnamese regime have given a new and grave turn to the already serious situation in southeast Asia. Our commitments in that area are well known to the Congress. They were first made in 1954 by President Eisenhower [Geneva Conference Protocols]. They were further defined in the Southeast Asia Collective Defense Treaty [creating SEATO (the Southeast Asia Treaty Organization)] approved by the Senate in February 1955.

This treaty with its accompanying protocol obligates the United States and other members to act in accordance with their constitutional processes to meet Communist aggression against any of the parties or protocol states.

Our policy in southeast Asia has been consistent and unchanged since 1954. I summarized it on June 2 in four simple propositions:

1. America keeps her word. Here as elsewhere, we must and shall honor our commitments.

2. The issue is the future of southeast Asia as a whole. A threat to any nation in that region is a threat to all, and a threat to us.

3. Our purpose is peace. We have no military, political or territorial ambitions in the area.

4. This is not just a jungle war, but a struggle for freedom on every front of human activity. Our military and economic assistance to South Vietnam and Laos in particular has the purpose of helping these countries to repel aggression and strengthen their independence.

The threat to the free nations of southeast Asia has long been clear. The North Vietnamese regime has constantly sought to take over South Vietnam and Laos. This Communist regime has violated the Geneva accords for Vietnam. It has systematically conducted a campaign of subversion, which includes the direction, training, and supply of personnel and arms for the conduct of guerrilla warfare in South Vietnamese territory. In Laos, the North Vietnamese regime has maintained military forces, used Laotian territory for infiltration into South Vietnam, and most recently carried out combat operations—all in direct violation of the Geneva agreements of 1962.

In recent months, the actions of the North Vietnamese regime have become steadily more threatening. In May, following new acts of Communist aggression in Laos, the United States undertook reconnaissance flights over Laotian territory, at the request of the Government of Laos. These flights had the essential mission of determining the situation in territory where Communist forces were preventing inspection by the

International Control Commission. When the Communists attacked these aircraft, I responded by furnishing escort fighters with instructions to fire when fired upon. Thus, these latest North Vietnamese attacks on our naval vessels are not the first direct attack on armed forces of the United States.

As President of the United States I have concluded that I should now ask the Congress, on its part, to join in affirming the national determination that all such attacks will be met, and that the United States will continue in its basic policy of assisting the free nations of the area to defend their freedom.

As I have repeatedly made clear, the United States intends no rashness, and seeks no wider war. We must make it clear to all that the United States is united in its determination to bring about the end of Communist subversion and aggression in the area. We seek the full and effective restoration of the international agreements signed in Geneva in 1954, with respect to South Vietnam, and again in Geneva in 1962, with respect to Laos.

I recommend a resolution expressing the support of the Congress for all necessary action to protect our Armed Forces and to assist nations covered by the SEATO Treaty. At the same time, I assure the Congress that we shall continue readily to explore any avenues of political solution that will effectively guarantee the removal of Communist subversion and the preservation of the independence of the nations of the area.

The resolution could well be based upon similar resolutions enacted by the Congress in the past—to meet the threat to Formosa in 1955, to meet the threat to the Middle East in 1957, and to meet the threat in Cuba in 1962. It could state in the simplest terms the resolve and support of the Congress for action to deal appropriately with attacks against our Armed Forces and to defend freedom and preserve peace in southeast Asia in accordance with the obligations of the United States under the Southeast Asia Treaty. I urge the Congress to enact such a resolution promptly and thus to give convincing evidence to the aggressive Communist nations, and to the world as a whole, that our policy in southeast Asia will be carried forward—and that the peace and security of the area will be preserved.

The events of this week would in any event have made the passage of a congressional resolution essential. But there is an additional reason for doing so at a time when we are entering on 3 months of political campaigning. Hostile nations must understand that in such a period the United States will continue to protect its national interests, and that in these matters there is no division among us.

SOURCE: *Bulletin* 51, no. 1313 (August 24, 1964): 261–63.

DOCUMENT 61

PRESIDENT JOHNSON'S SPEECH AT SYRACUSE UNIVERSITY ON THE GULF OF TONKIN INCIDENT AND U.S. RESPONSE IN SOUTHEAST ASIA. AUGUST 5, 1964.

. . . On this occasion it is fitting, I think, that we are meeting here to dedicate this new center to better understanding among all men. For that is my purpose in speaking to you.

Last night I spoke to the people of the Nation. This morning I speak to the people of all nations so that they may understand without mistake our purpose in the action that we have been required to take.

On August 2d the United States destroyer *Maddox* was attacked on the high seas in the Gulf of Tonkin by hostile vessels of the Government of North Viet-Nam.

On August 4th that attack was repeated in those same waters against two United States destroyers.

The attacks were deliberate.

The attacks were unprovoked.

The attacks have been answered.

Throughout last night, and within the last 12 hours, air units of the United States 7th Fleet have sought out the hostile vessels and certain of their supporting facilities. Appropriate armed action has been taken against them. The United States is now asking that this be brought immediately and urgently before the Security Council of the United Nations.

We welcome—and we invite the scrutiny of all men who seek peace, for peace is the only purpose of the course that America pursues.

The Gulf of Tonkin may be distant, but none can be detached about what has happened there.

Aggression—deliberate, willful, and systematic aggression—has unmasked its face to the entire world. The world remembers—the world must never forget—that aggression unchallenged is aggression unleashed.

We of the United States have not forgotten. That is why we have answered this aggression with action.

America's course is not precipitate.

America's course is not without long provocation.

For 10 years, three American Presidents—President Eisenhower, President Kennedy, and your present President—and the American people have been actively concerned with threats to the peace and security of the peoples of Southeast Asia from the Communist government of North Viet-Nam.

President Eisenhower sought—and President Kennedy sought—the same objective that I still seek:

That the governments of Southeast Asia honor the international agreements which apply in the area;

That those governments leave each other alone;

That they resolve their differences peacefully;

That they devote their talents to bettering the lives of their peoples by working against poverty and disease and ignorance.

In 1954 we made our position clear toward Viet-Nam.

In July of that year we stated we would view any renewal of the aggression in violation of the 1954 agreements [Geneva Protocols] "with grave concern and as seriously threatening international peace and security."

In September of that year the United States signed the Manila Pact, on which our participation in SEATO [Southeast Asia Treaty Organization] is based. That pact recognized that aggression by means of armed attack on South Viet-Nam would endanger the peace and the safety of the nations signing that solemn agreement.

In 1962 we made our position clear toward Laos. We signed the Declaration on the Neutrality of Laos. That accord provided for the withdrawal of all foreign forces and respect for the neutrality and independence of that little country.

The agreements of 1954 and 1962 were also signed by the government of North Viet-Nam.

In 1954 that government pledged that it would respect the territory under the military control of the other party and engage in no hostile act against the other party.

In 1962 that government pledged that it would "not introduce into the Kingdom of Laos foreign troops or military personnel."

That government also pledged that it would "not use the territory of the Kingdom of Laos for interference in the internal affairs of other countries."

That government of North Viet-Nam is now willfully and systematically violating those agreements of both 1954 and 1962.

To the south, it is engaged in aggression against the Republic of Viet-Nam.

To the west, it is engaged in aggression against the Kingdom of Laos.

To the east, it has now struck out on the high seas in an act of aggression against the United States of America.

There can be and there must be no doubt about the policy and no doubt about the purpose.

So there can be no doubt about the responsibilities of men and the responsibilities of nations that are devoted to peace.

Peace cannot be assured merely by assuring the safety of the United States destroyer *Maddox* or the safety of other vessels of other flags.

Peace requires that the existing agreements in the area be honored.

Peace requires that we and all our friends stand firm against the present aggressions of the government of North Viet-Nam.

The government of North Viet-Nam is today flouting the will of the world for peace. The world is challenged to make its will against war known and to make it known clearly and to make it felt and to make it felt decisively.

So, to our friends of the Atlantic alliance, let me say this this morning. The challenge that we face in Southeast Asia today is the same challenge that we have faced with courage and that we have met with strength in Greece and Turkey [1946], in Berlin [1948] and Korea [1950], in Lebanon [1958] and in Cuba [1962], and to any who may be tempted to support or to widen the present aggression I say this: There is no threat to any peaceful power from the United States of America. But there can be no peace by aggression and no immunity from reply. That is what is meant by the actions that we took yesterday.

Finally, my fellow Americans, I would like to say to ally and to adversary alike: Let no friend needlessly fear—and no foe vainly hope—that this is a nation divided in this election year. Our free elections—our full and free debate—are America's strength, not America's weakness.

There are no parties and there is no partisanship when our peace or the peace of the world is imperiled by aggressors in any part of the world.

We are one nation, united and indivisible. And united and indivisible we shall remain.

SOURCE: *Bulletin* 51, no. 1313 (August 24, 1964): 260–61.

DOCUMENT 62

PRESIDENT JOHNSON'S REMARKS AT THE SIGNING OF THE GULF OF TONKIN RESOLUTION. AUGUST 10, 1964.

My Fellow Americans:

One week ago, half a world away, our nation was faced by the challenge of deliberate and unprovoked acts of aggression in Southeast Asia. The cause of peace clearly required that we respond with a prompt and unmistakable reply.

As Commander in Chief, the responsibility was mine and mine alone. I gave the orders for that reply, and it has been given.

But, as President, there rested upon me still another responsibility—the responsibility of submitting our course to the representatives of the people for them to verify it or veto it. I directed that to be done last Tuesday, too.

Within 24 hours, the resolution before me now had been placed before each House of Congress. In each House, the resolution was promptly examined in committee and reported for action. In each House, there followed free and serious debate. In each House, the resolution was passed on Friday last—with a total of 502 votes in support and 2 opposed.

Thus, today our course is clearly known in every land. There can be no mistake—no miscalculation—of where America stands or what this generation of Americans stands for. The unanimity of the Congress reflects the unanimity of the country.

This resolution is short. It is straightforward. I hope it will be read around the world. The position of the United States is stated plainly.

To any armed attack upon our forces, we shall reply.

To any in Southeast Asia who ask our help in defending their freedom, we shall give it.

In that region, there is nothing we covet, nothing we seek—no territory, no military position, no political ambition. Our one desire—our one determination—is that the people of Southeast Asia be left in peace to work out their own destinies in their own way.

This resolution stands squarely within the four corners of the Constitution of the United States. It is clearly consistent with the principles and purposes of the Charter of the United Nations.

This is another new page in the outstanding record of accomplishment the 88th Congress is writing.

Americans of all parties and philosophies can be justly proud and justly grateful: proud that democracy has once again demonstrated its capacity to act swiftly and decisively against aggressors; grateful that there is in our National Government understanding, accord, and unity between the Executive and the Legislative branches—without regard to partisanship. This is a great strength that we must preserve.

This resolution confirms and reinforces powers of the Presidency. I pledge to all Americans to use those powers with all the wisdom and judgment God grants to me.

It is everlastingly right that we should be resolute in reply to aggression and steadfast in support of our friends.

But it is everlastingly necessary that our actions should be careful and measured. We are the most powerful of all nations—we must strive also to be the most responsible of nations.

So, in this spirit, and with this pledge, I now sign this resolution.

SOURCE: *Bulletin* 51, no. 1313 (August 24, 1964): 302–3.

DOCUMENT 63

PRESIDENT JOHNSON'S SPEECH TO THE NATIONAL LEGISLATIVE CONFERENCE ON AMERICA'S MISSION IN VIETNAM. SEPTEMBER 29, 1967.

I deeply appreciate this opportunity to appear before an organization whose members contribute every day such important work to the public affairs of our state and of our country.

This evening I came here to speak to you about Vietnam.

I do not have to tell you that our people are profoundly concerned about that struggle.

There are passionate convictions about the wisest course for our nation to follow. There are many sincere and patriotic Americans who harbor doubts about sustaining the commitment that three presidents and half a million of our young men have made.

Doubt and debate are enlarged because the problems of Vietnam are quite complex. They are a mixture of political turmoil—of poverty—of religious and factional strife—of ancient servitude and modern longing for freedom. Vietnam is all of these things.

Vietnam is also the scene of a powerful aggression that is spurred by an appetite for conquest.

It is the arena where communist expansionism is most aggressively at work in the world today—where it is crossing international frontiers in violation of international agreements; where it is killing and kidnapping; where it is ruthlessly attempting to bend free people to its will.

Into this mixture of subversion and war, of terror and hope, America has entered—with its material power and with its moral commitment.

Why?

Why should three presidents and the elected representatives of our people have chosen to defend this Asian nation more than 10,000 miles from American shores?

We cherish freedom—yes. We cherish self-determination for all people —yes. We abhor the political murder of any state by another, and the bodily murder of any people by gangsters of whatever ideology. And for twenty-seven years—since the days of Lend-Lease—we have sought to strengthen free people against domination by aggressive foreign powers.

But the key to all that we have done is really our own security. At times of crisis—before asking Americans to fight and die to resist aggression in a foreign land—every American president has finally had to answer this question:

Is the aggression a threat—not only to the immediate victim—but to the United States of America and to the peace and security of the entire world of which we in America are a very vital part?

That is the question which Dwight Eisenhower and John Kennedy and Lyndon Johnson had to answer in facing the issue in Vietnam.

That is the question that the Senate of the United States answered by a vote of 82 to 1 when it ratified and approved the SEATO treaty in 1955, and to which the members of the United States Congress responded in a resolution that it passed in 1964 by a vote of 504 to 2: "the United States is, therefore, prepared, as the president determines, to take all necessary steps, including the use of armed force, to assist any member or protocol state of the Southeast Asia Collective Defense Treaty requesting assistance in defense of its freedom."

Those who tell us now that we should abandon our commitment—that securing South Vietnam from armed domination is not worth the price we are paying—must also answer this question. And the test they must meet is this: What would be the consequences of letting armed aggression against South Vietnam succeed? What would follow in the time ahead? What kind of world are they prepared to live in five months or five years from tonight?

For those who have borne the responsibility for decision during these past 10 years, the stakes to us have seemed clear—and have seemed high.

President Dwight Eisenhower said in 1959:

"Strategically, South Vietnam's capture by the communists would bring their power several hundred miles into a hitherto free region. The remaining countries in Southeast Asia would be menaced by a great flanking movement. The freedom of twelve million people would be lost immediately, and that of one hundred fifty million in adjacent lands would be seriously endangered. The loss of South Vietnam would set in motion a crumbling process that could, as it progressed, have grave consequences for us and for freedom."

And President John F. Kennedy said in 1962:

"Withdrawal in the case of Vietnam and the case of Thailand might mean a collapse of the entire area."

A year later, he reaffirmed that:

"We are not going to withdraw from that effort. In my opinion, for us to withdraw from that effort would mean a collapse not only of South Vietnam, but Southeast Asia. So we are going to stay there," said President Kennedy.

This is not simply an American viewpoint, I would have you legislative leaders know. I am going to call the roll now of those who live in that part of the world—in the great arc of Asian and Pacific nations—and who bear the responsibility for leading their people, and the responsibility for the fate of their people.

The president of the Philippines [Ferdinand Marcos] had this to say:

"Vietnam is the focus of attention now. . . . It may happen to Thailand or the Philippines, or anywhere, wherever there is misery, disease, ignorance. . . . For you to renounce your position of leadership in Asia is to allow the Red Chinese to gobble up all of Asia."

The Foreign Minister of Thailand [Thanom Kittikachorn] said:

"(The American) decision will go down in history as the move that prevented the world from having to face another major conflagration."

The Prime Minister of Australia [Harold Holt] said:

"We are there because while communist aggression persists the whole of Southeast Asia is threatened."

President [Chung Hee] Park of Korea said:

"For the first time in our history, we decided to dispatch our combat troops overseas . . . because in our belief any aggression against the Republic of Vietnam represented a direct and grave menace against the security and peace of free Asia, and therefore directly jeopardized the very security and freedom of our own people.". . .

The Prime Minister of New Zealand [Keith Holyoake] said:

"We can thank God that America at least regards aggression in Asia with the same concern as it regards aggression in Europe—and is prepared to back up its concern with action.". . .

I cannot tell you tonight as your president—with certainty—that a communist conquest of South Vietnam would be followed by a communist conquest of Southeast Asia. But I do know that there are North Vietnamese troops in Laos. I do know that there are North Vietnamese trained guerrillas tonight in northeast Thailand. I do know that there are communist-supported guerrilla forces operating in Burma. And a communist coup was barely averted in Indonesia, the fifth largest nation in the world.[1]

So your American president cannot tell you—with certainty—that a Southeast Asia dominated by communist power would bring a third world war much closer to terrible reality. One could hope that this would not be so.

But all that we have learned in this tragic century strongly suggests to me that it would be so. As president of the United States, I am not prepared to gamble on the chance that it is not so. I am not prepared to risk the security—indeed, the survival—of this American nation on mere hope and wishful thinking. I am convinced that by seeing this struggle through now, we are greatly reducing the chances of a much larger war—perhaps a nuclear war. I would rather stand in Vietnam, in our time, and by meeting this danger now, and facing up to it, thereby reduce the danger for our children and for our grandchildren.

I want to turn now to the struggle in Vietnam itself.

There are questions about this difficult war that must trouble every really thoughtful person. I am going to put some of these questions to you. And I am going to give you the very best answers that I can give you.

First, are the Vietnamese—with our help and that of their other allies—really making any progress? Is there a forward movement? The reports I see make it clear that there is. Certainly there is a positive movement toward constitutional government. Thus far the Vietnamese have met the political schedule that they laid down in January 1966.

The people wanted an elected, responsive government. They wanted it strongly enough to brave a vicious campaign of communist terror and assassination to vote for it. It has been said that they killed more civilians in four weeks trying to keep them from voting before the election than our American bombers have killed in the big cities of North Vietnam in bombing military targets.

On November 1, subject to the action, of course, of the Constituent Assembly, an elected government will be inaugurated and an elected Senate and Legislature will be installed. Their responsibility is clear: To answer the desires of the South Vietnamese people for self-determination and for peace, for an attack on corruption, for economic development, and for social justice.

---

[1] Indonesian Communists attempted a coup on October 1, 1965, but were routed by loyalist military units.

There is progress in the war itself, steady progress considering the war that we are fighting; rather dramatic progress considering the situation that actually prevailed when we sent our troops there in 1965, when we intervened to prevent the dismemberment of the country by the Vietcong[2] and the North Vietnamese.

The campaigns of the last year drove the enemy from many of their major interior bases. The military victory almost within Hanoi's grasp in 1965 has now been denied them. The grip of the Vietcong on the people is being broken.

Since our commitment of major forces in July 1965 the proportion of the population living under communist control has been reduced to well under twenty percent. Tonight the secure proportion of the population has grown from about forty-five percent to sixty-five percent—and in the contested areas, the tide continues to run with us.

But the struggle remains hard. The South Vietnamese have suffered severely, as have we—particularly in the First Corps area in the north, where the enemy has mounted his heaviest attacks, and where his lines of communication to North Vietnam are shortest. Our casualties in the war have reached about 13,500 killed in action, and about 85,000 wounded. Of those 85,000 wounded, we thank God that 79,000 of the 85,000 have been returned, or will return to duty shortly, thanks to our great American medical science and the helicopter.

I know there are other questions on your minds, and on the minds of many sincere, troubled Americans: "Why not negotiate now?" so many ask me. The answer is that we and our South Vietnamese allies are wholly prepared to negotiate tonight.

I am ready to talk with [North Vietnamese President] Ho Chi Minh, and other chiefs of state concerned, tomorrow.

I am ready to have Secretary [of State Dean] Rusk meet with their foreign minister tomorrow.

I am ready to send a trusted representative of America to any spot on this earth to talk in public or private with a spokesman of Hanoi. We have twice sought to have the issue of Vietnam dealt with by the United Nations—and twice Hanoi has refused.

Our desire to negotiate peace—through the United Nations or not—has been made very, very clear to Hanoi—directly and many times through third parties.

---

[2]Vietnamese Communist units conducting guerrilla warfare in South Vietnam.

As we have told Hanoi time and time and time again, the heart of the matter is really this: The United States is willing to stop all aerial and naval bombardment of North Vietnam when this will lead promptly to productive discussions. We, of course, assume that while discussions proceed, North Vietnam would not take advantage of the bombing cessation or limitation.

But Hanoi has not accepted any of these proposals.

So it is by Hanoi's choice—and not ours, and not the rest of the world's—that the war continues.

Why, in the face of military and political progress in the South, and the burden of our bombing in the North, do they insist and persist with the war?

From many sources the answer is the same. They still hope that the people of the United States will not see this struggle through to the very end. As one Western diplomat reported to me only this week—he had just been in Hanoi—"They believe their staying power is greater than ours and that they can't lose." A visitor from a communist capital had this to say: "They expect the war to be long, and that the Americans in the end will be defeated by a breakdown in morale, fatigue, and psychological factors." The Premier of North Vietnam said as far back as 1962: "Americans do not like long, inconclusive war. . . . Thus we are sure to win in the end."

Are the North Vietnamese right about us?

I think not. No. I think they are wrong. I think it is the failing common to totalitarian regimes that they cannot really understand the nature of our democracy:

They mistake dissent for disloyalty.
They mistake restlessness for a rejection of policy.
They mistake a few committees for a country.
They misjudge individual speeches for public policy.

They are no better suited to judge the strength and perseverance of America than the Nazi and the Stalinist propagandists were able to judge it. It is a tragedy that they must discover these qualities in the American people, and discover them through a bloody war.

And, soon or late, they will discover them.

In the meantime, it shall be our policy to continue to seek negotiations—confident that reason will some day prevail; that Hanoi will realize that it just can never win; that it will turn away from fighting and start building for its own people.

Since World War II, this nation has met and has mastered many challenges—challenges in Greece and Turkey, in Berlin, in Korea, in Cuba.

We met them because brave men were willing to risk their lives for their nation's security. And braver men have never lived than those who carry our colors in Vietnam at this very hour.

The price of these efforts, of course, has been heavy. But the price of not having made them at all, not having seen them through, in my judgment would have been vastly greater.

Our goal has been the same—in Europe, in Asia, in our own hemisphere. It has been—and it is now—peace.

And peace cannot be secured by wishes; peace cannot be preserved by noble words and pure intentions. "Enduring peace," Franklin D. Roosevelt said, "cannot be bought at the cost of other people's freedom."

The late President Kennedy put it precisely in November 1961, when he said: "We are neither warmongers nor appeasers, neither hard nor soft. We are Americans determined to defend the frontiers of freedom by an honorable peace if peace is possible but by arms if arms are used against us."

The true peace-keepers in the world tonight are not those who urge us to retire from the field in Vietnam—who tell us to try to find the quickest, cheapest exit from that tormented land, no matter what the consequences to us may be.

The true peace-keepers are those men who stand out there on the DMZ [De-Militarized Zone] at this very hour, taking the worst that the enemy can give. The true peace-keepers are the soldiers who are breaking the terrorist's grip around the villages of Vietnam—the civilians who are bringing medical care and food and education to people who have already suffered a generation of war.

And so I report to you that we are going to continue to press forward. Two things we must do. Two things we shall do.

First, we must not mislead the enemy. Let him not think that debate and dissent will produce wavering and withdrawal. For I can assure you they won't. Let him not think that protests will produce surrender. Because they won't. Let him not think that he will wait us out. For he won't.

Second, we will provide all that our brave men require to do the job that must be done. And that job is going to be done.

These gallant men have our prayers—have our thanks—have our heartfelt praise—and our deepest gratitude.

Let the world know that the keepers of peace will endure through every trial—and that with the full backing of their countrymen, they are going to prevail.

SOURCE: Office of the Federal Register, *Weekly Compilation of Presidential Documents* 3, no. 40 (Washington, DC: Government Printing Office, October 9, 1967), 1372–77.

DOCUMENT 64

PRESIDENT JOHNSON'S STATEMENT ON U.S. INTERVENTION IN THE DOMINICAN REPUBLIC. APRIL 28, 1965.

I just concluded a meeting with the leaders of the Congress. I reported to them on the serious situation in the Dominican Republic. I reported the decisions this Government considers necessary in this situation in order to protect American lives.

The members of the leadership expressed their support in these decisions. The United States Government has been informed by military authorities in the Dominican Republic that American lives are in danger. These authorities are no longer able to guarantee their safety, and they have reported that the assistance of military personnel is now needed for that purpose.

I have ordered the Secretary of Defense [Robert S. McNamara] to put the necessary American troops ashore in order to give protection to hundreds of Americans who are still in the Dominican Republic and to escort them safely back to this country. This same assistance will be available to the nationals of other countries, some of whom have already asked for our help.

Pursuant to my instructions, 400 Marines have already landed. General [Earle G.] Wheeler, the Chairman of the Joint Chiefs of Staff, has just reported to me that there have been no incidents.

We have appealed repeatedly in recent days for a cease-fire between the contending forces of the Dominican Republic in the interests of all Dominicans and foreigners alike.

I repeat this urgent appeal again tonight. The Council of the OAS has been advised of the situation by the Dominican Ambassador [José Antonio Bonilla Atiles], and the Council will be kept fully informed.

SOURCE: *Bulletin* 52, no. 1351 (May 17, 1965): 738–39.

DOCUMENT 65

PRESIDENT JOHNSON'S TELEVISED SPEECH TO THE NATION ON U.S. INTERVENTION IN THE DOMINICAN REPUBLIC. APRIL 30, 1965.

Good Evening, Ladies and Gentlemen:

For 2 days American forces have been in Santo Domingo in an effort to protect the lives of Americans and the nationals of other countries in the face of increasing violence and disorder. With the assistance of these American forces, over 2,400 Americans and other nationals have been evacuated from the Dominican Republic. We took this step when, and only when, we were officially notified by police and military officials of the Dominican Republic that they were no longer in a position to guarantee the safety of American and foreign nationals and to preserve law and order.

In the last 24 hours violence and disorder have increased. There is great danger to the life of foreign nationals and of thousands of Dominican citizens, our fellow citizens of this hemisphere. By an outstanding effort of mediation the Papal Nuncio has achieved an agreement on a cease-fire which I have urged all those concerned to take. But this agreement is not now, as I speak, being fully respected. The maintenance of the cease-fire is essential to the hopes of all for peace and freedom in the Dominican Republic.

Meanwhile there are signs that people trained outside the Dominican Republic are seeking to gain control. Thus the legitimate aspirations of the Dominican people and most of their leaders for progress, democracy, and social justice are threatened and so are the principles of the inter-American system.

The inter-American system, and its principal organ, the Organization of American States, have a grave and immediate responsibility. It is important that prompt action be taken. I am informed that a representative of the OAS is leaving Washington very shortly for the Dominican Republic. It is very important that representatives of the OAS be sent to the Dominican Republic, just as soon as they can be sent there, in order to strengthen the cease-fire and in order to help clear a road to the return of constitutional processes and free elections. Loss of time may mean that it is too late to preserve freedom, which alone can lead to the establishment of true democracy. This, I am sure, is what the people of the Dominican Republic want. Late action, or delay, in such a case could mean a failure to accomplish the agreed objectives of the American states.

The eyes of the hemisphere are now on the OAS, both on its meeting today and on the meeting of its foreign ministers contemplated tomorrow. The wisdom, the statesmanship, and the ability to act decisively of the OAS are critical to the hopes of peoples in every land of this continent.

The United States will give its full support to the work of the OAS and will never depart from its commitment to the preservation of the right of all of the free people of this hemisphere to choose their own course without falling prey to international conspiracy from any quarter.

SOURCE: *Bulletin* 52, no. 1351 (May 17, 1965): 742–43.

DOCUMENT 66

PRESIDENT JOHNSON'S TELEVISED SPEECH TO THE NATION
ON U.S. INTERVENTION IN THE DOMINICAN REPUBLIC.
MAY 2, 1965.

Good Evening, Ladies and Gentlemen:

I have just come from a meeting with the leaders of both parties in the Congress, which was held in the Cabinet Room of the White House. I briefed them on the facts of the situation in the Dominican Republic. I want to make those same facts known to all the American people and to all the world.

There are times in the affairs of nations when great principles are tested in an ordeal of conflict and danger. This is such a time for the American nations.

At stake are the lives of thousands, the liberty of a nation, and the principles and the values of all the American Republics.

That is why the hopes and the concern of this entire hemisphere are on this Sabbath Sunday focused on the Dominican Republic.

In the dark mist of conflict and violence, revolution and confusion, it is not easy to find clear and unclouded truths.

But certain things are clear. And they require equally clear action. To understand, I think it is necessary to begin with the events of 8 or 9 days ago.

Last week our observers warned of an approaching political storm in the Dominican Republic. I immediately asked our Ambassador [W. Tapley Bennett, Jr.] to return to Washington at once so that we might discuss the situation and might plan a course of conduct. But events soon outran our hopes for peace.

Saturday, April 24—8 days ago—while Ambassador Bennett was conferring with the highest officials of your Government, revolution erupted in the Dominican Republic. Elements of the military forces of that country overthrew their government. However, the rebels themselves were divided. Some wanted to restore former President Juan Bosch.[1] Others opposed his restoration. President Bosch, elected after the fall of [dictator Rafael] Trujillo and his assassination [1961], had been driven from office by an earlier revolution in the Dominican Republic.

---

[1] A military junta had overthrown Bosch in September 1963.

Those who opposed Mr. Bosch's return formed a military committee in an effort to control that country. The others took to the street, and they began to lead a revolt on behalf of President Bosch. Control and effective government dissolved in conflict and confusion.

Meanwhile the United States was making a constant effort to restore peace. From Saturday afternoon onward, our Embassy urged a cease-fire, and I and all the officials of the American Government worked with every weapon at our command to achieve it.

On Tuesday the situation of turmoil was presented to the Peace Committee of the Organization of American States.

On Wednesday the entire Council of the Organization of American States received a full report from the Dominican Ambassador [Tapley Bennett].

Meanwhile, all this time, from Saturday to Wednesday, the danger was mounting. Even though we were deeply saddened by bloodshed and violence in a close and friendly neighbor, we had no desire to interfere in the affairs of a sister Republic.

On Wednesday afternoon there was no longer any choice for the man who is your President. I was sitting in my little office reviewing the world situation with Secretary Rusk, Secretary McNamara, and [National Security Adviser] Mr. McGeorge Bundy. Shortly after 3 o'clock I received a cable from our Ambassador, and he said that things were in danger; he had been informed the chief of police and governmental authorities could no longer protect us. We immediately started the necessary conference calls to be prepared.

At 5:14, almost 2 hours later, we received a cable that was labeled "critic," a word that is reserved for only the most urgent and immediate matters of national security.

The cable reported that Dominican law enforcement and military officials had informed our Embassy that the situation was completely out of control and that the police and the government could no longer give any guarantee concerning the safety of Americans or any foreign nationals.

Ambassador Bennett, who is one of our most experienced Foreign Service officers, went on in that cable to say that only an immediate landing of American forces could safeguard and protect the lives of thousands of Americans and thousands of other citizens of some 30 other countries. Ambassador Bennett urged your President to order an immediate landing.

In this situation hesitation and vacillation could mean death for many of our people, as well as many of the citizens of other lands.

I thought that we could not and we did not hesitate. Our forces, American forces, were ordered in immediately to protect American lives.

They have done that. They have attacked no one, and although some of our servicemen gave their lives, not a single American civilian or the civilian of any other nation, as a result of this protection, lost their lives.

There may be those in our own country who say that such action was good but we should have waited, or we should have delayed, or we should have consulted further, or we should have called a meeting. But from the very beginning, the United States, at my instructions, had worked for a cease-fire beginning the Saturday the revolution took place. The matter was before the OAS Peace Committee on Tuesday, at our suggestion. It was before the full Council on Wednesday, and when I made my announcement to the American people that evening, I announced then I was notifying the Council.

When that cable arrived, when our entire country team in the Dominican Republic, made up of nine men—one from the Army, Navy, and Air Force, our Ambassador, our AID [Agency for International Development] man, and others—said to your President unanimously: Mr. President, if you do not send forces immediately, men and women—Americans and those of other lands—will die in the streets—well, I knew there was no time to talk, to consult, or to delay. For in this situation delay itself would be decision—the decision to risk and to lose the lives of thousands of Americans and thousands of innocent people from all lands.

I want you to know that it is not a light or an easy matter to send our American boys to another country, but I do not think that the American people expect their President to hesitate or to vacillate in the face of danger, just because the decision is hard when life is in peril.

Meanwhile, the revolutionary movement took a tragic turn. Communist leaders, many of them trained in Cuba, seeing a chance to increase disorder, to gain a foothold, joined the revolution. They took increasing control. And what began as a popular democratic revolution, committed to democracy and social justice, very shortly moved and was taken over and really seized and placed into the hands of a band of Communist conspirators.

Many of the original leaders of the rebellion, the followers of President Bosch, took refuge in foreign embassies because they had been superseded by other evil forces, and the Secretary General of the rebel government, Martínez Francisco, appealed for a cease-fire. But he was ignored. The revolution was now in other and dangerous hands.

When these new and ominous developments emerged, the OAS met again, and it met at the request of the United States. I am glad to say they responded wisely and decisively. A five-nation OAS team is now in the Dominican Republic, acting to achieve a cease-fire to insure the safety of innocent people, to restore normal conditions, and to open a path to democratic progress.

That is the situation now.

I plead, therefore, with every person and every country in this hemisphere that would choose to do so, to contact their ambassador in the Dominican Republic directly and to get firsthand evidence of the horrors and the hardship, the violence and the terror, and the international conspiracy from which United States servicemen have rescued the people of more than 30 nations from that war-torn land.

Earlier today I ordered two additional battalions—2,000 extra men— to proceed immediately to the Dominican Republic. In the meeting that I have just concluded with the congressional leaders—following that meeting—I directed the Secretary of Defense and the Chairman of the Joint Chiefs of Staff [General Earle G. Wheeler] to issue instructions to land an additional 4,500 men at the earliest possible moment. The distribution of food to people who have not eaten for days, the need of medical supplies and attention for the sick and wounded, the health requirements to avoid an epidemic because there are hundreds that have been dead for days that are now in the streets, and other protection and security of each individual that is caught on that island require the attention of the additional forces which I have ordered to proceed to the Dominican Republic.

In addition, our servicemen have already, since they landed on Wednesday night, evacuated 3,000 persons from 30 countries in the world from this little island. But more than 5,000 people, 1,500 of whom are Americans—the others are foreign nationals—are tonight awaiting evacuation as I speak. We just must get on with that job immediately. . . .

The American nations cannot, must not, and will not permit the establishment of another Communist government in the Western Hemisphere. This was the unanimous view of all the American nations when, in January 1962, they declared, and I quote:

"The principles of communism are incompatible with the principles of the Inter- American system."

This is what our beloved President John F. Kennedy meant when, less than a week before his death, he told us: "We in this hemisphere must also use every resource at our command to prevent the establishment of another Cuba in this hemisphere."

This is and this will be the common action and the common purpose of the democratic forces of the hemisphere. For the danger is also a common danger, and the principles are common principles.

So we have acted to summon the resources of this entire hemisphere to this task. We have sent, on my instructions the night before last, special emissaries such as Ambassador [Teodoro] Moscoso of Puerto Rico, our very able Ambassador Averell Harriman, and others to Latin America to explain the situation, to tell them the truth, and to warn them that joint action is necessary. We are in contact with such distinguished Latin American statesmen as Romulo Betancourt [former president of Venezuela] and José Figueres [former president of Costa Rica]. We are seeking their wisdom and their counsel and their advice. We have also maintained communication with President Bosch, who has chosen to remain in Puerto Rico.

We have been consulting with the Organization of American States, and our distinguished Ambassador—than whom there is no better— Ambassador [Ellsworth] Bunker, has been reporting to them at great length all the actions of this Government, and we have been acting in conformity with their decisions.

We know that many who are now in revolt do not seek a Communist tyranny. We think it is tragic indeed that their high motives have been misused by a small band of conspirators who receive their directions from abroad.

To those who fight only for liberty and justice and progress I want to join with the Organization of American States in saying—in appealing to you tonight to lay down your arms and to assure you there is nothing to fear. The road is open for you to share in building a Dominican democracy, and we in America are ready and anxious and willing to help you. Your courage and your dedication are qualities which your country and all the hemisphere need for the future. You are needed to help shape that future. And neither we nor any other nation in this hemisphere can or should take it upon itself to ever interfere with the affairs of your country or any other country.

We believe that change comes, and we are glad it does, and it should come through peaceful process. But revolution in any country is a matter for that country to deal with. It becomes a matter calling for hemispheric action only—repeat, only—when the object is the establishment of a Communist dictatorship.

Let me also make clear tonight that we support no single man or any single group of men in the Dominican Republic. Our goal is a simple one. We are there to save the lives of our citizens and to save the lives of all people. Our goal, in keeping with the great principles of the inter-American system, is to help prevent another Communist state in this hemisphere. And we would like to do this without bloodshed or without large-scale fighting.

The form and the nature of the free Dominican government, I assure you, is solely a matter for the Dominican people, but we do know what kind of government we hope to see in the Dominican Republic. For that is carefully spelled out in the treaties and the agreements which make up the fabric of the inter-American system. It is expressed, time and time again, in the words of our statesmen and the values and hopes which bind us all together.

We hope to see a government freely chosen by the will of all the people.

We hope to see a government dedicated to social justice for every citizen.

We hope to see a government working, every hour of every day, to feed the hungry, to educate the ignorant, to heal the sick—a government whose only concern is the progress and the elevation and the welfare of all the people.

For more than three decades the people of that tragic little island suffered under the weight of one of the most brutal and despotic dictatorships of the Americas. We enthusiastically supported condemnation of that government by the Organization of American States. We joined in applying sanctions, and, when Trujillo was assassinated by his fellow citizens, we immediately acted to protect freedom and to prevent a new tyranny, and since that time we have taken the resources from all of our people at some sacrifice to many, and we have helped them with food and with other resources, with the Peace Corps volunteers, with the AID technicians; we have helped them in the effort to build a new order of progress.

How sad it is tonight that a people so long oppressed should once again be the targets of the forces of tyranny. Their long misery must weigh heavily on the heart of every citizen of this hemisphere. So I think it is our mutual responsibility to help the people of the Dominican Republic toward the day when they can freely choose the path of liberty and justice and progress. This is required of us by the agreements that we are party to and that we have signed. This is required of us by the values which bind us together.

Simón Bolívar once wrote from exile: "The veil has been torn asunder. We have already seen the light and it is not our desire to be thrust back into the darkness."[2]

---

[2]During the early decades of the nineteenth century, Simón Bolívar (1783–1830) fought to liberate the peoples of South America from Spanish colonial rule.

Well, after decades of night the Dominican people have seen a more hopeful light, and I know that the nations of this hemisphere will not let them be thrust back into the darkness.

And before I leave you, my fellow Americans, I want to say this personal word: I know that no American serviceman wants to kill anyone. I know that no American President wants to give an order which brings shooting and casualties and death. I want you to know, and I want the world to know, that as long as I am President of this country, we are going to defend ourselves. We will defend our soldiers against attackers. We will honor our treaties. We will keep our commitments. We will defend our nation against all those who seek to destroy not only the United States but every free country of this hemisphere. We do not want to bury anyone,[3] as I have said so many times before. But we do not intend to be buried.

Thank you. God bless you. Good night.

SOURCE: *Bulletin* 52, no. 1351 (May 17, 1965): 744–48.

---

[3] A reference to Soviet premier Nikita Khrushchev's famous threat in 1956 to the capitalist states: "We will bury you."

18

RICHARD M. NIXON

DOCUMENT 67

PRESIDENT RICHARD NIXON'S TELEVISED SPEECH TO THE NATION ON THE INVASION OF CAMBODIA. APRIL 30, 1970.

Ten days ago, in my report to the nation on Vietnam, I announced a decision to withdraw an additional 150,000 Americans from Vietnam over the next year. I said then that I was making that decision despite our concern over increased enemy activity in Laos, in Cambodia, and in South Vietnam.

At that time, I warned that if I concluded that increased enemy activity in any of these areas endangered the lives of Americans remaining in Vietnam, I would not hesitate to take strong and effective measures to deal with that situation.

Despite that warning, North Vietnam has increased its military aggression in all these areas, and particularly in Cambodia.

After full consultation with the National Security Council, Ambassador [Ellsworth] Bunker, General [Creighton] Abrams, and my other advisers, I have concluded that the actions of the enemy in the last 10 days clearly endanger the lives of Americans who are in Vietnam now and would constitute an unacceptable risk to those who will be there after withdrawal of another 150,000.

To protect our men who are in Vietnam and to guarantee the continued success of our withdrawal and Vietnamization programs, I have concluded that the time has come for action.

Tonight, I shall describe the actions of the enemy, the actions I have ordered to deal with that situation, and the reasons for my decision.

Cambodia, a small country of seven million people, has been a neutral nation since the Geneva Agreement of 1954—an agreement, incidentally, which was signed by the government of North Vietnam.

American policy since then has been to scrupulously respect the neutrality of the Cambodian people. We have maintained a skeleton diplomatic mission of fewer than 15 in Cambodia's capital, and that only since last August. For the previous four years, from 1965 to 1969, we did not have any diplomatic mission whatever in Cambodia. And for the past five years, we have provided no military assistance whatever and no economic assistance to Cambodia.

North Vietnam, however, has not respected that neutrality.

For the past five years—as indicated on this map that you see here [not included]—North Vietnam has occupied military sanctuaries all along the Cambodian frontier with South Vietnam. Some of these extend up to 20 miles into Cambodia. The sanctuaries are in red and, as you note, they are on both sides of the border. They are used for hit and run attacks on American and South Vietnamese forces in South Vietnam.

These Communist-occupied territories contain major base camps, training sites, logistics facilities, weapons and ammunition factories, air strips, and prisoner-of-war compounds.

For five years, neither the United States nor South Vietnam has moved against these enemy sanctuaries because we did not wish to violate the territory of a neutral nation. Even after the Vietnamese Communists began to expand these sanctuaries four weeks ago, we counseled patience to our South Vietnamese allies and imposed restraints on our own commanders.

In contrast to our policy, the enemy in the past two weeks has stepped up his guerrilla actions and he is concentrating his main forces in these sanctuaries that you see on this map where they are building up to launch massive attacks on our forces and those of South Vietnam.

North Vietnam in the last two weeks has stripped away all pretense of respecting the sovereignty or the neutrality of Cambodia. Thousands of their soldiers are invading the country from the sanctuaries; they are encircling the capital of Phnom Penh. Coming from these sanctuaries, as you see here, they have moved into Cambodia and are encircling the capital.

Cambodia, as a result of this, has sent out a call to the United States, to a number of other nations, for assistance. Because if this enemy effort succeeds, Cambodia would become a vast enemy staging area and a springboard for attacks on South Vietnam along 600 miles of frontier—a refuge where enemy troops could return from combat without fear of retaliation.

North Vietnamese men and supplies could then be poured into that country, jeopardizing not only the lives of our own men but the people of South Vietnam as well.

Now confronted with this situation, we have three options.

First, we can do nothing. Well, the ultimate result of that course of action is clear. Unless we indulge in wishful thinking, the lives of Americans remaining in Vietnam after our next withdrawal of 150,000 would be gravely threatened.

Let us go to the map again. Here is South Vietnam. Here is North Vietnam. North Vietnam already occupies this part of Laos. If North Vietnam also occupied this whole band in Cambodia, or the entire country, it would mean that South Vietnam was completely outflanked and the forces of Americans in this area, as well as the South Vietnamese, would be in an untenable military position.

Our second choice is to provide massive military assistance to Cambodia itself. Now unfortunately, while we deeply sympathize with the plight of seven million Cambodians whose country is being invaded, massive amounts of military assistance could not be rapidly and effectively utilized by the small Cambodian army against the immediate threat.

With other nations, we shall do our best to provide the small arms and other equipment which the Cambodian army of 40,000 needs and can use for its defense. But the aid we will provide will be limited to the purpose of enabling Cambodia to defend its neutrality and not for the purpose of making it an active belligerent on one side or the other.

Our third choice is to go to the heart of the trouble. That means cleaning out major North Vietnamese and Vietcong-occupied territories, these sanctuaries which serve as bases for attacks on both Cambodia and American and South Vietnamese forces in South Vietnam. Some of these, incidentally, are as close to Saigon as Baltimore is to Washington.

This one, for example, is called the Parrot's Beak. It is only 33 miles from Saigon.

Now faced with these three options, this is the decision I have made.

In cooperation with the armed forces of South Vietnam, attacks are being launched this week to clean out major enemy sanctuaries on the Cambodia-Vietnam border.

A major responsibility for the ground operations is being assumed by South Vietnamese forces. For example, the attacks in several areas, including the Parrot's Beak that I referred to a moment ago, are exclusively South Vietnamese ground operations under South Vietnamese command with the United States providing air and logistical support.

There is one area, however, immediately above Parrot's Beak, where I have concluded that a combined American and South Vietnamese operation is necessary.

Tonight, American and South Vietnamese units will attack the headquarters for the entire communist military operation in South Vietnam. This key control center has been occupied by the North Vietnamese and Vietcong for five years in blatant violation of Cambodia's neutrality.

This is not an invasion of Cambodia. The areas in which these attacks will be launched are completely occupied and controlled by North Vietnamese forces. Our purpose is not to occupy the areas. Once enemy forces are driven out of these sanctuaries and once their military supplies are destroyed, we will withdraw.

These actions are in no way directed at the security interests of any nation. Any government that chooses to use these actions as a pretext for harming relations with the United States will be doing so on its own responsibility, and on its own initiative, and we will draw the appropriate conclusions.

Now let me give you the reasons for my decision.

A majority of the American people, a majority of you listening to me, are for the withdrawal of our forces from Vietnam. The action I have taken tonight is indispensable for the continuing success of that withdrawal program.

A majority of the American people want to end this war rather than to have it drag on interminably. The action I have taken tonight will serve that purpose.

A majority of the American people want to keep the casualties of our brave men in Vietnam at an absolute minimum. The action I take tonight is essential if we are to accomplish that goal.

We take this action not for the purpose of expanding the war into Cambodia but for the purpose of ending the war in Vietnam and winning the just peace we all desire. We have made and we will continue to make every possible effort to end this war through negotiation at the conference table rather than through more fighting on the battlefield.

Let us look again at the record. We have stopped the bombing of North Vietnam. We have cut air operations by over 20 percent. We have announced withdrawal of over 250,000 of our men. We have offered to withdraw all of our men if they will withdraw theirs. We have offered to negotiate all issues with only one condition—and that is that the future of South Vietnam be determined not by North Vietnam, not by the United States, but by the people of South Vietnam themselves.

The answer of the enemy has been intransigence at the conference table, belligerence in Hanoi, massive military aggression in Laos and Cambodia, and stepped-up attacks in South Vietnam, designed to increase American casualties.

This attitude has become intolerable. We will not react to this threat to American lives merely by plaintive diplomatic protests. If we did, the credibility of the United States would be destroyed in every area of the world where only the power of the United States deters aggression.

Tonight, I again warn the North Vietnamese that if they continue to escalate the fighting when the United States is withdrawing its forces, I shall meet my responsibility as commander in chief of our armed forces to take the action I consider necessary to defend the security of our American men.

The action that I have announced tonight puts the leaders of North Vietnam on notice that we will be patient in working for peace, we will be conciliatory at the conference table, but we will not be humiliated. We will not be defeated. We will not allow American men by the thousands to be killed by an enemy from privileged sanctuaries.

The time came long ago to end this war through peaceful negotiations. We stand ready for those negotiations. We have made major efforts, many of which must remain secret. I say tonight that all the offers and approaches made previously remain on the conference table whenever Hanoi is ready to negotiate seriously.

But if the enemy response to our most conciliatory offers for peaceful negotiation continues to be to increase its attacks and humiliate and defeat us, we shall react accordingly.

My fellow Americans, we live in an age of anarchy both abroad and at home. We see mindless attacks on all the great institutions which have been created by free civilizations in the last 500 years. Even here in the United States, great universities are being systematically destroyed. Small nations all over the world find themselves under attack from within and from without.

If, when the chips are down, the world's most powerful nation, the United States of America, acts like a pitiful, helpless giant, the forces of totalitarianism and anarchy will threaten free nations and free institutions throughout the world.

It is not our power but our will and character that is being tested tonight. The question all Americans must ask and answer tonight is this: Does the richest and strongest nation in the history of the world have the character to meet a direct challenge by a group which rejects every effort to win a just peace, ignores our warning, tramples on solemn agreements, violates the neutrality of an unarmed people, and uses our prisoners as hostages?

If we fail to meet this challenge, all other nations will be on notice that despite its overwhelming power the United States, when a real crisis comes, will be found wanting.

During my campaign for the presidency, I pledged to bring Americans home from Vietnam. They are coming home.

I promised to end this war. I shall keep that promise.

I promised to win a just peace. I shall keep that promise.

We shall avoid a wider war. But we are also determined to put an end to this war.

In this room [the Oval Office], Woodrow Wilson made the great decisions which led to victory in World War I. Franklin Roosevelt made the decisions which led to our victory in World War II. Dwight D. Eisenhower made the decisions which ended the war in Korea and avoided war in the Middle East. John F. Kennedy, in his finest hour, made the great decision which removed Soviet nuclear missiles from Cuba and the Western Hemisphere.

I have noted that there has been a great deal of discussion with regard to this decision that I have made and I should point out that I do not contend that it is in the same magnitude as these decisions that I have just mentioned. But between those decisions and this decision there is a difference that is very fundamental. In those decisions, the American people were not assailed by counsels of doubt and defeat from some of the most widely known opinion leaders of the nation.

I have noted, for example, that a Republican senator has said that this action I have taken means that my party has lost all chance of winning the November elections. And others are saying today that this move against enemy sanctuaries will make me a one-term president.

No one is more aware than I am of the political consequences of the action I have taken. It is tempting to take the easy political path: to blame this war on previous administrations and to bring all of our men home immediately, regardless of the consequences, even though that would mean defeat for the United States; to desert 18 million South Vietnamese people, who have put their trust in us and to expose them to the same slaughter and savagery which the leaders of North Vietnam inflicted on hundreds of thousands of North Vietnamese who chose freedom when the Communists took over North Vietnam in 1954; to get peace at any price now, even though I know that a peace of humiliation for the United States would lead to a bigger war or surrender later.

I have rejected all political considerations in making this decision.

Whether my party gains in November is nothing compared to the lives of 400,000 brave Americans fighting for our country and for the cause of peace and freedom in Vietnam. Whether I may be a one-term president is insignificant compared to whether by our failure to act in this crisis the United States proves itself to be unworthy to lead the forces of freedom in this critical period in world history. I would rather be a one-term president and do what I believe is right than to be a two-term president at the cost of seeing America become a second-rate power and to see this nation accept the first defeat in its proud 190-year history.

I realize that in this war there are honest and deep differences in this country about whether we should have become involved, that there are differences as to how the war should have been conducted. But the decision I announce tonight transcends those differences.

For the lives of American men are involved. The opportunity for 150,000 Americans to come home in the next 12 months is involved. The future of 18 million people in South Vietnam and seven million people in Cambodia is involved. The possibility of winning a just peace in Vietnam and in the Pacific is at stake.

It is customary to conclude a speech from the White House by asking support for the president of the United States. Tonight, I depart from that precedent. What I ask is far more important. I ask for your support for our brave men fighting tonight halfway around the world—not for territory—not for glory—but so that their younger brothers and their sons and your sons can have a chance to grow up in a world of peace and freedom and justice.

SOURCE: Office of the Federal Register, *Weekly Compilation of Presidential Documents* 6, no. 18 (Washington, DC: Government Printing Office, May 4, 1970), 596–601.

19

GERALD R. FORD

DOCUMENT 68

PRESIDENT GERALD FORD'S LETTER TO CONGRESS
REPORTING U.S. ACTIONS IN THE RECOVERY OF THE
SS *MAYAGUEZ*. MAY 15, 1975.

On May 12, 1975, I was advised that the S.S. *Mayaguez*, a merchant vessel of United States registry en route from Hong Kong to Thailand with a U.S. citizen crew, was fired upon, stopped, boarded, and seized by Cambodian naval patrol boats of the Armed Forces of Cambodia in international waters in the vicinity of Poulo Wai Island. The seized vessel was then forced to proceed to Koh Tang Island where it was required to anchor. This hostile act was in clear violation of international law.

In view of this illegal and dangerous act, I ordered, as you have been previously advised, United States military forces to conduct the necessary reconnaissance and to be ready to respond if diplomatic efforts to secure the return of the vessel and its personnel were not successful. Two United States reconnaissance aircraft in the course of locating the *Mayaguez* sustained minimal damage from small firearms. Appropriate demands for the return of the *Mayaguez* and its crew were made, both publicly and privately, without success.

In accordance with my desire that the Congress be informed on this matter and taking note of Section 4(a) (1) of the War Powers Resolution,* I wish to report to you that at about 6:20 A.M., May 13, pursuant to my instructions to prevent the movement of the *Mayaguez* into a mainland port, U.S. aircraft fired warning shots across the bow of the ship and gave visual signals to small craft approaching the ship. Subsequently, in order to

---

*Largely as a result of presidential deployment of U.S. forces to Vietnam and Southeast Asia during the 1960s, in 1973 Congress passed the War Powers Resolution, which restricted the chief executive's authority to commit U.S. armed forces without a formal declaration of war.

stabilize the situation and in an attempt to preclude removal of the American crew of the *Mayaguez* to the mainland, where their rescue would be more difficult, I directed the United States Armed Forces to isolate the island and interdict any movement between the ship or the island and the mainland, and to prevent movement of the ship itself, while still taking all possible care to prevent loss of life or injury to the U.S. captives. During the evening of May 13, a Cambodian patrol boat attempting to leave the island disregarded aircraft warnings and was sunk. Thereafter, two other Cambodian patrol craft were destroyed and four others were damaged and immobilized. One boat, suspected of having some U.S. captives aboard, succeeded in reaching Kompong Som after efforts to turn it around without injury to the passengers failed.

Our continued objective in this operation was the rescue of the captured American crew along with the retaking of the ship *Mayaguez*. For that purpose, I ordered late this afternoon [May 14] an assault by United States Marines on the island of Koh Tang to search out and rescue such Americans as might still be held there, and I ordered retaking of the *Mayaguez* by other marines boarding from the destroyer escort *Holt*. In addition to continued fighter and gunship coverage of the Koh Tang area, these Marine activities were supported by tactical aircraft from the *Coral Sea*, striking the military airfield at Ream and other military targets in the area of Kompong Som in order to prevent reinforcement or support from the mainland of the Cambodian forces detaining the American vessel and crew.

At approximately 9:00 P.M. EDT on May 14, the *Mayaguez* was retaken by United States forces. At approximately 11:30 P.M. the entire crew of the *Mayaguez* was taken aboard the *Wilson*. U.S. forces have begun the process of disengagement and withdrawal.

This operation was ordered and conducted pursuant to the President's constitutional Executive power and his authority as Commander-in-Chief of the United States Armed Forces.

SOURCE: *Public Papers of the Presidents: Gerald R. Ford, 1975*, 2 vols. (Washington, DC: Government Printing Office, 1977), 1:669–70.

20

JIMMY CARTER

DOCUMENT 69

PRESIDENT JIMMY CARTER'S ADDRESS TO THE NATION ON THE RESCUE ATTEMPT OF AMERICAN HOSTAGES IN IRAN. APRIL 25, 1980.

Late yesterday I canceled a carefully planned operation which was under way in Iran to position our rescue team for a later withdrawal of American hostages who have been held captive there since November 4.*

Equipment failure in the rescue helicopter made it necessary to end the mission. As our team was withdrawing after my order to do so, two of our American aircraft collided on the ground following a refueling operation in a remote desert location in Iran.

Other information about this rescue mission will be made available to the American people when it is appropriate to do so.

There was no fighting. There was no combat. But to my deep regret eight of the crewmen of the two aircraft which collided were killed and several other Americans were hurt in the accident.

Our people were immediately airlifted from Iran. Those who were injured have gotten medical treatment and all of them are expected to recover.

---

*On November 4, 1979, a mob of Islamic militants stormed the U.S. embassy in Tehran and captured sixty-three (later reduced to fifty-two) Americans, all but two of them embassy personnel. Three days later the Iranian government demanded the return of deposed Shah Reza Pahlavi, who had been admitted to the United States for medical treatment, as a precondition for the release of the hostages. President Carter refused and over the next ten days stopped delivery of military supplies to Iran, suspended imports of Iranian oil, froze Iranian assets, and began assembling U.S. naval forces in the Indian Ocean near the Persian Gulf. After secret negotiations failed to gain the hostages' release, the United States broke off relations with Iran on April 7, 1980. A military rescue was then attempted on April 25 that resulted in the resignation of Secretary of State Cyrus Vance and the deaths of eight servicemen. After 444 days of captivity the last of the hostages was released just minutes before Jimmy Carter left office on January 20, 1981.

No knowledge of this operation by any Iranian officials or authorities was evident to us until several hours after all Americans were withdrawn from Iran.

Our rescue team knew and I knew that the operation was certain to be difficult and it was certain to be dangerous. We were all convinced that if and when the rescue operation had been commenced, it had an excellent chance of success.

They were all volunteers. They were all highly trained. I met with their leaders before they went on this operation. They knew then what hopes of mine and of all Americans they carried with them.

To the families of those who died and who were wounded, I want to express the admiration I feel for the courage of their loved ones and the sorrow that I feel personally for their sacrifice.

The mission on which they were involved was a humanitarian mission. It was not directed against Iran. It was not directed against the people of Iran. It was not undertaken with any feeling of hostility toward Iran or its people. It has caused no Iranian casualties.

Planning for this rescue effort began shortly after our embassy was seized, but for a number of reasons I waited until now to put those rescue plans into effect.

To be feasible this complex operation had to be the product of intensive planning and intensive training and repeated rehearsal.

However, a resolution of this crisis through negotiations and with voluntary action on the part of Iranian officials was obvious then, has been and will be preferable.

This rescue attempt had to await my judgment that the Iranian authorities could not or would not resolve this crisis on their own initiative.

With the steady unraveling of authority in Iran and the mounting dangers that were posed to the safety of the hostages themselves and the growing realization that their early release was highly unlikely, I made a decision to commence the rescue operations plans.

This attempt became a necessity and a duty. The readiness of our team to undertake the rescue made it completely practical. Accordingly, I made a decision to set our long-developed plans into operation.

I ordered this rescue mission prepared in order to safeguard American lives and protect America's national interests and to reduce the tensions in the world that have been caused among many nations as this crisis has continued.

It was my decision to attempt the rescue operation. It was my decision to cancel it when problems developed in the placement of our rescue team for a future rescue operation. The responsibility is fully my own.

In the aftermath of the attempt, we continue to hold the government of Iran responsible for the safety and for the early release of the American hostages who have been held so long.

The United States remains determined to bring about their safe release at the earliest date possible.

As president I know that our entire nation feels deep gratitude for the brave men who were prepared to rescue their fellow Americans from captivity. And as president I also know that the nation shares not only my disappointment that the rescue effort could not be mounted because of mechanical difficulties, but also my determination to persevere and to bring all of our hostages home to freedom.

We have been disappointed before. We will not give up in our efforts.

Throughout this extraordinarily difficult period, we have pursued and will continue to pursue every possible avenue to secure the release of the hostages.

In these efforts, the support of the American people and of our friends throughout the world has been a most crucial element. That support of other nations is even more important now. We will seek to continue along with other nations and the officials of Iran a prompt resolution of the crisis without any loss of life and through peaceful and diplomatic means.

SOURCE: Office of the Federal Register, *Weekly Compilation of Presidential Documents* 16, no. 17 (Washington, DC: Government Printing Office, April 28, 1980), 772–73.

DOCUMENT 70
PRESIDENT CARTER'S WAR POWERS REPORT TO THE CONGRESS ON THE ABORTIVE HOSTAGE RESCUE OPERATION IN IRAN. APRIL 26, 1980.

Dear Mr. Speaker, Dear Mr. President:

. . . Beginning approximately 10:30 A.M. EST on April 24, six U.S. C-130 transport aircraft and eight RH-53 helicopters entered Iran airspace. Their crews were not equipped for combat. Some of the C-130 aircraft carried a force of approximately 90 members of the rescue team equipped for combat, plus various support personnel.

From approximately 2 to 4 P.M. EST the six transports and six of the eight helicopters landed at a remote desert site in Iran approximately 200 miles from Tehran where they disembarked the rescue team, commenced refueling operations and began to prepare for the subsequent phases.

During the flight to the remote desert site, two of the eight helicopters developed operating difficulties. One was forced to return to the carrier *Nimitz*; the second was forced to land in the desert, but its crew was taken aboard another of the helicopters and proceeded on to the landing site. Of the six helicopters which landed at the remote desert site, one developed a serious hydraulic problem and was unable to continue with the mission. The operational plans called for a minimum of six helicopters in good operational condition able to proceed from the desert site. Eight helicopters had been included in the force to provide sufficient redundancy without imposing excessive strains on the refueling and exit requirements of the operation. When the number of helicopters available to continue dropped to five, it was determined that the operation could not proceed as planned. Therefore, on the recommendation of the force commander and my military advisers, I decided to cancel the mission and ordered the United States Armed Forces involved to return from Iran.

During the process of withdrawal, one of the helicopters accidentally collided with one of the C-130 aircraft, which was preparing to take off, resulting in the death of eight personnel and the injury of several others. At this point, the decision was made to load all surviving personnel aboard the remaining C-130 aircraft and to abandon the remaining helicopters at the landing site. Altogether, the United States Armed Forces remained on the ground for a total of approximately three hours. The five remaining aircraft took off about 5:45 P.M. EST and departed from Iran airspace without further incident at about 8:00 P.M. EST on April 24. No United States Armed Forces remain in Iran.

The remote desert area was selected to conceal this phase of the mission from discovery. At no time during the temporary presence of United States Armed Forces in Iran did they encounter Iranian forces of any type. We believe, in fact, that no Iranian military forces were in the desert area, and that the Iranian forces were unaware of the presence of United States Armed Forces until after their departure from Iran. As planned, no hostilities occurred during this phase of the mission—the only phase that was executed.

At one point during the period in which United States Armed Forces elements were on the ground at the desert landing site a bus containing forty-four Iranian civilians happened to pass along a nearby road. The bus was stopped and then disabled. Its occupants were detained by United States Armed Forces until their departure, and then released unharmed. One truck closely followed by a second vehicle also passed by while United States Armed Forces elements were on the ground. These elements stopped the truck by a shot into its headlights. The driver ran to the second vehicle which then escaped across the desert. Neither of these incidents affected the subsequent decision to terminate the mission.

Our rescue team knew, and I knew, that the operation was certain to be dangerous. We were all convinced that if and when the rescue phase of the operation had been commenced, it had an excellent chance of success. They were all volunteers; they were all highly trained. I met with their leaders before they went on this operation. They knew then what hopes of mine and of all Americans they carried with them. I share with the nation the highest respect and appreciation for the ability and bravery of all who participated in the mission.

To the families of those who died and who were injured, I have expressed the admiration I feel for the courage of their loved ones and the sorrow that I feel personally for their sacrifice.

The mission on which they were embarked was a humanitarian mission. It was not directed against Iran. It was not directed against the people of Iran. It caused no Iranian casualties.

This operation was ordered and conducted pursuant to the President's powers under the Constitution as Chief Executive and as Commander-in-Chief of the United States Armed Forces, expressly recognized in Section 8(d)(1) of the War Powers Resolution.* In carrying out this operation, the United States was acting wholly within its right in accordance with Article 51 of the United Nations Charter, to protect and rescue its citizens where the government of the territory in which they are located is unable or unwilling to protect them.

SOURCE: Office of the Federal Register, *Weekly Compilation of Presidential Documents* 16, no. 18 (Washington, DC: Government Printing Office, May 5, 1980), 777–80.

*Provides the commander in chief with authority to protect the lives of U.S. citizens in immediate distress.

21

RONALD REAGAN

DOCUMENT 71

PRESIDENT RONALD REAGAN'S TELEVISED SPEECH TO THE NATION ON THE TERRORIST BOMBING AGAINST U.S. MARINES IN BEIRUT, LEBANON, AND THE INVASION OF GRENADA. OCTOBER 27, 1983.

My Fellow Americans:

Some two months ago we were shocked by the brutal massacre of 269 men, women and children, in the shooting down of a Korean airliner.[1] Now, in these past several days, violence has erupted again, in Lebanon and Grenada.

In Lebanon we have some 1,600 marines, part of a multinational force that's trying to help the people of Lebanon restore order and stability to that troubled land. Our marines are assigned to the south of the city of Beirut near the only airport operating in Lebanon. Just a mile or so to the north is the Italian contingent and not far from them the French and a company of British soldiers.

This past Sunday, at 22 minutes after six, Beirut time, with dawn just breaking, a truck looking like a lot of other vehicles in the city approached the airport on a busy main road. There was nothing in its appearance to suggest it was any different than the truck or cars that were normally seen on and around the airport. But this one was different.

At the wheel was a young man on a suicide mission. The truck carried some 2,000 pounds of explosives, but there was no way our marine guard could know this. Their first warning that something was wrong came when the truck crashed through a series of barriers, including a chain link fence and barbed wire entanglements. The guards opened fire but it was too late.

---

[1] A Soviet jet fighter shot down a South Korean commercial airliner, whose passengers included sixty Americans, after it strayed into Soviet airspace over the Sea of Japan.

The truck smashed through the doors of the headquarters building in which our marines were sleeping and instantly exploded. The four-story concrete building collapsed in a pile of rubble.

More than 200 of the sleeping men were killed in that one hideous insane attack. Many others suffered injury and are hospitalized here or in Europe. This was not the end of the horror.

At almost the same instant another vehicle on a suicide and murder mission crashed into the headquarters of the French peacekeeping force, an eight-story building, destroying and killing more than 50 French soldiers.

Prior to this day of horror there had been several tragedies for our men in the multinational force; attacks by snipers and mortar fire had taken their toll. I called the bereaved parents and/or widows of the victims to express on behalf of all of us our sorrow and sympathy. Sometimes there were questions. And now many of you are asking: Why should our young men be dying in Lebanon? Why is Lebanon important to us?

Well, it's true Lebanon is a small country more than five and a half thousand miles from our shores, on the edge of what we call the Middle East. But every president who has occupied this office in recent years has recognized that peace in the Middle East is of vital concern to our nation and, indeed, to our allies in Western Europe and Japan. We've been concerned because the Middle East is a powder keg. Four times in the last 30 years the Arabs and Israelis have gone to war and each time the world has teetered near the edge of catastrophe. The area is the key to the economic and political life of the West. Its strategic importance, its energy resources, the Suez Canal, the well-being of the nearly 200 million people living there: all are vital to us and to world peace.

If that key should fall into the hands of a power or powers hostile to the free world, there would be a direct threat to the United States and to our allies.

We have another reason to be involved. Since 1948, our nation has recognized and accepted a moral obligation to assure the continued existence of Israel as a nation. Israel shares our democratic values and is a formidable force an invader of the Middle East would have to reckon with. For several years, Lebanon has been torn by internal strife. Once a prosperous, peaceful nation, its government had become ineffective in controlling the militias that warred on each other.

Sixteen months ago we were watching on our TV screens the shelling and bombing of Beirut, which was being used as a fortress by P.L.O. [Palestine Liberation Organization] bands. Hundreds and hundreds of civilians were being killed and wounded in the daily battles. Syria, which makes no secret of its claim that Lebanon should be part of a greater Syria, was occupying a large part of Lebanon. Today, Syria has become a home for 7,000 Soviet advisers and technicians who man a massive amount of Soviet weaponry, including SS-21 ground-to-ground missiles capable of reaching vital areas of Israel.

A little over a year ago, hoping to build on the Camp David accords which have led to peace between Israel and Egypt,[2] I proposed a peace plan for the Middle East to end the wars between the Arab states and Israel. It was based on U.N. Resolutions 242 and 338 and called for a fair and just solution to the Palestinian problem, as well as a fair and just settlement of issues between the Arab states and Israel.[3]

Before the necessary negotiations could begin, it was essential to get all foreign forces out of Lebanon and to end the fighting there. So why are we there? Well, the answer is straight-forward: to help bring peace to Lebanon and stability to the vital Middle East. To that end the multinational force was created to help stabilize the situation in Lebanon until a government could be established and the Lebanese army mobilized to restore Lebanese sovereignty over its own soil as the foreign forces withdrew.

Israel agreed to withdraw as did Syria. But Syria then reneged on its promise. Over 10,000 Palestinians who had been bringing ruin down on Beirut, however, did leave the country. Lebanon has formed a government under the leadership of President [Amin] Gemayel and that government, with our assistance and training, has set up its own army. In only a year's time that army has been rebuilt. It's a good army composed of Lebanese of all factions. A few weeks ago the Israeli army pulled back to the Awali River in southern Lebanon. Despite fierce resistance by Syrian-backed forces the Lebanese army was able to hold the line and maintain the defensive perimeter around Beirut. In the year that our marines have been there Lebanon has made important steps toward stability and order. The physical presence of the marines lends support to both the Lebanese government and its army. It allows the hard work of diplomacy to go forward. Indeed,

---

[2] A 1978 statement of principles between Israel and Egypt, with agreed-upon U.S. participation, for a negotiated settlement of territorial sovereignty over the Sinai Peninsula and other bilateral issues. The presidential retreat at Camp David, Maryland, was the site of talks hosted by Jimmy Carter between Menachem Begin and Anwar Sadat.

---

[3] Adopted in November 1967, Resolution 242 stipulated the withdrawal of Israeli armed forces from occupied Palestinian territory for Palestinian recognition of the state of Israel and termination of threats or acts of force, known as the "land for peace" compromise. Resolution 338 agreed not to recognize Israeli acquisition of Arab territory, including the city of Jerusalem, by aggression.

without peacekeepers from the U.S., France, Italy and Britain, the efforts to find a peaceful solution in Lebanon would collapse.

As for that narrower question, what exactly is the operational mission of the marines, the answer is to secure a piece of Beirut; to keep order in their sector and to prevent the area from becoming a battlefield. Our marines are not just sitting in an airport. Part of their task is to guard that airport. Because of their presence the airport has remained operational. In addition they patrol the surrounding area. This is their part—a limited but essential part—in a larger effort that I described.

If our marines must be there, I'm asked, why can't we make them safer? Who committed this latest atrocity against them and why? Well, we'll do everything we can to insure that our men are as safe as possible. We ordered the battleship *New Jersey* to join our naval forces offshore. Without even firing them, the threat of its 16-inch guns silenced those who once fired down on our marines from the hills. And they're a good part of the reason we suddenly had a cease-fire. We're doing our best to make our forces less vulnerable to those who want to snipe at them or send in future suicide missions.

Secretary [of State George] Shultz called me today from Europe, where he was meeting with the foreign ministers of our allies, and the multinational force. They remain committed to our task, and plans were made to share information as to how we can improve security for all our men.

We have strong circumstantial evidence that the attack on the marines was directed by terrorists who used the same method to destroy our embassy in Beirut.[4] Those who directed this atrocity must be dealt justice, and they will be. The obvious purpose behind the sniping and now this attack was to weaken American will and force the withdrawal of U.S. and French forces from Lebanon.

The clear intent of the terrorists was to limit our support of the Lebanese government and to destroy the ability of the Lebanese people to determine their own destiny. To answer those who ask if we're serving any purpose in being there, let me answer a question with a question: would the terrorists have launched their suicide attacks against the multinational force if it were not doing its job?

The multinational force was attacked precisely because it is doing the job it was sent to do in Beirut. It is accomplishing its mission.

Now then, where do we go from here?

---

[4] On April 18, 1983, a Shiite fundamentalist rammed a van loaded with several hundred pounds of TNT into the front of the U.S. embassy in West Beirut. Sixty-seven people were killed. Seventeen of the dead were Americans, including several CIA officers.

What can we do now to help Lebanon gain greater stability so that our marines can come home? I believe we can take three steps now that will make a difference.

First, we will accelerate the search for peace and stability in that region. Little attention is being paid to the fact that we have had special envoys there working literally around the clock to bring the warring factions together. This coming Monday in Geneva President Gemayel of Lebanon will sit down with other factions from his country to see if national reconciliation can be achieved. He has our firm support.

I will soon be announcing a replacement for Bud [National Security Council Aide Robert] McFarlane who was preceded by [State Department diplomat] Phil Habib. Both worked tirelessly and must be credited for much, if not most, of the progress we've made.

Second, we'll work even more closely with our allies in providing support for the government of Lebanon and for the rebuilding of a national consensus.

Third, we will insure that the multinational peacekeeping forces, our marines, are given the greatest possible protection. Our Commandant of the Marine Corps, General [Paul] Kelley, returned from Lebanon today and will be advising us on steps we can take to improve security.

Vice President [George] Bush returned just last night from Beirut and gave me a full report of his brief visit.

Beyond our progress in Lebanon let us remember that our main goal and purpose is to achieve a broader peace in all of the Middle East. The factions and bitterness that we see in Lebanon are just a microcosm of the difficulties that are spread across much of that region. A peace initiative for the entire Middle East, consistent with the Camp David accords and U.N. Resolutions 242 and 338, still offers the best hope for bringing peace to the region. Let me ask those who say we should get out of Lebanon: If we were to leave Lebanon now, what message would that send to those who foment instability and terrorism? If Americans were to walk away from Lebanon, what chance would there be for a negotiated settlement producing the unified, democratic Lebanon? If we turned our backs on Lebanon now, what would be the future of Israel? At stake is the fate of only the second Arab country to negotiate a major agreement with Israel. That's another accomplishment of this past year, the May 17 accord signed by Lebanon and Israel.[5]

---

[5]This agreement provided Israel with a security buffer zone against terrorist safe havens in Lebanon's Bekaa Valley.

If terrorism and intimidation succeed, it'll be a devastating blow to the peace process and to Israel's search for genuine security. It won't just be Lebanon sentenced to a future of chaos. Can the United States, or the free world, for that matter, stand by and see the Middle East incorporated into the Soviet bloc? What of Western Europe and Japan's dependence on Middle East oil for the energy to fuel their industries? The Middle East is, as I said, vital to our national security and economic well-being.

Brave young men have been taken from us. Many others have been grievously wounded. Are we to tell them their sacrifice was wasted or that they gave their lives in defense of our national security every bit as much as any man who ever died fighting in a war?

We must not strip every ounce of meaning and purpose from their courageous sacrifice. We are a nation with global responsibilities, we're not somewhere else in the world protecting someone else's interest. We're there protecting our own.

I received a message from the father of a marine in Lebanon. He told me: "In a world where we speak of human rights, there is a sad lack of acceptance of responsibility. My son has chosen the acceptance of responsibility for the privilege of living in this country."

Certainly in this country one does not inherently have rights unless the responsibility for these rights is accepted.

Dr. Kenneth Morrison said that while he was waiting to learn if his son was one of the dead. I was thrilled for him to learn today that his son, Ross, is alive and well and carrying on his duties in Lebanon.

Let us meet our responsibilities. For longer than any of us can remember, the people of the Middle East have lived from war to war with no prospect for any other future. That dreadful cycle must be broken.

Why are we there? When a Lebanese mother told one of our ambassadors that her little girl had only attended school two of the last eight years. Now, because of our presence there, she said her daughter could live a normal life. With patience and firmness we can help bring peace to that strife-torn region and make our own lives more secure.

Our role is to help the Lebanese put their country together, not to do it for them.

Now I know another part of the world is very much on our minds. A place much closer to our shores. Grenada. The island is only twice the size of the District of Columbia with a total population of about 110,000 people. Grenada and a half-dozen other Caribbean islands here were, until recently, British colonies. They are now independent states and members of the British Commonwealth.

While they respect each other's independence they also feel a kinship with each other and think of themselves as one people. In 1979 trouble came to Grenada. Maurice Bishop, a protégé of Fidel Castro, staged a military coup and overthrew the government which had been elected under the constitution left to the people by the British.

He sought the help of Cuba in building an airport, which he claimed was for tourist trade, but which looked suspiciously suitable for military aircraft, including Soviet-built long-range bombers. The six sovereign countries and one remaining colony are joined together in what they call the Organization of Eastern Caribbean States.[6] The six became increasingly alarmed as Bishop built an army greater than all of theirs combined.

Obviously it was not purely for defense. In this last year or so, Prime Minister Bishop gave indications that he might like better relations with the United States. He even made a trip to our country and met with senior officials at the White House and the State Department. Whether he was serious or not we'll never know.

On October 12, a small group of his militia seized him and put him under arrest. They were, if anything, even more radical and more devoted to Castro's Cuba than he had been. Several days later, a crowd of citizens appeared before Bishop's home, freed him and escorted him toward the headquarters of the Military Council. They were fired upon. A number, including some children, were killed and Bishop was seized. He and several members of his Cabinet were subsequently executed and a 24-hour shoot-to-kill curfew was put in effect. Grenada was without a government, its only authority exercised by a self-proclaimed band of military men.

There were then about 1,000 of our citizens on Grenada, 800 of them students in St. George's University Medical School. Concern that they'd be harmed or held as hostages, I ordered a flotilla of ships then on its way to Lebanon with marines—part of our regular rotation program—to circle south on a course that would put them somewhere in the vicinity of Grenada in case there should be a need to evacuate our people.

Last weekend I was awakened in the early morning hours and told that six members of the Organization of Eastern Caribbean States joined by Jamaica and Barbados had sent an urgent request that we join them in a military operation to restore order and democracy to Grenada.

---

[6] Established in 1981 as a regional mutual defense league against Cuba within the framework of the OAS, this organization was primarily composed of the English-speaking democracies of the region: Dominica, St. Lucia, St. Vincent, Montserrat, St. Christopher-Nevis, and Grenada.

They were proposing this action under the terms of a treaty, a mutual assistance pact that existed among them. These small peaceful nations needed our help. Three of them don't have armies at all and the others have very limited forces.

The legitimacy of their request plus my own concern for our citizens dictated my decision. I believe our government has a responsibility to go to the aid of its citizens if their right to life and liberty is threatened. The nightmare of our hostages in Iran must never be repeated.

We knew we had little time and that complete secrecy was vital to insure both the safety of the young men who would undertake this mission and the Americans they were about to rescue.

The Joint Chiefs worked around the clock to come up with a plan. They had little intelligence information about conditions on the island. We had to assume that several hundred Cubans working on the airport could be military reserves. As it turned out the number was much larger and they were a military force. Six hundred of them have been taken prisoner and we have discovered a complete base with weapons and communications equipment which makes it clear a Cuban occupation of the island had been planned.

Two hours ago we released the first photos from Grenada. They included pictures of a warehouse of military equipment, one of three we've uncovered so far. This warehouse contained weapons and ammunition stacked almost to the ceiling, enough to supply thousands of terrorists.

Grenada, we were told, was a friendly island paradise for tourism. Well it wasn't. It was a Soviet-Cuban colony being readied as a major military bastion to export terror and undermine democracy.

We got there just in time.

I can't say enough in praise of our military—Army rangers and paratroopers, navy, marine and air force personnel, those who planned a brilliant campaign and those who carried it out.

Almost instantly our military seized the two airports, secured the campus where most of our students were and they're now in the mopping-up phase.

It should be noted that in all the planning, a top priority was to minimize risk, to avoid casualties to our own men and also the Grenadian forces as much as humanly possible. But there were casualties. And we all owe a debt to those who lost their lives or were wounded. They were few in number but even one is a tragic price to pay.

It's our intention to get our men out as soon as possible.

Prime Minister Eugenia Charles of Dominica—I called that wrong, she pronounces it Dom-in-EEE-kuh—she is chairman of O.E.C.S. She's calling for help from Commonwealth nations in giving the people their right to establish a constitutional government on Grenada. We anticipate that the governor general, a Grenadian, will participate in setting up a provisional government in the interim.

The events in Lebanon and Grenada, though oceans apart, are closely related. Not only has Moscow assisted and encouraged the violence in both countries, but it provides direct support through a network of surrogates and terrorists. It is no coincidence that when the thugs tried to wrest control of Grenada, there were 30 Soviet advisers and hundreds of Cuban military and paramilitary forces on the island. At the moment of our landing we communicated with the governments of Cuba and the Soviet Union and told them we would offer shelter and security to their people on Grenada. Regrettably, Castro ordered his men to fight to the death and some did. The others will be sent to their homelands.

Now there was a time when our national security was based on a standing army here within our own borders and shore batteries of artillery along our coast, and of course a navy to keep the sea lanes open for the shipping of things necessary to our well being. The world has changed. Today our national security can be threatened in far-away places. It's up to all of us to be aware of the strategic importance of such places and to be able to identify them.

Sam Rayburn once said that freedom is not something a nation can work for once and win forever.[7] He said it's like an insurance policy; its premiums must be kept up-to-date. In order to keep it we have to keep working for it and sacrificing for it just as long as we live. If we do not, our children may not know the pleasure of working to keep it for it may not be theirs to keep.

In these last few days, I've been more sure than I've ever been that we Americans of today will keep freedom and maintain peace. I've been made to feel that by the magnificent spirit of our young men and women in uniform, and by something here in our nation's capital.

In this city, where political strife is so much a part of our lives, I've seen Democratic leaders in the Congress join their Republican colleagues, send a message to the world that we're all Americans before we're anything else, and when our country is threatened, we stand shoulder to shoulder in support of men and women in the armed forces.

May I share something with you I think you'd like to know? It's something that happened to the Commandant of our Marine Corps, General

---

[7] Congressman from Texas and former Speaker of the U.S. House of Representatives.

Paul Kelley, while he was visiting our critically injured marines in an air force hospital. It says more than any of us could ever hope to say about the gallantry and heroism of these young men, young men who served so willingly so that others might have a chance at peace and freedom in their own lives and in the life of their country.

I'll let General Kelley's words describe the incident. He spoke of a "young marine with more tubes going in and out of his body than I have ever seen in one body. He couldn't see very well. He reached up and grabbed my four stars just to make sure I was who I said I was. He held my hand with a firm grip. He was making signals and we realized he wanted to tell me something. We put a pad of paper in his hand and he wrote, 'semper fi.'"

Well, if you've been a marine, or if, like myself, you're an admirer of the marines, you know those words are a battle cry, a greeting and a legend in the marine corps. They're marine shorthand for the motto of the corps: Semper Fidelis, Always Faithful.

General Kelley has a reputation for being a very sophisticated general and a very tough marine, but he cried when he saw those words, and who can blame him. That marine, and all those like him living and dead, have been faithful to their ideals. They've given willingly of themselves so that a nearly defenseless people in a region of great strategic importance to the free world will have a chance someday to live lives free of murder and mayhem and terrorism. I think that young marine and all of his comrades have given every one of us something to live up to.

They were not afraid to stand up for their country or, no matter how difficult and slow the journey might be, to give to others that last best hope of a better future.

We cannot and will not dishonor them now and the sacrifices they made by failing to remain as faithful to the cause of freedom and the pursuit of peace as they have been.

I will not ask you to pray for the dead because they are safe in God's loving arms and beyond need of our prayers.

I would like to ask you all, wherever you may be in this blessed land, to pray for these wounded young men and to pray for the bereaved families of those who gave their lives for our freedom.

God bless you and God bless America.

SOURCE: *Public Papers of the Presidents: Ronald W. Reagan, 1983,* 2 vols. (Washington, DC: Government Printing Office, 1984), 2:1517–22.

DOCUMENT 72
PRESIDENT REAGAN'S ADDRESS TO THE NATION CONCERNING THE U.S. AIR STRIKE AGAINST LIBYA. APRIL 14, 1986.

My Fellow Americans:

At 7 o'clock this evening Eastern Time air and naval forces of the United States launched a series of strikes against the headquarters, terrorist facilities, and military assets that support Muammar Qadhafi's subversive activities. The attacks were concentrated and carefully targeted to minimize casualties among the Libyan people with whom we have no quarrel. From initial reports, our forces have succeeded in their mission.

Several weeks ago in New Orleans, I warned Colonel Qadhafi we would hold his regime accountable for any new terrorist attacks launched against American citizens. More recently I made it clear we would respond as soon as we determined conclusively who was responsible for such attacks. On April 5th in West Berlin a terrorist bomb exploded in a nightclub frequented by American servicemen. Sergeant Kenneth Ford and a young Turkish woman were killed and 230 others were wounded, among them some 50 American military personnel. This monstrous brutality is but the latest act in Colonel Qadhafi's reign of terror. The evidence is now conclusive that the terrorist bombing of La Belle discothèque was planned and executed under the direct orders of the Libyan regime. On March 25th, more than a week before the attack, orders were sent from Tripoli to the Libyan People's Bureau in East Berlin to conduct a terrorist attack against Americans to cause maximum and indiscriminate casualties. Libya's agents then planted the bomb. On April 4th the People's Bureau alerted Tripoli that the attack would be carried out the following morning. The next day they reported back to Tripoli on the great success of their mission.

Our evidence is direct; it is precise; it is irrefutable. We have solid evidence about other attacks Qadhafi has planned against the United States installations and diplomats and even American tourists. Thanks to close cooperation with our friends, some of these have been prevented. With the help of French authorities, we recently aborted one such attack: a planned massacre, using grenades and small arms, of civilians waiting in line for visas at an American Embassy.

Colonel Qadhafi is not only an enemy of the United States. His record of subversion and aggression against the neighboring states in Africa is well documented and well known. He has ordered the murder of fellow

Libyans in countless countries. He has sanctioned acts of terror in Africa, Europe, and the Middle East, as well as the Western Hemisphere. Today we have done what we had to do. If necessary, we shall do it again. It gives me no pleasure to say that, and I wish it were otherwise. Before Qadhafi seized power in 1969, the people of Libya had been friends of the United States. And I'm sure that today most Libyans are ashamed and disgusted that this man has made their country a synonym for barbarism around the world. The Libyan people are a decent people caught in the grip of a tyrant.

To our friends and allies in Europe who cooperated in today's mission, I would only say: you have the permanent gratitude of the American people. Europeans who remember history understand better than most that there is no security, no safety, in the appeasement of evil. It must be the core of Western policy that there be no sanctuary for terror. And to sustain such a policy, free men and free nations must unite and work together. Sometimes it is said that by imposing sanctions against Colonel Qadhafi or by striking at his terrorist installations we only magnify the man's importance, that the proper way to deal with him is to ignore him. I do not agree.

Long before I came into this office, Colonel Qadhafi had engaged in acts of international terror, acts that put him outside the company of civilized men. For years, however, he suffered no economic or political or military sanction; and the atrocities mounted in number, as did the innocent dead and wounded. And for us to ignore by inaction the slaughter of American civilians and American soldiers, whether in nightclubs or airline terminals, is simply not in the American tradition. When our citizens are abused or attacked anywhere in the world on the direct orders of a hostile regime, we will respond so long as I'm in this Oval Office. Self-defense is not only our right, it is our duty. It is the purpose behind the mission undertaken tonight, a mission fully consistent with Article 51 of the United Nations Charter.

We believe that this preemptive action against his terrorist installations will not only diminish Colonel Qadhafi's capacity to export terror, it will provide him with incentives and reasons to alter his criminal behavior. I have no illusion that tonight's action will ring down the curtain on Qadhafi's reign of terror. But this mission, violent though it was, can bring closer a safer and more secure world for decent men and women. We will persevere. This afternoon we consulted with the leaders of Congress regarding what we were about to do and why. Tonight I salute the skill and professionalism of the men and women of our Armed Forces who carried out this mission. It's an honor to be your Commander in Chief.

We Americans are slow to anger. We always seek peaceful avenues before resorting to the use of force—and we did. We tried quiet diplomacy, public condemnation, economic sanctions, and demonstrations of military force. None succeeded. Despite our repeated warnings, Qadhafi continued his reckless policy of intimidation, his relentless pursuit of terror. He counted on America to be passive. He counted wrong. I warned that there should be no place on Earth where terrorists can rest and train and practice their deadly skills. I meant it. I said that we would act with others, if possible, and alone if necessary to ensure that terrorists have no sanctuary anywhere. Tonight, we have.

Thank you, and God bless you.

SOURCE: *Public Papers of the Presidents: Ronald W. Reagan, 1986*, 2 vols. (Washington, DC: Government Printing Office, 1988), 1:468–69.

DOCUMENT 73
PRESIDENT REAGAN'S LETTER TO CONGRESS ON U.S. AIR STRIKE AGAINST LIBYA. APRIL 16, 1986.

Commencing at about 7:00 P.M. (EST) on April 14, air and naval forces of the United States conducted simultaneous bombing strikes on headquarters, terrorist facilities and military installations that support Libyan subversive activities. These strikes were completed by approximately 7:30 P.M. (EST).

The United States Air Force element, which launched from bases in the United Kingdom, struck targets at Tripoli Military Air Field, Tarabulus (Aziziyah) Barracks, and Sidi Bilal Terrorist Training Camp. The United States Navy element, which launched from the USS *Coral Sea* and the USS *America*, struck targets at Benina Military Air Field and Benghazi Military Barracks. One F-111 with its two crew members is missing. These targets were carefully chosen, both for their direct linkage to Libyan support of terrorist activities and for the purpose of minimizing collateral damage and injury to innocent civilians.

These strikes were conducted in the exercise of our right of self-defense under Article 51 of the United Nations Charter. This necessary and appropriate action was a preemptive strike, directed against the Libyan terrorist infrastructure and designed to deter acts of terrorism by Libya, such as the Libyan-ordered bombing of a discothèque in West Berlin on April 5. Libya's cowardly and murderous act resulted in the death of two innocent people—an American soldier and a young Turkish woman—and the wounding of 50 United States Armed Forces personnel and 180 other innocent persons. This was the latest in a long series of terrorist attacks against United States installations, diplomats and citizens carried out or attempted with the support and direction of Muammar Qadhafi.

Should Libyan-sponsored terrorist attacks against United States citizens not cease, we will take appropriate measures necessary to protect United States citizens in the exercise of our right of self-defense.

In accordance with my desire that Congress be informed on this matter, and consistent with the War Powers Resolution, I am providing this report on the employment of the United States Armed Forces. These self-defense measures were undertaken pursuant to my authority under the Constitution, including my authority as Commander in Chief of United States Armed Forces.

SOURCE: *Public Papers: Reagan, 1986,* 1:478.

DOCUMENT 74
PRESIDENT REAGAN'S STATEMENT ON U.S. REPRISAL RAID ON IRANIAN PLATFORMS IN THE PERSIAN GULF. OCTOBER 19, 1987.

Acting pursuant to my authority as Commander in Chief, United States naval vessels at 7 A.M. (EDT) today struck an Iranian military platform in international waters in the central Persian Gulf. This platform has been used to assist in a number of Iranian attacks against nonbelligerent shipping. Iran's unprovoked attacks upon U.S. and other nonbelligerent shipping, and particularly deliberate laying of mines and firing of Silkworm missiles, which have hit U.S.-flag vessels, have come in spite of numerous messages from the Government of the United States to the Government of Iran warning of the consequences.

The action against the Iranian military platform came after consultations with congressional leadership and friendly governments. It is a prudent yet restrained response to this unlawful use of force against the United States and to numerous violations of the rights of other nonbelligerents. It is a lawful exercise of the right of self-defense enshrined in Article 51 of the United Nations Charter and is being so notified to the President of the United Nations Security Council.

The United States has no desire for a military confrontation with Iran, but the Government of Iran should be under no illusion about our determination and ability to protect our ships and our interests against unprovoked attacks. We have informed the Government of Iran of our desire for an urgent end to tensions in the region and an end to the Iran-Iraq war through urgent implementation of Security Council Resolution 598.

SOURCE: *Public Papers of the Presidents: Ronald W. Reagan, 1987*, 2 vols. (Washington, DC: Government Printing Office, 1989), 2:1201–02.

DOCUMENT 75

PRESIDENT REAGAN'S LETTER TO CONGRESS ON THE REPRISAL RAID AGAINST IRAN. OCTOBER 20, 1987.

Dear Mr. Speaker, Dear Mr. President:

At approximately 10:45 P.M. (EDT) on October 15, 1987, a Silkworm missile fired by Iranian forces from Iranian-occupied Iraqi territory struck the *Sea Isle City*, a U.S.-flag tanker, in Kuwaiti territorial waters. This action is the latest in a series of such missile attacks against targets in Kuwait, including neutral vessels engaged in peaceful commerce. It also is the latest in a series of acts by Iranian forces against the United States, as described in my letters of September 23 and October 10, 1987.

At approximately 7:00 A.M. (EDT) on October 19, 1987, Armed Forces of the United States assigned to the Middle East Joint Task Force, after warning Iranian naval personnel and allowing them to depart, attacked Rashadat Platform, an armed platform equipped with radar and communications devices which is used for surveillance and command and control. This platform, located in international waters, also has been used to stage helicopter and small boat attacks and to support mine-laying operations targeted against non-belligerent shipping in the Persian Gulf. It is now believed that this platform also was the source of fire directed at a U.S. helicopter on October 8, 1987. United States Navy ships fired upon and destroyed the platform. Additionally, U.S. forces briefly boarded another platform in the area, which had been abandoned by the Iranians when the operation began.

United States forces have returned to their prior state of alert readiness in the Persian Gulf region. They will remain prepared to take any additional action necessary to protect U.S. forces, U.S.-flag vessels, and U.S. lives.

These restrained and measured actions by U.S. forces were taken at my specific direction in accordance with our inherent right of self-defense, as recognized in Article 51 of the United Nations Charter, and pursuant to my constitutional authority with respect to the conduct of foreign relations and as Commander in Chief.

Since March 1987, I and members of my Administration have provided to the Congress letters, reports, briefings, and testimony in connection with developments in the Persian Gulf and activities of U.S. Armed Forces in that region. Additionally, congressional leaders were consulted on Sunday, October 18, 1987, concerning this operation. In accordance with my desire that the Congress continue to be fully informed in this matter, I am providing this report consistent with the War Powers Resolution. I look forward to cooperating with the Congress in pursuit of our mutual, overriding aim of peace and stability in the Persian Gulf region.

SOURCE: *Public Papers: Reagan, 1987,* 2:1212.

22

GEORGE H. W. BUSH

DOCUMENT 76

PRESIDENT GEORGE BUSH'S ADDRESS TO THE NATION ANNOUNCING OPERATION JUST CAUSE IN PANAMA. DECEMBER 20, 1989.

My Fellow Citizens:

Last night I ordered U.S. military forces to Panama. No President takes such action lightly. This morning I want to tell you what I did and why I did it.

For nearly 2 years, the United States, nations of Latin America and the Caribbean have worked together to resolve the crisis in Panama. The goals of the United States have been to safeguard the lives of Americans, to defend democracy in Panama, to combat drug trafficking, and to protect the integrity of the Panama Canal treaty. Many attempts have been made to resolve this crisis through diplomacy and negotiations. All were rejected by the dictator of Panama, General Manuel Noriega, an indicted drug trafficker.

Last Friday, Noriega declared his military dictatorship to be in a state of war with the United States and publicly threatened the lives of Americans in Panama. The very next day, forces under his command shot and killed an unarmed American serviceman [Marine Lieutenant Robert Paz]; wounded another; arrested and brutally beat a third American serviceman [Navy Lieutenant Adam J. Curtis]; and then brutally interrogated his wife [Bonnie], threatening her with sexual abuse. That was enough.

General Noriega's reckless threats and attacks upon Americans in Panama created an imminent danger to the 35,000 American citizens in Panama. As President, I have no higher obligation than to safeguard the lives of American citizens. And that is why I directed our Armed Forces to protect the lives of American citizens in Panama and to bring General Noriega to justice in the United States. I contacted the bipartisan leadership of Congress last night and informed them of this decision, and after taking this action, I also talked with leaders in Latin America, the Caribbean, and those of other U.S. allies.

At this moment, U.S. forces, including forces deployed from the United States last night, are engaged in action in Panama. The United States intends to withdraw the forces newly deployed to Panama as quickly as possible. Our forces have conducted themselves courageously and selflessly. And as Commander in Chief, I salute every one of them and thank them on behalf of our country.

Tragically, some Americans have lost their lives in defense of their fellow citizens, in defense of democracy. And my heart goes out to their families. We also regret and mourn the loss of innocent Panamanians.

The brave Panamanians elected by the people of Panama in the elections last May, President Guillermo Endara and Vice President [Guillermo] Ford, have assumed the rightful leadership of their country. You remember those horrible pictures of newly elected Vice President Ford, covered head to toe with blood, beaten mercilessly by so-called "dignity battalions." Well, the United States today recognizes the democratically elected government of President Endara. I will send our Ambassador back to Panama immediately.

Key military objectives have been achieved. Most organized resistance has been eliminated, but the operation is not over yet: General Noriega is in hiding. And nevertheless, yesterday a dictator ruled Panama, and today constitutionally elected leaders govern.

I have today directed the Secretary of the Treasury and the Secretary of State to lift the economic sanctions with respect to the democratically elected government of Panama and, in cooperation with that government, to take steps to effect an orderly unblocking of Panamanian Government assets in the United States. I'm fully committed to implement the Panama Canal treaties and turn over the Canal to Panama in the year 2000.* The actions we have taken and the cooperation of a new, democratic government in Panama will permit us to honor these commitments. As soon as the new government recommends a qualified candidate—Panamanian— to be Administrator of the Canal, as called for in the treaties, I will submit this nominee to the Senate for expedited consideration.

I am committed to strengthening our relationship with the democratic nations in this hemisphere. I will continue to seek solutions to the problems of this region through dialog and multilateral diplomacy. I took this

---

*In 1978 the Carter administration won Senate approval of turning the Canal Zone over to Panama in 2000.

action only after reaching the conclusion that every other avenue was closed and the lives of American citizens were in grave danger. I hope that the people of Panama will put this dark chapter of dictatorship behind them and move forward together as citizens of a democratic Panama with this government that they themselves elected.

The United States is eager to work with the Panamanian people in partnership to rebuild their economy. The Panamanian people want democracy, peace, and the chance for a better life in dignity and freedom. The people of the United States seek only to support them in pursuit of these noble goals.

SOURCE: *Public Papers of the Presidents: George Bush, 1989,* 2 vols. (Washington, DC: Government Printing Office, 1990), 2:1722–23.

DOCUMENT 77

PRESIDENT BUSH'S LETTER TO CONGRESS CONCERNING U.S. MILITARY ACTION IN PANAMA. DECEMBER 21, 1989.

Dear Mr. Speaker, Dear Mr. President:

On December 15, 1989, at the instigation of Manuel Noriega, the illegitimate Panamanian National Assembly declared that a state of war existed between the Republic of Panama and the United States. At the same time, Noriega gave a highly inflammatory anti-American speech. A series of vicious and brutal acts directed at U.S. personnel and dependents followed these events.

On December 16, 1989, a U.S. Marine officer was killed without justification by Panama Defense Forces (PDF) personnel. Other elements of the PDF beat a U.S. naval officer and unlawfully detained, physically abused, and threatened the officer's wife. These acts of violence are directly attributable to Noriega's dictatorship, which created a climate of aggression that places American lives and interests in peril.

These and other events over the past two years have made it clear that the lives and welfare of American citizens in Panama were increasingly at risk, and that the continued safe operation of the Panama Canal and the integrity of the Canal Treaties would be in serious jeopardy if such lawlessness were allowed to continue.

Under these circumstances, I ordered the deployment of approximately 11,000 additional U.S. Forces to Panama. In conjunction with the 13,000

U.S. Forces already present, military operations were initiated on December 20, 1989, to protect American lives, to defend democracy in Panama, to apprehend Noriega and bring him to trial on the drug-related charges for which he was indicted in 1988, and to ensure the integrity of the Panama Canal Treaties.

In the early morning of December 20, 1989, the democratically elected Panamanian leadership announced formation of a government, assumed power in a formal swearing-in ceremony, and welcomed the assistance of U.S. Armed Forces in removing the illegitimate Noriega regime. The deployment of U.S. Forces is an exercise of the right of self-defense recognized in Article 51 of the United Nations Charter and was necessary to protect American lives in imminent danger and to fulfill our responsibilities under the Panama Canal Treaties. It was welcomed by the democratically elected government of Panama. The military operations were ordered pursuant to my constitutional authority with respect to the conduct of foreign relations and as Commander in Chief.

In accordance with my desire that Congress be fully informed on this matter, and consistent with the War Powers Resolution, I am providing this report on the deployment of U.S. Armed Forces to Panama.

Although most organized opposition has ceased, it is not possible at this time to predict the precise scope and duration of the military operations or how long the temporary increase of U.S. Forces in Panama will be required. Nevertheless, our objectives are clear and largely have been accomplished. Our additional Forces will remain in Panama only so long as their presence is required.

SOURCE: *Public Papers: Bush, 1989*, 2:1734.

DOCUMENT 78
PRESIDENT BUSH'S ANNOUNCEMENT OF THE DEPLOYMENT OF U.S. ARMED FORCES TO SAUDI ARABIA FOR OPERATION DESERT SHIELD. AUGUST 8, 1990.

In the life of a nation, we're called upon to define who we are and what we believe. Sometimes these choices are not easy. But today as President, I ask for your support in a decision I've made to stand up for what's right and condemn what's wrong, all in the cause of peace.

At my direction, elements of the 82d Airborne Division as well as key units of the United States Air Force are arriving today to take up defensive positions in Saudi Arabia. I took this action to assist the Saudi Arabian Government in the defense of its homeland. No one commits America's Armed Forces to a dangerous mission lightly, but after perhaps unparalleled international consultation and exhausting every alternative, it became necessary to take this action. Let me tell you why.

Less than a week ago, in the early morning hours of August 2d, Iraqi Armed Forces, without provocation or warning, invaded a peaceful Kuwait. Facing negligible resistance from its much smaller neighbor, Iraq's tanks stormed in blitzkrieg fashion through Kuwait in a few short hours. With more than 100,000 troops, along with tanks, artillery, and surface-to-surface missiles, Iraq now occupies Kuwait. This aggression came just hours after Saddam Hussein specifically assured numerous countries in the area that there would be no invasion. There is no justification whatsoever for this outrageous and brutal act of aggression.

A puppet regime imposed from the outside is unacceptable. The acquisition of territory by force is unacceptable. No one, friend or foe, should doubt our desire for peace; and no one should underestimate our determination to confront aggression.

Four simple principles guide our policy. First, we seek the immediate, unconditional, and complete withdrawal of all Iraqi forces from Kuwait. Second, Kuwait's legitimate government must be restored to replace the puppet regime. And third, my administration, as has been the case with every President from President Roosevelt to President Reagan, is committed to the security and stability of the Persian Gulf. And fourth, I am determined to protect the lives of American citizens abroad.

Immediately after the Iraqi invasion, I ordered an embargo of all trade with Iraq and, together with many other nations, announced sanctions that both freeze all Iraqi assets in this country and protect Kuwait's assets. The stakes are high. Iraq is already a rich and powerful country that possesses the world's second largest reserves of oil and over a million men under arms. It's the fourth largest military in the world. Our country now imports nearly half the oil it consumes and could face a major threat to its economic independence. Much of the world is even more dependent upon imported oil and is even more vulnerable to Iraqi threats.

We succeeded in the struggle for freedom in Europe because we and our allies remained stalwart. Keeping the peace in the Middle East will require no less. We're beginning a new era. This new era can be full of promise, an age of freedom, a time of peace for all peoples. But if history teaches us anything, it is that we must resist aggression or it will destroy our freedoms. Appeasement does not work.* As was the case in the 1930s, we see in Saddam Hussein an aggressive dictator threatening his neighbors. Only 14 days ago, Saddam Hussein promised his friends he would not invade Kuwait. And 4 days ago, he promised the world he would withdraw. And twice we have seen what his promises mean: His promises mean nothing.

In the last few days, I've spoken with political leaders from the Middle East, Europe, Asia, and the Americas; and I've met with [British] Prime Minister [Margaret] Thatcher, [Canadian] Prime Minister [Brian] Mulroney, and NATO Secretary General [Manfred] Woerner. And all agree that Iraq cannot be allowed to benefit from its invasion of Kuwait.

We agree that this is not an American problem or a European problem or a Middle East problem: It is the world's problem. And that's why, soon after the Iraqi invasion, the United Nations Security Council, without dissent, condemned Iraq, calling for the immediate and unconditional withdrawal of its troops from Kuwait. The Arab world, through both the Arab League and the Gulf Cooperation Council, courageously announced its opposition to Iraqi aggression. Japan, the United Kingdom, and France, and other governments around the world have imposed severe sanctions. The Soviet Union and China ended all arms sales to Iraq.

And this past Monday, the United Nations Security Council approved for the first time in 23 years mandatory sanctions under Chapter VII of the United Nations Charter. These sanctions, now enshrined in international law, have the potential to deny Iraq the fruits of aggression while sharply limiting its ability to either import or export anything of value, especially oil.

I pledge here today that the United States will do its part to see that these sanctions are effective and to induce Iraq to withdraw without delay from Kuwait.

But we must recognize that Iraq may not stop using force to advance its ambitions. Iraq has massed an enormous war machine on the Saudi border capable of initiating hostilities with little or no additional preparation. Given the Iraqi government's history of aggression against its own citizens as well as its neighbors, to assume Iraq will not attack again would be unwise and unrealistic.

---

*Because of the agreements signed by France and Britain with Adolf Hitler at the 1938 Munich Conference, appeasement has become a word of disgrace associated with Western democracies not confronting the military aggression of totalitarian regimes.

And therefore, after consulting with King Fahd, I sent Secretary of Defense Dick Cheney to discuss cooperative measures we could take. Following those meetings, the Saudi Government requested our help, and I responded to that request by ordering U.S. air and ground forces to deploy to the Kingdom of Saudi Arabia.

Let me be clear: The sovereign independence of Saudi Arabia is of vital interest to the United States. This decision, which I shared with the congressional leadership, grows out of the long-standing friendship and security relationship between the United States and Saudi Arabia. U.S. forces will work together with those of Saudi Arabia and other nations to preserve the integrity of Saudi Arabia and to deter further Iraqi aggression. Through their presence, as well as through training and exercises, these multinational forces will enhance the overall capability of Saudi Armed Forces to defend the Kingdom.

I want to be clear about what we are doing and why. America does not seek conflict, nor do we seek to chart the destiny of other nations. But America will stand by her friends. The mission of our troops is wholly defensive. Hopefully, they will not be needed long. They will not initiate hostilities, but they will defend themselves, the Kingdom of Saudi Arabia, and other friends in the Persian Gulf.

We are working around the clock to deter Iraqi aggression and to enforce U.N. sanctions. I'm continuing my conversations with world leaders. Secretary of Defense Cheney has just returned from valuable consultations with President [Hosni] Mubarak of Egypt and King Hassan [II] of Morocco. Secretary of State [James] Baker has consulted with his counterparts in many nations, including the Soviet Union, and today he heads for Europe to consult with President [Turgut] Ozal of Turkey, a staunch friend of the United States. And he'll then consult with the NATO Foreign Ministers.

I will ask oil-producing nations to do what they can to increase production in order to minimize any impact that oil flow reductions will have on the world economy. And I will explore whether we and our allies should draw down our strategic petroleum reserves. Conservation measures can also help; Americans everywhere must do their part. And one more thing: I'm asking the oil companies to do their fair share. They should show restraint and not abuse today's uncertainties to raise prices.

Standing up for our principles will not come easy. It may take time and possibly cost a great deal. But we are asking no more of anyone than of the brave young men and women of our Armed Forces and their families. And I ask that in the churches around the country prayers be said for those who are committed to protect and defend America's interests.

Standing up for our principles is an American tradition. As it has so many times before, it may take time and tremendous effort, but most of all, it will take unity of purpose. As I've witnessed throughout my life in both war and peace, America has never wavered when her purpose is driven by principle. And in this August day, at home and abroad, I know she will do no less.

Thank you, and God bless the United States of America.

SOURCE: *Public Papers of the Presidents: George Bush, 1990,* 2 vols. (Washington, DC: Government Printing Office, 1991), 2:1107–8.

DOCUMENT 79

PRESIDENT BUSH'S ADDRESS BEFORE CONGRESS ON THE PERSIAN GULF CRISIS. SEPTEMBER 11, 1990.

Mr. President [Dan Quayle] and Mr. Speaker [Thomas Foley] and Members of the United States Congress:

Thank you very much for that warm welcome. We gather tonight, witness to events in the Persian Gulf as significant as they are tragic. In the early morning hours of August 2d, following negotiations and promises by Iraq's dictator Saddam Hussein not to use force, a powerful Iraqi army invaded its trusting and much weaker neighbor, Kuwait. Within 3 days, 120,000 Iraqi troops with 850 tanks had poured into Kuwait and moved south to threaten Saudi Arabia. It was then that I decided to act to check that aggression.

At this moment, our brave servicemen and women stand watch in that distant desert and on distant seas, side by side with the forces of more than 20 other nations. They are some of the finest men and women of the United States of America. And they're doing one terrific job. These valiant Americans were ready at a moment's notice to leave their spouses and their children, to serve on the front line halfway around the world. They remind us who keeps America strong: they do. In the trying circumstances of the Gulf, the morale of our service men and women is excellent. In the face of danger, they're brave, they're well-trained, and dedicated.

A soldier, Private First Class Wade Merritt of Knoxville, Tennessee, now stationed in Saudi Arabia, wrote his parents of his worries, his love of family, and his hope for peace. But Wade also wrote, "I am proud of my country and its firm stance against inhumane aggression. I am proud of my army and its men. I am proud to serve my country." Well, let me just say, Wade, America is proud of you and is grateful to every soldier, sailor, marine, and airman serving the cause of peace in the Persian Gulf. I also want to thank the Chairman of the Joint Chiefs of Staff, General [Colin] Powell; the Chiefs here tonight; our commander in the Persian Gulf, General [H. Norman] Schwarzkopf; and the men and women of the Department of Defense. What a magnificent job you all are doing. And thank you very, very much from a grateful people. I wish I could say that their work is done. But we all know it's not.

So, if there ever was a time to put country before self and patriotism before party, the time is now. And let me thank all Americans, especially those here in this Chamber tonight, for your support for our armed forces and for their mission. That support will be even more important in the days to come. So, tonight I want to talk to you about what's at stake—what we must do together to defend civilized values around the world and maintain our economic strength at home.

Our objectives in the Persian Gulf are clear, our goals defined and familiar: Iraq must withdraw from Kuwait completely, immediately, and without condition. Kuwait's legitimate government must be restored. The security, and stability, of the Persian Gulf must be assured. And American citizens abroad must be protected. These goals are not ours alone. They've been endorsed by the United Nations Security Council five times in as many weeks. Most countries share our concern for principle. And many have a stake in the stability of the Persian Gulf. This is not, as Saddam Hussein would have it, the United States against Iraq. It is Iraq against the world.

As you know, I've just returned from a very productive meeting with Soviet President [Mikhail] Gorbachev. And I am pleased that we are working together to build a new relationship. In Helsinki, our joint statement affirmed to the world our shared resolve to counter Iraq's threat to peace. Let me quote: "We are united in the belief that Iraq's aggression must not be tolerated. No peaceful international order is possible if larger states can devour their smaller neighbors." Clearly, no longer can a dictator count on East/West confrontation to stymie concerted United Nations action against aggression. A new partnership of nations has begun.

We stand today at a unique and extraordinary moment. The crisis in the Persian Gulf, as grave as it is, also offers a rare opportunity to move toward an historic period of cooperation. Out of these troubled times, our fifth objective—a new world order—can emerge: a new era—freer from the threat of terror, stronger in the pursuit of justice, and more secure in the quest for peace. An era in which the nations of the world, East and West, North and South, can prosper and live in harmony. A hundred generations have searched for this elusive path to peace, while a thousand wars raged across the span of human endeavor. Today that new world is struggling to be born, a world quite different from the one we've known. A world where the rule of law supplants the rule of the jungle. A world in which nations recognize the shared responsibility for freedom and justice. A world where the strong respect the rights of the weak. This is the vision that I shared with President Gorbachev in Helsinki. He and other leaders from Europe, the Gulf, and around the world understand that how we manage this crisis today could shape the future for generations to come.

The test we face is great, and so are the stakes. This is the first assault on the new world that we seek, the first test of our mettle. Had we not responded to this first provocation with clarity of purpose, if we do not continue to demonstrate our determination, it would be a signal to actual and potential despots around the world. America and the world must defend common vital interests—and we will. America and the world must support the rule of law—and we will. America and the world must stand up to aggression—and we will. And one thing more: In the pursuit of these goals America will not be intimidated.

Vital issues of principle are at stake. Saddam Hussein is literally trying to wipe a country off the face of the Earth. We do not exaggerate. Nor do we exaggerate when we say Saddam Hussein will fail. Vital economic interests are at risk as well. Iraq itself controls some 10 percent of the world's proven oil reserves. Iraq plus Kuwait controls twice that. An Iraq permitted to swallow Kuwait would have the economic and military power, as well as the arrogance, to intimidate and coerce its neighbors—neighbors who control the lion's share of the world's remaining oil reserves. We cannot permit a resource so vital to be dominated by one so ruthless. And we won't.

Recent events have surely proven that there is no substitute for American leadership. In the face of tyranny, let no one doubt American credibility and reliability. Let no one doubt our staying power. We will stand by our friends. One way or another, the leader of Iraq must learn this fundamental truth. From the outset, acting hand in hand with others, we've sought to fashion the broadest possible international response to Iraq's aggression. The level of world cooperation and condemnation of Iraq is unprecedented. Armed forces from countries spanning four continents are there at the request of King Fahd of Saudi Arabia to deter and, if need be, to defend against attack. Moslems and non-Moslems, Arabs and non-Arabs, soldiers from many nations stand shoulder to shoulder, resolute against Saddam Hussein's ambitions.

We can now point to five United Nations Security Council resolutions that condemn Iraq's aggression. They call for Iraq's immediate and unconditional withdrawal, the restoration of Kuwait's legitimate government, and categorically reject Iraq's cynical and self-serving attempt to annex Kuwait. Finally, the United Nations has demanded the release of all foreign nationals held hostage against their will and in contravention of international law. It is a mockery of human decency to call these people "guests." They are hostages, and the whole world knows it.

Prime Minister Margaret Thatcher, a dependable ally, said it all: "We do not bargain over hostages. We will not stoop to the level of using human beings as bargaining chips ever." Of course, of course, our hearts go out to the hostages and to their families. But our policy cannot change, and it will not change. America and the world will not be blackmailed by this ruthless policy.

We're now in sight of a United Nations that performs as envisioned by its founders. We owe much to the outstanding leadership of Secretary-General Javier Pérez de Cuellar. The United Nations is backing up its words with action. The Security Council has imposed mandatory economic sanctions on Iraq, designed to force Iraq to relinquish the spoils of its illegal conquest. The Security Council has also taken the decisive step of authorizing the use of all means necessary to ensure compliance with these sanctions. Together with our friends and allies, ships of the United States Navy are today patrolling Mideast waters. They've already intercepted more than 700 ships to enforce the sanctions. Three regional leaders I spoke with just yesterday told me that these sanctions are working. Iraq is feeling the heat. We continue to hope that Iraq's leaders will recalculate just what their aggression has cost them. They are cut off from world trade, unable to sell their oil. And only a tiny fraction of goods gets through.

The communique with President Gorbachev made mention of what happens when the embargo is so effective that children of Iraq literally need milk or the sick truly need medicine. Then, under strict international supervision that guarantees the proper destination, then food will be permitted.

At home, the material cost of our leadership can be steep. That's why Secretary of State [James] Baker and Treasury Secretary [William] Brady met with many world leaders to underscore that the burden of this collective effort must be shared. We are prepared to do our share and more to help carry that load; we insist that others do their share as well.

The response of most of our friends and allies has been good. To help defray costs, the leaders of Saudi Arabia, Kuwait, and the UAE—the United Arab Emirates—have pledged to provide our deployed troops with all the food and fuel they need. Generous assistance will also be provided to stalwart front-line nations, such as Turkey and Egypt. I am also heartened to report that this international response extends to the neediest victims of this conflict—those refugees. For our part, we've contributed $28 million for relief efforts. This is but a portion of what is needed. I commend, in particular, Saudi Arabia, Japan, and several European nations who have joined us in this purely humanitarian effort.

There's an energy-related cost to be borne as well. Oil-producing nations are already replacing lost Iraqi and Kuwaiti output. More than half of what was lost has been made up. And we're getting superb cooperation. If producers, including the United States, continue steps to expand oil and gas production, we can stabilize prices and guarantee against hardship. Additionally, we and several of our allies always have the option to extract oil from our strategic petroleum reserves if conditions warrant. As I've pointed out before, conservation efforts are essential to keep our energy needs as low as possible. And we must then take advantage of our energy sources across the board: coal, natural gas, hydro, and nuclear. Our failure to do these things has made us more dependent on foreign oil than ever before. Finally, let no one even contemplate profiteering from this crisis. We will not have it.

I cannot predict just how long it will take to convince Iraq to withdraw from Kuwait. Sanctions will take time to have their full intended effect. We will continue to review all options with our allies, but let it be clear: we will not let this aggression stand.

Our interest, our involvement in the Gulf is not transitory. It predated Saddam Hussein's aggression and will survive it. Long after all our troops come home—and we all hope it's soon, very soon—there will be a lasting role for the United States in assisting the nations of the Persian Gulf. Our role then: to deter future aggression. Our role is to help our friends in their own self-defense. And something else: to curb the proliferation of chemical, biological, ballistic missile and, above all, nuclear technologies.

Let me also make clear that the United States has no quarrel with the Iraqi people. Our quarrel is with Iraq's dictator and with his aggression. Iraq will not be permitted to annex Kuwait. That's not a threat, that's not a boast, that's just the way it's going to be.

Our ability to function effectively as a great power abroad depends on how we conduct ourselves at home. Our economy, our Armed Forces, our energy dependence, and our cohesion all determine whether we can help our friends and stand up to our foes. For America to lead, America must remain strong and vital. Our world leadership and domestic strength are mutual and reinforcing; a woven piece, as strongly bound as Old Glory. To revitalize our leadership, our leadership capacity, we must address our budget deficit—not after election day, or next year, but now.

Higher oil prices slow our growth, and higher defense costs would only make our fiscal deficit problem worse. That deficit was already greater than it should have been—a projected $232 billion for the coming year. It must—it will—be reduced.

To my friends in Congress, together we must act this very month—before the next fiscal year begins on October 1st—to get America's economic house in order. The Gulf situation helps us realize we are more economically vulnerable than we ever should be. Americans must never again enter any crisis, economic or military, with an excessive dependence on foreign oil and an excessive burden of Federal debt.

Most Americans are sick and tired of endless battles in the Congress and between the branches over budget matters. It is high time we pulled together and get the job done right. It's up to us to straighten this out. This job has four basic parts. First, the Congress should, this month, within a budget agreement, enact growth-oriented tax measures—to help avoid recession in the short term and to increase savings, investment, productivity, and competitiveness for the longer term. These measures include extending incentives for research and experimentation; expanding the use of IRAs for new homeowners; establishing tax-deferred family savings accounts; creating incentives for the creation of enterprise zones and initiatives to encourage more domestic drilling; and, yes, reducing the tax rate on capital gains.

And second, the Congress should, this month, enact a prudent multiyear defense program, one that reflects not only the improvement in East-West relations but our broader responsibilities to deal with the continuing risks of outlaw action and regional conflict. Even with our obligations in the Gulf, a sound defense budget can have some reduction in real terms; and we're prepared to accept that. But to go beyond such levels, where cutting defense would threaten our vital margin of safety, is something I will never accept. The world is still dangerous. And surely, that is now clear. Stability's not secure. American interests are far reaching. Interdependence has increased. The consequences of regional instability can be global. This is no time to risk America's capacity to protect her vital interests.

And third, the Congress should, this month, enact measures to increase domestic energy production and energy conservation in order to reduce dependence on foreign oil. These measures should include my proposals to increase incentives for domestic oil and gas exploration, fuel-switching, and to accelerate the development of the Alaskan energy resources without damage to wildlife. As you know, when the oil embargo was imposed in the early 1970s, the United States imported almost 6 million barrels of oil a day. This year, before the Iraqi invasion, U.S. imports had risen to nearly 8 million barrels per day. And we'd moved in the wrong direction. And now we must act to correct that trend.

And fourth, the Congress should, this month, enact a 5-year program to reduce the projected debt and deficits by $500 billion—that's by half a trillion dollars. And if, with the Congress, we can develop a satisfactory program by the end of the month, we can avoid the ax of sequester—deep across-the-board cuts that would threaten our military capacity and risk substantial domestic disruption. I want to be able to tell the American people that we have truly solved the deficit problem. And for me to do that, a budget agreement must meet these tests: It must include the measures I've recommended to increase economic growth and reduce dependence on foreign oil. It must be fair. All should contribute, but the burden should not be excessive for any one group of programs or people. It must address the growth of government's hidden liabilities. It must reform the budget process and, further, it must be real.

I urge Congress to provide a comprehensive 5-year deficit reduction program to me as a complete legislative package, with measures to assure that it can be fully enforced. America is tired of phony deficit reduction or promise-now, save-later plans. It is time for a program that is credible and real. And finally, to the extent that the deficit reduction program includes new revenue measures, it must avoid any measure that would threaten economic growth or turn us back toward the days of punishing income tax rates. That is one path we should not head down again.

I have been pleased with recent progress, although it has not always seemed so smooth. But now it's time to produce. I hope we can work out a responsible plan. But with or without agreement from the budget summit, I ask both Houses of the Congress to allow a straight up-or-down vote on a complete $500-billion deficit reduction package not later than September 28. If the Congress cannot get me a budget, then Americans will have to face a tough, mandated sequester. I'm hopeful, in fact, I'm confident that the Congress will do what it should. And I can assure you that we in the Executive branch will do our part.

In the final analysis, our ability to meet our responsibilities abroad depends upon political will and consensus at home. This is never easy in democracies, for we govern only with the consent of the governed. And although free people in a free society are bound to have their differences, Americans traditionally come together in times of adversity and challenge.

Once again, Americans have stepped forward to share a tearful goodbye with their families before leaving for a strange and distant shore. At this very moment, they serve together with Arabs, Europeans, Asians, and Africans in defense of principle and the dream of a new world order. That's why they sweat and toil in the sand and the heat and the sun. If they can come together under such adversity, if old adversaries like the Soviet Union and the United States can work in common cause, then surely, we who are so fortunate to be in this great Chamber—Democrats, Republicans, liberals, conservatives—can come together to fulfill our responsibilities here.

Thank you. Good night. And God bless the United States of America.

SOURCE: *Public Papers: Bush, 1990,* 2:1218–22.

DOCUMENT 80

PRESIDENT BUSH'S LETTER TO CONGRESS CONCERNING U.S. MILITARY DEPLOYMENT TO THE PERSIAN GULF. NOVEMBER 16, 1990.

Dear Mr. Speaker, Dear Mr. President:

There have been a number of important developments in the Persian Gulf region since my letter of August 9, 1990, informing you of the deployment of U.S. Armed Forces in response to Iraq's invasion of Kuwait. In the spirit of consultation and cooperation between our two branches of Government and in the firm belief that working together as we have we can best protect and advance the Nation's interests, I wanted to update you on these developments.

As you are aware, the United States and Allied and other friendly governments have introduced elements of their Armed Forces into the region in response to Iraq's unprovoked and unlawful aggression and at the request of regional governments. In view of Iraq's continued occupation of Kuwait, defiance of 10 U.N. Security Council resolutions demanding unconditional withdrawal, and sustained threat to other friendly countries in the region, I determined that the U.S. deployments begun in August should continue. Accordingly, on November 8, after consultations with our Allies and coalition partners, I announced the continued deployment of U.S. Armed Forces to the Persian Gulf region. These Forces include a heavy U.S. Army Corps and a Marine expeditionary force with an additional brigade. In addition, three aircraft carriers, a battleship, appropriate escort ships, a naval amphibious landing group, and a squadron of maritime prepositioning ships will join other naval units in the area.

I want to emphasize that this deployment is in line with the steady buildup of U.S. Armed Forces in the region over the last 3 months and is a continuation of the deployment described in my letter of August 9. I also want to emphasize that the mission of our Armed Forces has not changed. Our Forces are in the Gulf region in the exercise of our inherent right of individual and collective self-defense against Iraq's aggression and consistent with U.N. Security Council resolutions related to Iraq's ongoing occupation of Kuwait. The United States and other nations continue to seek a peaceful resolution of the crisis. We and our coalition partners share the common goals of achieving the immediate, complete, and unconditional withdrawal of Iraqi forces from Kuwait, the restoration of Kuwait's legitimate government, the protection of the lives of citizens held hostage by Iraq both in Kuwait and Iraq, and the restoration of security and stability in the region. The deployment will ensure that the coalition has an adequate offensive military option should that be necessary to achieve our common goals.

In my August 9 letter, I indicated that I did not believe that involvement in hostilities was imminent. Indeed, it was my belief that the deployment would facilitate a peaceful resolution of the crisis. I also stated that our Armed Forces would remain in the Persian Gulf region so long as required to contribute to the security of the region and desired by host governments. My view on these matters has not changed.

I appreciate the views you and other members of the congressional leadership have expressed throughout the past 3 months during our consultations. I look forward to continued consultation and cooperation with the Congress in pursuit of peace, stability, and security in the Gulf region.

SOURCE: *Public Papers: Bush, 1990,* 2:1617–18.

DOCUMENT 81

PRESIDENT BUSH'S REMARKS TO U.S. TROOPS AT
DHAHRAN, SAUDI ARABIA. NOVEMBER 22, 1990.

Thank you all. Thank you for that warm welcome. I'm just delighted to be here, and so is Barbara [Mrs. Barbara Bush, the First Lady]. And I don't normally speak for the joint leadership of the United States Congress, but it is most fitting that on this Thanksgiving Day we have with me here the Speaker of the House, Tom Foley; Bob Michel, the minority leader in our House; Senator [George] Mitchell, the leader in the United States Senate; and Bob Dole, the minority leader in the Senate. I'm just delighted they're out here with us.

And, of course, I salute not only Colonel [John] McBroom but also General [Norman] Schwarzkopf. And, Norm, we have a little present [teddy bear suit] for you. It comes from the families and friends of our troops around the world, and it's just your size. This thing will fit you. [Laughter]

Well, Barbara and I are very proud to be sharing this Thanksgiving with the men and women of our allied forces. And later we're going to visit your partners in the Army, the Navy, Coast Guard, Marines—together, the finest Armed Forces in the entire world. And we are here because we believe in freedom: our freedom and the freedom of others. And we're here because we believe in principle. And we're here because we believe in you.

And I'm very impressed with the Air Force—people like Airman First Class Wade West. He was home on leave to get married when this got started. On August 7th he was called up. Within an hour he had the ceremony performed—his wedding ceremony—and left for the Middle East. You talk about a guy who gets things done. [Laughter] Fantastic.

Over the past 4 months, you have launched what history will judge as one of the most important deployments of allied military power since 1945. And I'm here today to personally thank you—the Saudi, Kuwaiti, British, and American air men and women here today, and the forces from 23 other nations—here to see that an unprecedented series of U.N. resolutions is honored.

Thanksgiving is indeed the oldest, some say the most American of holidays, dating back to our very origins as a people. It's a day apart from all others—a day of peace, a day of thanks, a day to remember what we stand for and, this Thanksgiving, why we're here. It isn't all that complicated. Earlier this week I set out the key reasons why we're here, making a stand in defense of peace and freedom. And we're here to protect freedom, here to protect the future, and here to protect innocent lives.

First, freedom: Protecting freedom means standing up to aggression. The brutality inflicted on the people of Kuwait and on innocent citizens of every country must not be rewarded. Kuwait is small, but one conquered nation is one too many. And remember, remember, the invasion of Kuwait was without provocation. The invasion of Kuwait was without excuse. And the invasion of Kuwait simply will not stand.

Second: Protecting our future means protecting our national security and the stability and security of the Gulf area that is so vital to all nations. Today the worldwide march of freedom is threatened by a man hell-bent on gaining a choke-hold on the world's economic lifeline. And that's why Iraq's aggression is not just a challenge to the security of our friends in the Gulf but to the new partnership of nations we're all hoping to build. Energy security is national security for us and for every country.

And third: We're here to protect innocent lives, including American lives. Every diplomat and every citizen of every country held hostage must be freed.

Three simple reasons—protecting freedom, protecting our future, protecting innocent lives—any one is reason enough why Iraq's unprincipled, unprovoked aggression must not go unchallenged. Together, as 10 United Nations Security Council resolutions made clear, they are a compelling case for your mission.

What we're confronting is a classic bully who thinks he can get away with kicking sand in the face of the world. And so far, we have acted with restraint, as is our way. But Saddam is making the mistake of his life if he confuses an abundance of restraint and patience with a lack of resolve. And every day that passes brings Saddam Hussein one step closer to realizing his goal of a nuclear weapons arsenal. And that's another reason, frankly, why, more and more, our mission is marked by a real sense of urgency.

Our objectives in the Gulf have never varied. We want a free and restored Kuwait, protect American citizens, safeguard the security and stability of the region. To force Iraq to comply, we and our allies have forged a strong, diplomatic, economic and, yes, military strategy. No President, none at all, is quick to order American troops abroad. But there are times when all nations that value freedom must confront aggression.

Sometimes it's a question of some pain—some pain now to avoid even worse pain later. In World War II, the world paid dearly for appeasing an aggressor who could have been stopped early on. We're not going to make that mistake again. We will not appease this aggressor.

The world is still a dangerous place, and those in uniform will always bear the heaviest burden. And we want every single American home. And this we promise: No American will be kept in the Gulf a single day longer than necessary. But we won't pull punches. We're not here on some exercise. This is a real world situation, and we're not walking away until our mission is done, until the invader is out of Kuwait.

There is no way Americans can forget the contribution you are making to world peace and to our country. Year after year on this very special day, special to every American, no doubt each of you has given thanks to your country. This year your country gives thanks to you. We think of you with pride in our hearts and a prayer on our lips.

May God bless you and watch over you. To those with whom we stand shoulder to shoulder, our friends from other lands, may God bless each and every one of you. And may God bless the United States of America.

SOURCE: *Public Papers: Bush, 1990*, 2:1666–67.

DOCUMENT 82
PRESIDENT BUSH'S REMARKS ON SIGNING THE RESOLUTION AUTHORIZING THE USE OF FORCE AGAINST IRAQ. JANUARY 14, 1991.

Today, I am signing H.J. Res. 77, the "Authorization for Use of Military Force Against Iraq Resolution." By passing H.J. Res. 77, the Congress of the United States has expressed its approval of the use of U.S. Armed Forces consistent with U.N. Security Council Resolution 678. I asked the Congress to support implementation of U.N. Security Council Resolution 678 because such action would send the clearest possible message to Saddam Hussein that he must withdraw from Kuwait without condition or delay. I am grateful to those of both political parties who joined in the expression of resolve embodied in this resolution. To all, I emphasize again my conviction that this resolution provides the best hope for peace.

The debate on H.J. Res. 77 reflects the profound strength of our constitutional democracy. In coming to grips with the issues at stake in the Gulf, both Houses of Congress acted in the finest traditions of our country. This resolution provides unmistakable support for the international community's determination that Iraq's ongoing aggression against, and occupation of, Kuwait shall not stand. As I made clear to congressional leaders at the outset, my request for congressional support did not, and my signing this resolution does not, constitute any change in the long-standing positions of the Executive branch on either the President's constitutional authority to use the Armed Forces to defend vital U.S. interests or the constitutionality of the War Powers Resolution. I am pleased, however, that differences on these issues between the President and many in the Congress have not prevented us from uniting in a common objective. I have had the benefit of extensive and meaningful consultations with the Congress throughout this crisis, and I shall continue to consult closely with the Congress in the days ahead.

SOURCE: *Public Papers of the Presidents: George Bush, 1991*, 2 vols. (Washington, DC: Government Printing Office, 1992), 1:40.

DOCUMENT 83

PRESIDENT BUSH'S ADDRESS TO THE NATION ANNOUNCING ALLIED MILITARY ACTION IN THE PERSIAN GULF AGAINST IRAQI FORCES. JANUARY 16, 1991.

Just 2 hours ago, allied air forces began an attack on military targets in Iraq and Kuwait. These attacks continue as I speak. Ground forces are not engaged.

This conflict started August 2d when the dictator of Iraq invaded a small and helpless neighbor. Kuwait—a member of the Arab League and a member of the United Nations—was crushed; its people, brutalized. Five months ago, Saddam Hussein started this cruel war against Kuwait. Tonight, the battle has been joined.

This military action, taken in accord with United Nations resolutions and with the consent of the United States Congress, follows months of constant and virtually endless diplomatic activity on the part of the United Nations, the United States, and many, many other countries. Arab leaders sought what became known as an Arab solution, only to conclude that Saddam Hussein was unwilling to leave Kuwait. Others traveled to Baghdad in a variety of efforts to restore peace and justice. Our Secretary of State, James Baker, held an historic meeting in Geneva, only to be totally rebuffed. This past weekend, in a last-ditch effort, the Secretary-General of the United Nations went to the Middle East with peace in his heart—his second such mission. And he came back from Baghdad with no progress at all in getting Saddam Hussein to withdraw from Kuwait.

Now the 28 countries with forces in the Gulf area have exhausted all reasonable efforts to reach a peaceful resolution—have no choice but to drive Saddam from Kuwait by force. We will not fail.

As I report to you, air attacks are under way against military targets in Iraq. We are determined to knock out Saddam Hussein's nuclear bomb potential. We will also destroy his chemical weapons facilities. Much of Saddam's artillery and tanks will be destroyed. Our operations are designed to best protect the lives of all the coalition forces by targeting Saddam's vast military arsenal. Initial reports from General Schwarzkopf are that our operations are proceeding according to plan.

Our objectives are clear: Saddam Hussein's forces will leave Kuwait. The legitimate government of Kuwait will be restored to its rightful place, and Kuwait will once again be free. Iraq will eventually comply with all relevant United Nations resolutions, and then, when peace is restored, it is our hope that Iraq will live as a peaceful and cooperative member of the family of nations, thus enhancing the security and stability of the Gulf.

Some may ask: Why act now? Why not wait? The answer is clear: The world could wait no longer. Sanctions, though having some effect, showed no signs of accomplishing their objective. Sanctions were tried for well over 5 months, and we and our allies concluded that sanctions alone would not force Saddam from Kuwait.

While the world waited, Saddam Hussein systematically raped, pillaged, and plundered a tiny nation, no threat to his own. He subjected the people of Kuwait to unspeakable atrocities—and among those maimed and murdered, innocent children.

While the world waited, Saddam sought to add to the chemical weapons arsenal he now possesses, an infinitely more dangerous weapon of mass destruction—a nuclear weapon. And while the world waited, while the world talked peace and withdrawal, Saddam Hussein dug in and moved massive forces into Kuwait.

While the world waited, while Saddam stalled, more damage was being done to the fragile economies of the Third World, emerging democracies of Eastern Europe, to the entire world, including to our own economy.

The United States, together with the United Nations, exhausted every means at our disposal to bring this crisis to a peaceful end. However, Saddam clearly felt that by stalling and threatening and defying the United Nations, he could weaken the forces arrayed against him.

While the world waited, Saddam Hussein met every overture of peace with open contempt. While the world prayed for peace, Saddam prepared for war.

I had hoped that when the United States Congress, in historic debate, took its resolute action, Saddam would realize he could not prevail and would move out of Kuwait in accord with the United Nations resolutions. He did not do that. Instead, he remained intransigent, certain that time was on his side.

Saddam was warned over and over again to comply with the will of the United Nations: Leave Kuwait, or be driven out. Saddam has arrogantly rejected all warnings. Instead, he tried to make this a dispute between Iraq and the United States of America.

Well, he failed. Tonight, 28 nations—countries from 5 continents, Europe and Asia, Africa, and the Arab League—have forces in the Gulf area standing shoulder to shoulder against Saddam Hussein. These countries had hoped the use of force could be avoided. Regrettably, we now believe that only force will make him leave.

Prior to ordering our forces into battle, I instructed our military commanders to take every necessary step to prevail as quickly as possible, and with the greatest degree of protection possible for American and allied service men and women. I've told the American people before that this will not be another Vietnam, and I repeat this here tonight. Our troops will have the best possible support in the entire world, and they will not be asked to fight with one hand tied behind their back. I'm hopeful that this fighting will not go on for long and that casualties will be held to an absolute minimum.

This is an historic moment. We have in this past year made great progress in ending the long era of conflict and cold war. We have before us the opportunity to forge for ourselves and for future generations a new world order—a world where the rule of law, not the law of the jungle, governs the conduct of nations. When we are successful—and we will be—we have a real chance at this new world order, an order in which a credible United Nations can use its peacekeeping role to fulfill the promise and vision of the U.N.'s founders.

We have no argument with the people of Iraq. Indeed, for the innocents caught in this conflict, I pray for their safety. Our goal is not the conquest of Iraq. It is the liberation of Kuwait. It is my hope that somehow the Iraqi people can, even now, convince their dictator that he must lay down his arms, leave Kuwait, and let Iraq itself rejoin the family of peace-loving nations.

Thomas Paine wrote many years ago: "These are the times that try men's souls." Those well-known words are so very true today. But even as planes of the multinational forces attack Iraq, I prefer to think of peace, not war. I am convinced not only that we will prevail but that out of the horror of combat will come the recognition that no nation can stand against a world united, no nation will be permitted to brutally assault its neighbor.

No President can easily commit our sons and daughters to war. They are the Nation's finest. Ours is an all-volunteer force, magnificently trained, highly motivated. The troops know why they're there. And listen to what they say, for they've said it better than any President or Prime Minister ever could.

Listen to Hollywood Huddleston, Marine lance corporal. He says, "Let's free these people, so we can go home and be free again." And he's right. The terrible crimes and tortures committed by Saddam's henchmen against the innocent people of Kuwait are an affront to mankind and a challenge to the freedom of all.

Listen to one of our great officers out there, Marine Lieutenant General Walter Boomer. He said: "There are things worth fighting for. A world in which brutality and lawlessness are allowed to go unchecked isn't the kind of world we're going to want to live in."

Listen to Master Sergeant J.P. Kendall of the 82d Airborne: "We're here for more than just the price of a gallon of gas. What we're doing is going to chart the future of the world for the next 100 years. It's better to deal with this guy now than 5 years from now."

And finally, we should all sit up and listen to Jackie Jones, an Army lieutenant, when she says, "If we let him get away with this, who knows what's going to be next?"

I have called upon Hollywood and Walter and J.P. and Jackie and all their courageous comrades-in-arms to do what must be done. Tonight, America and the world are deeply grateful to them and to their families. And let me say to everyone listening or watching tonight: When the troops we've sent in finish their work, I am determined to bring them home as soon as possible.

Tonight, as our forces fight, they and their families are in our prayers. May God bless each and every one of them, and the coalition forces at our side in the Gulf, and may He continue to bless our nation, the United States of America.

SOURCE: *Public Papers: Bush, 1991*, 1:42–44.

DOCUMENT 84

PRESIDENT BUSH'S ADDRESS TO THE NATION ON THE DEPLOYMENT OF U.S. FORCES TO SOMALIA FOR OPERATION RESTORE HOPE. DECEMBER 4, 1992.

I want to talk to you today about the tragedy in Somalia and about a mission that can ease suffering and save lives. Every American has seen the shocking images from Somalia. The scope of suffering there is hard to imagine. Already, over a quarter of a million people, as many people as live in Buffalo, New York, have died in the Somali famine. In the months ahead 5 times that number, 1½ million people, could starve to death.

For many months now, the United States has been actively engaged in the massive international relief effort to ease Somalia's suffering. All told, America has sent Somalia 200,000 tons of food, more than half the world total. This summer, the distribution system broke down. Truck convoys from Somalia's ports were blocked. Sufficient food failed to reach the starving in the interior of Somalia.

So in August, we took additional action. In concert with the United Nations, we sent in the U.S. Air Force to help fly food to the towns. To date, American pilots have flown over 1,400 flights, delivering over 17,000 tons of food aid. And when the U.N. authorized 3,500 U.N. guards to protect the relief operation, we flew in the first of them, 500 soldiers from Pakistan.

But in the months since then, the security situation has grown worse. The U.N. has been prevented from deploying its initial commitment of troops. In many cases, food from relief flights is being looted upon landing; food convoys have been hijacked; aid workers assaulted; ships with food have been subject to artillery attacks that prevented them from docking. There is no government in Somalia. Law and order have broken down. Anarchy prevails.

One image tells the story. Imagine 7,000 tons of food aid literally bursting out of a warehouse on a dock in Mogadishu, while Somalis starve less than a kilometer away because relief workers cannot run the gauntlet of armed gangs roving the city. Confronted with these conditions, relief groups called for outside troops to provide security so they could feed people. It's now clear that military support is necessary to ensure the safe delivery of the food Somalis need to survive.

It was this situation which led us to tell the United Nations that the United States would be willing to provide more help to enable relief to be delivered. Last night the United Nations Security Council, by unanimous vote and after the tireless efforts of Secretary-General [Boutros] Boutros-Ghali, welcomed the United States offer to lead a coalition to get the food through.

After consulting with my advisers, with world leaders, and the congressional leadership, I have today told Secretary-General Boutros-Ghali that America will answer the call. I have given the order to Secretary Cheney to move a substantial American force into Somalia. As I speak, a Marine amphibious ready group, which we maintain at sea, is offshore Mogadishu. These troops will be joined by elements of the 1st Marine Expeditionary

Force, based out of Camp Pendleton, California, and by the Army's 10th Mountain Division out of Fort Drum, New York. These and other American forces will assist in Operation Restore Hope. They are America's finest. They will perform this mission with courage and compassion, and they will succeed.

The people of Somalia, especially the children of Somalia, need our help. We're able to ease their suffering. We must help them live. We must give them hope. America must act.

In taking this action, I want to emphasize that I understand the United States alone cannot right the world's wrongs. But we also know that some crises in the world cannot be resolved without American involvement, that American action is often necessary as a catalyst for broader involvement of the community of nations. Only the United States has the global reach to place a large security force on the ground in such a distant place quickly and efficiently and thus save thousands of innocents from death.

We will not, however, be acting alone. I expect forces from about a dozen countries to join us in this mission. When we see Somalia's children starving, all of America hurts. We've tried to help in many ways. And make no mistake about it, now we and our allies will ensure that aid gets through. Here is what we and our coalition partners will do:

First, we will create a secure environment in the hardest hit parts of Somalia, so that food can move from ships over land to the people in the countryside now devastated by starvation.

Second, once we have created that secure environment, we will withdraw our troops, handing the security mission back to a regular U.N. peacekeeping force. Our mission has a limited objective: To open the supply routes, to get food moving, and to prepare the way for a U.N. peacekeeping force to keep it moving. This operation is not open-ended. We will not stay one day longer than is absolutely necessary.

Let me be very clear: Our mission is humanitarian, but we will not tolerate armed gangs ripping off their own people, condemning them to death by starvation. General [Joseph] Hoar and his troops have the authority to take whatever military action is necessary to safeguard the lives of our troops and the lives of Somalia's people. The outlaw elements in Somalia must understand this is serious business. We will accomplish our mission. We have no intent to remain in Somalia with fighting forces, but we are determined to do it right, to secure an environment that will allow food to get to the starving people of Somalia.

To the people of Somalia I promise this: We do not plan to dictate political outcomes. We respect your sovereignty and independence. Based on my conversations with other coalition lenders, I can state with confidence: We come to your country for one reason only, to enable the starving to be fed.

Let me say to the men and women of our Armed Forces: We are asking you to do a difficult and dangerous job. As Commander in Chief I assure you, you will have our full support to get the job done, and we will bring you home as soon as possible.

Finally, let me close with a message to the families of the men and women who take part in this mission: I understand it is difficult to see your loved ones go, to send them off knowing they will not be home for the holidays, but the humanitarian mission they undertake is in the finest traditions of service. So, to every sailor, soldier, airman, and marine who is involved in this mission, let me say, you're doing God's work. We will not fail.

Thank you, and may God bless the United States of America.

SOURCE: *Public Papers of the Presidents: George Bush, 1992–93*, 2 vols. (Washington, DC: Government Printing Office, 1993), 2:2174–76.

DOCUMENT 85

PRESIDENT BUSH'S LETTER TO CONGRESS CONCERNING U.S. MILITARY ACTION IN SOMALIA. DECEMBER 21, 1992.

Beginning in January of this year with the adoption of U.N. Resolution 733, the United Nations has been actively addressing the humanitarian crisis in Somalia. The United States has been assisting the U.N. effort to deal with a human catastrophe. Over 300,000 Somalis have died of starvation. Five times that number remain at risk, beyond the reach of international relief efforts in large part because of the security situation. As a result, voluntary relief organizations from the United States and other countries have appealed for assistance from outside security forces.

On November 29, 1992, the Secretary-General of the United Nations [Boutros Boutros-Ghali] reported to the Security Council that the deteriorating security conditions in Somalia had severely disrupted international relief efforts and that an immediate military operation under U.N. authority was urgently required. On December 3, the Security Council adopted Resolution 794, which determined that the situation in Somalia constituted a threat to international peace and security, and, invoking Chapter VII of the U.N. Charter, authorized Member States to use all necessary means to establish a secure environment for humanitarian relief operations in Somalia. In my judgment, the deployment of U.S. Armed Forces under U.S. command to Somalia as part of this multilateral response to the Resolution is necessary to address a major humanitarian calamity, avert related threats to international peace and security, and protect the safety of Americans and others engaged in relief operations.

In the evening, Eastern Standard Time, on December 8, 1992, U.S. Armed Forces entered Somalia to secure the airfield and port facility of Mogadishu. Other elements of the U.S. Armed Forces and the Armed Forces of other Members of the United Nations are being introduced into Somalia to achieve the objectives of U.N. Security Council Resolution 794. No organized resistance has been encountered to date.

U.S. Armed Forces will remain in Somalia only as long as necessary to establish a secure environment for humanitarian relief operations and will then turn over the responsibility of maintaining this environment to a U.N. peacekeeping force assigned to Somalia. Over 15 nations have already offered to deploy troops. While it is not possible to estimate precisely how long the transfer of responsibility may take, we believe that prolonged operations will not be necessary.

We do not intend that U.S. Armed Forces deployed to Somalia become involved in hostilities. Nonetheless, these forces are equipped and ready to take such measures as may be needed to accomplish their humanitarian mission and defend themselves, if necessary; they also will have the support of any additional U.S. Armed Forces necessary to ensure their safety and the accomplishment of their mission.

I have taken these actions pursuant to my constitutional authority to conduct our foreign relations and as Commander in Chief and Chief Executive, and in accordance with applicable treaties and laws. In doing so, I have taken into account the views expressed in H. Con. Res. 370, S. Con. Res. 132, and the Horn of Africa Recovery and Food Security Act, Public Law 102-274, on the urgent need for action in Somalia.

I am providing this report in accordance with my desire that Congress be fully informed and consistent with the War Powers Resolution. I look forward to cooperating with Congress in the effort to relieve human suffering and to restore peace and stability to the region.

SOURCE: *Public Papers: Bush, 1992–93*, 2:2179–80.

23

WILLIAM J. CLINTON

DOCUMENT 86

PRESIDENT BILL CLINTON'S RADIO ADDRESS CONCERNING
U.S. MILITARY ACTION IN SOMALIA. JUNE 12, 1993.

———◆———

Good morning. Last night the United Nations, acting with American and other coalition forces, successfully attacked the military positions in Somalia of the warlord Mohamed Farah Aideed. Our forces, thankfully, have sustained no casualties.

The UN's action was a response to a savage attack this past week by Aideed's forces carried out on UN peacekeepers. Aideed's attack killed 23 Pakistanis and injured 3 Americans serving in the UN's force. It was a cold-blooded ambush on UN forces who were delivering food and building peace for the people of Somalia. The United Nations and the United States refuse to tolerate this ruthless disregard for the will of the international community. Therefore, following a request from the UN and pursuant to a UN Security Council resolution, I ordered the participation of our troops in this action. I commend the decisive leadership of the UN Secretary-General [Boutros] Boutros-Ghali, the commander of the UN force, Turkish General Bir, and United States Major General Thomas Montgomery.

With this action, the world community moves to restore order in Somalia's capital and to underscore its commitment to preserve the security of UN forces. For if UN peacekeepers are to be effective agents for peace and stability in Somalia and elsewhere, they must be capable of using force when necessary to defend themselves and accomplish their goals.

We need to recall why U.S. forces were in Somalia to begin with and how much has been accomplished since they first arrived. Last December the United States first sent troops to Somalia to help the United Nations answer a desperate call for help. By the time we arrived over 350,000 Somalis already had died in a bloody civil war, shrouding the nation in famine and disease. Over 30,000 American men and women, both military and civilian, joined with troops and relief workers from all over the world in an effort to end the starvation and the hopelessness. They worked with courage and dedication to quell the violence, rein in the warlords, and deliver tons of urgently needed food and medicine. That humanitarian effort restored hope, advanced our interests, and represented the very best of America's ideals.

Today in Somalia, crops are growing, starvation has ended, refugees are beginning to return, schools and hospitals are reopening, a civil police force has been recreated, and Somalia has begun a process of national reconciliation with the goal of creating the institutions of democracy. As a result, over recent months, we have been able to reduce our troop presence in Somalia down to fewer than 4,000, a small fraction of the total UN force.

While American and UN efforts in Somalia have been successful, there remains a small but dangerous minority of Somalis who are determined to provoke terror and chaos. Last night's action was essential to send a clear message to the armed gangs, to protect the vast majority of Somalis who long for peace, to enhance the security of our forces still in Somalia, to hasten the day when they can safely return home, and to strengthen the effectiveness and the credibility of UN peacekeeping in Somalia and around the world.

The UN's action holds an important lesson about how our Nation can accomplish our own security goals in this new era. Although the cold war is over, the world remains a dangerous place. The United States cannot be the world's policeman, but we also cannot turn a blind eye to the world's problems, for they affect our own security, our own interests, and our own ideals. The U.S. must continue to play its unique role of leadership in the world. But now we can increasingly express that leadership through multilateral means such as the United Nations, which spread the costs and expressed the unified will of the international community. That was one of the lessons of Desert Storm. And clearly, that was one of the lessons last night in Somalia.

On behalf of all Americans, I am proud of the American forces who once again have demonstrated extraordinary courage and skill. The world thanks them and all of the UN forces in Somalia for their service, for striking a blow against lawlessness and killing, and for advancing the world's commitment to justice and security.

SOURCE: *Public Papers of the Presidents: William J. Clinton, 1993*, 2 vols. (Washington, DC: Government Printing Office, 1994), 1:839–40.

DOCUMENT 87

PRESIDENT CLINTON'S TELEVISED ADDRESS TO THE NATION CONCERNING U.S. MILITARY INVOLVEMENT IN SOMALIA. OCTOBER 7, 1993.

Today I want to talk with you about our Nation's military involvement in Somalia. A year ago, we all watched with horror as Somali children and their families lay dying by the tens of thousands, dying the slow, agonizing death of starvation, a starvation brought on not only by drought, but also by the anarchy that then prevailed in that country.

This past weekend we all reacted with anger and horror as an armed Somali gang desecrated the bodies of our American soldiers and displayed a captured American pilot, all of them soldiers who were taking part in an international effort to end the starvation of the Somali people themselves. These tragic events raise hard questions about our effort in Somalia. Why are we still there? What are we trying to accomplish? How did a humanitarian mission turn violent? And when will our people come home?

These questions deserve straight answers. Let's start by remembering why our troops went into Somalia in the first place. We went because only the United States could help stop one of the great human tragedies of this time. A third of a million people had died of starvation and disease. Twice that many more were at risk of dying. Meanwhile, tons of relief supplies piled up in the capital of Mogadishu because a small number of Somalis stopped food from reaching their own countrymen.

Our consciences said, enough. In our Nation's best tradition, we took action with bipartisan support. President Bush sent in 28,000 American troops as part of a United Nations humanitarian mission. Our troops created a secure environment so that food and medicine could get through. We saved close to one million lives. And throughout most of Somalia, everywhere but in Mogadishu, life began returning to normal. Crops are growing. Markets are reopening. So are schools and hospitals. Nearly a million Somalis still depend completely on relief supplies, but at least the starvation is gone. And none of this would have happened without American leadership and America's troops.

Until June, things went well, with little violence. The United States reduced our troop presence from 28,000 down to less than 5,000, with other nations picking up where we left off. But then in time, the people who caused much of the problem in the beginning started attacking

American, Pakistani, and other troops who were there just to keep the peace.

Rather than participate in building the peace with others, these people sought to fight and to disrupt, even if it means returning Somalia to anarchy and mass famine. And make no mistake about it, if we were to leave Somalia tomorrow, other nations would leave, too. Chaos would resume. The relief effort would stop, and starvation soon would return.

That knowledge has led us to continue our mission. It is not our job to rebuild Somalia's society or even to create a political process that can allow Somalia's clans to live and work in peace. The Somalis must do that for themselves. The United Nations and many African states are more than willing to help. But we, we in the United States must decide whether we will give them enough time to have a reasonable chance to succeed.

We started this mission for the right reasons, and we're going to finish it in the right way. In a sense, we came to Somalia to rescue innocent people in a burning house. We've nearly put the fire out, but some smoldering embers remain. If we leave them now, those embers will reignite into flames, and people will die again. If we stay a short while longer and do the right things, we've got a reasonable chance of cooling off the embers and getting other fire-fighters to take our place.

We also have to recognize that we cannot leave now and still have all our troops present and accounted for. And I want you to know that I am determined to work for the security of those Americans missing or held captive. Anyone holding an American right now should understand, above all else, that we will hold them strictly responsible for our soldiers' well-being. We expect them to be well-treated, and we expect them to be released.

So now we face a choice. Do we leave when the job gets tough, or when the job is well done? Do we invite a return of mass suffering, or do we leave in a way that gives the Somalis a decent chance to survive?

Recently, General Colin Powell said this about our choices in Somalia: "Because things get difficult, you don't cut and run. You work the problem and try to find a correct solution." I want to bring our troops home from Somalia. Before the events of this week, as I said, we had already reduced the number of our troops there from 28,000 to less than 5,000. We must complete that withdrawal soon, and I will. But we must also leave on our terms. We must do it right. And here is what I intend to do.

This past week's events make it clear that even as we prepare to withdraw from Somalia, we need more strength there. We need more armor, more air power, to ensure that our people are safe and that we can do our job. Today I have ordered 1,700 additional Army troops and 104 additional armored vehicles to Somalia to protect our troops and to complete our mission. I've also ordered an aircraft carrier and two amphibious groups with 3,600 combat Marines to be stationed offshore. These forces will be under American command.

Their mission, what I am asking these young Americans to do, is the following:

First, they are there to protect our troops and our bases. We did not go to Somalia with a military purpose. We never wanted to kill anyone. But those who attack our soldiers must know they will pay a very heavy price.

Second, they are there to keep open and secure the roads, the port, and the lines of communication that are essential for the United Nations and the relief workers to keep the flow of food and supplies and people moving freely throughout the country so that starvation and anarchy do not return.

Third, they are there to keep the pressure on those who cut off relief supplies and attacked our people, not to personalize the conflict but to prevent a return to anarchy.

Fourth, through their pressure and their presence, our troops will help to make it possible for the Somali people, working with others, to reach agreements among themselves so that they can solve their problems and survive when we leave. That is our mission.

I am proposing this plan because it will let us finish leaving Somalia on our own terms and without destroying all that two administrations have accomplished there. For, if we were to leave today, we know what would happen. Within months, Somali children again would be dying in the streets. Our own credibility with friends and allies would be severely damaged. Our leadership in world affairs would be undermined at the very time when people are looking to America to help promote peace and freedom in the post-cold war world. And all around the world, aggressors, thugs, and terrorists will conclude that the best way to get us to change our policies is to kill our people. It would be open season on Americans.

That is why I am committed to getting this job done in Somalia, not only quickly but also effectively. To do that, I am taking steps to ensure troops from other nations are ready to take the place of our own soldiers. We've already withdrawn some 20,000 troops, and more than that number have replaced them from over two dozen other nations. Now we will intensify efforts to have other countries deploy more troops to Somalia to assure that security will remain when we're gone.

And we'll complete the replacement of U.S. military logistics personnel with civilian contractors who can provide the same support to the United Nations. While we're taking military steps to protect our own people and to help the UN maintain a secure environment, we must pursue new diplomatic efforts to help the Somalis find a political solution to their problems. That is the only kind of outcome that can endure.

For fundamentally, the solution to Somalia's problems is not a military one, it is political. Leaders of the neighboring African states, such as Ethiopia and Eritrea, have offered to take the lead in efforts to build a settlement among the Somali people that can preserve order and security. I have directed my representatives to pursue such efforts vigorously. And I've asked Ambassador Bob Oakley, who served effectively in two administrations as our representative in Somalia, to travel again to the region immediately to advance this process.

Obviously, even then there is no guarantee that Somalia will rid itself of violence and suffering. But at least we will have given Somalia a reasonable chance. This week some 15,000 Somalis took to the streets to express sympathy for our losses, to thank us for our effort. Most Somalis are not hostile to us but grateful. And they want to use this opportunity to rebuild their country.

It is my judgment and that of my military advisers that we may need up to 6 months to complete these steps and to conduct an orderly withdrawal. We'll do what we can to complete the mission before then. All American troops will be out of Somalia no later than March the 31st, except for a few hundred support personnel in noncombat roles.

If we take these steps, if we take the time to do the job right, I am convinced we will have lived up to the responsibilities of American leadership in the world. And we will have proved that we are committed to addressing the new problems of a new era.

When our troops in Somalia came under fire this last weekend, we witnessed a dramatic example of the heroic ethic of our American military. When the first Black Hawk helicopter was downed this weekend, the other American troops didn't retreat although they could have. Some 90 of them formed a perimeter around the helicopter, and they held that ground under intensely heavy fire. They stayed with their comrades. That's the kind of soldiers they are. That's the kind of people we are.

So let us finish the work we set out to do. Let us demonstrate to the world, as generations of Americans have done before us, that when Americans take on a challenge, they do the job right.

Let me express my thanks and my gratitude and my profound sympathy to the families of the young Americans who were killed in Somalia. My message to you is, your country is grateful and so is the rest of the world, and so are the vast majority of the Somali people. Our mission from this day forward is to increase our strength, do our job, bring our soldiers out, and bring them home.

Thank you, and God bless America.

SOURCE: *Public Papers: Clinton, 1993,* 2:1702–6.

DOCUMENT 88
PRESIDENT CLINTON'S MESSAGE TO CONGRESS REPORTING U.S. MILITARY OPERATIONS IN SOMALIA. OCTOBER 13, 1993.

In response to the request made by the House and Senate for certain information on our military operations in Somalia, I am pleased to forward the attached report [not included here].

In transmitting this report, I want to reiterate the points that I made on October 6 and to the American people in remarks on October 7. We went to Somalia on a humanitarian mission. We saved approximately a million lives that were at risk of starvation brought on by civil war that had degenerated into anarchy. We acted after 350,000 already had died.

Ours was a gesture of a great nation, carried out by thousands of American citizens, both military and civilian. We did not then, nor do we now, plan to stay in that country. The United Nations agreed to assume our military mission and take on the additional political and rehabilitation activities required so that the famine and anarchy do not resume when the international presence departs.

For our part, we agreed with the United Nations to participate militarily with a much smaller U.S. force for a period of time, to help the United Nations create a secure environment in which it could ensure the free flow of humanitarian relief. At the request of the United Nations and the United States, approximately 30 nations deployed over 20,000 troops as we reduced our military presence.

With the recent tragic casualties to American forces in Somalia, the American people want to know why we are there, what we are doing, why we cannot come home immediately, and when we will come home. Although the report answers those questions in detail, I want to repeat concisely my answers:

We went to Somalia because without us a million people would have died. We, uniquely, were in a position to save them, and other nations were ready to share the burden after our initial action.

What the United States is doing there is providing for a limited period of time, logistics support and security so that the humanitarian and political efforts of the United Nations, relief organizations, and others can have a reasonable chance of success. The United Nations, in turn, has a longer-term political, security, and relief mission designed to minimize the likelihood that famine and anarchy will return when the United Nations leaves. The U.S. military mission is not now nor was it ever one of "nation building."

We cannot leave immediately because the United Nations has not had an adequate chance to replace us, nor have the Somalis had a reasonable opportunity to end their strife. We want other nations to assume more of the burden of international peace. To have them do so, they must think that they can rely on our commitments when we make them. Moreover, having been brutally attacked, were American forces to leave now we would send a message to terrorists and other potential adversaries around the world that they can change our policies by killing our people. It would be open season on Americans.

We will, however, leave no later than March 31, 1994, except for a few hundred support troops. That amount of time will permit the Somali people to make progress toward political reconciliation and allow the United States to fulfill our obligations properly, including the return of any Americans being detained. We went there for the right reasons and we will finish the job in the right way.

While U.S. forces are there, they will be fully protected with appropriate American military capability.

Any Americans detained will be the subject of the most complete and thorough efforts of which this Government is capable, with the unrelenting goal of returning them home and returning them to health.

I want to thank all those who have expressed their support for this approach during the last week. At difficult times such as these, when we face international challenges, bipartisan unity among our two branches of government is vital.

SOURCE: *Public Papers: Clinton, 1993*, 1: 1739–40.

DOCUMENT 89

PRESIDENT CLINTON'S ADDRESS TO THE NATION CONCERNING THE STRIKE ON THE IRAQI INTELLIGENCE HEADQUARTERS IN BAGHDAD. JUNE 26, 1993.

My Fellow Americans:

This evening I want to speak with you about an attack by the Government of Iraq against the United States and the actions we have just taken to respond.

This past April, the Kuwaiti Government uncovered what they suspected was a car bombing plot to assassinate former President George Bush while he was visiting Kuwait City. The Kuwaiti authorities arrested 16 suspects, including 2 Iraqi nationals. Following those arrests, I ordered our own intelligence and law enforcement agencies to conduct a thorough and independent investigation. Over the past several weeks, officials from those agencies reviewed a range of intelligence information, traveled to Kuwait and elsewhere, extensively interviewed the suspects, and thoroughly examined the forensic evidence.

This Thursday, Attorney General [Janet] Reno and Director of Central Intelligence [R. James] Woolsey gave me their findings. Based on their investigation there is compelling evidence that there was, in fact, a plot to assassinate former President Bush and that this plot, which included the use of a powerful bomb made in Iraq, was directed and pursued by the Iraqi intelligence service.

We should not be surprised by such deeds, coming as they do from a regime like Saddam Hussein's, which is ruled by atrocity, slaughtered its own people, invaded two neighbors, attacked others, and engaged in chemical and environmental warfare. Saddam has repeatedly violated the will and conscience of the international community. But this attempt at revenge by a tyrant against the leader of the world coalition that defeated him in war is particularly loathsome and cowardly. We thank God it was unsuccessful. The authorities who foiled it have the appreciation of all Americans.

It is clear that this was no impulsive or random act. It was an elaborate plan devised by the Iraqi Government and directed against a former President of the United States because of actions he took as President. As such, the Iraqi attack against President Bush was an attack against our country and against all Americans. We could not and have not let such action against our Nation go unanswered.

From the first days of our Revolution, America's security has depended on the clarity of this message: Don't tread on us. A firm and commensurate response was essential to protect our sovereignty, to send a message to those who engage in state-sponsored terrorism, to deter further violence against our people, and to affirm the expectation of civilized behavior among nations.

Therefore, on Friday I ordered our forces to launch a cruise missile attack on the Iraqi intelligence service's principal command-and-control facility in Baghdad. Those missiles were launched this afternoon at 4:22 Eastern Daylight Time. They landed approximately an hour ago. I have discussed this action with the congressional leadership and both our allies and friends in the region. And I have called for an emergency meeting of the United Nations Security Council to expose Iraq's crime.

These actions were directed against the Iraqi Government, which was responsible for the assassination plot. Saddam Hussein has demonstrated repeatedly that he will resort to terrorism or aggression if left unchecked. Our intent was to target Iraq's capacity to support violence against the United States and other nations and to deter Saddam Hussein from supporting such outlaw behavior in the future. Therefore, we directed our action against the facility associated with Iraq's support of terrorism, while making every effort to minimize the loss of innocent life.

There should be no mistake about the message we intend these actions to convey to Saddam Hussein, to the rest of the Iraqi leadership, and to any nation, group, or person who would harm our leaders or our citizens. We will combat terrorism. We will deter aggression. We shall protect our people.

The world has repeatedly made clear what Iraq must do to return to the community of nations. And Iraq has repeatedly refused. If Saddam and his regime contemplate further illegal provocative actions, they can be certain of our response.

Let me say to the men and women in our Armed Forces and in our intelligence and law enforcement agencies who carried out the investigation and our military response: You have my gratitude and the gratitude of all Americans. You have performed a difficult mission with courage and professionalism.

Finally, I want to say this to all the American people: While the cold war has ended, the world is not free of danger. And I am determined to take the steps necessary to keep our Nation secure. We shall keep our forces ready to fight. We will work to head off emerging threats, and we will take action when action is required. That is precisely what we have done today.

Thank you, and God bless America.

SOURCE: *Public Papers: Clinton, 1993*, 1:938–39.

DOCUMENT 90
PRESIDENT CLINTON'S LETTER TO CONGRESS CONCERNING THE STRIKE ON THE IRAQI INTELLIGENCE HEADQUARTERS IN BAGHDAD. JUNE 28, 1993.

Commencing at approximately 4:22 P.M. (EST) on June 26, 1993, at my direction, U.S. naval forces launched a Tomahawk cruise missile strike on the Iraqi Intelligence Service's (IIS) principal command and control complex in Baghdad. This facility is the headquarters for the IIS, which planned the failed attempt to assassinate former President Bush during his visit to Kuwait in April of this year. This U.S. military action was completed upon impact of the missiles on target at approximately 6 P.M. (EST).

Operating under the United States Central Command, two U.S. Navy surface ships launched a total of 23 precision-guided Tomahawk missiles in this coordinated strike upon the key facilities in the IIS compound. The USS *Peterson* (DD 969) launched 14 missiles from its position in the Red Sea, while the USS *Chancellorsville* (CG 62) in the Arabian Gulf launched nine missiles. The timing of this operation, with missiles striking at approximately 2:00 A.M. local Iraqi time, was chosen carefully so as to minimize risks to innocent civilians. Initial reports indicate that heavy damage was inflicted on the complex. Regrettably, there were some collateral civilian casualties.

I ordered this military response only after I considered the results of a thorough and independent investigation by U.S. intelligence and law enforcement agencies. The reports by Attorney General Reno and Director of Central Intelligence Woolsey provided compelling evidence that the operation that threatened the life of President Bush in Kuwait City in April was directed and pursued by the Iraqi Intelligence Service and that the government of Iraq bore direct responsibility for this effort.

The Government of Iraq acted unlawfully in attempting to carry out Saddam Hussein's threats against former President Bush because of actions he took as President. The evidence of the Government of Iraq's violence and terrorism demonstrates that Iraq poses a continuing threat to United States nationals and shows utter disregard for the will of the international community as expressed in Security Council Resolutions and the United Nations Charter. Based on the Government of Iraq's pattern of disregard for international law, I concluded that there was no reasonable prospect that new diplomatic initiatives or economic measures could influence the current Government of Iraq to cease planning future attacks against the United States.

Consequently, in the exercise of our inherent right of self-defense as recognized in Article 51 of the United Nations Charter and pursuant to my constitutional authority with respect to the conduct of foreign relations and as Commander in Chief, I ordered a military strike that directly targeted a facility of Iraqi intelligence implicated in the plot against the former Chief Executive. In accordance with Article 51 of the United Nations Charter, this action was reported immediately to the Security Council on June 26. On June 27, [UN] Ambassador [Madeleine] Albright provided evidence of Iraq's assassination attempts to the United Nations Security Council, which had been convened in emergency session at our request.

I am certain that you share my sincere hope that the limited and proportionate action taken by the United States Government will frustrate and help deter and prevent future unlawful actions on the part of the Government of Iraq. Nonetheless, in the event that Iraqi violence, aggression, or state-sponsored terrorism against the United States continues, I will direct such additional measures in our exercise of the right of self-defense as may be necessary and appropriate to protect United States citizens.

I remain committed to ensuring that the Congress is kept fully informed regarding significant employments of the U.S. Armed Forces. Accordingly, I am providing this report on the U.S. military actions of June 26, consistent with the War Powers Resolution. I appreciate your thoughts and continued support as we address these important concerns.

SOURCE: *Public Papers: Clinton, 1993,* 1:940–41.

DOCUMENT 91

PRESIDENT CLINTON'S LETTER TO CONGRESSIONAL LEADERS ON THE USE OF U.S. ARMED FORCES IN INTERNATIONAL OPERATIONS. OCTOBER 18, 1993.

—◆◈◆—

Dear Mr. Leader:

I am writing to express grave concern about a number of amendments that may be offered to H.R. 3116, the Defense Appropriations bill for FY [Fiscal Year] 94, regarding Haiti, Bosnia and the use of United States armed forces in international operations.

I am fundamentally opposed to amendments which improperly limit my ability to perform my constitutional duties as Commander-in-Chief, which may well have unconstitutional provisions, and which if adopted, could weaken the confidence of our allies in the United States. Such amendments would provide encouragement to aggressors and repressive rulers around the world who seek to operate without fear of reprisal.

America's adversaries and allies must know with certainty that the United States can respond decisively to protect the lives of Americans and to address cases that challenge American interests. Successive administrations have found it critical in world affairs to be able to state that no option has been ruled out.

I respect and acknowledge the importance of cooperation between the Executive and Legislative branches. There will inevitably be give and take between the Executive branch and Congress as we work to redefine our role in the post-Cold War world. But it is wrong and even dangerous to allow the questions of the moment to undercut the strength of our national security policies and to produce a fundamental shift in the proper relationship between our two branches of government.

The amendment regarding command and control of U.S. forces, which already has been introduced, would insert Congress into the detailed execution of military contingency planning in an unprecedented manner. The amendment would make it unreasonably difficult for me or any President to operate militarily with other nations when it is in our interest to do so—and as we have done effectively for half a century through NATO. It could lead to an all-or-nothing approach that causes the United States to shoulder the entire burden of a conflict even when a multinational approach would be most effective from the standpoint of military planning, burden sharing and other American national interests.

With regard to potential amendments on Haiti, let me caution against action that could aggravate that nation's violent conflict and undermine American interests. The situation on the ground in Haiti is highly unstable. Limiting my ability to act—or even creating the perception of such a limitation—could signal a green light to Haiti's military and police authorities in their brutal efforts to resist a return of democracy, could limit my ability to protect the more than 1,000 Americans currently in Haiti, and could trigger another mass exodus of Haitians, at great risk to their lives and great potential cost and disruption to our nation and others.

With regard to potential Bosnia amendments, our nation has worked with NATO to prepare to help implement a fair and enforceable peace settlement. This amendment thus could undermine our relationship with our NATO allies and frustrate the negotiation of an end to the aggression and ethnic cleansing in the former Yugoslavia. As you know, I have placed strict conditions on any U.S. involvement in Bosnia with which I believe most members of Congress would agree.

I am committed to full consultation with Congress on our foreign policy. As I have clearly stated for the record, I welcomed congressional authorization for U.S. operations in Somalia and would welcome similar action regarding U.S. efforts in Bosnia, should that become necessary. Further, as this Administration has done and is continuing to do, we will consult with and keep Congress fully informed on these and other issues that affect American national security.

SOURCE: *Public Papers: Clinton, 1993*, 2:1770.

DOCUMENT 92

PRESIDENT CLINTON'S LETTER TO CONGRESS ANNOUNCING THE DEPLOYMENT OF U.S. NAVAL FORCES OFF THE COAST OF HAITI. OCTOBER 20, 1993.

Dear Mr. Speaker, Dear Mr. President:

I have directed the deployment of U.S. Naval Forces to participate in the implementation of the petroleum and arms embargo of Haiti. At 11:59 P.M. E.S.T., October 18, units under the command of the Commander in Chief, U.S. Atlantic Command, began enforcement operations in the waters around Haiti, including the territorial sea of that country, pursuant to my direction and consistent with United Nations Security Council Resolutions 841, 873, and 875. I am providing this report, consistent with the War Powers Resolution, to ensure that the Congress is kept fully informed about this important U.S. action to support multilateral efforts to restore democracy in Haiti and thereby promote democracy throughout the hemisphere.

During the past week, the world has witnessed lawless, brutal actions by Haiti's military and police authorities to thwart the Haitian people's manifest desire for democracy to be returned to their country. With our full support, the United Nations Security Council has responded resolutely to these events. On October 16, the Security Council, acting under Chapters VII and VIII of the United Nations Charter, adopted Resolution 875. This resolution calls upon Member States, "acting nationally or through regional agencies or arrangements, cooperating with the legitimate Government of

Haiti, to use such measures commensurate with the specific circumstances as may be necessary" to ensure strict implementation of sanctions imposed by Resolutions 841 and 873. The maritime interception operations I have directed are conducted under U.S. command and control. In concert with allied navies, U.S. Naval Forces will ensure that merchant vessels proceeding to Haiti are in compliance with the embargo provisions set forth in the Security Council resolutions.

The initial deployment includes six U.S. Navy ships and supporting elements under the command of the U.S. Atlantic Command. These U.S. forces and others as may be necessary, combined with those forces that other Member States have committed to this operation, will conduct intercept operations to ensure that merchant ships proceeding to Haiti are in compliance with United Nations Security Council sanctions. On the first day of the operation, one of our ships, with U.S. Navy and Coast Guard personnel aboard, carried out an interception of a Belize-flag vessel and allowed it to proceed to its destination after determining that it was in compliance with the embargo. In addition, the forces of the U.S. Atlantic Command will remain prepared to protect U.S. citizens in Haiti and, acting in cooperation with the U.S. Coast Guard, to support the Haitian Alien Migrant Interdiction Operations (AMIO) of the United States, as may be necessary.

The United States strongly supports the Governors Island Agreement and restoration of democracy in Haiti. The measures I have taken to deploy U.S. Armed Forces in "Operation Restore Democracy" are consistent with United States goals and interests and constitute crucial support for the world community's strategy to overcome the persistent refusal of Haitian military and police authorities to fulfill their commitments under the Governors Island Agreement. I have ordered the deployment of U.S. Armed Forces for these purposes pursuant to my constitutional authority to conduct foreign relations and as Commander in Chief and Chief Executive.

Close cooperation between the President and the Congress is imperative for effective U.S. foreign policy and especially when the United States commits our Armed Forces abroad. I remain committed to consulting closely with Congress on our foreign policy, and I will continue to keep Congress fully informed about significant deployments of our Nation's Armed Forces.

SOURCE: *Public Papers: Clinton, 1993*, 2:1782–83.

DOCUMENT 93

PRESIDENT CLINTON'S ADDRESS TO THE NATION
REPORTING THE SITUATION IN HAITI. SEPTEMBER 15, 1994.

My Fellow Americans:

Tonight I want to speak with you about why the United States is leading the international effort to restore democratic government in Haiti.

Haiti's dictators, led by General Raoul Cédras, control the most violent regime in our hemisphere. For 3 years, they have rejected every peaceful solution that the international community has proposed. They have broken an agreement that they made to give up power. They have brutalized their people and destroyed their economy. And for 3 years, we and other nations have worked exhaustively to find a diplomatic solution, only to have the dictators reject each one.

Now the United States must protect our interests, to stop the brutal atrocities that threaten tens of thousands of Haitians, to secure our borders, and to preserve stability and promote democracy in our hemisphere and to uphold the reliability of the commitments we make and the commitments others make to us.

Earlier today, I ordered Secretary of Defense [William] Perry to call up the military reserve personnel necessary to support United States troops in any action we might undertake in Haiti. I have also ordered two aircraft carriers, the U.S.S. *Eisenhower* and the U.S.S. *America*, into the region. I issued these orders after giving full consideration to what is at stake. The message of the United States to the Haitian dictators is clear: Your time is up. Leave now, or we will force you from power.

I want the American people to understand the background of the situation in Haiti, how what has happened there affects our national security interests and why I believe we must act now. Nearly 200 years ago, the Haitian people rose up out of slavery and declared their independence. Unfortunately, the promise of liberty was quickly snuffed out, and ever since, Haiti has known more suffering and repression than freedom. In our time, as democracy has spread throughout our hemisphere, Haiti has been left behind.

Then, just 4 years ago, the Haitian people held the first free and fair elections since their independence. They elected a parliament and a new President, Father Jean-Bertrand Aristide, a Catholic priest who received almost 70 percent of the vote. But 8 months later, Haitian dreams of democracy became a nightmare of bloodshed. General Raoul Cédras led a military coup that overthrew President Aristide, the man who had appointed Cédras to lead the army. Resistors were beaten and murdered. The dictators launched a horrible intimidation campaign of rape, torture, and mutilation. People starved; children died; thousands of Haitians fled their country, heading to the United States across dangerous seas. At that time, President Bush declared, the situation posed, and I quote, "an unusual and extraordinary threat to the national security, foreign policy, and economy of the United States."

Cédras and his armed thugs have conducted a reign of terror, executing children, raping women, killing priests. As the dictators have grown more desperate, the atrocities have grown ever more brutal. Recent news reports have documented the slaying of Haitian orphans by the nation's deadly police thugs. The dictators are said to suspect the children of harboring sympathy toward President Aristide for no other reason than he ran an orphanage in his days as a parish priest. The children fled the orphanages for the streets. Now they can't even sleep there because they're so afraid. As one young boy told a visitor, "I do not care if the police kill me because it only brings an end to my suffering."

International observers uncovered a terrifying pattern of soldiers and policemen raping the wives and daughters of suspected political dissidents, young girls, 13, 16 years old; people slain and mutilated, with body parts left as warnings to terrify others; children forced to watch as their mothers' faces are slashed with machetes. A year ago, the dictators assassinated the Minister of Justice. Just last month, they gunned down Father Jean-Marie Vincent, a peasant leader and close friend of Father Aristide. Vincent was executed on the doorstep of his home, a monastery. He refused to give up his ministry, and for that, he was murdered.

Let me be clear: General Cédras and his accomplices alone are responsible for this suffering and terrible human tragedy. It is their actions that have isolated Haiti.

Neither the international community nor the United States has sought a confrontation. For nearly 3 years, we've worked hard on diplomatic efforts. The United Nations, the Organization of American States, the Caribbean community, the six Central American Presidents all have sought a peaceful end to this crisis. We have tried everything: persuasion and negotiation, mediation and condemnation. Emissaries were dispatched to Port-au-Prince and were turned away. The United Nations labored for months to reach an agreement acceptable to all parties.

Then last year, General Cédras himself came here to the United States and signed an agreement on Governors Island in New York in which he pledged to give up power, along with the other dictators. But when the day came for the plan to take effect, the dictators refused to leave and instead increased the brutality they are using to cling to power.

Even then, the nations of the world continued to seek a peaceful solution while strengthening the embargo we had imposed. We sent massive amounts of humanitarian aid, food for a million Haitians and medicine to try to help the ordinary Haitian people, as the dictators continued to loot the economy. Then this summer, they threw out the international observers who had blown the whistle on the regime's human rights atrocities.

In response to that action, in July the United Nations Security Council approved a resolution that authorizes the use of all necessary means, including force, to remove the Haitian dictators from power and restore democratic government. Still, we continued to seek a peaceful solution, but the dictators would not even meet with the United Nations Special Envoy. In the face of this continued defiance and with atrocities rising, the United States has agreed to lead an international force to carry out the will of the United Nations.

More than 20 countries from around the globe, including almost all the Caribbean community and nations from as far away as Poland, which has so recently won its own freedom, Israel and Jordan, which have been struggling for decades to preserve their own security, and Bangladesh, a country working on its own economic problems, have joined nations like Belgium and Great Britain. They have all agreed to join us because they think this problem in our neighborhood is important to their future interests and their security.

I know that the United States cannot, indeed we should not, be the world's policemen. And I know that this is a time with the cold war over that so many Americans are reluctant to commit military resources and our personnel beyond our borders. But when brutality occurs close to our shores, it affects our national interests. And we have a responsibility to act.

Thousands of Haitians have already fled toward the United States, risking their lives to escape the reign of terror. As long as Cédras rules, Haitians will continue to seek sanctuary in our Nation. This year, in less than 2 months, more than 21,000 Haitians were rescued at sea by our Coast Guard and Navy. Today, more than 14,000 refugees are living at our naval base in Guantánamo [in Cuba]. The American people have already expended almost $200 million to support them, to maintain the economic embargo. And the prospect of millions and millions more being spent every month for an indefinite period of time looms ahead unless we act.

Three hundred thousand more Haitians, 5 percent of their entire population, are in hiding in their own country. If we don't act, they could be the next wave of refugees at our door. We will continue to face the threat of a mass exodus of refugees and its constant threat to stability in our region and control of our borders.

No American should be surprised that the recent tide of migrants seeking refuge on our shores comes from Haiti and from Cuba. After all, they're the only nations left in the Western Hemisphere where democratic government is denied, the only countries where dictators have managed to hold back the wave of democracy and progress that has swept over our entire region and that our own Government has so actively promoted and supported for years.

Today, 33 of the 35 countries in the Americas have democratically elected leaders. And Haiti is the only nation in our hemisphere where the people actually elected their own government and chose democracy, only to have tyrants steal it away.

There's no question that the Haitian people want to embrace democracy; we know it because they went to the ballot box and told the world. History has taught us that preserving democracy in our own hemisphere strengthens America's security and prosperity. Democracies here are more likely to keep the peace and to stabilize our region. They're more likely to create free markets and economic opportunity, and to become strong, reliable trading partners. And they're more likely to provide their own people with the opportunities that will encourage them to stay in their nation and to build their own futures. Restoring Haiti's democratic government will help lead to more stability and prosperity in our region, just as our actions in Panama and Grenada did.

Beyond the human rights violations, the immigration problems, the importance of democracy, the United States also has strong interests in not letting dictators, especially in our own region, break their word to the United States and the United Nations. In the post-cold war world, we will assure the security and prosperity of the United States with our military strength, our economic power, our constant efforts to promote peace and growth. But when our national security interests are threatened, we will use diplomacy when possible and force when necessary.

In Haiti, we have a case in which the right is clear, in which the country in question is nearby, in which our own interests are plain, in which the mission is achievable and limited, and in which the nations of the world stand with us. We must act.

Our mission in Haiti, as it was in Panama and Grenada, will be limited and specific. Our plan to remove the dictators will follow two phases. First, it shall remove dictators from power and restore Haiti's legitimate, democratically elected government. We will train a civilian-controlled

Haitian security force that will protect the people rather than repress them. During this period, police monitors from all around the world will work with the authorities to maximize basic security and civil order and minimize retribution.

The Haitian people should know that we come in peace. And you, the American people, should know that our soldiers will not be involved in rebuilding Haiti or its economy. The international community, working together, must provide that economic, humanitarian, and technical assistance necessary to help the Haitians rebuild.

When this first phase is completed, the vast majority of our troops will come home, in months, not years. I want our troops and their families to know that we'll bring them home just as soon as we possibly can.

Then, in the second phase, a much smaller U.S. force will join forces from other members of the United Nations. And their mission will leave Haiti after elections are held next year and a new Haitian government takes office in early 1996.

Tonight I can announce that President Aristide has pledged to step down when his term ends, in accordance with the constitution he has sworn to uphold. He has committed himself to promote reconciliation among all Haitians and to set an historic example by peacefully transferring power to a duly elected successor. He knows, as we know, that when you start a democracy, the most important election is the second election. President Aristide has told me that he will consider his mission fulfilled not when he regains office but when he leaves office to the next democratically elected President of Haiti. He has pledged to honor the Haitian voters who put their faith in the ballot box.

In closing, let me say that I know the American people are rightfully concerned whenever our soldiers are put at risk. Our volunteer military is the world's finest, and its leaders have worked hard to minimize risks to all our forces. But the risks are there, and we must be prepared for that.

I assure you that no President makes decisions like this one without deep thought and prayer. But it's my job as President and Commander in Chief to take those actions that I believe will best protect our national security interests.

Let me say again, the nations of the world have tried every possible way to restore Haiti's democratic government peacefully. The dictators have rejected every possible solution. The terror, the desperation, and the instability will not end until they leave. Once again, I urge them to do so. They can still move now and reduce the chaos and disorder, increase the security, the stability, and the safety in which this transfer back to democracy can occur.

But if they do not leave now, the international community will act to honor our commitments; to give democracy a chance, not to guarantee it; to remove stubborn and cruel dictators, not to impose a future.

I know many people believe that we shouldn't help the Haitian people recover their democracy and find their hard-won freedoms, that the Haitians should accept the violence and repression as their fate. But remember, the same was said of a people who more than 200 years ago took up arms against a tyrant whose forces occupied their land. But they were a stubborn bunch, a people who fought for their freedoms and appealed to all those who believed in democracy to help their cause. And their cries were answered, and a new nation was born, a nation that ever since has believed that the rights of life, liberty, and the pursuit of happiness should be denied to none.

May God bless the people of the United States and the cause of freedom. Good night.

SOURCE: *Public Papers of the Presidents: William J. Clinton, 1994*, 2 vols. (Washington, DC: Government Printing Office, 1995), 2:1558–61.

DOCUMENT 94
PRESIDENT CLINTON'S WEEKLY RADIO MESSAGE ANNOUNCING THE CARTER-POWELL-NUNN DIPLOMATIC MISSION TO HAITI. SEPTEMBER 17, 1994.

Good morning. The night before last, I spoke with you about why America's interests compel us to help restore democratic government in Haiti.

For 3 years, the United Nations, the Caribbean community, and the Organization of American States have pursued every diplomatic avenue possible. But the dictators rejected all of our efforts, and their reign of terror, a campaign of murder, rape, and mutilation, gets worse with every passing day. Now we must act.

Our reasons are clear: to stop the horrific atrocities that threaten thousands of men, women, and children in Haiti, here in our own neighborhood; to affirm our determination that we keep our commitments and we expect others to keep their commitments to us; to avert the flow of thousands of more refugees and to secure our borders; and to preserve the stability of democracy in our hemisphere.

Today I'd like to speak with you about the steps we are now taking to ensure that these brutal dictators leave and leave now. The preparations of the extraordinary international coalition we have assembled are proceeding without delay. Even as I speak with you, our Armed Forces, in coordination with personnel from 24 other nations from all around the world, are poised to end the reign of terror that has plagued Haiti since the military coup 3 years ago. I have great pride and confidence in our troops. Our leaders have prepared their mission very, very carefully, and our forces are clearly the finest in the world.

At the same time, it is the responsibility of any American President to pursue every possible alternative to the use of force in order to avoid bloodshed and the loss of American lives. That is why this morning, at my request, President [Jimmy] Carter, former chairman of the Joint Chiefs of Staff General Colin Powell, and chairman of the Senate Armed Services Committee Senator Sam Nunn left for Haiti. Their mission is to make one last best effort to provide a peaceful, orderly transfer of power, to minimize the loss of life, and to maximize the chances of security for all Haitians and, of course, for our own troops in the coalition force.

On Thursday night, I stated that the Cédras regime's time is up. Their time is up. The remaining question is not whether they will leave but how they will leave. They can go peacefully and increase the chances for a peaceful future and a more stable future for Haiti in the near term, not only for all those whose democracy they stole but for themselves as well. They can do that, or they will be removed by force.

Yesterday leaders of the international coalition gathered at the White House. They come not only from our hemisphere and from our neighborhood here in the Caribbean but also from Europe, Asia, Africa, and the Middle East, from countries as diverse as Israel and Poland, Belgium and Bangladesh, countries with problems of their own, economic problems, political problems, even security problems. But each and every one of them believes it's important enough for them to come here to participate, to stand united with us in insisting that the dictators who terrorize Haiti must be removed and that the democratically elected government must be returned to power now.

As Prime Minister Owen Arthur of Barbados stated so eloquently yesterday, "The Haitian people have wished for democracy. They have suffered for it. They have voted for it. And now they are dying for it."

The goals of the international coalition are clear and limited. Once the military regime is removed from power, the coalition will help the democratic government establish basic security. It will begin the process of placing the Haitian police under civilian control and monitor them to help ensure that they respect human rights. Then, in months, not years, the coalition will pass the baton on to the United Nations. The UN mission in Haiti will take over and continue to professionalize Haiti's police and military. It will leave Haiti no later than 18 months from now, after elections are held and a new government takes office.

Over time, the coalition countries as well as the international financial institutions will provide Haiti with economic, humanitarian, and technical assistance that the country needs to stay on the democratic track, to put people back to work, and to begin the work of progress.

They can get assistance from other countries but we all know that in the end the job of rebuilding Haiti belongs to the Haitian people.

Yesterday at the White House, President Aristide took a long step toward the job of rebuilding, in the spirit of reconciliation. He put it very well when he said, "We say and we will be saying again and again, no to vengeance and no to retaliation; let us embrace peace." President Aristide also reiterated his pledge to transfer power peacefully to a duly elected successor. He said that in the formative years of any democracy, the most important election is not the first one but the second. That's a sentiment that should become a staple of civics books in our country and throughout the world.

My fellow Americans, at this very hour, we are taking important steps in the journey back to democracy in Haiti. We still hope to end this journey peacefully. But let me say one last time: The cause is right, the mission is achievable and limited, and we will succeed. The dictators must leave.

SOURCE: *Public Papers: Clinton, 1994*, 2:1567–68.

DOCUMENT 95
PRESIDENT CLINTON'S LETTER TO CONGRESS ON DEPLOYMENT OF U.S. ARMED FORCES TO HAITI. SEPTEMBER 18, 1994.

Dear Mr. Speaker, Dear Mr. President:

I am providing this report, consistent with the sense of Congress in section 8147(c) of the Department of Defense Appropriations Act, 1994 (Public Law 103-139), to advise you of the objectives and character of the planned deployment of U.S. Armed Forces into Haiti.

(1) The deployment of U.S. Armed Forces into Haiti is justified by United States national security interests: to restore democratic government to Haiti; to stop the brutal atrocities that threaten tens of thousands of Haitians; to secure our borders; to preserve stability and promote democracy in our hemisphere; and to uphold the reliability of the commitments we make and the commitments others make to us.

From the very beginning of the coup against the democratic government of Haiti, the United States and the rest of the international community saw the regime as a threat to our interests in this hemisphere. Indeed President Bush declared that the coup "constituted an unusual and extraordinary threat to the national security, foreign policy, and economy of the United States."

The United States' interest in Haiti is rooted in a consistent U.S. policy, since the 1991 coup, to help restore democratic government to that nation. The United States has a particular interest in responding to gross abuses of human rights when they occur so close to our shores.

The departure of the coup leaders from power is also the best way to stem another mass outflow of Haitians, with consequences for the stability of our region and control of our borders. Continuing unconstitutional rule in Haiti would threaten the stability of other countries in this hemisphere by emboldening elements opposed to democracy and freedom.

The agreement regarding the transition between the *de facto* government and the elected government, negotiated by former President Jimmy Carter, Senator Sam Nunn, and General Colin Powell, will achieve the objective of facilitating the departure of the coup leaders. Their departure will substantially decrease the likelihood of armed resistance.

(2) Despite this agreement, this military operation is not without risk. Necessary steps have been taken to ensure the safety and security of U.S. Armed Forces. Our intention is to deploy a force of sufficient size to serve as a deterrent to armed resistance. The force will have a highly visible and robust presence and firepower ample to overwhelm any localized threat. This will minimize casualties and maximize our capability to ensure that essential civil order is maintained and the agreement arrived at is implemented. The force's rules of engagement allow for the use of necessary and proportionate force to protect friendly personnel and units and to provide for individual self-defense, thereby ensuring that our forces can respond effectively to threats and are not made targets by reason of their rules of engagement.

(3) The proposed mission and objectives are most appropriate for U.S. Armed Forces, and the forces proposed for deployment are necessary and

sufficient to accomplish the objectives of the proposed mission. Pursuant to UN Security Council Resolution 940, a multinational coalition has been assembled to use "all necessary means" to restore the democratic government to Haiti and to provide a stable and secure environment for the implementation of the Governors Island Accords. The deployment of U.S. Armed Forces is required to ensure that United States national security interests with respect to Haiti remain unchallenged and to underscore the reliability of U.S. and UN commitments.

This crisis affects the interests of the United States and other members of the world community alike, and thus warrants and has received the participation of responsible states in the coalition to redress the situation. The United States is playing a predominant role because it is the leading military power in the hemisphere, and accordingly, has the influence and military capability to lead such an operation. The coalition is made up of representatives from 25 member nations, including the United States. During the initial phase of the operation, the force will be of sufficient size to overwhelm any opposition that might arise despite the existence of the agreement. In the follow-on, transitional phase, forces from other members of the coalition will assume increasingly important roles. At all times when U.S. forces are deployed in whatever phase, they will be equipped, commanded, and empowered so as to ensure their own protection.

(4) Clear objectives for the deployment have been established. These limited objectives are: to facilitate the departure of the military leadership, the prompt return of the legitimately elected President and the restoration of the legitimate authorities of the Government of Haiti. We will assist the Haitian government in creating a civilian-controlled security force. We will also ensure the protection of U.S. citizens and U.S. facilities.

(5) An exit strategy for ending the deployment has been identified. Our presence in Haiti will not be open-ended. After a period of months the coalition will be replaced by a UN peacekeeping force (UNMIH). By that time, the bulk of U.S. forces will have departed. Some U.S. forces will make up a portion of the UNMIH and will be present in Haiti for the duration of the UN mission. The entire UN mission will withdraw from Haiti after elections are held next year and a new Haitian Government takes office in early 1996, consistent with UN Security Council Resolution 940.

(6) The financial costs of the deployment are estimated to be the following. A conservative, preliminary estimate of Department of Defense and Department of State incremental costs for U.S. military operations, U.S. support for the multinational coalition, and the follow-on UN peacekeeping operation is projected at $500-$600 million through February 1996.

This covers potential costs to be incurred in FY 1994, FY 1995, and FY 1996. Final deployment-related costs could vary from this estimate depending on how operations proceed in the first few weeks, how fast civic order is restored, and when the operation is replaced by a UN peacekeeping operation. A preliminary estimate of U.S. nondeployment costs—migrant operations, sanctions enforcement, police training, and economic reconstruction—will be provided separately. The Congress will be provided more complete estimates as they become available.

SOURCE: *Public Papers: Clinton, 1994*, 2:1572–73.

DOCUMENT 96

PRESIDENT CLINTON'S LETTER TO CONGRESS REPORTING ON THE NO-FLY ZONE IN BOSNIA-HERZEGOVINA. OCTOBER 13, 1993.

Dear Mr. Speaker [Thomas Foley], Dear Mr. President:

Six months ago I provided you with my initial report on the deployment of U.S. combat-equipped aircraft to support NATO's enforcement of the no-fly zone in Bosnia-Herzegovina. I am now providing this follow-up report, consistent with the War Powers Resolution, to keep Congress fully informed on our enforcement effort.

The United Nations Security Council has been actively addressing the humanitarian and ethnic crisis in the Balkans since adopting Resolution 713 on September 25, 1991. As it is a significant part of the extensive United Nations effort in the region, the Security Council acted through Resolutions 781 and 786 to establish a ban on all unauthorized flights over Bosnia-Herzegovina. In response to blatant violations of these Resolutions, the Security Council adopted Resolution 816, which authorized Member States, acting nationally or through regional organizations or arrangements, to take all necessary measures to ensure compliance with the no-fly zone. NATO and its North Atlantic Council (NAC) agreed to provide NATO air assets to enforce the declared no-fly zone.

As I stated in my April 13 report, this enforcement effort began on April 12, 1993. Since that time, the participating nations have conducted phased air operations to prevent flights over Bosnia-Herzegovina that are not authorized by the United Nations Protection Forces (UNPROFOR). The United States has played a major role by contributing combat-equipped fighter aircraft as well as electronic combat and supporting tanker aircraft to these operations in the airspace over Bosnia-Herzegovina.

Militarily, enforcement of the no-fly zone has been effective. Since the operations pursuant to Resolution 816 began, we have seen no recurrence of air-to-ground bombing of villages or other air-to-ground combat activity in Bosnia-Herzegovina. Although nearly 400 violations have occurred, most have been rotary-wing aircraft. These flights are difficult to detect because they are of short duration and are flown slowly, at low altitudes, and in mountainous terrain. Consequently, such flights sometimes can complete missions after being detected but before being intercepted. In addition, the violators appear to have learned the limits of our rules of engagement (ROE) and have become adept at playing "cat-and-mouse" games with the interceptors. When intercepted, violators heed the warnings to land, but sometimes the flights continue after the interceptors depart.

These enforcement operations have been conducted safely, with no casualties to date. Consideration has been given to strengthening the ROE to enforce the no-fly zone more aggressively. Because the violations have been militarily insignificant, however, the ROE have not been changed.

The United States continues to make extensive and valuable contributions to the United Nations efforts in the former Yugoslavia. More than 50 U.S. aircraft are now available to NATO for the continued conduct of no-fly zone enforcement operations and possible provision of close air support to UNPROFOR in the future. In addition, U.S. airlift missions to Sarajevo have numbered more than 1,900, and we have completed nearly 1,000 airdrop missions to safe areas, including Mostar. U.S. medical and other support personnel are providing vital services in support of UNPROFOR, while our U.S. Army light infantry battalion deployed to Macedonia has become an integral part of the UNPROFOR monitoring operations there. Finally, U.S. naval forces have completed more than 14 months of enforcement operations as part of a multinational effort to implement the Security Council's mandate with respect to economic sanctions and the arms embargo covering the former Yugoslavia.

Although the no-fly zone enforcement operations have been militarily effective and have reduced potential air threats to our humanitarian aircraft and airdrop flights, this is only part of a much larger, continuing effort to resolve the extremely difficult situation in the former Yugoslavia. I therefore am not able to indicate at this time how long our participation in no-fly zone enforcement operations will be necessary. I have continued the deployment of U.S. Armed Forces for these purposes pursuant to my constitutional authority to conduct U.S. foreign relations and as Commander in Chief.

I am grateful for the continuing support of Congress for this important deployment, and I look forward to continued cooperation as we move forward toward attainment of our goals in this region.

SOURCE: *Public Papers: Clinton, 1993,* 2:1740–41.

DOCUMENT 97

PRESIDENT CLINTON'S REQUEST TO U.S. SENATE LEADERS FOR A RESOLUTION IN SUPPORT OF MILITARY OPERATIONS IN BOSNIA. OCTOBER 20, 1993.

Dear Mr. Leader [Senator George Mitchell of Maine]:

The violent conflict in the former Yugoslavia continues to be a source of deep concern. As you know, my Administration is committed to help stop the bloodshed and implement a fair and enforceable peace agreement, if the parties to the conflict can reach one. I have stated that such enforcement potentially could include American military personnel as part of a NATO operation. I have also specified a number of conditions that would need to be met before our troops would participate in such an operation.

I also have made clear that it would be helpful to have a strong expression of support from the United States Congress prior to the participation of U.S. forces in implementation of a Bosnian peace accord. For that reason, I would welcome and encourage congressional authorization of any military involvement in Bosnia.

The conflict in Bosnia ultimately is a matter for the parties to resolve, but the nations of Europe and the United States have significant interests at stake. For that reason, I am committed to keep our nation engaged in the search for a fair and workable resolution to this tragic conflict.

I want to express my lasting gratitude for the leadership you have shown in recent days as we have worked through difficult issues affecting our national security. With your help we have built a broad coalition that should provide the basis for proceeding constructively in the months ahead. Once again you have earned our respect and appreciation.

SOURCE: *Public Papers: Clinton, 1993,* 2:1781.

DOCUMENT 98

PRESIDENT CLINTON'S REMARKS ON SUSTAINING AMERICA'S NATO LEADERSHIP THROUGH U.S. FORCES IN BOSNIA. OCTOBER 25, 1995.

Because of the meetings I have just had at the United Nations and the work that we are doing 50 years after its beginning, I thought it might be worth sharing with you a few thoughts about Harry Truman's legacy and what it means for today and tomorrow.

Every American President . . . has followed in Harry Truman's footsteps in carrying forward America's leadership in the world. This tradition of sustained American leadership and involvement has been so successful and so consistently maintained by Democratic and Republican presidents alike that some of us forget what a bold departure it was.

Just before I came here tonight, I was with Prime Minister [Yitzhak] Rabin at another meeting talking about peace in the Middle East. Harry Truman was the first world leader to recognize the State of Israel. His commitment to giving us the capacity to lead and work for peace started a single silver thread that runs right through the terrific accomplishments of President Carter and all of the things which have been done since. But we forget what a bold departure it was. The Truman Doctrine, the Marshall Plan, the NATO alliance—each was a step unlike anything before.

Indeed, NATO, which President Truman rightly considered one of his finest achievements, was our very first peacetime alliance ever. We never had a military alliance in peacetime before NATO. This decisive change grew out of the belief that was shared by General [George C.] Marshall, Senator [Arthur H.] Vandenberg, [Secretary of State] Dean Acheson, and so many others that we could never again remain apart from the world. We had, after all, isolated ourselves after the First World War, and because of that, we had to fight another. Harry Truman was determined that that would not happen again. He had to face, almost immediately, the chilling prospect of the Cold War and to make all of the decisions which set in motion the policies which ultimately enabled freedom to prevail in that war.

He had to do it with a nation that was weary from war and weary from engagement, where people were longing to just focus on the little everyday things of life that mean the most to most of us. But because he did it, we just celebrated 50 years of the United Nations, with no more world war, no nuclear device ever dropped again, and now we see the movement for peace and freedom and democracy all over the world.

What are we going to do to build on his achievement? What do we have to do to secure a peace for the next century? Freedom's new gains, I believe, make it possible for us to help build a Europe that is democratic, that is peaceful, and that, for the first time since nation states appeared on that continent, is undivided.

We can build a Europe committed to freedom, democracy, and prosperity; genuinely secure throughout the continent; and aligned with other like-minded people throughout the world for the first time ever. I am committed to doing what we can to build that kind of Europe based on three principles:

First, to support democracy in Europe's newly free nations.

Second, to work to increase economic vitality in Europe with America and other partners through open markets and expanded trade, and to help the former communist countries complete their transition to market economies—a move that will strengthen democracy there and help block the advance of ultranationalism and ethnic hatred.

Finally, we are building a transatlantic community of tomorrow by deepening, not withdrawing, from our security cooperation. Today, with the overarching threat of communism gone, the faces of hatred and intolerance are still there with different faces—ethnic and religious conflicts, organized crime and drug dealing, state-sponsored terrorism, and the spread of weapons of mass destruction. America cannot insulate itself from these threats any more than it could insulate itself after World War II. Indeed, we have fewer options to do so because the world is becoming a global village.

By joining with our allies and embracing others who share our values, we cannot insulate ourselves from these threats, but we can surely create a better defense. NATO's success gives us proof of what we can do when we work together. NATO binds the Western democracies in a common purpose with shared values. I strongly believe that NATO does not depend upon an ever-present enemy to maintain its unity or its usefulness. The alliance strengthens all of its members from within and defends them from threats without. If you just compare the stability, the economic strength, the harmony in Western Europe today with the conditions that existed just a few decades ago—in President Truman's time—you can see that. The alliance has brought former foes together; strengthened democracy; and, along with the Marshall Plan, it sheltered fragile economies and got them going again. It gave countries confidence to look past their ancient hatreds. It gave them the safety to sow the prosperity they enjoy today.

By establishing NATO, of course, America also did something even more important from our point of view. We established the security that we require to flourish and to grow. Now, we have to build upon President Truman's accomplishments. He said when he announced the Truman Doctrine:

> The world is not static, the status quo is not sacred. We have to adapt NATO, and I believe we should open NATO's doors to new members.

The end of the Cold War cannot mean the end of NATO, and it cannot mean a NATO frozen in the past, because there is no other cornerstone for an integrated, secure, and stable Europe for the future.

NATO's success has involved promoting security interests, advancing values, and supporting democracy and economic opportunity. We literally have created a community of shared values and shared interests, as well as an alliance for the common defense. Now, the new democracies of Central and Eastern Europe and the former Soviet Union want to be a part of enlarging the circle of common purpose, and in so doing, increasing our own security. That is why we established the Partnership for Peace—PfP. In less than two years, we have brought 26 nations into a program to create confidence and friendship—former enemies now joining in field exercises throughout the year, building bonds together instead of battle plans against one another. This has been good for us and good for Europe.

Now those nations in the region that maintain their democracies and continue to promote economic reform and behave responsibly should be able to become members of NATO. That will give them the confidence to consolidate their freedom, to build their economies, and to make us more secure.

NATO has completed a study of how it should bring on new members. We intend to move carefully, deliberately, and openly, and share the conclusions of that study with all of those who have joined us in the PfP. But we have to move to the next phase in a steady, careful way, to consider who the new members should be and when they would be invited to join the alliance. Throughout this, I will engage with the Congress and the American people and seek the kind of bipartisan partnership that made Harry Truman's important work possible.

Let me emphasize one important point: Bringing new members into this alliance will enhance, not undermine, the security of everyone in Europe, including Russia, Ukraine, and the other former Soviet Republics. We have assured Russia that NATO is as it has always been—a defensive alliance. Extending the zone of security and democracy in Europe can help prevent new conflicts that have been building up, in many cases, for centuries. For Russia and all of her neighbors, this is a better path than the alternative.

I also want you to know, as you saw from the laughing photograph with [Russian] President [Boris] Yeltsin, we are still building a positive relationship with Russia. Those of you familiar with the history of that great country know that its heroic effort to become a confident and stable democracy is one of the most significant developments of our time.

One of our former colleagues, President Nixon, who is no longer with us, wrote me a letter about Russia a month to the day before he died—which I still have and re-read from time to time emphasizing the extraordinary historic significance of Russia's courageous reach for democracy and liberty.

Russia, too, has a contribution to make in the new Europe, and we have offered them a strong alliance with NATO and working through the PfP. Let me just tell you, that partnership is going to deepen. Tomorrow, U.S. and Russian armed forces will begin a peacekeeping exercise together at Fort Riley, Kansas, under the auspices of the PfP. We want our relationships with them to be daily, comprehensive, and routine. We want to go every step of the way to build confidence and security and a democratic Russia. But we do not think NATO's opening to the east and our relationship with Russia are mutually exclusive choices.

I want to emphasize one other thing. NATO is at work for us right now, as we speak, demonstrating in Bosnia how vital it is to securing the peace in Europe. The efforts of our negotiators, the military changes on the ground, and NATO's air strikes have brought these parties to the negotiating table and to an agreement on the basic principles of a settlement and a nationwide cease-fire.

Next week, in a historic meeting, the presidents of Bosnia, Croatia, and Serbia will travel to Dayton, Ohio, to resolve the remaining issues. The political settlement that is taking shape will preserve Bosnia as a single state and provide for a fair territorial compromise. It will commit the parties to hold free elections, establish democratic institutions, and respect human rights.

There are many people who have played a role in bringing this process this far. I want to thank one of them tonight for his extraordinary efforts—President Carter. Thank you so much for what you have done.

I want to say to all of you, there is no guarantee of peace, but it is possible —in large measure, because of NATO. Let me ask you one final thing. If the peace is negotiated, NATO must be prepared to help implement the agreement. There will be no peace without an international military presence in Bosnia—a presence that must be credible. NATO is indispensable to this to give the parties the reassurance they need to make peace.

The question I have is this: If Harry Truman were President, would he expect the United States as the leader of NATO to be a part of the force in Bosnia? I think you know what the answer is—the answer is yes. And so must we answer.

My fellow Americans, make no mistake about this—if we are not there, many of our partners will reconsider their commitments. If we are not there, America will sacrifice its leadership in NATO. If we are not there, we will be making a sad mistake. I am determined that we will be part of this NATO mission.

I am working with Congress, engaging in an important dialogue. I met not very long ago with a bipartisan group of leaders, and I want to say a special word of thanks to Senator [Sam] Nunn for his remarkable contribution to that meeting and for his remarkable contributions to our country, which we will all miss when he is gone.

My fellow Americans, if you want four years of bloody conflict to end, you have to support the United States being involved with NATO in enforcing the peace agreement. We have not sent troops into battle. We have not taken sides. We have not been a part of the UNPROFOR mission on the ground. But we must do this if you want your country and NATO to be as effective in our time as it was in President Truman's vision and in his time.

Let me also say again, if we do not do this, the consequences for our country could be grave indeed. This is the most serious conflict on the continent of Europe since World War II. NATO must help end it. If we fail to secure this peace, how can we achieve an integrated, peaceful, and united Europe? If we fail to secure this peace, our success around the world and much of our success at home, which has come from American leadership, will be weakened. If we fail to secure this peace, the conflict in the former Yugoslavia could spread to other nations and involve our sons and daughters in a conflict in Europe.

Let me say in closing that just a few days ago, we were fortunate to have a visit in the United States from His Holiness Pope John Paul II. I spent about half an hour with him alone, and he started into the most unusual conversation I have ever had with him or, in some ways, with any other world leader. He said, "I want to talk about the world, and I want to know what you think." I said, "The world?" He said, "Yes, the whole deal." I said,

"Well, where shall I start?" He said, "Start in Bosnia." So we talked about Bosnia. Then we went around the world. At the end he said,

> You know, I am not a young man. I have lived through most of this century. The 20th century began with a war in Sarajevo. Mr. President, you must not let it end with a war in Sarajevo.

I ask you to think of this, my fellow Americans, that first war in Sarajevo—that was Harry Truman's war. That is the war that he joined even though he was old enough and his eyesight was bad enough for him to get out of it. That is the war where he showed people the kind of leadership capacity he had. Our failures after that war led Franklin Roosevelt into another war and led Harry Truman to end that war with a set of difficult, painful decisions—including dropping the atomic bomb—and led him to determine that it would never happen again. That is why he did all the things we celebrate tonight. If he were here he would say, "If you really want to honor me, prepare for the future as I did."

SOURCE: U.S. Department of State, *Dispatch* 6, no. 45 (Washington, DC: Government Printing Office, 1995): 813–15.

DOCUMENT 99
PRESIDENT CLINTON'S ADDRESS TO THE NATION ON U.S. MILITARY OPERATIONS IN BOSNIA. NOVEMBER 27, 1995.

Good evening. Last week, the warring factions in Bosnia reached a peace agreement as a result of our efforts in Dayton, Ohio, and the support of our European and Russian partners. Tonight, I want to speak with you about implementing the Bosnian peace agreement and why our values and interests as Americans require that we participate.

Let me say at the outset that America's role will not be about fighting a war. It will be about helping the people of Bosnia to secure their own peace agreement. Our mission will be limited, focused, and under the command of an American general.

In fulfilling this mission, we will have the chance to help stop the killing of innocent civilians—especially children—and, at the same time, to bring stability to Central Europe, a region of the world that is vital to our national interests. It is the right thing to do.

From our birth, America has always been more than just a place. America has embodied an idea that has become the ideal for billions of people throughout the world. Our founders said it best: America is about life, liberty, and the pursuit of happiness.

In this century especially, America has done more than simply stand for these ideals. We have acted on them and sacrificed for them. Our people fought two world wars so that freedom could triumph over tyranny. After World War I, we pulled back from the world, leaving a vacuum that was filled by the forces of hatred. After World War II, we continued to lead the world. We made the commitments that kept the peace, that helped to spread democracy, that created unparalleled prosperity, and that brought victory in the Cold War.

Today, because of our dedication, America's ideals—liberty, democracy, and peace—are more and more the aspirations of people everywhere in the world. It is the power of our ideas—even more than our size, our wealth, and our military might—that makes America a uniquely trusted nation.

With the Cold War over, some people now question the need for our continued active leadership in the world. They believe that, much like after World War I, America can now step back from the responsibilities of leadership. They argue that to be secure we need only to keep our own borders safe and that the time has come now to leave to others the hard work of leadership beyond our borders; I strongly disagree.

As the Cold War gives way to the global village, our leadership is needed more than ever because problems that start beyond our borders can quickly become problems within them. We are all vulnerable to the organized forces of intolerance and destruction; terrorism; ethnic, religious, and regional rivalries; the spread of organized crime; weapons of mass destruction; and drug trafficking. Just as surely as fascism and communism, these forces also threaten freedom and democracy, peace and prosperity. And they, too, demand American leadership.

Nowhere has the argument for our leadership been more clearly justified than in the struggle to stop or prevent war and civil violence. From Iraq to Haiti, from South Africa to Korea, from the Middle East to Northern Ireland, we have stood up for peace and freedom because it is in our interest to do so and because it is the right thing to do.

Now, that doesn't mean we can solve every problem. My duty as President is to match the demands for American leadership to our strategic interest and to our ability to make a difference. America cannot and must not be the world's policeman. We cannot stop all war for all time, but we can stop some wars. We cannot save all women and all children, but we can save many of them. We can't do everything, but we must do what we can.

There are times and places where our leadership can mean the difference between peace and war and where we can defend our fundamental values as a people and serve our most basic, strategic interests. My fellow Americans, in this new era there are still times when America and America alone can and should make the difference for peace. The terrible war in Bosnia is such a case. Nowhere today is the need for American leadership more stark or more immediate than in Bosnia.

For nearly four years, a terrible war has torn Bosnia apart. Horrors we prayed had been banished from Europe forever have been seared into our minds again. Skeletal prisoners caged behind barbed-wire fences; women and girls raped as a tool of war; defenseless men and boys shot down into mass graves, evoking visions of World War II concentration camps; and endless lines of refugees marching toward a future of despair.

When I took office, some were urging immediate intervention in the conflict. I decided that American ground troops should not fight a war in Bosnia because the United States could not force peace on Bosnia's warring ethnic groups—the Serbs, Croats, and Muslims. Instead, America has worked with our European allies in searching for peace, stopping the war from spreading, and easing the suffering of the Bosnian people.

We imposed tough economic sanctions on Serbia. We used our air power to conduct the longest humanitarian airlift in history and to enforce a no-fly zone that took the war out of the skies. We helped to make peace between two of the three warring parties—the Muslims and the Croats. But as the months of war turned into years, it became clear that Europe alone could not end the conflict.

This summer, Bosnian Serb shelling once again turned Bosnia's playgrounds and marketplaces into killing fields. In response, the United States led NATO's heavy and continuous air strikes, many of them flown by skilled and brave American pilots. Those air strikes—together with the renewed determination of our European partners and the Bosnian and Croat gains on the battlefield—convinced the Serbs, finally, to start thinking about making peace.

At the same time, the United States initiated an intensive diplomatic effort that forged a Bosnia-wide cease-fire and got the parties to agree to the basic principles of peace. Three dedicated American diplomats—Bob Frasure, Joe Kruzel, and Nelson Drew—lost their lives in that effort. Tonight, we remember their sacrifice and that of their families. And we will never forget their exceptional service to our nation.

Finally, just three weeks ago, the Muslims, Croats, and Serbs came to Dayton, Ohio, in America's heartland, to negotiate a settlement. There, exhausted by war, they made a commitment to peace. They agreed to put down their guns; to preserve Bosnia as a single state; to investigate and prosecute war criminals; to protect the human rights of all citizens; to try to build a peaceful, democratic future. And they asked for America's help as they implement this peace agreement.

America has a responsibility to answer that request; to help to turn this moment of hope into an enduring reality. To do that, troops from our country and around the world would go into Bosnia to give them the confidence and support they need to implement their peace plan. I refuse to send American troops to fight a war in Bosnia, but I believe we must help to win the Bosnian peace.

I want you to know tonight what is at stake, exactly what our troops will be asked to accomplish, and why we must carry out our responsibility to help implement the peace agreement. Implementing the agreement in Bosnia can end the terrible suffering of the people—the warfare, the mass executions, the ethnic cleansing, the campaigns of rape and terror. Let us never forget that a quarter of a million men, women, and children have been shelled, shot, and tortured to death. Two million people—half of the population—were forced from their homes and into a miserable life as refugees. And these faceless numbers hide millions of real personal tragedies; for each of those victims was a mother or daughter, a father or son, a brother or sister.

Now the war is over. American leadership created the chance to build a peace and stop the suffering. Securing peace in Bosnia will also help to build a free and stable Europe. Bosnia lies at the very heart of Europe, next door to many of its fragile new democracies and some of our closest allies. Generations of Americans have understood that Europe's freedom and Europe's stability is vital to our own national security. That's why we fought two wars in Europe, that's why we launched the Marshall Plan to restore Europe, that's why we created NATO and waged the Cold War, and that's why we must help the nations of Europe to end their worst nightmare since World War II—now.

The only force capable of getting this job done is NATO—the powerful, military alliance of democracies that has guaranteed our security for half a century now. And as NATO's leader and the primary broker of the peace agreement, the United States must be an essential part of the mission. If we're not there, NATO will not be there. The peace will collapse, the war will reignite, and the slaughter of innocents will begin again. A conflict that already has claimed so many victims could spread like poison throughout the region, eat away at Europe's stability, and erode our partnership with our European allies.

America's commitment to leadership will be questioned if we refuse to participate in implementing a peace agreement that we brokered right here in the United States, especially since the Presidents of Bosnia, Croatia, and Serbia all asked us to participate and all pledged their best efforts to the security of our troops.

When America's partnerships are weak and our leadership is in doubt, it undermines our ability to secure our interests and to convince others to work with us. If we do maintain our partnerships and our leadership, we need not act alone. As we saw in the Gulf war and in Haiti, many other nations that share our goals will also share our burdens. But when America does not lead, the consequences can be very grave—not only for others, but eventually for us as well.

As I speak to you, NATO is completing its planning for IFOR, an international force for peace in Bosnia of about 60,000 troops. Already, more than 25 other nations, including our major NATO allies, have pledged to take part. They will contribute about two-thirds of the total implementation force—some 40,000 troops. The United States would contribute the rest—about 20,000 soldiers.

Later this week, the final NATO plan will be submitted to me for review and approval. Let me make clear what I expect it to include—and what it must include—for me to give final approval to the participation of our armed forces.

First, the mission will be precisely defined with clear, realistic goals that can be achieved in a definite period of time. Our troops will make sure that each side withdraws its forces behind the front lines and keeps them there. They will maintain the cease-fire to prevent the war from accidentally starting again. These efforts, in turn, will help to create a secure environment so that the people of Bosnia can return to their homes, vote in free elections, and begin to rebuild their lives. Our Joint Chiefs of Staff have concluded that this mission should and will take about one year.

Second, the risks to our troops will be minimized. American troops will take their orders from the American general who commands NATO. They will be heavily armed and thoroughly trained. By making an overwhelming show of force, they will lessen the need to use force. But unlike the UN forces, they will have the authority to respond immediately and the training and equipment to respond with overwhelming force to any threat to their own safety or any violations of the military provisions of the peace agreement.

If the NATO plan meets with my approval, I will immediately send it to Congress and request its support. I will also authorize the participation of a small number of American troops in a NATO advance mission that will lay the groundwork for IFOR, starting sometime next week. They will establish headquarters and set up the sophisticated communication systems that must be in place before NATO can send in its troops, tanks, and trucks to Bosnia.

The implementation force itself would begin deploying in Bosnia in the days following the formal signature of the peace agreement in mid-December. The international community will help to implement arms control provisions of the agreement so that future hostilities are less likely and armaments are limited, while the world community—the United States and others—will also make sure that the Bosnian Federation has the means to defend itself once IFOR withdraws. IFOR will not be a part of this effort.

Civilian agencies from around the world will begin a separate program of humanitarian relief and reconstruction, principally paid for by our European allies and other interested countries. This effort is also absolutely essential to making the peace endure. It will bring the people of Bosnia the food, shelter, clothing, and medicine so many have been denied for so long. It will help them to rebuild—to rebuild their roads and schools, their power plants and hospitals, their factories and shops. It will reunite children with their parents and families with their homes. It will allow the Bosnians to freely choose their own leaders. It will give all the people of Bosnia a much greater stake in peace than war, so that peace takes on a life and a logic of its own.

In Bosnia, we can and will succeed because our mission is clear and limited and our troops are strong and very well-prepared. But, my fellow Americans, no deployment of American troops is risk-free, and this one may well involve casualties. There may be accidents in the field or incidents with people who have not given up their hatred. I will take every measure possible to minimize these risks, but we must be prepared for that possibility.

As President, my most difficult duty is to put the men and women who volunteer to serve our nation in harm's way when our interests and values demand it. I assume full responsibility for any harm that may come to them. But anyone contemplating any action that would endanger our troops should know this: America protects its own. Anyone—anyone— who takes on our troops will suffer the consequences. We will fight fire with fire—and then some.

After so much bloodshed and loss, after so many outrageous acts of inhuman brutality, it will take an extraordinary effort of will for the people of Bosnia to pull themselves from their past and start building a future of peace. But with our leadership and the commitment of our allies, the people of Bosnia can have the chance to decide their future in peace. They have a chance to remind the world that just a few short years ago, the mosques and churches of Sarajevo were a shining symbol of multi-ethnic tolerance; that Bosnia once found unity in its diversity. Indeed, the cemetery in the center of the city was just a few short years ago a magnificent stadium which hosted the Olympics—our universal symbol of peace and harmony. Bosnia can be that kind of place again. We must not turn our backs on Bosnia now.

And so I ask all Americans, and I ask every Member of Congress—Democrat and Republican alike—to make the choice for peace. In the choice between peace and war, America must choose peace.

My fellow Americans, I ask you to think just for a moment about this century that is drawing to a close and the new one that will soon begin. Because previous generations of Americans stood up for freedom and because we continue to do so, the American people are more secure and more prosperous. All around the world, more people than ever before live in freedom; more people than ever before are treated with dignity; more people than ever before can hope to build a better life. That is what America's leadership is all about.

We know that these are the blessings of freedom, and America has always been freedom's greatest champion. If we continue to do everything we can to share these blessings with people around the world, if we continue to be leaders for peace, then the next century can be the greatest time our nation has ever known.

A few weeks ago, I was privileged to spend some time with His Holiness, Pope John Paul II, when he came to America. At the very end of our meeting, the Pope looked at me and said,

> I have lived through most of this century. I remember that it began with a war in Sarajevo. Mr. President, you must not let it end with a war in Sarajevo.

In Bosnia, this terrible war has challenged our interests and troubled our souls. Thankfully, we can do something about it. I say again, our mission will be clear, limited, and achievable. The people of Bosnia, our NATO allies, and people all around the world are now looking to America for leadership. So let us lead. That is our responsibility as Americans.

Goodnight, and God bless America.

SOURCE: *Dispatch* 6, no. 48 (1995): 867–69.

DOCUMENT 100
PRESIDENT CLINTON'S ADDRESS TO THE NATION ON
AIR STRIKES AGAINST SERBIAN TARGETS IN KOSOVO.
MARCH 24, 1999.

My Fellow Americans:

Today our Armed Forces joined our NATO Allies in airstrikes against Serbian forces responsible for the brutality in Kosovo. We have acted with resolve for several reasons.

We act to protect thousands of innocent people in Kosovo from a mounting military offensive. We act to prevent a wider war, to defuse a powder keg at the heart of Europe that has exploded twice before in this century with catastrophic results. And we act to stand united with our allies for peace. By acting now, we are upholding our values, protecting our interests, and advancing the cause of peace.

Tonight I want to speak to you about the tragedy in Kosovo and why it matters to America that we work with our allies to end it. First, let me explain what it is we are responding to. Kosovo is a province of Serbia, in the middle of southeastern Europe, about 160 miles east of Italy. That's less than the distance between Washington and New York and only about 70 miles north of Greece. Its people are mostly ethnic Albanian and mostly Muslim.

In 1989 Serbia's leader, Slobodan Milosevic, the same leader who started the wars in Bosnia and Croatia and moved against Slovenia in the last decade, stripped Kosovo of the constitutional autonomy its people enjoyed, thus denying them their right to speak their language, run their schools, shape their daily lives. For years, Kosovars struggled peacefully to get their rights back. When President Milosevic sent his troops and police to crush them, the struggle grew violent.

Last fall our diplomacy, backed by the threat of force from our NATO Alliance, stopped the fighting for a while and rescued tens of thousands of people from freezing and starvation in the hills where they had fled to save their lives. And last month, with our allies and Russia, we proposed a peace agreement to end the fighting for good. The Kosovar leaders signed that agreement last week. Even though it does not give them all they want, even though their people were still being savaged, they saw that a just peace is better than a long and unwinnable war.

The Serbian leaders, on the other hand, refused even to discuss key elements of the peace agreement. As the Kosovars were saying yes to peace,

Serbia stationed 40,000 troops in and around Kosovo in preparation for a major offensive—and in clear violation of the commitments they had made.

Now they've started moving from village to village, shelling civilians and torching their houses. We've seen innocent people taken from their homes, forced to kneel in the dirt, and sprayed with bullets; Kosovar men dragged from their families, fathers and sons together, lined up and shot in cold blood. This is not war in the traditional sense. It is an attack by tanks and artillery on a largely defenseless people whose leaders already have agreed to peace.

Ending this tragedy is a moral imperative. It is also important to America's national interest. . . . Kosovo is a small place, but it sits on a major fault line between Europe, Asia, and the Middle East, at the meeting place of Islam and both the Western and Orthodox branches of Christianity. To the south are our allies Greece and Turkey; to the north, our new democratic allies in central Europe. And all around Kosovo, there are other small countries struggling with their own economic and political challenges, countries that could be overwhelmed by a large, new wave of refugees from Kosovo. All the ingredients for a major war are there: ancient grievances; struggling democracies; and in the center of it all, a dictator in Serbia who has done nothing since the cold war ended but start new wars and pour gasoline on the flames of ethnic and religious division.

Sarajevo, the capital of neighboring Bosnia, is where World War I began. World War II and the Holocaust engulfed this region. In both wars, Europe was slow to recognize the dangers, and the United States waited even longer to enter the conflicts. Just imagine if leaders back then had acted wisely and early enough, how many lives could have been saved, how many Americans would not have had to die.

We learned some of the same lessons in Bosnia just a few years ago. The world did not act early enough to stop that war, either. And let's not forget what happened: innocent people herded into concentration camps, children gunned down by snipers on their way to school, soccer fields and parks turned into cemeteries; a quarter of a million people killed, not because of anything they have done but because of who they were. Two million Bosnians became refugees. This was genocide in the heart of Europe, not in 1945 but in 1995; not in some grainy newsreel from our parents' and grandparents' time but in our own time, testing our humanity and our resolve.

At the time, many people believed nothing could be done to end the bloodshed in Bosnia. They said, "Well, that's just the way those people in the Balkans are." But when we and our allies joined with courageous

Bosnians to stand up to the aggressors, we helped to end the war. We learned that in the Balkans, inaction in the face of brutality simply invites more brutality, but firmness can stop armies and save lives. We must apply that lesson in Kosovo before what happened in Bosnia happens there, too.

Over the last few months we have done everything we possibly could to solve this problem peacefully. Secretary [of State Madeleine] Albright has worked tirelessly for a negotiated agreement. Mr. Milosevic has refused. On Sunday I sent Ambassador Dick Holbrooke to Serbia to make clear to him again, on behalf of the United States and our NATO Allies, that he must honor his own commitments and stop his repression, or face military action. Again, he refused.

Today we and our 18 NATO Allies agreed to do what we said we would do, what we must do to restore the peace. Our mission is clear: to demonstrate the seriousness of NATO's purpose so that the Serbian leaders understand the imperative of reversing course; to deter an even bloodier offensive against innocent civilians in Kosovo; and, if necessary, to seriously damage the Serbian military's capacity to harm the people of Kosovo. In short, if President Milosevic will not make peace, we will limit his ability to make war.

Now, I want to be clear with you, there are risks in this military action, risks to our pilots and the people on the ground. Serbia's air defenses are strong. It could decide to intensify its assault on Kosovo or to seek to harm us or our allies elsewhere. If it does, we will deliver a forceful response.

Hopefully, Mr. Milosevic will realize that his present course is self-destructive and unsustainable. If he decides to accept the peace agreement and demilitarize Kosovo, NATO has agreed to help to implement it with a peacekeeping force. If NATO is invited to do so, our troops should take part in that mission to keep the peace. But I do not intend to put our troops in Kosovo to fight a war.

Do our interests in Kosovo justify the dangers to our Armed Forces? I've thought long and hard about that question. I am convinced that the dangers of acting are far outweighed by the dangers of not acting—dangers to defenseless people and to our national interests. If we and our allies were to allow this war to continue with no response, President Milosevic would read our hesitation as a license to kill. There would be many more massacres, tens of thousands more refugees, more victims crying out for revenge.

Right now our firmness is the only hope the people of Kosovo have to be able to live in their own country without having to fear for their own lives. Remember, we asked them to accept peace, and they did. We asked them to promise to lay down their arms, and they agreed. We pledged that we, the United States and the other 18 nations of NATO, would stick by them if they did the right thing. We cannot let them down now.

Imagine what would happen if we and our allies instead decided just to look the other way, as these people were massacred on NATO's doorstep. That would discredit NATO, the cornerstone on which our security has rested for 50 years now.

We must also remember that this is a conflict with no natural national boundaries. . . . The movement of refugees north, east, and south . . . is threatening the young democracy in Macedonia, which has its own Albanian minority and a Turkish minority. Already, Serbian forces have made forays into Albania from which Kosovars have drawn support. Albania has a Greek minority. Let a fire burn here in this area, and the flames will spread. Eventually, key U.S. allies could be drawn into a wider conflict, a war we would be forced to confront later, only at far greater risk and greater cost.

I have a responsibility as President to deal with problems such as this before they do permanent harm to our national interests. America has a responsibility to stand with our allies when they are trying to save innocent lives and preserve peace, freedom, and stability in Europe. That is what we are doing in Kosovo.

If we've learned anything from the century drawing to a close, it is that if America is going to be prosperous and secure, we need a Europe that is prosperous, secure, undivided, and free. We need a Europe that is coming together, not falling apart, a Europe that shares our values and shares the burdens of leadership. That is the foundation on which the security of our children will depend.

That is why I have supported the political and economic unification of Europe. That is why we brought Poland, Hungary, and the Czech Republic into NATO, and redefined its missions, and reached out to Russia and Ukraine for new partnerships.

Now, what are the challenges to that vision of a peaceful, secure, united, stable Europe? The challenge of strengthening a partnership with a democratic Russia that, despite our disagreements, is a constructive partner in the work of building peace; the challenge of resolving the tension between Greece and Turkey and building bridges with the Islamic world; and finally, the challenge of ending instability in the Balkans so that these bitter ethnic problems in Europe are resolved by the force of argument, not the force of arms, so that future generations of Americans do not have to cross the Atlantic to fight another terrible war.

It is this challenge that we and our allies are facing in Kosovo. That is why we have acted now: because we care about saving innocent lives; because we have an interest in avoiding an even crueler and costlier war; and because our children need and deserve a peaceful, stable, free Europe.

Our thoughts and prayers tonight must be with the men and women of our Armed Forces who are undertaking this mission for the sake of our values and our children's future.

May God bless them, and may God bless America.

SOURCE: *Public Papers of the Presidents: William J. Clinton, Book 1—January 1 to June 30, 1999* (Washington, DC: Government Printing Office, 2000), 451–53.

DOCUMENT 101
PRESIDENT CLINTON'S LETTER TO CONGRESSIONAL LEADERS REPORTING ON AIR STRIKES AGAINST SERBIAN TARGETS IN KOSOVO. MARCH 26, 1999.

Dear Mr. Speaker, Dear Mr President:

At approximately 1:30 P.M. Eastern Standard Time, on March 24, 1999, U.S. military forces, at my direction and in coalition with our NATO allies, began a series of air strikes in the Federal Republic of Yugoslavia (FRY) in response to the FRY government's continued campaign of violence and repression against the ethnic Albanian population in Kosovo. The mission of the air strikes is to demonstrate the seriousness of NATO's purpose so that the Serbian leaders understand the imperative of reversing course; to deter an even bloodier offensive against innocent civilians in Kosovo; and, if necessary, to seriously damage the Serbian military's capacity to harm the people of Kosovo. In short, if President Milosevic will not make peace, we will limit his ability to make war.

As you are aware, the Government of the FRY has been engaged in a brutal conflict in Kosovo. In this conflict, thousands of innocent Kosovar civilians have been killed or injured by FRY government security forces. The continued repression of Kosovars by the FRY military and security police forces constitutes a threat to regional security, particularly to Albania and Macedonia and, potentially, to Greece and to Turkey. Tens of thousands of others have been displaced from their homes, and many of them have fled to the neighboring countries of Bosnia, Albania, and Macedonia. These actions are the result of policies pursued by President Milosevic, who started the wars in Bosnia and Croatia, and moved against Slovenia in the last decade.

The United States, working closely with our European allies and Russia, have pursued a diplomatic solution to this crisis since last fall. The Kosovar leaders agreed to the interim settlement negotiated at Rambouillet, but the FRY government refused even to discuss key elements of the peace agreement. Instead, the Government of the FRY continues its attacks on the Kosovar population and has deployed 40,000 troops in and around Kosovo in preparation for a major offensive and in clear violation of the commitments it had made.

The FRY government has failed to comply with U.N. Security Council resolutions, and its actions are in violation of its obligations under the U.N. Charter and its other international commitments. The FRY government's actions in Kosovo are not simply an internal matter. The Security Council has condemned FRY actions as a threat to regional peace and security. The FRY government's violence creates a conflict with no natural boundaries, pushing refugees across borders and potentially drawing in neighboring countries. The Kosovo region is a tinder-box that could ignite a wider European war with dangerous consequences to the United States.

United States and NATO forces have targeted the FRY government's integrated air defense system, military and security police command and control elements, and military and security police facilities and infrastructure. United States naval ships and aircraft and U.S. Air Force aircraft are participating in these operations. Many of our NATO allies are also contributing aircraft and other forces.

In addition, since this air operation began, the U.S. Embassy in Skopje, Macedonia, has been subjected to increasingly hostile demonstrations by a large number of Serbian sympathizers. In response, I have authorized a unit consisting of about 100 combat-equipped Marines from the USS *Nassau* (LHA 4), which is supporting the air operations in Kosovo, to deploy to Skopje to enhance security at our embassy. These Marines will remain deployed so long as is necessary to protect our embassy and U.S. persons.

We cannot predict with certainty how long these operations will need to continue. Milosevic must stop his offensive, stop the repression, and agree to a peace accord based on the framework from Rambouillet. If he does not comply with the demands of the international community, NATO operations will seriously damage Serbia's military capacity to harm the people of Kosovo. NATO forces will also use such force as is necessary to defend themselves in the accomplishment of their mission.

I have taken these actions pursuant to my constitutional authority to conduct U.S. foreign relations and as Commander in Chief and Chief Executive. In doing so, I have taken into account the views and support expressed by the Congress in S. Con. Res. 21 and H. Con. Res. 42.

I am providing this report as part of my efforts to keep the Congress fully informed, consistent with the War Powers Resolution. I appreciate the support of the Congress in this action.

SOURCE: *Public Papers: Clinton, 1999*, 1:459–60.

24

GEORGE W. BUSH

DOCUMENT 102
PRESIDENT GEORGE BUSH'S ADDRESS TO A JOINT SESSION
OF CONGRESS AND THE AMERICAN PEOPLE.
SEPTEMBER 20, 2001.

———◆———

Mr. Speaker, Mr. President pro tempore, Members of Congress, and Fellow Americans:

In the normal course of events, Presidents come to this chamber to report on the state of the Union. Tonight no such report is needed. It has already been delivered by the American people.

We have seen it in the courage of passengers, who rushed terrorists to save others on the ground—passengers like an exceptional man named Todd Beamer.[1] Please help me to welcome his wife, Lisa Beamer, here tonight.

We have seen the state of our Union in the endurance of rescuers, working past exhaustion. We have seen the unfurling of flags, the lighting of candles, the giving of blood, the saying of prayers—in English, Hebrew, and Arabic. We have seen the decency of a loving and giving people, who have made the grief of strangers their own.

My fellow citizens, for the last nine days, the entire world has seen for itself the state of our Union—and it is strong.

Tonight we are a country awakened to danger and called to defend freedom. Our grief has turned to anger, and anger to resolution. Whether we

---

[1] Todd Beamer was a passenger on United Airlines Flight 93 from Newark to San Francisco on the morning of September 11, 2001. Four terrorists hijacked the plane with the intention of flying it to Washington and ramming it into a government building, possibly the White House. Apparently, Beamer was one of the leaders of an attempt to overpower the hijackers. The plane crashed in a field near Shanksville, Pennsylvania, about eighty miles southeast of Pittsburgh.

bring our enemies to justice, or bring justice to our enemies, justice will be done.

I thank the Congress for its leadership at such an important time. All of America was touched on the evening of the tragedy to see Republicans and Democrats, joined together on the steps of this Capitol, singing "God Bless America." And you did more than sing, you acted, by delivering forty billion dollars to rebuild our communities and meet the needs of our military.

Speaker Hastert and Minority Leader Gephardt—Majority Leader Daschle and Senator Lott—I thank you for your friendship and your leadership and your service to our country.[2]

And on behalf of the American people, I thank the world for its outpouring of support. America will never forget the sounds of our National Anthem playing at Buckingham Palace, and on the streets of Paris, and at Berlin's Brandenburg Gate. We will not forget South Korean children gathering to pray outside our embassy in Seoul, or the prayers of sympathy offered at a mosque in Cairo. We will not forget moments of silence and days of mourning in Australia and Africa and Latin America.

Nor will we forget the citizens of eighty other nations who died with our own. Dozens of Pakistanis. More than 130 Israelis. More than 250 citizens of India. Men and women from El Salvador, Iran, Mexico, and Japan. And hundreds of British citizens. America has no truer friend than Great Britain. Once again, we are joined together in a great cause. The British Prime Minister has crossed an ocean to show his unity of purpose with America, and tonight we welcome Tony Blair.

On September the eleventh, enemies of freedom committed an act of war against our country. Americans have known wars—but for the past 136 years, they have been wars on foreign soil, except for one Sunday in 1941. Americans have known the casualties of war—but not at the center of a great city on a peaceful morning. Americans have known surprise attacks —but never before on thousands of civilians. All of this was brought upon us in a single day—and night fell on a different world, a world where freedom itself is under attack.

Americans have many questions tonight. Americans are asking: Who attacked our country?

---

[2]Dennis Hastert, Republican of Illinois, Speaker of the U.S. House of Representatives; Richard Gephart, Democrat from Missouri, Minority Leader of the House; Thomas Daschle, Democrat of South Dakota, Majority Leader of the U.S. Senate; Trent Lott, Republican of Mississippi, Minority Leader of the Senate.

The evidence we have gathered all points to a collection of loosely affiliated terrorist organizations known as al-Qaida. They are the same murderers indicted for bombing American embassies in Tanzania and Kenya, and responsible for the bombing of the U.S.S. *Cole*.

Al-Qaida is to terror what the mafia is to crime. But its goal is not making money; its goal is remaking the world—and imposing its radical beliefs on people everywhere.

The terrorists practice a fringe form of Islamic extremism that has been rejected by Muslim scholars and the vast majority of Muslim clerics—a fringe movement that perverts the peaceful teachings of Islam. The terrorists' directive commands them to kill Christians and Jews, to kill all Americans, and make no distinctions among military and civilians, including women and children.

This group and its leader—a person named Usama bin Ladin—are linked to many other organizations in different countries, including the Egyptian Islamic Jihad and the Islamic Movement of Uzbekistan.

There are thousands of these terrorists in more than sixty countries. They are recruited from their own nations and neighborhoods, and brought to camps in places like Afghanistan where they are trained in the tactics of terror. They are sent back to their homes or sent to hide in countries around the world to plot evil and destruction.

The leadership of al-Qaida has great influence in Afghanistan, and supports the Taliban regime in controlling most of that country. In Afghanistan, we see al-Qaida's vision for the world.

Afghanistan's people have been brutalized—many are starving and many have fled. Women are not allowed to attend school. You can be jailed for owning a television. Religion can be practiced only as their leaders dictate. A man can be jailed in Afghanistan if his beard is not long enough.

The United States respects the people of Afghanistan—after all, we are currently its largest source of humanitarian aid—but we condemn the Taliban regime. It is not only repressing its own people, it is threatening people everywhere by sponsoring and sheltering and supplying terrorists. By aiding and abetting murder, the Taliban regime is committing murder. And tonight, the United States of America makes the following demands on the Taliban:

Deliver to United States authorities all the leaders of al-Qaida who hide in your land.

Release all foreign nationals—including American citizens—you have unjustly imprisoned, and protect foreign journalists, diplomats, and aid workers in your country.

Close immediately and permanently every terrorist training camp in Afghanistan and hand over every terrorist, and every person in their support structure, to appropriate authorities.

Give the United States full access to terrorist training camps, so we can make sure they are no longer operating.

These demands are not open to negotiation or discussion. The Taliban must act and act immediately. They will hand over the terrorists, or they will share in their fate.

I also want to speak tonight directly to Muslims throughout the world: We respect your faith. It is practiced freely by many millions of Americans, and by millions more in countries that America counts as friends. Its teachings are good and peaceful, and those who commit evil in the name of Allah blaspheme the name of Allah. The terrorists are traitors to their own faith, trying, in effect, to hijack Islam itself. The enemy of America is not our many Muslim friends; it is not our many Arab friends. Our enemy is a radical network of terrorists, and every government that supports them.

Our war on terror begins with al-Qaida, but it does not end there. It will not end until every terrorist group of global reach has been found, stopped, and defeated.

Americans are asking: Why do they hate us?

They hate what we see right here in this chamber—a democratically elected government. Their leaders are self-appointed. They hate our freedoms—our freedom of religion, our freedom of speech, our freedom to vote and assemble and disagree with each other.

They want to overthrow existing governments in many Muslim countries, such as Egypt, Saudi Arabia, and Jordan. They want to drive Israel out of the Middle East. They want to drive Christians and Jews out of vast regions of Asia and Africa.

These terrorists kill not merely to end lives, but to disrupt and end a way of life. With every atrocity, they hope that America grows fearful, retreating from the world and forsaking our friends. They stand against us, because we stand in their way.

We are not deceived by their pretenses to piety. We have seen their kind before. They are the heirs of all the murderous ideologies of the twentieth century. By sacrificing human life to serve their radical visions—by abandoning every value except the will to power—they follow in the path of fascism, and Nazism, and totalitarianism. And they will follow that path all the way, to where it ends: in history's unmarked grave of discarded lies.

Americans are asking: How will we fight and win this war?

We will direct every resource at our command—every means of diplomacy, every tool of intelligence, every instrument of law enforcement, every financial influence, and every necessary weapon of war—to the disruption and defeat of the global terror network.

This war will not be like the war against Iraq a decade ago, with its decisive liberation of territory and its swift conclusion. It will not look like the air war above Kosovo two years ago, where no ground troops were used and not a single American was lost in combat.

Our response involves far more than instant retaliation and isolated strikes. Americans should not expect one battle, but a lengthy campaign, unlike any other we have seen. It may include dramatic strikes, visible on television, and covert operations, secret even in success. We will starve terrorists of funding, turn them one against another, drive them from place to place, until there is no refuge or rest. And we will pursue nations that provide aid or safe haven to terrorism. Every nation, in every region, now has a decision to make. Either you are with us, or you are with the terrorists. From this day forward, any nation that continues to harbor or support terrorism will be regarded by the United States as a hostile regime.

Our Nation has been put on notice: We are not immune from attack. We will take defensive measures against terrorism to protect Americans.

Today; dozens of federal departments and agencies, as well as state and local governments; have responsibilities affecting homeland security. These efforts must be coordinated at the highest level. So tonight I announce the creation of a Cabinet-level position reporting directly to me—the Office of Homeland Security.

These measures are essential. But the only way to defeat terrorism as a threat to our way of life is to stop it, eliminate it, and destroy it where it grows.

Many will be involved in this effort, from FBI agents to intelligence operatives to the reservists we have called to active duty. All deserve our thanks, and all have our prayers. And tonight, a few miles from the damaged Pentagon, I have a message for our military: Be ready. I have called the armed forces to alert, and there is a reason. The hour is coming when America will act, and you will make us proud.

This is not, however, just America's fight. And what is at stake is not just America's freedom. This is the world's fight. This is civilization's fight. This is the fight of all who believe in progress and pluralism, tolerance and freedom.

We ask every nation to join us. We will ask, and we will need, the help of police forces, intelligence services, and banking systems around the world. The United States is grateful that many nations and many international organizations have already responded—with sympathy and with support. Nations from Latin America, to Asia, to Africa, to Europe, to the Islamic world. Perhaps the NATO Charter reflects best the attitude of the world: an attack on one is an attack on all.

The civilized world is rallying to America's side. They understand that if this terror goes unpunished, their own cities, their own citizens may be next. Terror, unanswered, can not only bring down buildings, it can threaten the stability of legitimate governments. And we will not allow it.

Americans are asking: What is expected of us?

I ask you to live your lives and hug your children. I know many citizens have fears tonight, and I ask you to be calm and resolute, even in the face of a continuing threat.

I ask you to uphold the values of America, and remember why so many have come here. We are in a fight for our principles, and our first responsibility is to live by them. No one should be singled out for unfair treatment or unkind words because of their ethnic background or religious faith.

I ask you to continue to support the victims of this tragedy with your contributions. Those who want to give can go to a central source of information, libertyunites.org, to find the names of groups providing direct help in New York, Pennsylvania, and Virginia.

The thousands of FBI agents who are now at work in this investigation may need your cooperation, and I ask you to give it

I ask for your patience, with the delays and inconveniences that may accompany tighter security—and for your patience in what will be a long struggle.

1 ask your continued participation and confidence in the American economy. Terrorists attacked a symbol of American prosperity. They did not touch its source. America is successful because of the hard work, and creativity, and enterprise of our people. These were the true strengths of our economy before September eleventh, and they are our strengths today.

Finally, please continue praying for the victims of terror and their families, for those in uniform, and for our great country. Prayer has comforted us in sorrow, and will help strengthen us for the journey ahead.

Tonight I thank my fellow Americans for what you have already done and for what you will do. And ladies and gentlemen of the Congress, I thank you, their representatives, for what you have already done, and for what we will do together.

Tonight, we face new and sudden national challenges. We will come together to improve air safety, to dramatically expand the number of air marshals on domestic flights, and take new measures to prevent hijacking. We will come together to promote stability and keep our airlines flying with direct assistance during this emergency.

We will come together to give law enforcement the additional tools it needs to track down terror here at home. We will come together to strengthen our intelligence capabilities to know the plans of terrorists before they act, and find them before they strike.

We will come together to take active steps that strengthen America's economy, and put our people back to work.

Tonight we welcome here two leaders who embody the extraordinary spirit of all New Yorkers: Governor George Pataki, and Mayor Rudy Giuliani. As a symbol of America's resolve, my Administration will work with the Congress, and these two leaders, to show the world that we will rebuild New York City.

After all that has just passed—all the lives taken, and all the possibilities and hopes that died with them—it is natural to wonder if America's future is one of fear. Some speak of an age of terror. I know there are struggles ahead, and dangers to face. But this country will define our times, not be defined by them. As long as the United States of America is determined and strong, this will not be an age of terror; this will be an age of liberty, here and across the world.

Great harm has been done to us. We have suffered great loss. And in our grief and anger we have found our mission and our moment. Freedom and fear are at war. The advance of human freedom—the great achievement of our time, and the great hope of every time—now depends on us. Our Nation—this generation—will lift a dark threat of violence from our people and our future. We will rally the world to this cause, by our efforts and by our courage. We will not tire, we will not falter, and we will not fail.

It is my hope that in the months and years ahead, life will return almost to normal. We'll go back to our lives and routines, and that is good. Even grief recedes with time and grace. But our resolve must not pass. Each of us will remember what happened that day, and to whom it happened. We will remember the moment the news came—where we were and what we were doing. Some will remember an image of fire, or a story of rescue. Some will carry memories of a face and a voice gone forever.

And I will carry this. It is the police shield of a man named George Howard, who died at the World Trade Center trying to save others. It was given to me by his mom, Arlene, as a proud memorial to her son. This is my reminder of lives that ended, and a task that does not end.

I will not forget this wound to our country, or those who inflicted it. I will not yield—I will not rest—I will not relent in waging this struggle for the freedom and security of the American people.

The course of this conflict is not known, yet its outcome is certain. Freedom and fear, justice and cruelty, have always been at war, and we know that God is not neutral between them.

Fellow citizens, we will meet violence with patient justice—assured of the rightness of our cause, and confident of the victories to come. In all that lies before us, may God grant us wisdom, and may He watch over the United States of America.

Thank you.

SOURCE: U.S. Department of State, Office of International Information Programs, http:\\usinfo.state.gov.

DOCUMENT 103

PRESIDENT BUSH'S REPORT TO CONGRESSIONAL COMMITTEE ON INTERNATIONAL RELATIONS ON MILITARY RESPONSE TO TERRORISM. OCTOBER 9, 2001.

Dear Mr. Speaker:

At approximately 12:30 P.M. (EDT) on October 7, 2001, on my orders, U.S. Armed Forces began combat action in Afghanistan against Al Qaida terrorists and their Taliban supporters. This military action is a part of our campaign against terrorism and is designed to disrupt the use of Afghanistan as a terrorist base of operations.

We are responding to the brutal September 11 attacks on our territory, our citizens, and our way of life, and to the continuing threat of terrorist acts against the United States and our friends and allies. This follows the deployment of various combat-equipped and combat support forces to a number of locations in the Central and Pacific Command areas of operations, as I reported to the Congress on September 24, to prepare for the campaign to prevent and deter terrorism.

I have taken these actions pursuant to my constitutional authority to conduct U.S. foreign relations as Commander in Chief and Chief Executive. It is not possible to know at this time either the duration of combat operations or the scope and duration of the deployment of U.S. Armed Forces necessary to counter the terrorist threat to the United States. As I have stated previously, it is likely that the American campaign against terrorism will be lengthy. I will direct such additional measures as necessary in exercise of our right to self-defense and to protect U.S. citizens and interests.

I am providing this report as part of my efforts to keep the Congress informed, consistent with the War Powers Resolution and Public Law 107-40. Officials of my Administration and I have been communicating regularly with the leadership and other members of Congress, and we will continue to do so. I appreciate the continuing support of the Congress, including its enactment of Public Law 107-40, in these actions to protect the security of the United States of America and its citizens, civilian and military, here and abroad.

SOURCE: U.S. Congress, House, *Report on Military Actions Taken to Respond to the Threat of Terrorism*, October 9, 2001, 107th Cong., 1st sess., H. Doc. 107-131, 1.

SELECTED BIBLIOGRAPHY

A large corpus of scholarship exists on presidential oratory. Among the many books on the subject, three that were most useful for the introduction to this study are Halford Ryan, ed., *U.S. Presidents as Orators* (Westport, CT: Greenwood Press, 1995), a collection of scholarly essays on twenty-one presidents, which includes a masterful introduction and an essay on Franklin Roosevelt, both by Ryan; Jeffrey K. Tulis, *The Rhetorical Presidency* (Princeton, NJ: Princeton University Press, 1987), an overview of the subject; and Kenneth Cmiel, *Democratic Eloquence: The Fight for Popular Speech in Nineteenth-Century America* (New York: William Morrow, 1990).

Other books that were critical to the completion of the work are Gordon Silverstein, *Imbalance of Powers: Constitutional Interpretation and the Making of American Foreign Policy* (New York: Oxford University Press, 1997), a most helpful study in gaining an understanding of the evolution of the war powers issue; Gary M. Stern and Morton H. Halperin, eds., *The U.S. Constitution and the Power to Go to War: Historical and Current Perspectives* (Westport, CT: Greenwood Press, 1994), another collection of essays that includes two written by the editors, which focuses on prescriptions for the post–Cold War era; and Louis Fisher, *Presidential War Power* (Lawrence: University Press of Kansas, 1995), an expert survey of warmaking powers throughout U.S. history. Of the more than fifty books and two hundred and fifty articles on the war clause, this work draws most on those described above. Additional valuable titles include the following:

Behl, William B. "Theodore Roosevelt's Principles of Speech Preparation and Delivery." *Speech Monographs* 12 (1945): 112–22.

Berman, Eleanor Davidson, and E. C. McClintock Jr. "Thomas Jefferson and Rhetoric." *Quarterly Journal of Speech* 33 (1947): 1–8.

Bochin, Hal W. *Richard Nixon: Rhetorical Strategist.* New York: Greenwood Press, 1990.

Braden, Waldo W. *Abraham Lincoln, Public Speaker.* Baton Rouge: Louisiana State University Press, 1988.

Caraway, Demetrios, ed. *The President's War Powers.* New York: Academy of Political Science, 1984.

Corwin, Edward S. *Total War and the Constitution.* Freeport, NY: Books for Libraries Press, 1947.

Craig, Hardin. "Woodrow Wilson as an Orator." *Quarterly Journal of Speech* 38 (1952): 145–48.

Dawson, Joseph G., ed. *Commanders in Chief: Presidential Leadership in Modern Wars.* Lawrence: University Press of Kansas, 1993.

DeConde, Alexander. *The Quasi-War: The Politics and Diplomacy of the Undeclared War with France, 1797–1801.* New York: Scribner, 1966.

Erickson, Paul D. *Reagan Speaks: The Making of an American Myth.* New York: New York University Press, 1985.

Farrell, James M. "John Adams's *Autobiography*: The Ciceronian Paradigm and the Quest for Fame." *New England Quarterly* 62 (1989): 505–28.

Fields, Wayne. *Union of Words: A History of Presidential Eloquence.* New York: Free Press, 1996.

Franck, Thomas M., ed. *The Tethered Presidency: Congressional Restraints on Executive Power.* New York: New York University Press, 1981.

Friedenberg, Robert V. *Theodore Roosevelt and the Rhetoric of Militant Decency.* New York: Greenwood Press, 1990.

Henkin, Louis. *Constitutionalism, Democracy, and Foreign Affairs.* New York: Columbia University Press, 1990.

Keynes, Edward. *Undeclared War: Twilight Zone of Constitutional Power.* University Park: Pennsylvania State University Press, 1982.

Leckie, Robert. *The Wars of America.* New York: Harper and Row, 1968.

Medhurst, Martin J. *Dwight D. Eisenhower: Strategic Communicator.* Westport, CT: Greenwood Press, 1993.

Moore, Wilbur E. "James Madison the Speaker." *Quarterly Journal of Speech* 31 (1945): 155–62.

Rahskopf, Horace G. "John Quincy Adams: Speaker and Rhetorician." *Quarterly Journal of Speech* 32 (1946): 435–41.

———. "John Quincy Adams's Theory and Practice of Public Speaking." *Archives of Speech* 1 (1936): 7–98.

Reveley, W. Taylor, III. *War Powers of the President and Congress: Who Holds the Arrows and Olive Branch?* Charlottesville: University Press of Virginia, 1981.

Rossiter, Clinton. *The Supreme Court and the Commander in Chief.* Ithaca, NY: Cornell University Press, 1976.

Ryan, Halford R. *Franklin D. Roosevelt's Rhetorical Presidency.* New York: Greenwood Press, 1988.

Shuman, Howard E., and Walter R. Thomas, eds. *The U.S. Constitution and National Security.* Washington, DC: National Defense University Press, 1990.

White, Eugene E., and Clair R. Henderlider. "What Harry S. Truman Told Us about His Speaking." *Quarterly Journal of Speech* 40 (1954): 37–42.

Wills, Garry. *Lincoln at Gettysburg: The Words That Remade America.* New York: Simon and Schuster, 1992.

_____. *Nixon Agonistes*. Boston: Houghton Mifflin, 1970.

_____. *Reagan's America: Innocents at Home*. Garden City, NY: Doubleday, 1987.

Wormuth, Francis P., and Edwin B. Firmage. *To Chain the Dog of War: The War Powers of Congress in History and Law*. Dallas: Southern Methodist University Press, 1986.

Zarefsky, David. "Civil Rights and Civil Conflict: Presidential Communication in Crisis." *Communication Studies* 34 (1983): 59–66.

_____. "The Great Society as a Rhetorical Proposition." *Quarterly Journal of Speech* 65 (1979): 364–78.

ABOUT THE EDITOR

Russell D. Buhite has been professor of history as well as department head at the University of Oklahoma and the University of Tennessee. Since 1997 he has been dean of the College of Arts and Sciences and professor of history at the University of Missouri-Rolla. He has published nine previous books and numerous articles and reviews in the field of American foreign relations. His most recent monograph is *Lives at Risk: Hostages and Victims in American Foreign Policy* (1995).